Building Data with VXLAN BGP EVPN

A Cisco NX-OS Perspective

Lukas Krattiger, *CCIE No. 21921*

Shyam Kapadia

David Jansen, *CCIE No. 5952*

Cisco Press

800 East 96th Street

Indianapolis, IN 46240

Building Data Centers with VXLAN BGP EVPN

A Cisco NX-OS Perspective

Lukas Krattiger
Shyam Kapadia
David Jansen

Copyright© 2017 Cisco Systems, Inc.

Published by:
Cisco Press
800 East 96th Street
Indianapolis, IN 46240 USA

All rights reserved. No part of this book may be reproduced or transmitted in any form or by any means, electronic or mechanical, including photocopying, recording, or by any information storage and retrieval system, without written permission from the publisher, except for the inclusion of brief quotations in a review.

Printed in the United States of America

1   17

Library of Congress Cataloging-in-Publication Number: 2017931984

ISBN-10: 1-58714-467-0

ISBN-13: 978-1-58714-467-7

Warning and Disclaimer

This book is designed to provide information about data center network design. Every effort has been made to make this book as complete and as accurate as possible, but no warranty or fitness is implied.

The information is provided on an "as is" basis. The authors, Cisco Press, and Cisco Systems, Inc., shall have neither liability nor responsibility to any person or entity with respect to any loss or damages arising from the information contained in this book or from the use of the discs or programs that may accompany it.

The opinions expressed in this book belong to the author and are not necessarily those of Cisco Systems, Inc.

Trademark Acknowledgments

All terms mentioned in this book that are known to be trademarks or service marks have been appropriately capitalized. Cisco Press or Cisco Systems, Inc., cannot attest to the accuracy of this information. Use of a term in this book should not be regarded as affecting the validity of any trademark or service mark.

Special Sales

For information about buying this title in bulk quantities, or for special sales opportunities (which may include electronic versions; custom cover designs; and content particular to your business, training goals, marketing focus, or branding interests), please contact our corporate sales department at corpsales@pearsoned.com or (800) 382-3419.

For government sales inquiries, please contact governmentsales@pearsoned.com.

For questions about sales outside the U.S., please contact intlcs@pearson.com.

Feedback Information

At Cisco Press, our goal is to create in-depth technical books of the highest quality and value. Each book is crafted with care and precision, undergoing rigorous development that involves the unique expertise of members of the professional technical community.

Readers' feedback is a natural continuation of this process. If you have any comments regarding how we could improve the quality of this book or otherwise alter it to better suit your needs, you can contact by e-mail, at feedback@ciscopress.com. Please make sure to include the book title and ISBN in your message. We greatly appreciate your assistance.

Editor-in-Chief: Mark Taub

Alliances Manager, Cisco Press: Ron Fligge

Product Line Manager: Brett Bartow

Executive Editor: Mary Beth Ray

Managing Editor: Sandra Schroeder

Development Editor: Christopher Cleveland

Project Editor: Mandie Frank

Copy Editor: Kitty Wilson

Technical Editors: Scott Morris, Jeff Tantsura

Editorial Assistant: Vanessa Evans

Cover Designer: Okomon Haus

Composition: codeMantra

Indexer: Erika Millen

Proofreader: Abigail Manheim

CISCO

Americas Headquarters	Asia Pacific Headquarters	Europe Headquarters
Cisco Systems, Inc.	Cisco Systems (USA) Pte. Ltd.	Cisco Systems International BV
San Jose, CA	Singapore	Amsterdam, The Netherlands

Cisco has more than 200 offices worldwide. Addresses, phone numbers, and fax numbers are listed on the Cisco Website at **www.cisco.com/go/offices.**

CCDE, CCENT, Cisco Eos, Cisco HealthPresence, the Cisco logo, Cisco Lumin, Cisco Nexus, Cisco StadiumVision, Cisco TelePresence, Cisco WebEx, DCE, and Welcome to the Human Network are trademarks; Changing the Way We Work, Live, Play, and Learn and Cisco Store are service marks; and Access Registrar, Aironet, AsyncOS, Bringing the Meeting to You, Catalyst, CCDA, CCDP, CCIE, CCIP, CCNA, CCNP, CCSP, CCVP, Cisco, the Cisco Certified Internetwork Expert logo, Cisco IOS, Cisco Press, Cisco Systems, Cisco Systems Capital, the Cisco Systems logo, Cisco Unity, Collaboration Without Limitation, EtherFast, EtherSwitch, Event Center, Fast Step, Follow Me Browsing, FormShare, GigaDrive, HomeLink, Internet Quotient, IOS, iPhone, iQuick Study, IronPort, the IronPort logo, LightStream, Linksys, MediaTone, MeetingPlace, MeetingPlace Chime Sound, MGX, Networkers, Networking Academy, Network Registrar, PCNow, PIX, PowerPanels, ProConnect, ScriptShare, SenderBase, SMARTnet, Spectrum Expert, StackWise, The Fastest Way to Increase Your Internet Quotient, TransPath, WebEx, and the WebEx logo are registered trademarks of Cisco Systems, Inc. and/or its affiliates in the United States and certain other countries.

All other trademarks mentioned in this document or website are the property of their respective owners. The use of the word partner does not imply a partnership relationship between Cisco and any other company. (0812R)

About the Authors

Lukas Krattiger, CCIE No. 21921 *(Routing/Switching and Data Center)*, is principal engineer, Technical Marketing, with more than 15 years of experience in data center, Internet, and application networks. Within Cisco, he specializes in data center switching, overlay architectures, and solutions across platforms. Lukas is a double-CCIE (R&S and Data Center) with several other industry certifications and has participated in various technology leadership and advisory groups. Prior to joining Cisco, Lukas was a senior network engineer with System Integrators and Service Providers, where he was responsible for data center and Internet networks. Since joining Cisco, he has covered various technologies within the data center as well as enterprise networks portfolio, and he has built foundational solutions for customers and partners. He is from Switzerland and currently lives in California with his wife and one wonderful daughter. He can be found on Twitter at @ccie21921.

Shyam Kapadia is a principal engineer in the Data Center Group at Cisco Systems. With more than a decade of experience in the networking industry, Shyam holds more than 30 patents and has coauthored the book *Using TRILL, FabricPath, and VXLAN: Designing MSDC with Overlays*. In his 10 years at Cisco, Shyam has worked on a number of products, including the Catalyst and Nexus families of switches, with special emphasis on end-to-end data center solutions, including automation and orchestration. He holds a Ph.D. and master's degree from the University of Southern California in the field of computer science. Over the past 15 years, Shyam has been the Program Chair for the Southern California Linux Exposition (SCALE). He lives in California with his wife, enjoys watching international movies, and is passionate about sports including cricket, basketball, and football.

David Jansen, CCIE No. 5952 *(Routing/Switching)*, is a distinguished systems engineer (DSE) for Cisco, specializing in data center, campus, branch/WAN, and cloud architectures. He has 20 years of experience in the industry and has earned certifications from Novell, VMware, Microsoft, TOGAF, and Cisco. His focus is working with global enterprise customers to address their challenges with comprehensive end-to-end data center, enterprise, WAN/Internet, and cloud architectures. David has been with Cisco for more than 19 years; for the last 4 years or so as a DSE, he has gained unique experiences in building next generation data center solutions. David has a bachelor's degree in computer science engineering from the University of Michigan and a master's degree in adult education from Central Michigan University.

About the Technical Reviewers

Scott Morris, the world traveling Über-Geek has four CCIE certifications (Routing & Switching, ISP/Dial, Security and Service Provider) as well as the coveted CCDE. He also has several expert-level certifications from other major vendors, making him "multi-lingual" in the networking world.

Working on large-scale network designs, troubleshooting, and some very interesting CyberSecurity projects, has kept Scott occupied. Outside of challenging work, Scott can be found spending time with his family or finding new things to learn. Having more than 30 years of experience in just about all aspects of the industry has provided both an in-depth and an entertaining approach to disseminating knowledge. Whether involved in large-scale designs, interesting implementations, or expert-level training, you can often find Scott willing to share information.

Jeff Tantsura has been in the networking space for 20+ years and has authored/contributed to many RFCs and patents. He is the chair of the IETF Routing Working Group, chartered to work on new network architectures and technologies, including protocol independent YANG models and working on YANG modeling as the working group chair and contributor.

Jeff is a coauthor of a recently published book, *Navigating Network Complexity*, talking, among other existing topics, about why networking has become so complex and the urgent need for automation and programmable, model-driven networking.

Dedications

From Lukas Krattiger:

I want to dedicate this book to my family, especially my wife, Snjezi, and daughter, Nadalina. They have shown immense patience during nights, weekends, vacations, and other inconvenient times while this book project was being completed. I love you both!

From Shyam Kapadia:

I dedicate this book to my family, especially my wife, Rakhee, and my mother, for their constant love and support.

From David Jansen:

This book is dedicated to my loving wife, Jenise, and my three children, Kaitlyn, Joshua, and Jacob. You are the inspiration that gave me the determination to complete this project. To my three amazing children, you are learning the skills to be the best at what you do and to accomplish anything in life; keep up the great work. Thank you for all your love and support. I could not have completed yet another book without your help, support, and understanding. I would also like to further dedicate this book to my parents, Michael and Dolores. You have given me the proper tools, guidance, attitude, drive, and education to allow me to do what I do. I'm likewise grateful to God, who gives endurance, encouragement, and motivation to complete such a large project like this. In my last book dedication, I mentioned that I would not take on any additional projects like that one. As you can see, I had a hard time saying no when my good friend and colleague Lukas Krattiger convinced me to take on this project. Thank you, Lukas; it is always a pleasure, my friend. I truly enjoy working with you.

Acknowledgments

From Lukas Krattiger:

First, I'd like to thank my coauthors, Shyam Kapadia and David Jansen. Shyam, thank you for being such a great coworker and a true technical leader in our organization. I could not imagine anyone better. It has been truly wonderful sharing ideas with you, and I look forward to addressing additional challenges and innovations with you in the near future. David, thank you for stepping in to help tackle this project. You are an exceptional colleague, and it was a true pleasure working with you these many engagements, especially the video series. Each of us has unique insights and gifts to contribute, and both you and Shyam highlight the benefits the diversity in our community provides.

Likewise, I would like to send a special acknowledgment to the other team members with whom I am working. In particular, I would like to recognize Carl Solder as well as Yousuf Khan for all the support and timely guidance. Special thanks to Victor Moreno for all the discussions and the groundbreaking work with overlays.

I would also like to thank some individuals who are intimately involved with VXLAN EVPN. In particular, Ali Sajassi, Samir Thoria, Dhananjaya Rao, Senthil Kenchiah (and team), Neeraj Malhota, Rajesh Sharma, and Bala Ramaraj deserve special recognition. Similarly, all my engineering and marketing colleagues who support this innovative technology and have helped contribute to the completion of this book deserve special recognition.

A special shout-out goes to all my friends in Switzerland, Europe, Australia, the United States, and the rest of the globe. Mentioning all of you here would create an additional 11 chapters.

Finally, writing this book provided me with the opportunity to get to know some new acquaintances. I would like to thank Doug Childress for his continuous edits and reviews on the manuscript, and I would also like to thank our technical editors, Scott Morris and Jeff Tantsura, for all the feedback they provided. Finally, I would like to give a special thanks to Cisco Press for all the support on this project.

From Shyam Kapadia:

I would like to especially thank my coauthors, Lukas and David, for their collaboration and support. Lukas did the lion's share in putting together this publication, and he deserves substantial credit for that. It's hard to imagine this book coming together without his tremendous contribution. Our collaboration over the past several years has been extremely fruitful, and I look forward to additional joint innovations and deliverables in the future. In addition, I would like to thank David, who has been a good role model for many individuals at Cisco, including me.

I'd like to give a special acknowledgment to the engineering leadership team in the Data Center group at Cisco for their constant support and encouragement in pursuing this endeavor. This team includes Nilesh Shah, Ravi Amanaganti, Venkat Krishnamurthy, Dinesh Khurana, Naoshad Mehta, and Mahesh Chellappa.

Like Lukas, I want to recognize individuals at Cisco involved in taking VXLAN BGP EVPN to the summit where it is today. I would also like to acknowledge the contributions of the DCNM team for providing the management and controller aspects to the programmable fabric solution with VXLAN BGP EVPN. I would like to also thank Doug Childress for helping review and edit the book chapters, and I offer a special thanks to the reviewers and editors for their tremendous help and support in developing this book. This is my second collaboration with Cisco Press, and the experience has been even better than the first one.

From David Jansen:

This is my fourth book, and it has been a tremendous honor to work with the great people at Cisco Press. There are so many people to thank, I'm not sure where to begin. First, I would like to thank my friends and coauthors, Lukas Krattiger and Shyam Kapadia. Both of you are great friends as well as exceptional coworkers. I can't think of two better people with whom to work or complete such a project. Cisco is one of the most amazing places I've ever worked, and people like you who are exceptionally intelligent and an extreme pleasure to work with make it such a great place. I look forward to working with you on other projects in the future and growing our friendship further into as well.

I would also like to acknowledge Chris Cleveland, with whom it is always a pleasure to work. His expertise, professionalism, and follow-up as a development editor are unsurpassed. I would like to specifically thank him for all his hard work and quick turnaround times in meeting the deadlines.

To our technical editors, Jeff Tantsura and Scott Morris, I would like to offer a thank you for your time, sharp eyes, and excellent comments/feedback provided during this project. It was a pleasure having you both as part of the team.

I would like to also thank the heavy metal music world out there. It allowed me to stay focused when burning the midnight oil. I would not have been able to complete this without loud rock and roll music, air guitar, and air drums as well! So thank you.

I want to thank my family for their support and understanding while I was working on this project late at night. They were patient with me when my lack of rest may have made me a little less than pleasant to be around. I know it is also hard to sleep when Dad is downstairs writing and fails to realize how the decibel level of the music is interfering with the rest of the family's ability to sleep.

Most importantly, I would like to thank God for giving me the ability to complete such a task with the required dedication and determination and for providing me the skills, knowledge, and health needed to be successful in such a demanding profession.

Contents at a Glance

Contents

Introduction

Building Data Centers with VXLAN BGP EVPN is intended to provide a solid understanding of how data center network fabrics with VXLAN BGP EVPN function. It serves as both a technology compendium and a deployment guide.

Cisco's NX-OS-based data center switching portfolio provides a collection of networking protocols and features that are foundational to building data center networks as traditional networks evolve into fabric-based architectures, like VXLAN with the BGP EVPN control plane.

This book's goal is to explain how to understand and deploy this technology, and it begins with an introduction to the current data center challenges, before going into the technology building blocks and related semantics. It also provides an overview of the evolution of the data center fabric. The book takes a deep dive into the various fabric semantics, including the underlay, multitenancy, control and data plane interaction, unicast and multicast forwarding flows, and external, data center interconnect, and service appliance deployments.

Goals and Methods

The goal of this book is to provide a resource for readers who want to get familiar with data center overlay technologies, especially VXLAN with a control plane like BGP EVPN. This book describes a methodology that network architects and administrators can use to plan, design, and implement scalable data centers. You do not have to be a networking professional or data center administrator to benefit from this book. The book is geared toward understanding the functionality of VXLAN with BGP EVPN in data center fabric deployments. Our hope is that all readers, from university students to professors to networking experts, will benefit from this book.

Who Should Read This Book?

This book has been written with a broad audience in mind, while specifically targeting network architects, engineers, and operators. Additional audiences who will benefit from reading this book include help desk analysts, network administrators, and certification candidates. This book provides information on VXLAN with BGP EVPN for today's data centers.

For a network professional with in-depth understanding of various networking areas, this book serves as an authoritative guide, explaining detailed control and data plane concepts, with VXLAN and BGP EVPN being the primary focus. Detailed packet flows are presented, covering numerous functions, features, and deployments.

Regardless of your level of expertise or role in the IT industry, this book offers significant benefits. It presents VXLAN and BGP EVPN concepts in a consumable manner. It also describes design considerations for various fabric semantics and identifies the key benefits of adopting this technology.

How This Book Is Organized

Although this book slowly progresses conceptually from Chapter 1 to Chapter 11, you could also read individual chapters that cover only the material of interest. The first chapter provides a brief introduction to the evolution of data center networks, with an emphasis on the need for network overlays. Chapters 2 and 3 form the foundation for VXLAN BGP EVPN. The subsequent chapters describe underlying or adjacent building blocks to VXLAN BGP EVPN, with an emphasis on Layer 2 and Layer 3 services and the associated multitenancy. Chapter 10 describes the integration of Layer 4–7 services into a VXLAN network with BGP EVPN, while Chapter 11 concludes the book with an overview of fabric management and operations.

The chapter breakdown is as follows:

- **Chapter 1, "Introduction to Programmable Fabric."** This chapter provides a brief introduction to the Cisco VXLAN BGP EVPN fabric. It begins with a description of the requirements of today's data centers. It also gives an overview of how data centers evolved over the years, leading to a VXLAN BGP EVPN-based spine–leaf fabric. This chapter introduces common fabric-based terminology and describes what makes the fabric extremely scalable, resilient, and elastic.

- **Chapter 2, "VXLAN BGP EVPN Basics."** This chapter describes why overlays have become a prime design choice for next-generation data centers, with a special emphasis on VXLAN, which has become the de facto choice. The chapter describes the need for a control plane–based solution for distribution of host reachability between various edge devices and provides a comprehensive introduction to BGP EVPN. It describes the important message formats in BGP EVPN for supporting network virtualization overlays and presents representative use cases. The subsequent chapters build on this background and provide further details on the underlay, multitenancy, and single-destination and multidestination data packet flows in a VXLAN BGP EVPN–based data center network.

- **Chapter 3, "VXLAN/EVPN Forwarding Characteristics."** This chapter provides an in-depth discussion on the core forwarding capabilities offered by a VXLAN BGP EVPN fabric. For carrying broadcast, unknown unicast, and multicast (BUM) traffic, this chapter describes both multicast and ingress replication. It also discusses enhanced forwarding features that reduce flooding in the fabric on account of ARP and unknown unicast traffic. This chapter describes one of the key benefits of a BGP EVPN fabric: the realization of a Distributed Anycast Gateway at the ToR or leaf layer.

- **Chapter 4, "The Underlay."** This chapter describes the BGP EVPN VXLAN fabric underlay that needs to be able to transport both single-destination and multidestination overlay traffic. The primary objective of the underlay is to provide reachability among the various switches in the fabric. This chapter presents IP address allocation options for the underlay, using both point-to-point IP numbered options and the rather attractive IP unnumbered option. It also discusses choices of popular IGP routing protocols, such as OSPF, IS-IS, and BGP for unicast routing. The chapter also describes the two primary choices for multidestination traffic replication in the underlay: the unicast and multicast mode.

- **Chapter 5, "Multitenancy."** This chapter describes how multitenancy has become a prime feature for next-generation data centers and how it is realized in the data center network with VXLAN BGP EVPN. In addition to discussing multitenancy when using VLANs or Bridge Domains (BDs) in VXLAN this chapter covers modes of operation for both Layer 2 and Layer 3 multitenancy. Overall, this chapter provides a basic introduction to the main aspects of multitenancy when using data center networks with VXLAN BGP EVPN.

- **Chapter 6, "Unicast Forwarding."** This chapter provides a set of sample packet flows that indicate how bridging and routing operations occur in a VXLAN BGP EVPN network. Critical concepts related to IRB functionality, symmetric IRB, and distributed anycast gateway are described in action for real-world traffic flows. This chapter pays special attention to scenarios with silent hosts as well as dual-homed hosts.

- **Chapter 7, "Multicast Forwarding."** This chapter provides details about forwarding multicast data traffic in a VXLAN BGP EVPN network. It discusses vanilla Layer 2 multicast traffic forwarding over VXLAN, as well as topics related to its evolution with enhancements in IGMP snooping. It also presents special considerations for dual-homed and orphan multicast endpoints behind a vPC domain.

- **Chapter 8, "External Connectivity."** This chapter presents external connectivity options with a VXLAN BGP EVPN fabric. After introducing the border leaf and border spine variants, it provides details on options for external Layer 3 connectivity using VRF Lite, LISP, and MPLS L3 VPN. It also details Layer 2 external connectivity options, with an emphasis on vPC.

- **Chapter 9, "Multi-pod, Multifabric, and Data Center Interconnect (DCI)."** This chapter describes various concepts related to multi-pod and multifabric options with VXLAN BGP EVPN deployments. It provides a brief primer on the salient distinctions between OTV and VXLAN. Most practical deployments require some form of interconnection between different pods or fabrics. This chapter discusses various considerations that need to be taken into account when making a decision on when to use the multi-pod option versus the multifabric option.

- **Chapter 10, "Layer 4–7 Services Integration."** This chapter provides details on how Layer 4–7 services can be integrated into a VXLAN BGP EVPN network. It covers deployments with intra-tenant and inter-tenant firewalls, which can be deployed in both transparent and routed modes. In addition, this chapter presents a common deployment scenario with load balancers, with emphasis on the nuances associated with its integration into a VXLAN BGP EVPN network. The chapter concludes with a common load balancer and firewall service chain deployment example.

■ **Chapter 11, "Introduction to Fabric Management."** This chapter introduces the basic elements of fabric management, including POAP-based day-0 provisioning (using DCNM, NFM, and so on), incremental configuration using day-0.5 configuration, overlay configuration using day-1 provisioning (using DCNM, VTS, and NFM), and day-2 provisioning, which involves provisions for continuous monitoring, visibility, and troubleshooting capabilities in a VXLAN BGP EVPN fabric. It presents a brief primer on VXLAN OAM, which is an extremely efficient tool for debugging in overlay-based fabrics.

Command Syntax Conventions

The conventions used to present command syntax in this book are the same conventions used in the *NX-OS Command Reference*:

■ **Boldface** indicates commands and keywords that are entered literally, as shown. In actual configuration examples and output (not general command syntax), boldface indicates commands that are manually input by the user (such as a **show** command).

■ *Italics* indicate arguments for which you supply actual values.

■ Vertical bars (|) separate alternative, mutually exclusive elements.

■ Square brackets [ ] indicate optional elements.

■ Braces { } indicate a required choice.

■ Braces within brackets [{ }] indicate a required choice within an optional element.

## Chapter 1

Introduction to Programmable Fabric

In this chapter, the following topics will be covered:

- Requirements of today's data centers

- Evolution of data center technology from Spanning Tree Protocol (STP) to VXLAN BGP EVPN

- Programmable fabric concepts

Data centers have evolved significantly over the past few years. This evolution has occurred rapidly and within a relatively short time period, bringing popular technologies such as virtualization, the cloud (private, public, and hybrid), software defined networking (SDN),[1] and big data. For the mobile-first and cloud-native age, scale, agility, security, consolidation, and integration with compute/storage orchestrators are common data center requirements. In addition, visibility, automation, ease of management, operability, troubleshooting, and advanced analytics are also expected to be part of today's data center solutions

The shift away from a device-by-device management toward a more service-centric system has already taken place. Open application programming interfaces (APIs) and standards-based protocols that prevent single-vendor lock-in are prime criteria in most customer requests for proposals (RFPs). The Cisco Virtual Extensible LAN (VXLAN) with BGP Ethernet VPN (EVPN)–based fabric presents a unified data center solution composed of the data center Nexus family of switches[2] running NX-OS coupled with controllers.

While this book focuses on NX-OS-based EVPN, the information presented is also applicable for platforms running IOS-XE[3] and IOS-XR[4] operating systems. This chapter presents some of the challenges and requirements that led to the evolution of the data center network fabric. It provides a brief primer on the architecture and commonly used terms associated with the programmable fabric or Cisco's VXLAN BGP EVPN–based fabric.

Today's Data Center Challenges and Requirements

In the past, the desire for instant elasticity and agility was perhaps not as pervasive as it is today, considering the application expectations from data centers. It took days or weeks to deploy applications. But with the evolution of the data center—and the cloud in particular—deployment time today is expected to be minutes or even seconds.

Not only is the speed of deployment critical, but it is important to be able to scale-up as workload requirements expand. In addition, paying only for what is actively being used has become the norm. The requirements for high-availability access to applications and their associated data have become increasingly stringent. While the demand for availability has been driven by the widespread globalization of enterprises across continents, applications have also become increasingly sophisticated.

In this new landscape, where all workloads and applications are being moved over to the data centers, the traditional designs for data centers are no longer sufficient to address all the requirements. This is the case regardless of whether data centers exist in combination with a private cloud, public cloud, or hybrid cloud. Given the current environment, some of the key demands of today's data center deployments are as follows:

- **Agility:** Agility defines how long it takes for an application request to be fulfilled. An agile data center is one that is able to reduce this time to a minimum.

- **Scalability:** Scalability is of paramount importance, especially in cloud-based data centers. A data center should be able to house thousands of tenants and several thousand tenant networks. The 4096 (or 4K) network limitation imposed by the 12-bit VLAN field is not sufficient for supporting large multitenant data centers.

- **Elasticity:** A data center must be able to adapt to changing demands and requirements. This might involve the addition of compute workloads, additional storage, additional network bandwidth, and so on. A data center must be able to add capacity to address the increase in demand without affecting existing application workloads.

- **Availability:** A data center must be able to be constantly operational (24/7, 365 days a year). In addition, access to applications needs to be available from all types of devices (such as tablets, smart phones, and smart watches), which advances the bring-your-own-device (BYOD) model to an entirely new level. For high availability, disaster recovery (DR) requirements often specify that potential backup options are available that can take over whenever some kind of failure occurs at the primary data center site.

- **Low cost:** The total cost of ownership (TCO) for a data center comprises both the capital expenditure (CAPEX) and the operating expenditure (OPEX). While the CAPEX portion is amortized over time, the OPEX portion is a continuous expenditure. As a result, OPEX is under close scrutiny from most CIOs/CFOs. Reducing OPEX for data centers is thus commonly a high-priority item.

- **Openness:** To prevent a tie-in with a single vendor, a push toward building data centers with standards-based options exists from both hardware and software points of view. Most large-scale data centers have already moved to a white-box or branded white-box (Brite-box) model. Enterprise and service providers are also demanding open standards–based data center deployments.

- **Security:** Especially in multitenant data center deployments, a prime requirement is to impose effective security policies to ensure that traffic from a tenant is completely isolated from another tenant. Some of the other security-related requirements include enforcement of application policies, prevention of unauthorized access, detection of threats, isolation of infected devices, distribution of secure patches to affected devices, and consistent policy applications between the private cloud and public cloud.

- **Solution orientation:** The days of a box-by-box deployment within a data center have passed. Today's data centers demand a unified solution with various pieces in place from a network point of view, and they also require close integration with compute and storage orchestrators as well as service appliances (physical and virtual). In addition, sophisticated automation in conjunction with an SDN controller is required in this highly competitive space.

- **Ease of use:** Even with a solution-oriented approach, continuous management, monitoring, and visibility into the day-to-day operations of a data center is highly desirable. Ease of use has a direct impact on reducing the OPEX.

- **Support for hybrid deployments:** Both enterprises and service providers have already adopted the cloud model to some extent. As a result, one of the key require-ments of a data center is support for hybrid cloud deployments where resources from the public cloud can be extended over to the private enterprise data center in an elastic manner. Such operations must be seamless from the point of view of the applications. In other words, applications should be completely unaware of whether they are hosted on premises or off premises.

- **Power efficiency:** A large portion of the operational cost of a data center is attrib-uted to its electrical power requirements. The networking industry at large and data center vendors in particular are cognizant of this requirement, and the incentive to build progressively green data centers certainly exists.

The Data Center Fabric Journey

Figure 1-1 depicts the evolution of data center networks over the past several years. Spanning Tree Protocol (STP)–based networks served network requirements for several years. Virtual PortChannel (vPC)[5] was introduced to address some of the drawbacks of STP networks while also providing dual-homing abilities. Subsequently, overlay technologies such as FabricPath[6] and TRILL[7] came to the forefront, introducing routed Layer 2 networks with a MAC-in-MAC overlay encapsulation. This evolved into a MAC-in-IP overlay with the invention of VXLAN.[8]

While Layer 2 networks evolved beyond the loop-free topologies with STP, the first-hop gateway functions for Layer 3 also became more sophisticated. The traditional centralized gateways hosted at the distribution or aggregation layers have transitioned to *distributed gateway* implementations. This has allowed for scaling out and removal of choke points. This section provides an overview of why and how this evolution has occurred.

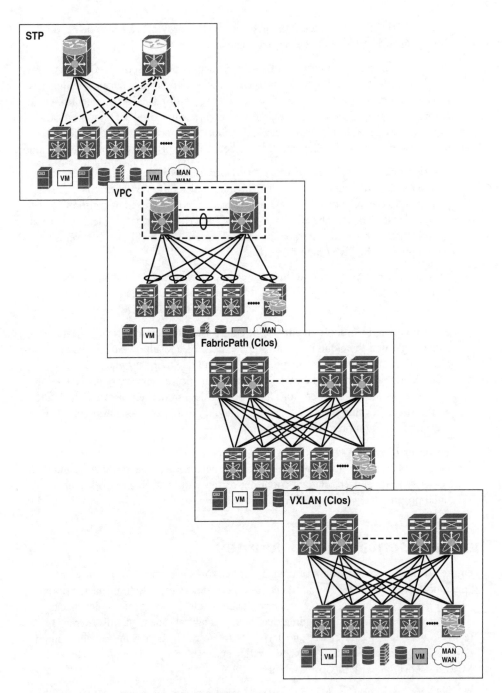

Figure 1-1 *Data Center Network Journey*

Building a loop-free Layer 2 network that enables devices in the same broadcast domain to communicate with each other, was the initial development that made local area networks (LANs) extremely popular. Within a broadcast domain, forwarding is based on a MAC address–based lookup. STP, which was standardized as IEEE 802.1D,[9] prescribed a methodology for creating a tree topology that is, by definition, loop free. By making this a plug-and-play function, STP-based networks with IEEE 802.1Q[10] support gained rapid adoption and are still being used today.

With many technologies, shortcomings become readily apparent when a technology or protocol is designed for one specific environment but is then applied to another environment that has a completely different set of requirements. This has been the case with STP-based networks. Various issues make the adoption of STP for a large data center network, difficult. Some of the major issues include the following:

■ **Convergence issues:** On a link failure or switch failure in STP-based networks, the tree needs to be recalculated. This can significantly impact traffic convergence times because topology change notifications result in clearing the MAC tables on the switches. As a result, relearning of the state is required. This problem becomes amplified when the root node goes down and a new one needs to be elected. While timers can be tweaked to reduce the effect of failures, the inherent problem persists. As link speeds go from 10G to 40G to 100G, even subsecond convergence times can result in significant traffic drops. High convergence times are thus one of the main drawbacks of STP-based networks.

■ **Unused links:** As mentioned earlier, STP builds a tree in order to ensure that the resultant network topology has no cycles or loops. One potential side effect of this is that many of the links between the various switches, which are part of the topology, are placed in a blocked state and rendered redundant. Consequently, network resources are not optimally utilized. Currently, having the ability to leverage all links and their corresponding bandwidth in order to attain optimal use of existing resources, is a desired goal.

■ **Suboptimal forwarding:** Because the tree is rooted at a particular switch with STP, all traffic from that switch to any other switch in the topology will be forwarded along a single path. Because traffic is always forwarded along this tree, a shorter path between a pair of non-root switches, if it exists, will not be utilized. Consequently, traffic between those switches will be suboptimally forwarded, and this is certainly a less-than-ideal situation.

■ **Lack of Equal-Cost MultiPath (ECMP) routing:** Because only one path is active between a source switch and a destination switch in a traditional STP-based Layer 2 network, ECMP options are absent. Layer 3 networks, on the other hand, provide the ability to leverage more than one equal-cost path between a pair of routers. This is extremely desirable and is one of the major reasons Layer 3 networks have gained popularity.

- **Traffic storm issues:** With a tree topology, traffic starting from a switch should not be sent back to that switch; however, traffic may still loop endlessly within a network in certain failure states. Such an occurrence could potentially bring down the entire network. This scenario has been termed a *broadcast storm*. Any kind of network storm can chew up unnecessary bandwidth within the network and should be avoided at all costs. Because there is no Time to Live (TTL) field in a Layer 2 header, once a storm is introduced, the traffic could flow endlessly. Layer 3 networks have a fail-safe mechanism due to the presence of the TTL field and an associated decrement at every routed hop. Once the TTL becomes 0, the packet is dropped. The lack of such a liveliness field in Layer 2 networks immensely limits scalability, especially as the size of the network grows.

- **Lack of dual-homing support:** STP inherently does not allow a device or host to be attached to more than one switch. When that is attempted, a loop is formed, and STP essentially blocks one of the links. Consequently, from a redundancy or fault tolerance point of view, if that switch goes down, traffic to and from the downstream device or host is black-holed until the tree is recalculated.

- **Network scale:** In the age of cloud computing, significant constraints can be introduced as a result of having only a 4K network namespace, especially with the addressing and numbering for tenant networks. Even a medium-sized data center deployment can host several tenants, each of which might have a set of networks that summed together exceeds this limit. Unfortunately, due to the 12-bit identifier that represents a VLAN or a broadcast domain in the IEEE 802.1Q or dot1q header, 4K is quite limiting. When dot1q was introduced a few decades ago, perhaps the inventors thought that 4K would be a large enough namespace; however, significant advances in networking technology resulted in this number being exceeded in a relatively short time period.

Technologies such as virtual PortChannel (vPC), Multichassis EtherChannel (MCEC)[11] and virtual switching system (VSS)[12] allow a downstream device (host or switch) to attach to a pair of switches. All these technologies fall under the umbrella of Multi-Chassis Link Aggregation (MC-LAG).[13] With vPC, a pair of switches (called *vPC peers*) is configured such that the rest of the network sees the pair as a single logical switch.

Figure 1-2 shows how a typical STP network can be made more efficient with vPC. The downstream device is attached to both vPC peers using a regular PortChannel or EtherChannel configuration. Both links are in an active state, thereby allowing active-active forwarding. Traffic from the downstream device may hash over to either peer and be appropriately forwarded. Similarly, traffic to the downstream device may flow through either peer. Multidestination traffic to the downstream device is sent via only one of the peers, thereby avoiding duplication.

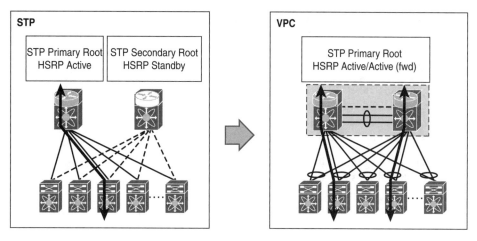

Figure 1-2 *STP to vPC Improvement*

Each vPC peer has a primary role and a secondary role. Information between the vPC peers is synchronized over a control channel termed the *vPC peer link*. This information includes MAC, ARP, and neighbor-discovery (ND) information as well as various configuration and consistency check parameters. Not only does vPC provide dual-homing from a Layer 2 perspective, but its active-active forwarding semantics also extend to first-hop redundancy protocols (FHRPs) like Hot-Standby Router Protocol (HSRP)[14] and Virtual Router Redundancy Protocol (VRRP).[15] This reflected a significant improvement over traditional FHRP deployments with active-standby behavior where only the active node was forwarding data traffic. With the presence of vPC, both vPC peers forward data traffic simultaneously, while the active FHRP vPC peer resolves ARP/ND requests from the control-plane perspective only. (For more information on vPC, see the Cisco vPC design best practices guide.[16])

While vPC addresses some limitations of STP, it remains limited to a pair of switches. A more generic multipath solution was desired, especially as the requirements of building an extremely large scalable Layer 2 domain developed. As the number of endpoints within Layer 2 networks expanded, it became impractical for all switches within a network to learn all endpoint MAC addresses.

In addition, the plug-and-play behavior of Layer 2 networks was still desirable. As a result, overlay technologies such as FabricPath and TRILL were introduced. Overlays in general provide a level of abstraction. With the separation of the host address space from the topology address space, overlays allow both of these to scale independently.

Cisco FabricPath is a MAC-in-MAC encapsulation that eliminates the use of STP in Layer 2 networks. It uses Layer 2 Intermediate System to Intermediate System (IS-IS) with appropriate extensions to distribute the topology information among the switches that are part of the network. In this way, switches behave like routers, building switch reachability tables and inheriting all the advantages of Layer 3 strategies such as ECMP. In addition, no unused links exist in this scenario, while optimal forwarding between any pair of switches is promoted. One of the salient features of FabricPath is the simplicity with respect to configuration and enablement. Only the global feature needs to be enabled, along with a couple of commands related to putting a VLAN and the network-facing ports in a specific mode. The switch ID allocation, the enablement of IS-IS, and the discovery of the switch topology happen under the hood.

At the same time, the IS-IS protocol is employed to build appropriate multidestination trees, thereby allowing optimal forwarding of Broadcast, Unknown Unicast, Multicast (BUM) traffic. vPC was extended to vPC+[17] for supporting dual-homed devices in FabricPath networks.

In FabricPath, every switch in the network has a unique switch identifier, or switch ID. Figure 1-3 provides a snapshot of the FabricPath header.

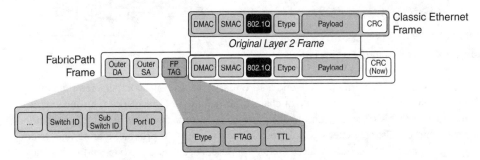

Figure 1-3 *FabricPath Header*

As shown in Figure 1-3, the outer MAC header encodes the destination and source switch ID. In addition, a forwarding tag (FTAG field) is used for topology identification.

For multidestination traffic, the FTAG field identifies the tree along which BUM traffic must be forwarded. In a FabricPath network, endpoints are attached to edge switches. Core switches interconnect various edge switches with each other. The edge switches learn about directly attached endpoints in a manner similar to traditional Layer 2 network learning. When traffic is sent over the FabricPath network, however, the edge switches add a FabricPath header with its own source switch ID and an appropriate destination switch ID. In that sense, MAC learning is still achieved via Flood and Learn (F&L) semantics, but in this situation, switches learn remote MAC addresses against the appropriate remote switch ID.

The core switches in the network only need to forward traffic based on the FabricPath header. They are completely unaware of the endpoints. The core switches can therefore be lean, and, in general, this helps the network scale.

For improving the scale on the edge switches, Layer 2 conversational learning is enabled by default in a FabricPath network. With Layer 2 conversational learning, switches only learn about remote endpoints in active conversation.

While Layer 2 ECMP became available with FabricPath, the scale-out of first-hop routing for endpoints (aka the default gateway) was also desired. With Anycast HSRP,[18] a four-way active-active FHRP for FabricPath was introduced, allowing a more scalable approach than the classic centralized two-way active-active approach with vPC.

While FabricPath has been immensely popular and adopted by thousands of customers, it has faced skepticism because it is associated with a single vendor, Cisco, as well as a lack of multivendor support. In addition, with IP being the de facto standard in the networking industry, a push for an IP-based overlay encapsulation occurred. As a result, VXLAN was introduced.

VXLAN, a MAC-in-IP/UDP encapsulation, is currently the most popular overlay encapsulation in use. As an open standard, it has received widespread adoption from networking vendors. Just like FabricPath, VXLAN addresses all the STP limitations previously described. However, in addition, with VXLAN, a 24-bit number identifies a virtual network segment, thereby allowing support for up to 16 million broadcast domains as opposed to the traditional 4K limitation imposed by VLANs.

Because VXLAN runs over an IP network, the ECMP feature of Layer 3 networks is innately available for use. In general, an overlay such as VXLAN running on top of Layer 3 can use hierarchical addressing with IP and any transport. However, an overlay such as FabricPath that uses a MAC-in-MAC encapsulation requires a transparent Layer 1 transport that cannot be addressed in a scalable manner because MAC addresses are represented by a flat address space. In essence, with VXLAN, data center networks have moved from being transport dependent to any-transport (aka transport independent) with the use of IP. As a result, the previous flat MAC-based addressing scheme for the underlay has moved to a hierarchical IP-based addressing scheme.

The edge switches in a VXLAN network are called *edge devices*, and they host the VXLAN Tunnel Endpoint (VTEP). The edge switches are responsible for encapsulation and decapsulation of the VXLAN header. The core switches that interconnect the various VTEPs are regular IP routers. Notably, these do not need to have any specialized hardware or software functionality. Also, the switches within a VXLAN network learn about each other using regular routing protocols such as OSPF, Layer 3 IS-IS, and so on.

The VTEPs learn about their directly attached endpoints using regular Layer 2 learning semantics. Remote endpoints are learned through a process known as VXLAN Flood and Learn (F&L). Toward the VXLAN core, VTEPs take the original Layer 2 frame from an endpoint and add a VXLAN header. This header contains the outer source IP address (SIP) set to its own VTEP IP and an outer destination IP address (DIP) set to the VTEP IP below which the destination endpoint is attached.

With VXLAN, the endpoint-to-VTEP binding is learned using F&L semantics. Typically, every network is identified with a unique Layer 2 virtual network identifier (L2 VNI) and associated with a multicast group. Multidestination traffic from a VTEP is forwarded toward the VXLAN core with the destination IP set to the multicast group associated with the corresponding Layer 2 network. In this way, remote VTEPs that are part of the same Layer 2 network will receive that traffic because they are part of the same multicast tree.

After decapsulation, VTEPs perform MAC learning of remote MAC addresses against the associated remote VTEPs (specifically L2 VNI, SMAC to VTEP SIP). As with any other overlay, the core switches forward traffic based only on the outer header, in this case, the outer IP header and are unaware of the endpoint addresses. With non-multicast options for VXLAN F&L, the IP core network does not need to support IP multicast.

With the non-multicast option, the VTEPs need to support ingress or head-end replication. Here, multiple replicas are generated and individually unicast to every member remote VTEP for every multidestination frame. With VXLAN F&L, a similar approach is performed for the first-hop gateway as with classic Ethernet. A two-way active-active FHRP in conjunction with vPC introduces a centralized gateway approach.

Today, VXLAN is one of the few overlay protocols that can be used both as a network overlay and a host overlay. This means the VXLAN header can be encapsulated/decapsulated and processed not only at the VXLAN-capable network switches but also at the server hosts themselves. This allows for extremely flexible implementation options with seamless physical-to-virtual integration. In addition, proposals are already in place for the next overlay evolution, in the form of Generic Protocol Encapsulation (GPE) and Network Service Header (NSH). However, ratification of these options may take some time.[19] For now, VXLAN remains the de facto overlay protocol for data center deployments.

Cisco Open Programmable Fabric

With the introduction of VXLAN as a competent standards-based data center overlay solution, learning within a VXLAN network was still based on F&L semantics. Years of networking experience showed that flooding-based approaches eventually present scalability challenges.

Regardless, flooding provided a mechanism to learn about endpoint, specifically remote MAC to VTEP bindings so that subsequent traffic can be unicast. However, if this same mapping could be distributed to the various edge devices or VTEPs employing a control protocol, then the need for flooding could potentially be completely eliminated.

With extensions to the BGP EVPN address family, it is now possible to distribute endpoint (IP, MAC)-to-VTEP bindings within a VXLAN network. In this way, the moment an endpoint is learned locally at a VTEP, using BGP EVPN, this reachability information can be distributed to all the interested VTEPs. Any traffic to this endpoint can then be optimally forwarded from any other VTEP without the need for any flood traffic.

While elimination of flooding for Layer 2 traffic certainly helps scalability to a large extent in a VXLAN network with BGP EVPN support, Layer 3 traffic can also be optimally forwarded in these networks, using specific methodologies. Before discussing these options, however, this chapter provides a brief primer regarding traditional Layer 3 traffic forwarding in a data center network.

The classic three-tier topology has served the networking industry for a fairly long time period (see Figure 1-4). Typically, endpoints or servers are attached to the access layer, which has Layer 2 support only with appropriate VLAN and switch port configurations. For inter-subnet communication, traffic from the endpoints is routed via the aggregation or distribution layer switches.

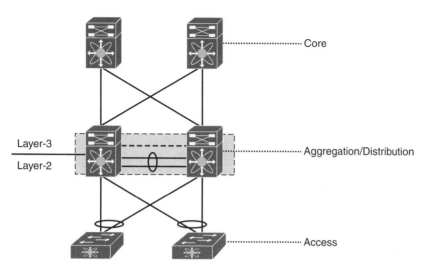

Figure 1-4 *Classic Three-Tier Topology*

The default gateway for the endpoints is hosted at the aggregation layer in the form of Layer 3 SVIs or IRB interfaces. For redundancy, aggregation layer switches are configured with FHRPs such as HSRP or VRRP. Various aggregation layer switches are in turn interconnected via core layer switches. Appropriate Layer 3 protocols allow exchange of prefix information between aggregation and core layer switches.

With large-scale data center deployments, three-tier topologies have become scale bottlenecks. As the number of endpoints within a network expands, the number of IP-MAC bindings stored within the aggregation layer switches also increases, consequently requiring support for a large FIB table. In addition, the control plane overhead in terms of ARP and ND refreshes that need to be handled by these switches also expands significantly. This issue, coupled with the number of Layer 3 interfaces and corresponding tenant VRFs that can be hosted at the aggregation layer switches, yields big problems.

With the agility and elasticity requirements, relocating any workload to areas where resources are available, is desirable. With three-tier topologies, unnecessary "tromboning" of traffic through aggregation switches, which host the corresponding default gateways, offers the best-case scenario. In the worst-case scenario, the workloads may only be brought up below servers that are behind the directly attached access layer switches in a given aggregation POD.

For 4K VLANs, the aggregation layer switches might suffer from huge scalability challenges. Therefore, with VXLAN in the picture, and its support for up to 16 million virtual networks, a traditional three-tier topology cannot survive such a burden. The industry at large recognized this limitation, and a strong push toward moving Layer 3 to the access layer and away from a centralized Layer 3 gateway approach has occurred.

Moving the default gateway to the access layer reduces the failure domains because the access switch only needs to support first-hop protocols for workloads below it. This certainly represents a more scalable model, compared to the case where a single or pair of aggregation switches have to support all endpoints below all the access switches. This has given rise to leaf-spine or spine-leaf topologies (see Figure 1-5).

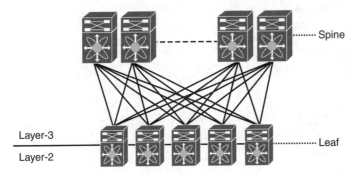

Figure 1-5   *Layer 3 Moved to the Access Layer in Clos Topology*

The access layer with Layer 3 support is typically called the *leaf layer*. The aggregation layer that provides the interconnection between the various leafs is called the *spine layer*. With VXLAN and the elimination of STP and its associated ill effects, the network has already moved toward greater stability. The aggregation or spine switches now become core switches, which are lean and only need to optimally forward traffic between the leafs. They are completely unaware of the endpoint addresses. In addition, with the BGP EVPN control protocol, the reason to flood any unknown unicast traffic is essentially eliminated.

The distribution of reachability information with BGP EVPN allows the realization of a distributed IP anycast gateway. The same default gateway can be simultaneously configured at any and all leaf switches as needed. In this way, when a workload moves between various leaf switches, it still finds its default gateway directly attached to it. Any workload can be placed below any leaf switch.

With the distributed IP anycast gateway, any routed traffic will be optimally forwarded from the source leaf to the destination leaf. The spines provide the required redundancy, thereby providing a simple network topology with enough redundancy.

The Cisco open programmable fabric employs this spine-leaf–based, multitier Clos[20] topology that employs open, standards-based protocols, specifically VXLAN for the data plane and BGP EVPN for the control plane. The fabric encompasses not only the optimal forwarding semantics but also the automation and manageability framework that accompanies the solution. In short, this involves (1) Day 0 bring-up of the fabric with the devices set up in the appropriate designated roles and the corresponding startup configuration; (2) Day 1 operations of the fabric, which involves provisioning of appropriate overlay configuration on the respective leaf switches based on active workloads; and (3) Day 2 operations of the fabric, which involves troubleshooting, manageability, and continuous monitoring of the fabric. This also includes integration of the fabric with various compute orchestrators as well as with Layer 4–7 service appliances.

Fabric-Related Terminology

Figure 1-6 shows some terminology that is used throughout this book. As mentioned earlier, the fabric is comprised of leaf switches hosting a VTEP. The leaf switches or leafs are also called *edge or Network Virtualization Edge (NVE) devices*. Physical and virtual endpoints are connected to the leafs.

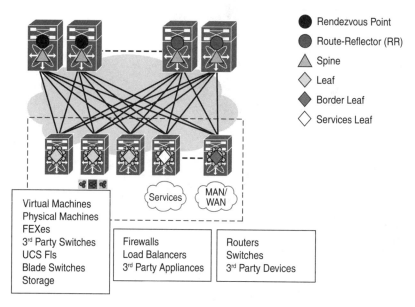

Figure 1-6   *Data Center Fabric Terminology*

The downstream interface from the leaf toward the endpoints is typically a Layer 2 port over which dot1q tagged or untagged traffic is carried. One or more spine switches provide connectivity between the leafs. Each switch within the fabric is part of an IP network that is termed the *underlay* (see Figure 1-7).

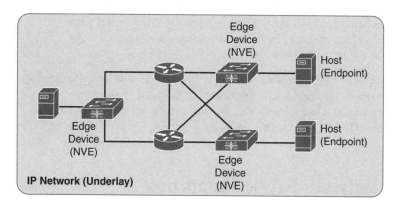

Figure 1-7   *Fabric Underlay*

All interleaf traffic is VXLAN encapsulated and sent over the overlay (see Figure 1-8). External reachability from the fabric occurs through special nodes called *borders*. The border functionality may either be hosted on a leaf (in which case it is termed a *border leaf*) or hosted on a spine (in which case it is called a *border spine*).

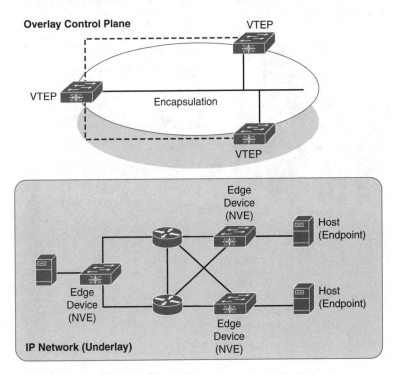

Figure 1-8   *Fabric Overlay*

VXLAN encapsulated traffic coming from the leaf switches is typically decapsulated at the VTEP on the border. Also, based on the configured Layer 2 or Layer 3 handoff, traffic is forwarded toward the external device. Sometimes the leaf to which service appliances are attached is termed a *service leaf*. Incidentally, different leaf roles are notably logical and not physical. The same leaf switch could perform all three functions—regular, border, and service leaf.

For efficient BGP EVPN overlay connectivity, one or more route reflectors (RRs) are also hosted within the fabric. Typically, RR functionality is configured on the spines or *super spines*. If IP multicast is employed for forwarding multidestination traffic, rendezvous points (RPs) also need to be hosted within the fabric. Typically, RPs are also hosted on the spines or super spines.

Data Center Network Fabric Properties

The Clos-based fabric has several desirable properties that are especially appealing for data center networks. This relatively simple topology offers enhanced scalability, resiliency, and efficiency. With no oversubscription and with equal uplink and downlink bandwidth at every leaf, the fabric offers high bisectional bandwidth that is especially appealing for data center applications.

With a two-tier Clos fabric, every leaf can reach every other leaf via a single hop through a selected spine. This provides deterministic latency for all traffic forwarded through the fabric. Adding an additional spine causes this number of equal-cost paths to increase by one. The ECMP applies equally to both unicast and multicast traffic as well as to both Layer 2 (bridged) and Layer 3 (routed) traffic with the distributed IP anycast gateway at the leaf layer.

The fabric is extremely resilient to link and node failures, and therefore it provides a high level of redundancy. Losing a spine reduces the available fabric bandwidth, but traffic continues to be forwarded in an optimal manner albeit at a reduced total rate. Similarly, on link failures, traffic is redirected to available paths, and the convergence time is governed by how fast the underlay and overlay protocols converge.

Within a fabric, any and all subnets can be simultaneously configured on any and all leafs, providing a true "any workload anywhere" option from a network point of view.

The fabric has a desirable scale-out property by which more leafs can be added if more servers, racks, or workloads are added. On the other hand, if the workloads require additional bandwidth, more spines can be added. And if higher bandwidth is required toward the external world, more border nodes can be added. In this way, the fabric can be extended as needed based on the demand.

The fabric can also be designed so that tens to hundreds to thousands of 10G server-facing ports can be supported. With desired oversubscription configuration, the fabric is malleable to support different kinds of workload environments with varying capacities.

Server or Endpoint Connectivity Options

The endpoints typically attached to a leaf may be bare-metal machines, virtual workloads, storage devices or service appliances. The endpoints may be attached to the leafs either directly or via fabric extenders (FEX)[21] or, in some cases, via blade switches. With the introduction of the Nexus 2K series of switches, FEX technology came to the forefront, and since then, it has gained widespread acceptance in a relatively short period of time.

Logically, a FEX module can be treated as an external line card that is completely managed from the parent switch to which it is attached. All management and configuration of the FEX module is done from the parent switch. Traffic to and from FEX-connected end hosts is switched and routed at the parent switch.

With FEX, the end-of-row (EoR) or middle-of-row (MoR) topologies are prevalent, where the FEX typically serves as the top-of-rack (ToR) switch per rack and where every FEX connects to a MoR or EoR switch. MoR deployments have the advantage of requiring shorter cables for connectivity compared to EoR deployments.

With respect to a fabric, various FEX connectivity combinations are possible, as shown in Figure 1-9. These combinations depend on whether the server is dual attached directly to the leaf or via the FEX. The FEX itself may even be dual attached to a pair of leaf switches configured as vPC peers.

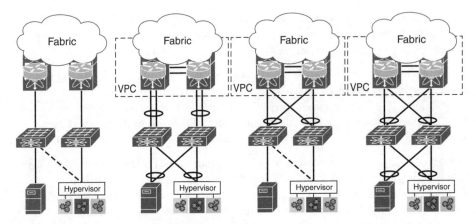

Figure 1-9   *Southbound FEX Connectivity Options*

Probably the most common option is to have straight-through FEX with one on each vPC peer while having a server dual attached to these FEXs via a PortChannel. This allows fault tolerance in case of a link failure, FEX failure, or vPC peer failure. If even more redundancy is required, enhanced vPC or EvPC deployments may be used, where both the servers and the FEXs are dual attached.

Blade chassis-based server deployments are extremely popular as well, providing the advantages of packing more compute power in the same rack space, simplifying management, and reducing the amount of cabling required. Blade switches such as the Cisco UCS Fabric Interconnect [FI] series of switches,[22] can also be connected southbound from the leafs. Figure 1-10 shows common southbound connectivity options with the UCS FI.

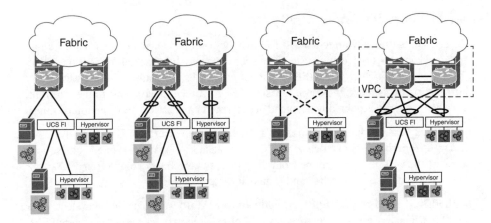

Figure 1-10   *Southbound UCS-FI Connectivity Options*

For a complete data center solution, along with compute and network features, storage also needs to be considered. The fabric is flexible enough to support both traditional Fibre Channel (FC)[23]–based storage and IP storage options. Cisco Nexus devices support the unified port option, where a port can be configured to carry either Ethernet or FC traffic.

Fibre Channel over Ethernet (FCoE)[24] technology eliminates the need for having a dedicated Ethernet link and a separate FC link. FCoE allows a converged southbound connectivity option to the servers, where the same link can carry both Ethernet and FC traffic. Upstream from the leafs, the traffic can be separated into Ethernet traffic that is carried over the VXLAN core, and storage traffic that is carried over a separate storage network.

With the popularity of IP storage and the rapid rise of hyperconvergence solutions, the need for having a separate storage network has been completely eliminated. The Cisco HyperFlex[25] solution provides an evolutionary approach for IP storage that is fully backward compatible with current deployments and easily integrated with a VXLAN BGP EVPN–based fabric. The fabric integrates well with both FC and IP storage devices.

This brief introduction to the VXLAN BGP EVPN–based fabric will allow acceleration to grasp the concepts discussed in subsequent chapters, which deal with the details of various control and data plane nuances and how traffic is forwarded within and outside the fabric. The VXLAN BGP EVPN–based fabric is a giant step toward realization of an extremely scalable network that is going to serve cloud-based data center environments for the foreseeable future.

Summary

This chapter provides a brief introduction to the Cisco VXLAN BGP EVPN fabric. The chapter begins with a description of the requirements of modern data centers. Subsequently, it gives an overview of how data centers evolved over the years leading to a VXLAN BGP EVPN–based spine-leaf fabric. Common fabric-based terminologies are introduced, along with a description on what makes the fabric extremely scalable, resilient, and elastic.

References

1. Open Networking Foundation. *Software-defined networking definition.* www.opennetworking.org/sdn-resources/sdn-definition.

2. Cisco. *Data center switches.* www.cisco.com/c/en/us/products/switches/data-center-switches/index.html.

3. Cisco. *Cisco IOS XE.* www.cisco.com/c/en/us/products/ios-nx-os-software/ios-xe/index.html.

4. Cisco. *Cisco IOS XR software.* www.cisco.com/c/en/us/products/ios-nx-os-software/ios-xr-software/index.html.

5. Cisco. *Design and configuration guide: Best practices for virtual PortChannels (vPC) on Cisco Nexus 7000 series switches.* 2016. www.cisco.com/c/dam/en/us/td/docs/switches/datacenter/sw/design/vpc_design/vpc_best_practices_design_guide.pdf.

6. Cisco. *Cisco's FabricPath*. www.cisco.com/c/en/us/solutions/
   data-center-virtualization/fabricpath/index.html.

7. Internet Engineering Task Force (IETF). *Routing bridges (RBridges): Base protocol specification*. 2011. tools.ietf.org/html/rfc6325.

8. Mahalingam, M., et al. *Virtual eXtensible local area network (VXLAN): A framework for overlaying virtualized Layer 2 networks over Layer 3 networks*. 2014. tools.ietf.org/html/rfc7348.

9. IEEE Standards Association. *802.1D-2004—IEEE standard for local and metropolitan area networks: Media access control (MAC) bridges*. 2004. standards.ieee.org/findstds/standard/802.1D-2004.html.

10. IEEE Standards Association. *802.1Q-2003—IEEE standards for local and metropolitan area networks: Virtual bridged local area networks*. 2003. standards.ieee.org/findstds/standard/802.1Q-2003.html.

11. Cisco. *Multichassis LACP*. 2015. www.cisco.com/c/en/us/td/docs/ios-xml/ios/
    cether/configuration/15-s/ce-15-s-book/ce-multichass-lacp.html.

12. Cisco. *Configuring virtual switching systems*. www.cisco.com/c/en/us/td/docs/
    switches/lan/catalyst6500/ios/12-2SX/configuration/guide/book/vss.pdf.

13. IEEE Standards Association. *802.1AX-2008—IEEE standard for local and metropolitan area networks: Link aggregation*. standards.ieee.org/findstds/
    standard/802.1AX-2008.html.

14. Internet Engineering Task Force (IETF). *Cisco hot standby router protocol (HSRP)*. 1998. www.ietf.org/rfc/rfc2281.txt.

15. Internet Engineering Task Force (IETF). *Virtual Router Redundancy Protocol (VRRP) version 3 for IPv4 and IPv6*. 2014. tools.ietf.org/html/rfc5798.

16. Cisco. *Design and configuration guide: Best practices for virtual PortChannels (vPC) on Cisco Nexus 7000 Series Switches*. 2016.
    www.cisco.com/c/dam/en/us/td/docs/switches/datacenter/sw/design/
    vpc_design/vpc_best_practices_design_guide.pdf.

17. Cisco. *Cisco FabricPath best practice*. 2016. www.cisco.com/c/dam/en/us/products/
    collateral/switches/nexus-7000-series-switches/white_paper_c07-728188.pdf.

18. Cisco. *Configuring an anycast bundle*. 2016. www.cisco.com/c/en/us/td/
    docs/switches/datacenter/sw/6_x/nx-os/fabricpath/configuration/guide/
    b-Cisco-Nexus-7000-Series-NX-OS-FP-Configuration-Guide-6x/
    b-Cisco-Nexus-7000-Series-NX-OS-FP-Configuration-Guide-6x_chapter_
    0100.html#task_BF30BB009250408E99FA8ED33D1FDB57.

19. Cisco. *Encapsulation techniques: Generic network virtualization encapsulation, VXLAN generic protocol extension, and network service header*. 2014.
    www.cisco.com/c/en/us/solutions/collateral/data-center-virtualization/
    application-centric-infrastructure/white-paper-c11-733127.html.

20. Clos, C. A study of non-blocking switching networks. *Bell System Technical Journal*, 32(2):406–424, 1953.

21. http://www.cisco.com/c/en/us/support/switches/nexus-2000-series-fabric-extenders/tsd-products-support-series-home.html

22. Cisco. *Servers: Unified computing.* www.cisco.com/c/en/us/products/servers-unified-computing/index.html.

23. Internet Engineering Task Force (IETF). *Fibre Channel (FC) frame encapsulation.* 2003. tools.ietf.org/html/rfc3643.

24. Cisco. *Fibre Channel over Ethernet (FCoE).* www.cisco.com/c/en/us/solutions/data-center-virtualization/fibre-channel-over-ethernet-fcoe/index.html.

25. Cisco. *Hyperconverged infrastructure.* www.cisco.com/c/en/us/products/hyperconverged-infrastructure/index.html.

## Chapter 2

VXLAN BGP EVPN Basics

In this chapter, you will learn about the following:

- VXLAN and its typical Flood and Learn (F&L) use case

- The evolution of a BGP EVPN control plane for VXLAN-based data center environments

- Basic Route type messages employed with BGP EVPN for network virtualization overlays

The paradigm shift toward cloud has included the adoption of an increasing degree of virtualization, where an array of physical servers and I/O devices can host multiple virtual servers that can all share the same logical network despite being in remote geographic locales. As opposed to the traditional north–south direction of data traffic between clients and servers, virtualization has facilitated greater east–west data traffic within the data center. East–west traffic describes data communications between servers and/or various applications all contained within the data center. Because much of the data required by the end user in a corporate network or on the Internet involves more complex data, certain preprocessing activities are required. As a means to demonstrate this preprocessing need, one example of east–west traffic involves access from a web server (via an app server) to the database.

Dynamic rendering of websites and/or business applications often uses a two- or three-tiered server architecture, where one tier must communicate with a second tier before delivering the requested data to the end user. When these tiers communicate with one another or need access to data storage or other data residing in the same data center, the term *east–west traffic* is used because this represents a more horizontal path profile (see Figure 2-1). Another example of east–west traffic is a user making a request to a social networking site (such as www.facebook.com), which results in a rapid set of exchanges between the servers sitting on the data center backend and returning a web page that has lots of information about the user, his friends' feeds, the associated advertisements that may match the user's preferences, and so on.

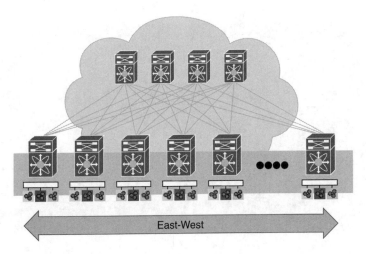

Figure 2-1   *East–West Communication Flow*

Typically, groups of devices are isolated into a broadcast domain using virtual local area networks (VLANs). A VLAN is assigned an IP subnet, and all the hosts within that VLAN have unique IP addresses within that subnet. A VLAN based on the IEEE 802.1Q standard is represented by a 12-bit tag.[1] This limits the maximum number of VLANs to 4096, thereby limiting the number of supported unique network identifiers or broadcast domains. In an era of multitenant cloud deployments, 4K VLANs are not enough. Because a single tenant might require several network IDs (VLANs) for different application tiers, saturation of these virtualized networks became a notable problem.

With virtualization, the number of end hosts, which now occupy virtual workloads or virtual machines within a broadcast domain, has skyrocketed. Scalability issues are paramount as a result. A typical 48-port access layer switch traditionally had 48 servers attached to it. With virtualization, this number has increased 20- to 30-fold. In some cases, this increase is even greater due to the fact that containers are becoming popular.[2] As a result, a switch now needs to cater to this increased capacity by having larger hardware forwarding table resources; this is a MAC table explosion problem from a data plane point of view.[3] In addition, the switches also have to service first-hop protocols (for example, DHCP, ARP, ND, IGMP) for these workloads, which results in an increase in the control plane overhead.

The classical protocol for establishing a loop-free environment in a Layer 2 broadcast domain has been the IEEE 802.1D Spanning Tree Protocol (STP) and the corresponding evolved revisions, Rapid Spanning Tree Protocol (RSTP; IEEE 802.1w) and Multiple Spanning Tree (MST; IEEE 802.1s).[4] STP has served networking environments for over 20 years. As discussed in Chapter 1, "Introduction to Programmable Fabric," STP has several drawbacks, such as increased convergence time on switch/link failures, non-optimal forwarding between switches since the packets traverse a tree, and no multipath or equal-cost multipath (ECMP) options (an attractive feature of Layer 3 networks). The increase in the host scale in a broadcast domain demands a better option than STP for supporting large data center environments.

Because virtualization permits decoupling of an end host from a physical server, migration and mobility demands of data centers, allowing movement from one physical server to another, have resulted in higher bandwidth requirements of such networks. This fact is further supported by the change in network communications, which adopt an "any-to-any" model, where any host can communicate with any other host on the network, logical or physical. In addition, agility, power efficiency, and ease of manageability are additional demands of data centers as utilization expands. Given these requirements, it is evident that traditional networking paradigms are insufficient.

The rise in horizontal data center traffic requires solutions to address the broadcast domain limitations exhibited by 12-bit VLANs. Overloading VLANs with different multiple IP subnets has not solved the problem because it does not provide the isolation required in multitenant environments. In addition, different tenants may have network identifiers with overlapping IP subnets. Thus any solution needs to somehow maintain Layer 2 bridging semantics while achieving better Layer 2 isolation of tenants with a higher capacity for network IDs. In order to accommodate the needed flexibility, scalability, mobility, and agility that data centers now require, an extended virtualized network solution was required. To fill this need, network virtualization overlays came to the forefront.

Overlays

Network virtualization overlays have become the de facto solution to address the problems just described related to data center expansion. Overlays provide a level of indirection, which allows the abstraction of the existing network technologies and extends classic network capabilities. As stated by David Wheeler, "All problems in computer science can be solved by another level of indirection, except of course for the problem of too many indirections."[5] This fundamental computer science idea supports the concept of network virtualization overlays.

The concept of overlays has been around in the networking world for quite a while. Chapter 1 describes the drawbacks of conventional networks that led to the evolution of overlays. As the name implies, an *overlay* is a static or dynamic tunnel that runs on top of a physical network infrastructure. In the 1990s, MPLS- and GRE-based encapsulations started to gain popularity.[6,7] Subsequently, other tunneling technologies, such as IPsec,[8] 6in4,[9] and L2TPv3,[10] also came to the forefront, but they were typically used at WAN edge devices. These tunnels were employed either for security purposes, for simplifying routing lookups, or in the case of 6in4 for example, for carrying payloads over a transport network that was not capable of supporting the payload type.

With overlays, the original packet or frame is packaged or encapsulated at a source edge device with an outer header and dispatched toward an appropriate destination edge device. The intermediate network devices all forward the packet based on the outer header and are not aware of the original payload. At the destination edge device, the overlay header is stripped off, and the packet is forwarded based on the inner payload.

Overlays have been used in data center environments only since 2008. That time frame also saw the rise of software defined networking (SDN) and the adoption of the cloud. Overlays in data center environments are referred to as *network virtualization overlays*. The name comes from the fact that most of the trends in data centers were revolutionized by the rapid adoption of server virtualization. When considering network virtualization overlays, a few distinct characteristics need to be considered. A primary feature that all these network virtualization overlays exhibit is related to the concept of location and identity. *Identity* identifies an end host and could be its IP address, its MAC address, and so on. *Location* identifies the tunnel edge device that is responsible for encapsulating and decapsulating tunnel traffic for that end host. As mentioned earlier, the end hosts themselves could be virtual machines, bare-metal servers, containers, or any other work-load. The outer header of the overlay references the source and destination locations, and the inner header references the source and destination end host identities.

The other notable feature pertains to the specific overlay service an overlay provides. This dictates the type of overlay as well as the associated header format. Overlay services are routinely offered as either Layer 2 (bridging) or Layer 3 (routing) services; however, many modern overlays provide both Layer 2 and Layer 3 services. The original packet (Layer 3) or frame (Layer 2) can be encapsulated into another packet (Layer 3) or frame (Layer 2). This provides potentially four combinations, depending on whether a packet/frame is carried in another packet/frame. If the outer header is a Layer 2 frame, the overlay approach is referred to as *frame encapsulation*. Examples of overlays that employ frame encapsulation are TRILL,[11] Cisco FabricPath,[12] and SPB (IEEE 802.1Qaq).[13] On the other hand, if the outer header is a Layer 3 packet, the overlay is referred to as *packet encapsulation*. Examples of overlays that employ packet encapsulation are LISP, VXLAN, and NvGRE.[14]

With Overlay services defined along with the different data-plane encapsulations, a method of transport to move the data across the physical network is required. This method of transport is typically an *underlay transport network* (or simply the *underlay*). In defining the underlay, we need to know the OSI layer where tunnel encapsulation occurs. In some sense, the overlay header type dictates the type of transport network. For example, with VXLAN, the underlying transport network (underlay) would be a Layer 3 network, which would transport the VXLAN-encapsulated packets between the source and destination tunnel edge devices. Thus, the underlay provides reachability between the various tunnel/overlay edge devices.

Usually reachability is distributed via an appropriate routing protocol. Discovery of these edge devices is a prerequisite to the operation of any overlay service. It should be noted that overlays incur a per-packet/frame overhead of *n* bytes, where *n* is the size of the overlay header along with the associated outer headers. The original payload encapsulated into the overlay header is transported over the underlay; hence, the underlay network must be provisioned with the appropriate maximum transmission unit (MTU) to ensure delivery of the overlay traffic.

Next, the network virtualization overlay requires a mechanism to know which end hosts are behind which overlay edge device. This allows the tunnel edge devices to build the location-identity mapping database. The mapping information may be facilitated via a central SDN controller (such as a Cisco APIC[15] or an OpenDaylight controller[16]) or via an overlay end host distribution protocol (such as BGP EVPN[17] or OVSDB[18]) or via a data plane–based discovery scheme (such as Flood and Learn [F&L]). Using this information for a destination end host lookup, the source edge device can push an overlay header with the appropriate fields so that the packet/frame can be delivered to the destination edge device and, subsequently, to the destination end host. Because end hosts typically belong to a certain tenant, it is imperative that the overlay header has some notion of tenancy. By pushing the appropriate tenant context information in the overlay header at the source device during encapsulation, the destination edge device can perform a per-tenant destination lookup post decapsulation, thereby ensuring isolation among tenant traffic. This is a primary requirement in multitenant data center environments.

The data plane for overlays, in addition to providing unicast encapsulated transport of Layer 2 or Layer 3 traffic, also needs to handle the transport of multidestination traffic. Multidestination traffic is typically referred to as "BUM," which stands for "broadcast, unknown unicast, or multicast." Handling these traffic types requires special capabilities to receive imposed multidestination packets from the overlay and then replicate and transport these packets accordingly in the underlay. The two most common methods that can accommodate this replication and transport in the underlay are IP multicast and ingress replication (also called head-end replication or unicast mode).

Network virtualization overlays can be initiated either from physical servers or network switches, typically the top-of-rack (ToR) switches connected to the servers. The physical servers are typically virtualized so that they can host a virtual switch/router that has enhanced capability of encapsulating and decapsulating the overlay header. This model requires the network switches to only provide connectivity between the virtualized servers, which in turn permits transport of data between the virtual end hosts, using what are called *host overlays*.

For deployments where there is a mix of bare-metal and virtualized workloads, the ToRs take care of pushing/popping the overlay headers for all kinds of workloads beneath them. These are termed *network overlays*. Both host overlays and network overlays are extremely popular and represent commonly deployed options for addressing the scale challenges in multitenant data center environments. Each has pros and cons, but the best of both worlds can be realized by using *hybrid overlay* environments, where both host overlays and network overlays are supported, allowing for optimized physical-to-virtual (P2V) communication (see Figure 2-2).

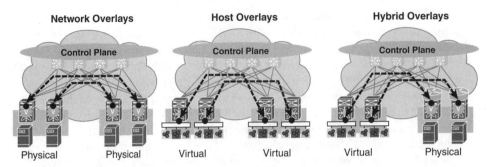

Figure 2-2   *Host, Network, and Hybrid Overlays*

With a basic understanding of essential features of overlay services, an overview of the commonly used taxonomy for both the underlay and the overlay, is presented. The underlying transport network, or underlay, is typically composed of transit devices that interconnect the edge devices. Edge devices serve as boundary devices for the underlay and are connected to end hosts and to non-overlay-speaking devices such as physical and virtual servers. Thus, edge devices connect LAN segments with the underlay.

Within the edge devices resides the functionality for encapsulation and decapsulation of overlay data traffic and for building the whole overlay network. In VXLAN terminology, this functionality on the edge device is termed a *VTEP*, which stands for *VXLAN Tunnel Endpoint*. Figure 2-3 illustrates the key terms and functions involved in a VXLAN underlay.

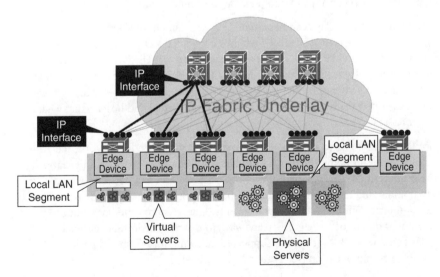

Figure 2-3   *Underlay Taxonomy*

While an edge device can host multiple VTEPs that may participate in different under-lays, typically an edge device hosts a single VTEP. As a result, throughout this book we frequently use the terms *VTEP* and *edge device* interchangeably. Between the VTEPs, tunnel encapsulation is used to provide the overlay services. In regard to VXLAN, these services are distinctively identified with a virtual network identifier (VNI), which significantly expands the ability to accommodate a much larger scale of broadcast domains within the network. These aspects make VXLAN very attractive. Figure 2-4 illustrates the key terms and functions involved in a VXLAN overlay.

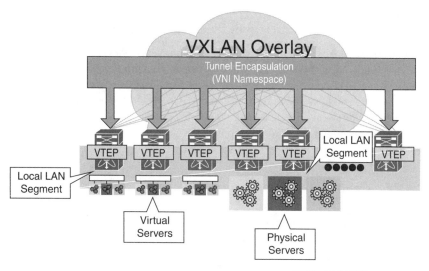

Figure 2-4   *Overlay Taxonomy*

Introduction to VXLAN

The scalability limitations of VLANs have created a need for alternative solutions as virtualization has expanded. Yet, at the same time, utilization of bridging semantics of OSI Layer 2 have needed to be preserved in order to link specific VMs and legacy devices within networks. In order to achieve this, VXLAN (Virtual Extensible Local Area Network) was developed. VXLAN extends the number of network IDs from 4096 to 16 million and provides a MAC-over-IP/UDP overlay that extends the existing VLAN namespace, thus increasing the number of broadcast domains exponentially. Hence, VXLAN represents a Layer 2-in-Layer 3 overlay. Edge devices are responsible for pushing and popping the VXLAN header through the hosted VTEP functionality.

In essence, a VXLAN connects two or more networks over Layer 3 while allowing workloads or servers on these different networks to continue sharing the same Layer 2 broadcast domain. Thus, while VLAN always operates in the Ethernet data link layer (Layer 2) only, VXLAN operates across Layer 3. In addition, as mentioned earlier, Layer 2 Ethernet networks employ STP for loop prevention, which creates a loop-free topology and hence a single active path for VLAN traffic. However, by using Layer 3 with VXLAN, all possible paths between the VTEPs can be employed via ECMP, which also greatly increases utilization of the fabric. Even by using ECMP in the underlay, a single distinct path between the VTEPs in the overlay is used while still leveraging all available ECMP paths. And by using an IP core as part of its underlay, VXLAN has made it easier to debug and maintain data centers by leveraging existing network expertise.

Inner aspects of the VXLAN header refer to Layer 2 components, while outer headers reflect the Layer 3 edge devices. Thus, the VXLAN header contains the original Layer 2 Ethernet frame of a workload, which includes the inner MAC source address as well as the inner MAC destination address, the original Ethernet payload, and the frame check sequence. In addition, the original inner 802.1Q header of the Layer 2 Ethernet frame is removed and mapped to a VNI to complete the VXLAN header, as illustrated in Figure 2-5.

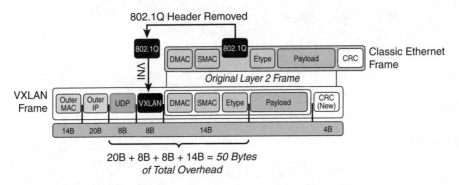

Figure 2-5   *VXLAN Frame Format*

The VXLAN header is preceded by an outer UDP header, an outer IP header, and an outer Ethernet header. The destination port number of the outer UDP header is set to 4789.[19] The UDP source port number is generated based on the fields of the original or inner header. The source IP address in the outer IP header is set to that of the source VTEP, while the destination IP address is set to that of the destination VTEP. The derivation of the outer Ethernet header is based on a routing lookup on the outer IP header, using regular Layer 3 lookup semantics. In this way, VXLAN adds a 50-byte overhead to the existing Ethernet frame or 54-byte overhead, if an optional IEEE 802.1Q tag is added. Figure 2-6 illustrates the VXLAN frame format.

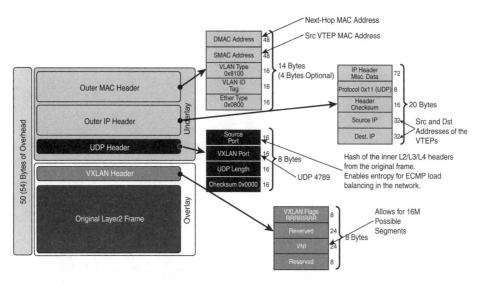

Figure 2-6   *VXLAN Frame Format Details*

Typically, in a Layer 3 network with ECMP, load balancing is achieved for forwarding traffic by choosing one of several equal-cost paths based on the popular 5-tuple input.[20] Typically, the 5-tuple comprises the source IP address, destination IP address, Layer 4 (L4) protocol, source L4 port, and destination L4 port. With VXLAN, for all traffic destined between workloads behind the same pair of source and destination VTEPs, all the other fields in the outer headers other than the UDP source port are identical. Since the UDP source port varies based on the contents of the inner packet/frame, it provides the necessary entropy to select different paths for different end host flows between the same source and destination VTEP pair. Hence, the ability to appropriately generate the UDP source port values is an important feature that should be supported by VTEPs, regardless of whether they are implemented in a software or hardware form factor. This is a critical differentiator of VXLAN compared to other overlays.

With an IP underlay, any appropriate routing protocols such as OSPF,[21] IS-IS,[22] etc. can be employed for all the VTEPs to establish connectivity to one another. The IP underlay needs to provide a means to transport overlay single-destination and multidestination traffic. One way to transport multidestination traffic is using IP multicast in the underlay. In this case, the underlay employs Protocol Independent Multicast (PIM), which is a family of multicast routing protocols for IP networks. Popular PIM options for IP multicast include PIM Any Source Multicast (ASM), PIM Single Source Multicast (SSM), and Bidirectional PIM (BIDIR).[23] Chapter 4, "The Underlay," goes into further detail on both unicast and multicast routing options for the IP underlay. A VXLAN VNI is mapped to an appropriate IP multicast group. This is done at configuration time, when the VNI is configured at a VTEP. As a result, the VTEP joins the corresponding multicast tree established via PIM. In this way, all VTEPs that are members of the same VNI are part of the same multicast group. Multidestination traffic originating from an end host that is part of a given VNI is transported to all other end hosts in that VNI over VXLAN where the outer destination IP address is set to the multicast group address associated with that VNI.

VXLAN Flood and Learn (F&L)

Consider the sample network topology shown in Figure 2-7, which illustrates a typical F&L-based communication in a VXLAN network.

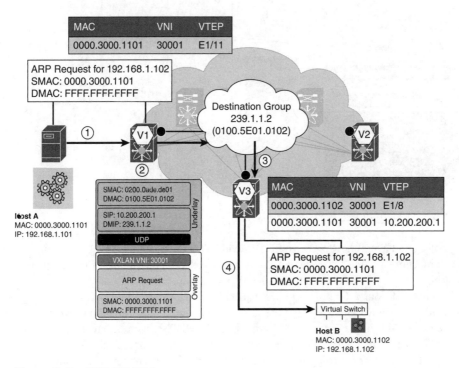

Figure 2-7   *VXLAN F&L*

Host A (IP 192.168.1.101) below VTEP V1 (10.200.200.1) and Host B (IP 192.168.1.102) below VTEP V3 (10.200.200.3) are part of the same VXLAN segment with VNI 30001. The network subnet associated with VNI 30001 is 192.168.1.0/24, and the associated multicast group is 239.1.1.2. When VNI 30001 is configured at V1 and V3, they both join the multicast group 239.1.1.2 as interested receivers. Assume that Host A wants to communicate with Host B.

As is usually the case, Host A will first try to resolve the IP-MAC binding associated with Host B, using Address Resolution Protocol (ARP). Host A sends out an ARP request with DMAC=FFFF.FFFF.FFFF and SMAC=00:00:30:00:11:01. VTEP V1 receives this ARP request and performs a Layer 2 lookup based on [VNI=30001, DMAC=FFFF.FFFF.FFFF]. VTEP V1 determines that this is a multidestination frame that needs to be sent out to all members of VNI 30001. Consequently, it encapsulates this packet with a VXLAN header with VNI=30001, Source IP=10.200.200.1, and Destination IP=239.1.1.2.

The VXLAN-encapsulated packet is sent out toward the IP core. The packet is forwarded over the multicast tree and then reaches all interested receivers, including V3.

The VXLAN-encapsulated packet is decapsulated at V3 because it has [VNI=30001, Group=239.1.1.2] configured locally. Layer 2 learning results in the entry [VNI=30001, MAC=00:00:30:00:11:01->10.200.200.1] being learned at V3. A Layer 2 lookup is performed at V3 based on [VNI=30001, DMAC=FFFF.FFFF.FFFF]. Because this is a broadcast packet, it is locally forwarded to all hosts below V3 that are part of VNI 30001, including Host B. On receiving the ARP request, Host B sends out an ARP response with DMAC=00:00:30:00:11:01 and SMAC= 00:00:30:00:11:02. V3 receives this packet, and it performs local learning and a destination lookup based on [VNI=30001, DMAC=00:00:30:00:11:01]. This results in a Layer 2 table HIT, and the packet is VXLAN encapsulated and sent toward V1.

The salient fields of interest in this packet are VNI=30001, Source IP=10.200.200.3, and Destination IP=10.200.200.1. The encapsulated packet is delivered to V1 via regular Layer 3 routing. V1 also performs Layer 2 learning and then the destination lookup based on [VNI, DMAC] results in the ARP response packet from Host B being delivered to Host A. In this way, the host MAC information is appropriately populated at both VTEPs, and Hosts A and B know about each other's MAC-IP binding. Subsequent traffic between Hosts A and B is then unicast over VXLAN between V1 and V3, respectively.

Through this mechanism, the multidestination traffic is *flooded* over the VXLAN between VTEPs to *learn* about the host MACs located behind the VTEPs so that subsequent traffic can be unicast. This is referred to as an *F&L* mechanism. Given this, communication within a VXLAN VNI follows regular Layer 2 forwarding semantics, just as is the case within a VLAN (see Figure 2-8). The main difference is that the VXLAN VNI domain spans Layer 3 networks over an IP underlay.

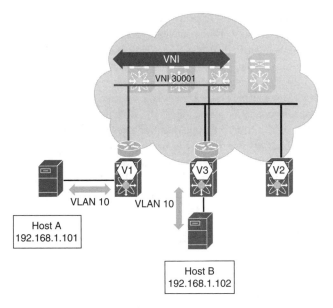

Figure 2-8 *VLAN-to-VNI Mapping*

Multiple VNIs may share the same multicast group. This is because having 16 million potential VNI options and having a unique 1:1 mapping between a VNI and a multicast group requires an exorbitant number of software and hardware resources, making it impractical for deployment. In fact, in most practical deployments, a maximum of 512 or 1024 multicast groups are supported. This means that a VTEP may receive VXLAN-encapsulated multidestination traffic for a VNI that is not locally configured. Isolation at the network level is still maintained, because every VXLAN network segment has a unique VNI, and the lookup key is always [VNI, DMAC]. One alternative to IP multicast for handling multidestination traffic in a VXLAN environment is to use ingress replication (IR), or head-end replication. With IR, every VTEP must be aware of other VTEPs that have membership in a given VNI. The source VTEP generates *n* copies for every multidestination frame, with each destined to other VTEPs that have membership in the corresponding VNI. This places an additional burden on the VTEPs, but it has the benefit of simplification since there is no need to run multicast in the IP underlay.

VXLAN is one of the few overlays that has been used both as a host overlay and as a network overlay. With the rise of SDN, VXLAN has been heavily used as a host overlay, with physical servers hosting software VTEPs that perform VXLAN encapsulation and decapsulation for traffic between virtualized workloads. To establish communication between legacy workloads that do not support VXLAN, Layer 2 VXLAN gateways come to the forefront, providing translation between legacy VLAN-based and virtualized VXLAN-based domains. Networking vendors started to support VXLAN in their hardware switches, thereby providing options for use of VXLAN as a network overlay. This paved the way for a hybrid environment where both software and hardware VTEPs can be simultaneously supported in the same data center environment.

VXLAN provided a notable solution for the issues of poor scalability, the need for enhanced network mobility, and preserved network manageability. However, some disadvantages with VXLAN have been identified. While VXLAN defined an extensible data plane for virtual networks, a control plane was not specified in this regard. Consequently, the native F&L-based approach employed by VXLAN is far from ideal since the broadcast domain for a VXLAN now spans Layer 3 boundaries. In general, any flooding-based mechanism will have serious concerns, especially as the scale increases. As discussed in Chapter 1, VXLAN F&L suffers from the same disadvantages as Ethernet F&L-based networks. Thus, while VXLAN offers significant advantages in some aspects related to the increasing data center demands, it fails to offer a comprehensive solution in total. The missing piece is a mechanism to learn about end hosts behind a VTEP without the need to flood traffic. This is accomplished using a BGP-based control protocol extension.

Introduction to BGP EVPN with VXLAN

Utilization of VXLAN clearly offers many advantages for multitenant data centers through advancing the number of network identifiers and through its Layer 3 overlay platform. But while STP is avoided by incorporating the IP core for data transport, multicast protocols are still required to emulate flooding over a Layer 3 network when seeking destination workloads before specific host-to-host identifiers are learned and defined.

Therefore, VXLANs traditionally have utilized F&L approaches when transporting data over a network. All logical and legacy devices within the network behind the destination VTEP addresses receive data from the originating workload in an effort to target the destination workload, and once received by its intended destination address, specific MAC address information is provided back to the originating workload so that host learning occurs. Once learned, a direct host-to-host connection is established within the VXLAN network segment.

With this in mind, the use of Border Gate Protocol (BGP)[24] and Ethernet VPN (EVPN)[25] addresses some problems related to learning via flooding by minimizing the extent to which this needs to occur. BGP is a longstanding, standardized protocol for Network Layer Reachability Information (NLRI) exchange to facilitate host-to-host reachability within the network. BGP has effectively demonstrated that it can scale at the Internet level. Being a hard-state protocol, one that initiates messaging only when there is a change of some sort in the network reachability information that it is advertising, BGP messaging has been extended in various ways. In the context of network virtualization overlays, BGP provides a data directory of all MAC and IP addresses of devices (logical and otherwise) behind a VTEP within a VXLAN network segment. As a result, BGP permits a clear structure of standardized numbering and naming of VXLAN destinations, which eliminates the need to flood in order to learn addressing information. Multiprotocol BGP has similarly been well established in operating in IP networks with multitenancy support,[26] and its use in combination with EVPN offers the needed control plane aspects.

The EVPN extensions that are part of BGP (or Multiprotocol BGP [MP-BGP])[27] add enough information within these standardized identifiers so data exchange may occur efficiently between workloads. EVPN transports information between source and destination VTEPs within a VXLAN, using BGP/MP-BGP formatting to identify reachability of specific IP and MAC address destinations behind a VTEP. Through integrated routing and switching,[28] EVPN facilitates transport for both Layer 2 and Layer 3, using known workload addresses present within the VXLAN network. As a result, the need for unnecessary flooding for learning can be notably reduced, and in some cases, it can be completely eliminated.

In a nutshell, the EVPN address family allows the host MAC, IP, network, VRF, and VTEP information to be carried over MP-BGP. In this way, as long as a VTEP learns about a host behind it (via ARP/ND/DHCP etc.), BGP EVPN distributes and provides this information to all other BGP EVPN–speaking VTEPs within the network. As long as the source VTEP continues to detect a host behind it, an EVPN update message is not sent out. As a result, other VTEPs need not "age out" any remote host reachability information. This prevents any kind of aging-related churn that may happen in typical F&L scenarios, thereby greatly enhancing network scalability.

To expand on this concept a bit further, it is sometimes presumed that BGP-EVPN eliminates the need for flooding altogether, but this is not actually valid. VXLAN operates as the data plane of the network and transports data. Hence, for handling BUM traffic over VXLAN, the sourcing VTEP is still required to send multidestination traffic to multiple VTEPs, either using IP multicast or ingress replication. While flooding due to unknown unicast traffic can perhaps be eliminated (if there are no "silent" hosts, or hosts that have not yet been discovered and only respond when spoken to), broadcast traffic due to ARP, DHCP, and other addressing protocols may still incur flooding. Examples of these include a web server, some firewalls, or some select service appliances. In the era of virtualization, the number of silent hosts has been reduced; however, these hosts have not been completely eliminated. Therefore, through the use of the EVPN control plane, the need for flooding is reduced, but EVPN does not remove the need for it entirely.

BGP EVPN differs from F&L in several ways. Both peer discovery and remote end host learning are handled in a completely different fashion because BGP EVPN distributes endpoint identifiers (MAC and optionally IP addresses) as well the endpoint-associated IP prefix information behind a VTEP. Likewise, peer VTEP authentication is different, with the control plane containing the required information rather than waiting for unicast learning responses. In addition, BGP EVPN narrows host route distribution through the use of this control plane. As a result, ARP requests are suppressed within the VXLAN network, which markedly enhances the efficiency of the data transport. Given these characteristics, the use of BGP EVPN with VXLAN offers an improved means by which data transport is facilitated and controlled so that the number of specific hosts being identified within a network can increase exponentially.

MP-BGP Features and Common Practices

The VXLAN BGP-EVPN solution is based on MP-BGP, as described in RFC 4760.[29] The main feature in MP-BGP is to allow a multiplex of address families and related NLRI into a single BGP peering session. As a result, MP-BGP also allows VPN services across this single BGP peering session and provides embedded logic for separating reachability information for the separate tenants. The terms *tenant*, *VPN*, and *VRF* are used interchangeably here.

MP-BGP address families are used to transport specific reachability information. Popular address families include VPNv4 and VPNv6, which are widely used for Multiprotocol Label Switching (MPLS) between different data center sites with Layer 3 VPNs. Other VPN address families (for example, Multicast VPN [MVPN]) are used to transport reachability of multicast group information within MPLS or other encapsulations in a multitenant environment. In case of VXLAN, the focus is on the address family L2VPN EVPN, which describes the method of transporting tenant-aware Layer 2 (MAC) and Layer 3 (IP) information across a single MP-BGP peering session.

In BGP, when using a single autonomous system (AS), the peering between BGP speakers is called internal BGP (iBGP). iBGP is mainly used to exchange information between all the speakers in a synchronous fashion across the entire AS. iBGP requires full-mesh peering as reachability information must be learned from an iBGP speaker and must not be relayed to any other iBGP speaker. In order to change this behavior, iBGP can utilize the function of a route reflector (RR). An RR is allowed to receive iBGP information and then "reflect" the information to any of its RR clients—that is, all known iBGP neighbors. With iBGP and RR function, BGP peerings can be optimized so the requirement of using a full-mesh BGP peering can be abandoned (see Figure 2-9). Likewise, this also permits the control plane to be scaled higher (that is, N sessions for N peers versus $N(N-1)/2$ or $O(N^2)$ sessions required with full-mesh connectivity).

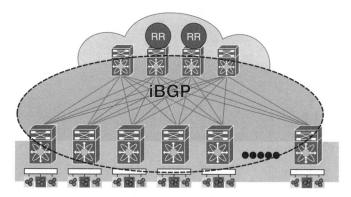

Figure 2-9   *iBGP with a Route Reflector*

With external BGP (eBGP), peering between BGP speakers is achieved between different autonomous systems. This means, for example, that a BGP speaker in AS 65500 can be peered with its neighbor BGP speaker, which resides in AS 65501 (see Figure 2-10). In eBGP, the rules for route exchange are slightly different. Unlike with iBGP, which requires full-mesh peering without the use of an RR, BGP reachability information received from an eBGP speaker is always sent to all its neighbors. In addition, compared to iBGP, eBGP has implicit next-hop self-semantics so that every route originated by the eBGP speaker is advertised with itself as the next hop.

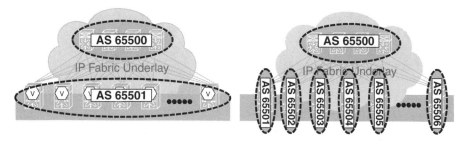

Figure 2-10   *eBGP with no Route Reflector*

MP-BGP is well known for its multitenancy and routing policy capabilities. In order to differentiate between routes stored in the BGP tables, MP-BGP uses Route Distinguishers (RDs). An RD is 8 bytes (64 bits) and composed of three fields. The first 2 bytes are the Type field, which determines how the Value field will be interpreted. The remaining 6 bytes are the Value field, which can be filled according to three well-known formats.

As illustrated in Figure 2-11, the first format is type 0, where a 2-byte autonomous system number plus a 4-byte individual number completes the Value field of the RD. For type 1 and type 2, the first portion of the Value field is similar in size (each 4 bytes), but the content of this portion differs: It is the IP address in type 1 and the AS number in type 2. The latter portion of the Value field for both type 1 and type 2 formats is again a 2-byte individual number field. As a common best practice for separation and path efficiency, a good rule of thumb is to use a unique RD on a per-VRF, per-router basis so each logical virtual router instance is individually identifiable.

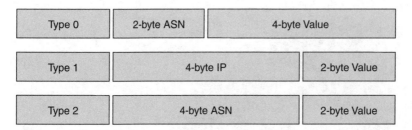

Figure 2-11 *Route Distinguisher Formats and Types*

In addition to providing unique identifiers for multiple tenants, MP-BGP also uses route policies to prioritize routes in a particular logical instance. This is achieved via an attribute called a Route Target (RT). An RT attribute can be thought of as identifying a set of sites, though it would be more precise to think of it as identifying a set of VRFs. Associating a particular RT attribute with a route allows that route to be placed in the VRFs that are used for routing traffic that is received from the corresponding sites.

The RT's notation is similar to that of the RD, but its function is rather different. While one is used to uniquely identify prefixes of entries in the BGP table, the other controls the import or export of these prefixes (see Figure 2-12). RTs essentially are tags placed on a route to identify routes, which may be preferentially important.

By using RTs, routes can be identified and placed in different VRF tables. With the control of an export RT, prefixes can be steered, at the ingress switch, to receive a special tag assigned in MP-BGP. Likewise, if the same RTs on the import side are being used, all the routes marked at the export can then be imported preferentially as well. RTs are also 8 bytes long, but formatting can be rather freely used, apart from the *prefix:suffix* notation. Cisco provides automated derivation of RDs and RTs for simplification.

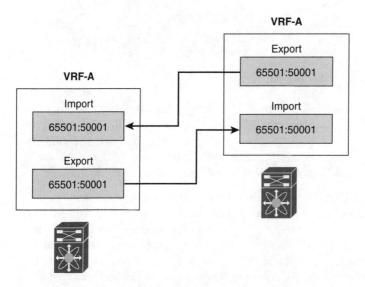

Figure 2-12 *Route Target Concept*

Note   Automated derivation of RD uses the type 1 format with RID Loopback IP: internal MAC/IP VRF ID (RD: 10.10.10.1:3). For automatic derivation of RT, the format is ASN: VNI (RT: 65501:50001).

Multiprotocol BGP contains many more features and functions. For the specifics of the VXLAN EVPN solution, the RD and RT fields are described to understand generic prefix advertisement. Further, extended community attributes are carried in MP-BGP to amend the existing prefixes with further information for forwarding. However, this information is beyond the scope of this introduction to MP-BGP and its associated common practices.

IETF Standards and RFCs

VXLAN EVPN pertains to multiple Internet Engineering Task Force (IETF) Requests for Comments (RFCs) or drafts. The generic control plane for EVPN is described in RFC 7432. This RFC defines the general rules of engagement of the MP-BGP EVPN address family and its NLRI for the different data plane implementations. While specific drafts exist to define the details for MPLS, for Provider Backbone Bridges (PBB), and for the network virtualization overlay (NVO) implementations, our main focus involves the implementation of BGP EVPN for the NVO data plane with VXLAN (see Figure 2-13).

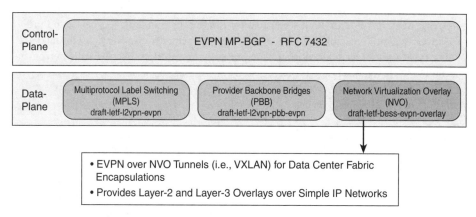

Figure 2-13   *IETF RFC/Draft for Control and Data Plane*

The relevant IETF draft describing the VXLAN implementation for EVPN is draft-ietf-bess-evpn-overlay. This draft is part of the BGP Enabled Services (BESS) working group[30] and defines functions like encapsulation markers, how to construct EVPN routes, and how subnets are mapped to an EVPN virtual instance (EVI). Subsequent implementation drafts are draft-ietf-bess-evpn-inter-subnet-forwarding and draft-ietf-bess-evpn-prefix-advertisement. Both of these additions describe how the Integrated Routing and Bridging (IRB) and Layer 3 routing operation in EVPN are handled. Table 2-1 lists the VXLAN BGP EVPN–related RFCs/drafts currently implemented on the Cisco Nexus operating system (NX-OS).

Table 2-1 *RFC/Draft Overview*

RFC/Draft	Title	Category
RFC 7348	Virtual Extensible Local Area Network	Data plane
RFC 7432	BGP MPLS Based Ethernet VPNs	Control plane
draft-ietf-bess-evpn-overlay	A Network Virtualization Overlay Solution Using EVPN	Control plane
draft-ietf-bess-evpn-inter-subnet-forwarding	Integrated Routing and Bridging in EVPN	Control plane
draft-ietf-bess-evpn-prefix-advertisement	IP Prefix Advertisement in EVPN	Control plane
draft-tissa-nvo3-oam-fm	NVO3 Fault Management/OAM	Management plane

Important sections for Cisco's NX-OS implementation of VXLAN EVPN are the sections on VLAN-based bundle services, symmetric IRB forwarding on NVEs for end hosts or subnets (that is, inter-subnet-forwarding, sections 5.1 and 5.2), and implementation of IP-VRF-to-IP-VRF (that is, prefix advertisement, Section 5.4).

It should be noted that MP-BGP EVPN has different NLRI definitions as part of RFC 7432. Likewise, MP-BGP EVPN Route types have different defining sections in RFC 7432 for Route types 1 through 4 and also for Route type 5 in draft-ietf-bess-evpn-prefix-advertisement (see Table 2-2). Route type 1 (Ethernet auto-discovery [A-D] route) and Route type 4 (Ethernet segment route) are presently not used in Cisco's EVPN implementation for VXLAN, but Route types 2, 3, and 5 are rather important.

Table 2-2 *BGP EVPN Route types*

RFC/Draft	Route type	Description
RFC 7432	1	Ethernet auto-discovery (AD) route
	2	MAC/IP advertisement route
	3	Inclusive multicast Ethernet tag route
	4	Ethernet segment route
draft-ietf-bess-evpn-prefix-advertisement	5	IP prefix route

Route type 2 defines the MAC/IP advertisement route and is responsible for the distribution of MAC and IP address reachability information in BGP EVPN (see Figure 2-14). Route type 2 has various fields that provide contexts for addressing information. Route type 2 has mandatory MAC Address and MAC Address Length fields. Likewise, one label has to be populated to define the Layer 2 VNI for the VXLAN data plane (MPLS label 1). This NLRI also allows for the optional fields, IP Address, and IP Address Length. While normally the IP Address Length field is variable, the length is intended to be 32 for IPv4 and 128 for IPv6 for Route type 2, which contains IP addressing information for a single endpoint or server.

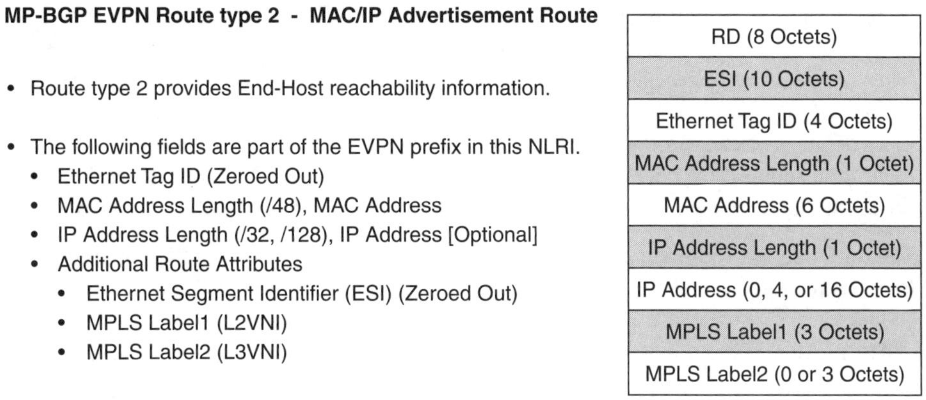

MP-BGP EVPN Route type 2 - MAC/IP Advertisement Route

- Route type 2 provides End-Host reachability information.

- The following fields are part of the EVPN prefix in this NLRI.
  - Ethernet Tag ID (Zeroed Out)
  - MAC Address Length (/48), MAC Address
  - IP Address Length (/32, /128), IP Address [Optional]
  - Additional Route Attributes
    - Ethernet Segment Identifier (ESI) (Zeroed Out)
    - MPLS Label1 (L2VNI)
    - MPLS Label2 (L3VNI)

RD (8 Octets)
ESI (10 Octets)
Ethernet Tag ID (4 Octets)
MAC Address Length (1 Octet)
MAC Address (6 Octets)
IP Address Length (1 Octet)
IP Address (0, 4, or 16 Octets)
MPLS Label1 (3 Octets)
MPLS Label2 (0 or 3 Octets)

Figure 2-14 *BGP EVPN Route type 2 NLRI*

When using Route type 2 for bridging information, additional community attributes can be present, such as the encapsulation type (Encap 8: VXLAN), Route Target, or MAC mobility sequence for endpoint mobility or duplicate host detection. Additional attributes or communities are also present for the routing case where the Router MAC of the next hop will be incorporated as an extended community as well as a second VNI (Layer 3 VNI) and Route Target, for the Layer 3 operation. Note that with Route type 2, individual RTs and VNIs are present with one each for Layer 2 and Layer 3 information. In case of the absence of IP information in a Route type 2 message, the optional fields IP Address and IP Address Length are "zeroed out," and the Layer 3 VNI (MPLS Label 2) is omitted.

Route type 3 is called "inclusive multicast Ethernet tag route" and is typically used to create the distribution list for ingress replication (see Figure 2-15). This provides a way to replicate multidestination traffic in a unicast way. Route type 3 is immediately generated and sent to all ingress replication–participating VTEPs as soon as a VNI is configured at the VTEP and is operational. This is different from Route type 2, which is only sent with MAC/IP information, once end hosts have been learned. In this way, every VTEP is aware of all the other remote VTEPs that need to be sent a copy of a BUM packet in a given VNI.

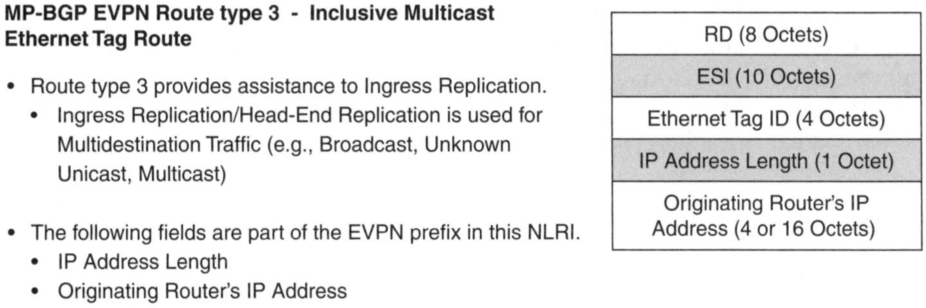

MP-BGP EVPN Route type 3 - Inclusive Multicast Ethernet Tag Route

- Route type 3 provides assistance to Ingress Replication.
  - Ingress Replication/Head-End Replication is used for Multidestination Traffic (e.g., Broadcast, Unknown Unicast, Multicast)

- The following fields are part of the EVPN prefix in this NLRI.
  - IP Address Length
  - Originating Router's IP Address

RD (8 Octets)
ESI (10 Octets)
Ethernet Tag ID (4 Octets)
IP Address Length (1 Octet)
Originating Router's IP Address (4 or 16 Octets)

Figure 2-15 *BGP EVPN Route type 3 NLRI*

Note that ingress replication is a functionality that not only has to be supported by the BGP EVPN control plane, but must also be supported by the data plane. In addition, the data plane must be able to generate *n* copies for every multidestination packet, where *n* is the remote VTEPs that have membership in the associated VNI. Because this data-plane capability depends on the specific hardware ASIC that hosts the VTEP, in the absence of ingress replication support, the only option for forwarding BUM traffic is IP multicast. As a result, the myth that EVPN removes the requirement of multicast in the underlay is nullified.

The third and last Route type to be discussed is Route type 5, the IP prefix route (see Figure 2-16).

MP-BGP EVPN Route type 5 - IP Route

- Route type 5 provides IP prefix advertisement in EVPN.
  - RT-5 decouples IP prefix from MAC (RT-2) and provides flexible advertisement of IPv4 and IPv6 prefixes with variable length.

- The following fields are part of the EVPN prefix in this NLRI.
  - IP Prefix Length (0-32 Bits for IPv4 or 0-128 Bits for IPv6)
  - IP Prefix (IPv4 or IPv6)
  - GW IP Address
  - MPLS Label (L3VNI)

RD (8 Octets)
ESI (10 Octets)
Ethernet Tag ID (4 Octets)
IP Prefix Length (1 Octet)
IP Prefix (4 or 16 Octets)
GW IP Address (4 or 16 Octets)
MPLS Label (3 Octets)

Figure 2-16   *BGP EVPN Route type 5 NLRI*

While EVPN was primarily built for transporting Layer 2 information and providing better efficiency in bridging operations, routing represents a generic demand in overlay networks for inter-subnet communication or communication across two Layer 2 VNIs. Route type 5 provides the capability of transporting IP prefix information within EVPN by allowing the transport of IPv4 and IPv6 prefixes with variable IP prefix length (0 to 32 for IPv4 and 0 to 128 for IPv6). IP prefix routes on Route type 5 do not contain Layer 2 MAC information within the NLRI, and therefore Route type 5 only incorporates the Layer 3 VNI needed for routing and integrated multitenancy. Furthermore, the extended communities of Route type 5 carry the Route Target, the encapsulation type, and the router MAC of the next-hop VTEP in the overlay. With a Route type 2, a MAC address is used for route identification within a MAC VRF, while for a Route type 5, the IP prefix is used for route identification in an IP VRF. This allows a clean separation for the BGP EVPN speakers, thereby preventing any MAC address–related processing for EVPN-advertised IP prefix routes (Route type 5).

Host and Subnet Route Distribution

With BGP EVPN, overlay end host and subnet reachability information is distributed in such a way that it is decoupled from the underlay. While the underlay provides the topology with reachability information from VTEP to VTEP, the overlay control protocol distributes end host information, like MAC addresses, IP addresses, or subnet prefixes with the associated location in the overlay. The VTEP is advertised as the next hop in all BGP EVPN prefix advertisements. BGP EVPN exchanges this information with all participating VTEPs to achieve end-to-end reachability on the Layer 2 bridging or Layer 3 routing layer. In addition to the reachability information itself, BGP EVPN also provides the respective context to which the respective addresses belong and the resulting multitenancy. As BGP provides a resilient way to distribute the information, the individual edge devices, or VTEPs, are required to inject the local known information of MAC, IP, and IP subnet into BGP for further distribution.

On detection of an end host connected to a VXLAN BGP EVPN–capable edge device or VTEP, the MAC information is learned on the local switch in a traditional way through Layer 2 MAC learning (such as [VLAN, SMAC] entry points to the Incoming_port). Through the process of MAC learning, the relationship to the Layer 2 VLAN will be known, and it maps to the Layer 2 VNI. Information about newly learned local MAC addresses is populated into the MP-BGP control protocol by filling the mandatory section of the Route type 2 message. At this stage, a BGP update, containing an EVPN Route type 2 NLRI, is created with the MAC address length (6 bytes), the MAC address itself, the Layer 2 VNI (label 1), and the respective Route Distinguisher and Route Target, derived through the configuration on the edge device itself (see Figure 2-17).

Furthermore, as BGP EVPNs for VXLAN are used, the encapsulation type 8 is incorporated to ensure that all neighboring devices understand that the data plane encapsulation being used is VXLAN.[31] Because the message shown in Figure 2-17 was triggered on a new MAC address learn event at the VTEP in the BGP EVPN–based network, the MAC mobility extended community is unpopulated.[32]

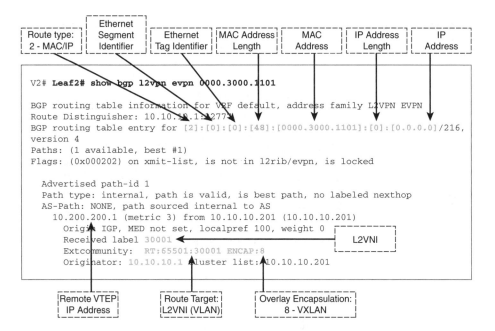

Figure 2-17   show bgp l2vpn evpn: *Route type 2 (MAC Only)*

Note   As a verification, the EVPN NLRI is being checked with the bit count of the populated fields. This bit count results as a / notation next to the respective prefix. A MAC-only Route type 2 is represented with a /216 prefix, while a MAC/IP Route type 2 is represented as a /272 prefix (that is, an additional 32 bits for IPv4 address plus 24 bits for L3VNI). When an IPv6 address is carried in Route type 2, it is represented as a /368 prefix (that is, an additional 128 bits for IPv6 address plus 24 bits for L3VNI). A Route type 5 EVPN route carrying an IPv4 prefix is represented by a /224 prefix, while one carrying an IPv6 address is represented by a /416 prefix.

Once the edge device receives an ARP request from a directly attached end host, the IP-MAC binding of the end host is learned at that edge device. The ingress Layer 3 interface on which the ARP request is received provides the associated context information for that end host. The context implicitly maps to the tenant VRF associated with the Layer 3 interface and, hence, the end host. Recall that every tenant VRF is associated with a unique Layer 3 VNI that is used for routing tenant traffic.

While the description thus far refers to ARP, similar operations are performed with IPv6 end hosts using Neighbor Discovery Protocol (ND). With the parameters required to configure the VRF for BGP EVPN, the Route Distinguisher for this VRF is also derived, along with the respective Route Targets. At this stage, all the related Layer 3 end host information can be populated into the Route type 2 NLRI in the BGP EVPN message. This includes the IP address length, the IP address, the Layer 3 VNI (label 2), and the Route Distinguisher and Route Target derived via the configuration. In addition, the Router MAC (RMAC) associated with the sourcing VTEP or edge device is also added as an extended community. This provides the neighboring edge devices the mapping information about the sourcing VTEP's IP address (Layer 3) and the associated MAC address (Layer 2).

The requirement of incorporating the RMAC in the BGP EVPN message comes from the fact that VXLAN is a MAC in IP/UDP encapsulation. By providing the inner MAC to be the RMAC for routing purposes, the information used during encapsulation appropriately identifies the neighboring VTEP not only at the Layer 3 (next-hop IP) level but also at the Layer 2 (destination VTEP MAC) level. Next to the RMAC, the encapsulation type 8 (VXLAN) is also added to the extended community to ensure that all neighboring VTEPs read this prefix as belonging to VXLAN. Additional fields in the BGP EVPN Route type 2 NLRI have to be considered. Figure 2-18 illustrates a sample **show** output for a typical Route type 2 entry with both MAC and IP fields populated. Because VLAN-based bundle services are employed, the Ethernet tag field in the MAC/IP advertisement (Route type 2) and inclusive multicast route (Route type 3) advertisement must be set to zero.[33]

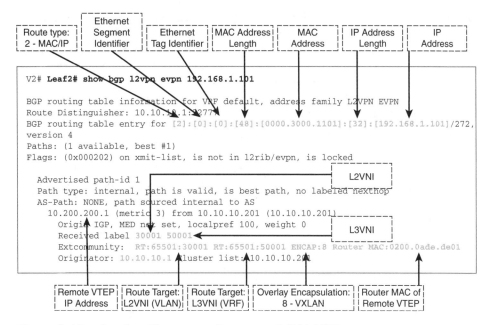

Figure 2-18 show bgp l2vpn evpn: *Route type 2 (MAC/IP)*

With the addition of the Layer 3 information to Route type 2, which previously only carried Layer 2 information, we now have a fully populated NLRI to perform bridging and routing operation within a VXLAN network using BGP EVPN. The information known is sent via BGP update to the route reflector (iBGP), which in turn forwards this update message to all its BGP peers. On receiving this update message, all the edge devices add the information of the newly learned remote end hosts to their respective local databases—aka end host (MAC/IP) bridging/routing tables. At this time, MAC addresses matching the Layer 2 VNI and the corresponding import Route Targets are populated in the hardware tables for MAC learning purposes (for example, [VLAN, MAC]->Remote_ VTEP_IP). Note that these MAC addresses are learned via BGP and not subjected to regular aging semantics. They are deleted only when a corresponding BGP delete message is received, signaling the removal of the endpoint.

A similar procedure is followed for populating the host IP prefixes into the hardware routing table, typically called the Forwarding Information Base (FIB). Specifically, the Layer 3 VNI, along with the associated import Route Targets, identifies the tenant VRF or VPN in which the /32 or /128 host IP prefix must be installed. Depending on the hardware capability of the edge device, the FIB may be divided into a host route table (HRT), which stores exact /32 (IPv4) or /128 (IPv6) host prefixes, and a Longest Prefix Match (LPM) table, which typically stores variable-length IP prefix information. The FIB entry, either from the HRT or LPM, points to an adjacency or next-hop entry. This is populated with the [BD, RMAC] entry, where BD is the hardware bridge domain that maps to the Layer 3 VNI and RMAC corresponds to the remote VTEP. Both of these pieces of information are carried in the BGP-EVPN Route type 2/5 advertisement.

It should be noted that the FIB HRT is typically implemented in hardware as a hash table since it only needs to support exact match semantics, while the FIB LPM is implemented as a true TCAM or algorithm TCAM, since it must support longest prefix match semantics. Because TCAMs are an expensive resource due to their larger power requirement, a relatively smaller LPM-based TCAM table is generally present in data center ToR ASICs with bigger HRT tables that can support a large number of endpoints or end hosts in massive-scale data center environments.

Only providing locally learned host routing information (with /32- or /128-based IP prefixes) via BGP EVPN is insufficient. Therefore, in addition to host bridging and routing capability, BGP EVPN also provides the classic semantics of IP prefix-based routing. IP prefixes are learned and redistributed by the sourcing edge devices into the BGP EVPN control protocol. To perform this operation, a specific EVPN NLRI format has been introduced (Route type 5). With Route type 5 messages, an edge device populates the IP prefix length with the IP prefix field corresponding to the route being advertised and the Layer 3 VNI associated with the VRF context to which the route belongs (see Figure 2-19). Based on the configuration of the VRF itself, the Route Distinguisher and Route Target associated with the route can be derived. Similar to the Route type 2 message, the RMAC and encapsulation type (that is, VXLAN) are also incorporated as an extended community into the Route type 5 message.

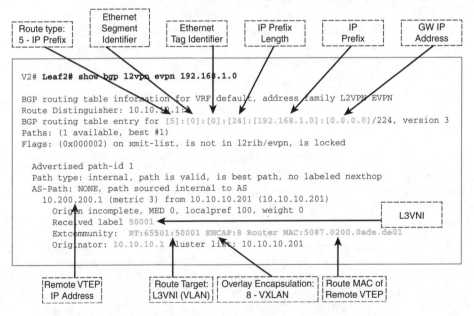

Figure 2-19   show bgp l2vpn evpn: *Route type 5 (IP)*

Once a Route type 5 message is received by an edge device or a VTEP, the IP prefix route carried in the update is imported into the routing tables only if the Layer 3 VNI and Route Target configured locally at the receiving VTEP matches the one carried in the message. If this match exists, the IP route is installed into the FIB table, typically as an LPM entry. The corresponding adjacency or next-hop entry is populated in a similar manner to the Route type 2 message.

There are two major use cases in which Route type 5 is utilized for carrying the IP prefix routing information in a VXLAN-based BGP EVPN network. The first involves advertising the IP subnet prefix information from every edge device performing first-hop routing service. In the case of first-hop routing, also referred to as Integrated Routing and Bridging (IRB), the edge device performs the default gateway service with the distributed IP anycast gateway (see Figure 2-20). As long as the gateway is configured, the IP subnet prefix is advertised via Route type 5. This helps in the discovery of undiscovered, or "silent," end hosts because the subnet prefix attracts routed traffic to the edge device below which the undiscovered host resides. This edge device generates an ARP request to discover the silent host, which in turn sends out an ARP response. After discovery, the IP-MAC binding of the end host is learned at the directly attached edge device (via ARP snooping) and advertised into BGP EVPN using Route type 2, as described earlier. In case the IP subnet prefix route was not advertised from all edge devices hosting the distributed IP anycast gateway for that subnet, the traffic toward that end host would be silently dropped instead of initiating the described host discovery process.

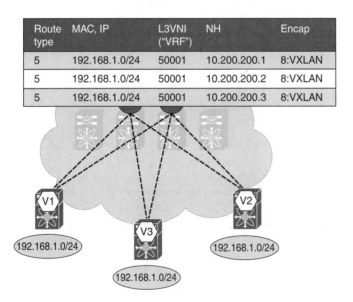

Route type	MAC, IP	L3VNI ("VRF")	NH	Encap
5	192.168.1.0/24	50001	10.200.200.1	8:VXLAN
5	192.168.1.0/24	50001	10.200.200.2	8:VXLAN
5	192.168.1.0/24	50001	10.200.200.3	8:VXLAN

Figure 2-20 *Integrated Route and Bridge (IRB)*

The second and probably more common use case for injection of IP prefix routes into the BGP EVPN fabric involves external routing. Routes are learned via peering established using eBGP (or other unicast routing protocols) and redistributed into the BGP EVPN address family using appropriate route map policies (see Figure 2-21). As part of this redistribution process, this information is advertised in the same routing context (VRF) in which it was learned. This means that using Inter-AS Option A[34] with subinterfaces is a viable way to keep multitenancy information even beyond the BGP EVPN network. An alternative solution for keeping this context awareness could be achieved by Locator/ID Separation Protocol (LISP)[35] or an MPLS Layer 3 VPN. Next to the integrated approach of receiving BGP EVPN information and advertising it to a multitenant-aware external network, LISP also provides the capability of FIB-space conservation (resource savings for host routes) for external sites and ingress route optimization with host granularity.[36]

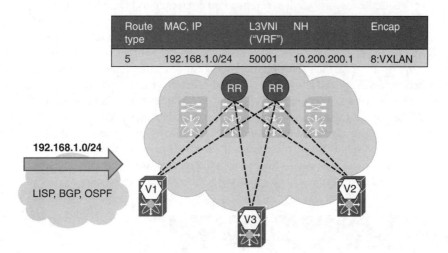

Figure 2-21   *External Route Learning*

Host Deletion and Move Events

So far, end host detection has been covered in addition to the advertisement of Layer 2 and Layer 3 reachability information about an end host into BGP EVPN. This section covers handling of end host deletion and move events. The deletion of end hosts follows almost the same process as learning a new end host, but in the opposite order. Once an end host gets detached from the VXLAN BGP EVPN–based network, on expiration of the ARP entry (the Cisco NX-OS default is 1500 seconds), Layer 3 information about that end host is removed from BGP EVPN. This means the Route type 2 advertisement providing the information for the end host's MAC and IP is withdrawn after the timeout of the related ARP entry.

Specifically, on expiration of the ARP entry, the NX-OS edge device performs a refresh operation. It sends out an ARP request toward the end host to detect its presence. If it receives an ARP response, the end host is deemed "alive," and the ARP refresh timer for that entry is reset to 1500 seconds. However, if no ARP response is received, the ARP entry is deleted, and the end host is deemed "dead." Then a Route type 2 deletion advertisement is sent out to let all other edge devices know that the corresponding end host is no longer reachable.

Even when the ARP entry is deleted, the MAC-only Route type 2 still resides in the BGP EVPN control plane until the MAC aging timer expires (the NX-OS default is 1800 seconds), and the MAC information is removed. On this expiration event, the MAC-only Route type 2 advertisement is withdrawn from the BGP EVPN control protocol. Subsequently, when that end host reappears by sending some ARP or other traffic, the information about the end host is relearned and advertised into the BGP-EVPN control plane. The EVPN prefixes are considered new and never seen before. Note that the ARP aging timer is slightly shorter than the MAC aging timer. As a best practice, the two timers should be configured in this way so that unnecessary unknown unicast flooding in the network is avoided. If the MAC aging timer is reduced, then it is important to also reduce the ARP aging timer.

Moving workloads is fairly common in today's cloud-based data centers, especially with the presence of virtualization. It entails moving an end host so that the same MAC and IP address can now be reached from a different edge device. From a network point of view, the control protocol can treat this as a deletion of the end host from the old edge device and a new learn event from the edge device to which the end host has moved.
This process can be time-consuming, especially in case of "hot" move events, where the end host is still "on" when it is moved to permit the resumption of its operations at the new location as soon as the move is complete. A faster option is required that allows for just-in-time end host move signaling so that the network is aware of the new location of the end host, which allows for faster convergence.

BGP EVPN has the logic for MAC mobility incorporated to cater to end host objects (like the same MAC and/or IP address) showing up behind two different locations (VTEPs) because of end host (aka VM) move operations. Initially, when a VM appears, the associated MAC and IP information is advertised by the VTEP that detected its presence. When the VM is moved from one server to another, the hypervisor at the destination server typically detects the VM move event. Once this detection is completed, the hypervisor sends out a broadcast Reverse ARP (RARP) message with the MAC address of the moved VM. In some cases, the hypervisor/virtual switch may send out a Gratuitous ARP (GARP) message signaling the move of both the IP and MAC associated with the moved VM. In either case, the VTEP connected to the destination server detects that the MAC and/or IP address that was originally remote has now become local, that is, reachable via one of its server-facing interfaces.

Given this information, the VTEP connected to the destination server, generates a Route type 2 BGP EVPN message similar to the one advertised during a new learn event. But in addition to advertising the MAC address, Layer 2 VNI, and VTEP IP address as the next-hop, the edge device also advertises an additional field in the form of a MAC mobility extended community. The sequence number in the MAC Mobility field is incremented by one to provide a tiebreaker for what Route type 2 advertisement is the most up-to-date, and hence it is used for forwarding by all the remote edge devices or VTEPs. When this Route type 2 message is received by the old VTEP that initially advertised the reachability of the VM, an additional validation step is performed to ensure that the information learned from the new VTEP is not caused by a duplicate MAC/IP situation. A duplicate address situation occurs when two end hosts are inadvertently configured with the same address.

Figure 2-22 illustrates a sample **show** output for a typical Route type 2 entry with the MAC Mobility Sequence Number field populated after a host mobility event. Once the validation step passes the duplicate check, the old VTEP withdraws the non-best BGP EVPN Route type 2 message (the one with the lower mobility sequence number). The BGP EVPN MAC mobility sequence numbering details are defined in RFC 7432, Section 7.7, which describes the handling of scenarios where the MAC mobility sequence number may wrap around due to a large number of move events.

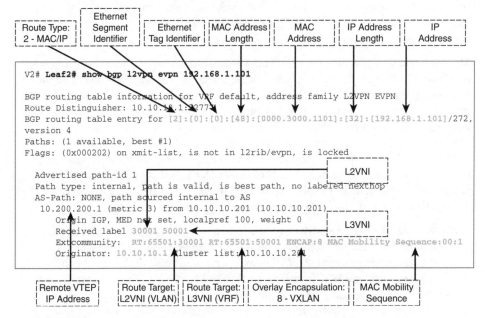

Figure 2-22 show bgp l2vpn evpn: *Route type 2 (MAC/IP and Mobility Sequence Number)*

Summary

This chapter describes why overlays have become a prime design choice for next-generation data centers. It places special emphasis on VXLAN, which has become the de facto choice. This chapter describes the need for a control plane–based solution for distribution of host reachability between various edge devices and provides a comprehensive introduction to BGP EVPN. It describes the important message formats in BGP EVPN for supporting network virtualization overlays, along with their representative use cases. The subsequent chapters build on this background, providing further details on the underlay, multitenancy, and single-destination and multidestination data packet flows in a VXLAN BGP EVPN–based data center topology.

References

1. Institute of Electrical and Electronics Engineers (IEEE). *802.1q—VLANs*. 2016. www.ieee802.org/1/pages/802.1Q.html.

2. Red Hat. *Linux containers with docker format*. 2016. access.redhat.com/ documentation/en-US/Red_Hat_Enterprise_Linux/7/html/7.0_Release_Notes/ chap-Red_Hat_Enterprise_Linux-7.0_Release_Notes-Linux_Containers_with_ Docker_Format.html.

3. Goransson, P., and C. Black. *Software defined networks: A comprehensive approach* (1st ed.). San Francisco, CA: Morgan Kaufmann Publishers Inc., 2014.

4. Institute of Electrical and Electronics Engineers (IEEE). *IEEE 802.1*. 2016. www.ieee802.org/1/.

5. Smith, K. Cython: The best of both worlds. *Computing in Science & Engineering*, 13(2):31–39, 2011.

6. Cisco. *Multiprotocol Label Switching (MPLS)*. www.cisco.com/c/en/us/products/ ios-nx-os-software/multiprotocol-label-switching-mpls/index.html.

7. Cisco. *GRE tunnel interface states and what impacts them*. 2014. www.cisco.com/c/en/us/support/docs/ip/generic-routing-encapsulation-gre/ 118361-technote-gre-00.html.

8. Cisco. *Cisco IOS IPsec*. www.cisco.com/c/en/us/products/ios-nx-os-software/ ios-ipsec/index.html.

9. Wilkins, S. *IPv6 tunneling technology configurations*. 2013. www.ciscopress.com/ articles/article.asp?p=2104948.

10. Internet Engineering Task Force (IETF). *Layer Two Tunneling Protocol—Version 3 (L2TPv3)*. 2005. tools.ietf.org/html/rfc3931.

11. Internet Engineering Task Force (IETF). *Routing bridges (RBridges): Base protocol specification*. 2011. tools.ietf.org/html/rfc6325.

12. Cisco. *Cisco FabricPath*. http://www.cisco.com/c/en/us/solutions/ data-center-virtualization/fabricpath/index.html.

13. Institute of Electrical and Electronics Engineers (IEEE). *802.1aq—Shortest path bridging*. 2012. www.ieee802.org/1/pages/802.1aq.html.

14. Internet Engineering Task Force (IETF). *NVGRE: Network virtualization using generic routing encapsulation*. 2015. tools.ietf.org/html/rfc7637.

15. Cisco. *Application policy infrastructure controller (APIC)*. www.cisco.com/c/en/us/products/cloud-systems-management/ application-policy-infrastructure-controller-apic/index.html.

16. Open Daylight. www.opendaylight.org.

17. Internet Engineering Task Force (IETF). *BGP MPLS-based Ethernet VPN*. 2015. tools.ietf.org/html/rfc7432.

18. Pfaff, B. *The open vSwitch database management protocol*. 2013. tools.ietf.org/html/rfc7047.

19. Internet Engineering Task Force (IETF). *Virtual eXtensible local area network (VXLAN): A framework for overlaying virtualized Layer 2 networks over Layer 3 networks*. 2014. tools.ietf.org/html/rfc7348.

20. Hogue, T. *The dreaded 5-tuple*. 2015. blogs.cisco.com/security/the-dreaded-5-tuple.

21. Cisco. *OSPF design guide*. 2005. www.cisco.com/c/en/us/support/docs/ip/open-shortest-path-first-ospf/7039-1.html#topic2.

22. Cisco. *Intermediate System-to-Intermediate System Protocol*. www.cisco.com/en/US/products/ps6599/products_white_paper09186a00800a3e6f.shtml.

23. Cisco. *Configuring PIM*. www.cisco.com/c/en/us/td/docs/switches/datacenter/nexus3548/sw/multicast/602_A1_1/multicast_cli/pim.html.

24. Cisco. *Border Gateway Protocol (BGP)*. www.cisco.com/c/en/us/products/ios-nx-os-software/border-gateway-protocol-bgp/index.html.

25. Cisco. *Ethernet VPN (EVPN) and provider backbone bridging-EVPN: Next generation solutions for MPLS-based Ethernet services*. www.cisco.com/c/en/us/products/collateral/routers/asr-9000-series-aggregation-services-routers/whitepaper_c11-731864.html.

26. Network Working Group. *BGP/MPLS IP virtual private networks (VPNs)*. 2006. tools.ietf.org/html/rfc4364.

27. Cisco. *Multiprotocol BGP*. http://www.cisco.com/c/en/us/td/docs/ios-xml/ios/mp_l3_vpns/configuration/15-mt/mp-l3-vpns-15-mt-book/mp-bgp-mpls-vpn.html.

28. Internet Engineering Task Force (IETF). *Integrated routing and bridging in EVPN*. 2014. www.ietf.org/archive/id/draft-sajassi-l2vpn-evpn-inter-subnet-forwarding-05.txt.

29. IETF Network Working Group. *Multiprotocol extensions for BGP-4*. 2007. tools.ietf.org/html/rfc4760.

30. BESS Working Group. *Interconnect solution for EVPN overlay networks draft-ietf-bess-dci-evpn-overlay-01*. 2016. tools.ietf.org/html/draft-ietf-bess-evpn-overlay-01.

31. L2VPN Work Group. *A network virtualization overlay solution using EVPN draft-ietf-bess-evpn-overlay-02*. 2015. tools.ietf.org/html/draft-ietf-bess-evpn-overlay-02#section-13.

32. Internet Engineering Task Force (IETF). *BGP MPLS-based Ethernet VPN: MAC mobility*. 2015. tools.ietf.org/html/rfc7432#section-15.

33. L2VPN Work Group. *A network virtualization overlay solution using EVPN draft-ietf-bess-evpn-overlay-02: Encapsulation options for EVPN overlays.* 2015. tools.ietf.org/html/draft-ietf-bess-evpn-overlay-02#section-5.

34. Internet Engineering Task Force (IETF). *BGP/MPLS IP virtual private networks.* 2006. tools.ietf.org/html/rfc4364#section-10.

35. Internet Engineering Task Force (IETF). *The Locator/ID Separation Protocol (LISP).* 2013. tools.ietf.org/html/rfc6830.

36. Cisco. *Optimizing ingress routing with LISP across multiple VXLAN/EVPN sites: White paper.* www.cisco.com/c/en/us/products/collateral/switches/nexus-7000-series-switches/white-paper-c11-734843.html.

## Chapter 3

VXLAN/EVPN Forwarding Characteristics

In this chapter, the following topics will be covered:

- Enhanced BGP EVPN features such as ARP suppression, unknown unicast suppression, and optimized IGMP snooping

- Distributed IP anycast gateway in the VXLAN EVPN fabric

- Anycast VTEP implementation with dual-homed deployments

VXLAN BGP EVPN has been extensively documented in various standardized references, including IETF drafts[1] and RFCs.[2] While that information is useful for implementing the protocol and related encapsulation, some characteristics regarding forwarding require additional attention and discussion. Unfortunately, a common misunderstanding is that VXLAN with BGP EVPN does not require any special treatment for multidestination traffic. This chapter describes how multidestination replication works using VXLAN with BGP EVPN for forwarding broadcast, unknown unicast, and multicast (BUM) traffic. In addition, methods to reduce BUM traffic are covered. This chapter also includes a discussion on enhanced features such as early Address Resolution Protocol (ARP) suppression, unknown unicast suppression, and optimized Internet Group Management Protocol (IGMP) snooping in VXLAN BGP EVPN networks. While the functions and features of Cisco's VXLAN BGP EVPN implementation support reduction of BUM traffic, the use case of silent host detection still requires special handling, which is also discussed.

In addition to discussing Layer 2 BUM traffic, this chapter talks about Layer 3 traffic forwarding in VXLAN BGP EVPN networks. VXLAN BGP EVPN provides Layer 2 overlay services as well as Layer 3 services. For Layer 3 forwarding or routing, the presence of a first-hop default gateway is necessary. The distributed IP anycast gateway enhances the first-hop gateway function by distributing the endpoints' default gateway across all available edge devices (or Virtual Tunnel Endpoints [VTEPs]). The distributed IP anycast gateway is implemented using the Integrated Routing and Bridging (IRB) functionality. This ensures that both bridged and routed traffic—to and from endpoints—is always optimally forwarded within the network with predictable latency, based on the BGP EVPN advertised reachability information. Because of this distributed approach for the Layer 2/Layer 3 boundary, virtual machine mobility is seamlessly handled from the network point of view by employing special mobility-related functionality in BGP EVPN. The distributed anycast gateway ensures that the IP-to-MAC binding for the default gateway does not change, regardless of where an end host resides or moves within the network. In addition, there is no hair-pinning of routed traffic flows to/from the endpoint after a move event. Host route granularity in the BGP EVPN control plane protocol facilitates efficient routing to the VTEP behind which an endpoint resides—at all times.

Data centers require high availability throughout all layers and components. Similarly, the data center fabric must provide redundancy as well as dynamic route distribution. VXLAN BGP EVPN provides redundancy from multiple angles. The Layer 3 routed underlay between the VXLAN edge devices or VTEPs provides resiliency as well as multipathing. Connecting classic Ethernet endpoints via multichassis link aggregation or virtual PortChannel (vPC) provides dual-homing functionality that ensures fault tolerance even in case of a VTEP failure. In addition, typically, Dynamic Host Configuration Protocol (DHCP) services are required for dynamic allocation of IP addresses to endpoints. In the context of DHCP handling, the semantics of centralized gateways are slightly different from those of the distributed anycast gateway. In a VXLAN BGP EVPN fabric, the DHCP relay needs to be configured on each distributed anycast gateway point, and the DHCP server configuration must support DHCP Option 82.[3] This allows a seamless IP configuration service for the endpoints in the VXLAN BGP EVPN fabric.

The aforementioned standards are specific to the interworking of the data plane and the control plane. Some components and functionalities are not inherently part of the standards, and this chapter provides coverage for them. The scope of the discussion in this chapter is specific to VXLAN BGP EVPN implementation on Cisco NX-OS-based platforms. Later chapters provide the necessary details, including detailed packet flows, for forwarding traffic in a VXLAN BGP EVPN network, along with the corresponding configuration requirements.

Multidestination Traffic

The VXLAN with BGP EVPN control plane has two different options for handling BUM or multidestination traffic. The first approach is to leverage multicast replication in the underlay. The second approach is to use a multicast-less approach called *ingress replication*, in which multiple unicast streams are used to forward multidestination traffic to the appropriate recipients. The following sections discuss these two approaches.

Leveraging Multicast Replication in the Underlying Network

The first approach to handling multidestination traffic requires the configuration of IP multicast in the underlay and leverages a network-based replication mechanism. With multicast, a single copy of the BUM traffic is sent from the ingress/source VTEP toward the underlay transport network. The network itself forwards this single copy along the multicast tree (that is, a shared tree or source tree) so that it reaches all egress/destination VTEPs participating in the given multicast group. As the single copy travels along the multicast tree, the copy is replicated at appropriate branch points only if receivers have joined the multicast group associated with the VNI. With this approach, a single-copy per-wire/link is kept within the network, thereby providing the most efficient way to forward BUM traffic.

A Layer 2 VNI is mapped to a multicast group. This mapping must be consistently configured on all VTEPs where this VNI is present, typically signifying the presence of some interested endpoint below that VTEP. Once it is configured, the VTEP sends out a corresponding multicast join expressing interest in the tree associated with the corresponding multicast group. When mapping a Layer 2 VNI to a multicast group, various options are available in the mapping provision for the VNI and multicast group. The simplest approach is to employ a single multicast group and map all Layer 2 VNIs to that group. An obvious benefit of this mapping is the reduction of the multicast state in the underlying network; however, it is also inefficient in the replication of BUM traffic. When a VTEP joins a given multicast group, it receives all traffic being forwarded to that group. The VTEP does not do anything with traffic in which no interest exists (for example, VNIs for which the VTEP is not responsible). In other words, it silently drops that traffic. The VTEP continues to receive this unnecessary traffic as an active receiver for the overall group. Unfortunately, there is no suboption for a VNI to prune back multicast traffic based on both group and VNI. Thus, in a scenario where all VTEPs participate in the same multicast group or groups, the scalability of the number of multicast outgoing interfaces (OIFs) needs to be considered.

At one extreme, each Layer 2 VNI can be mapped to a unique multicast group. At the other extreme, all Layer 2 VNIs are mapped to the same multicast group. Clearly, the optimal behavior lies somewhere in the middle. While theoretically there are 2^{24} = 16 million possible VNI values and more than enough multicast addresses (in the multicast address block 224.0.0.0–239.255.255.255), practical hardware and software factors limit the number of multicast groups used in most practical deployments to a few hundred. Setting up and maintaining multicast trees requires a fair amount of state maintenance and protocol exchange (PIM, IGMP, and so on) in the underlay. To better explain this concept, this chapter presents a couple of simple multicast group usage scenarios for BUM traffic in a VXLAN network. Consider the BUM flows shown in Figure 3-1.

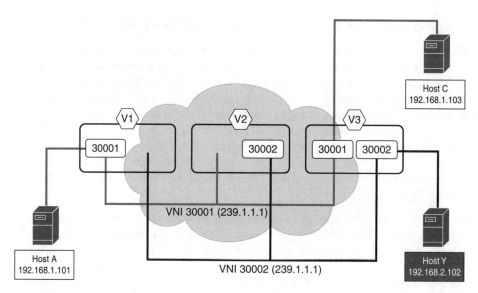

Figure 3-1   *Single Multicast Group for All VNIs*

Three edge devices participate as VTEPs in a given VXLAN-based network. These VTEPs are denoted V1 (10.200.200.1), V2 (10.200.200.2), and V3 (10.200.200.3). IP subnet 192.168.1.0/24 is associated with Layer 2 VNI 30001, and subnet 192.168.2.0/24 is associated with Layer 2 VNI 30002. In addition, VNIs 30001 and 30002 share a common multicast group (239.1.1.1), but the VNIs are not spread across all three VTEPs. As is evident from Figure 3-1, VNI 30001 spans VTEPs V1 and V3, while VNI 30002 spans VTEPs V2 and V3. However, the shared multicast group causes all VTEPs to join the same shared multicast tree. In the figure, when Host A sends out a broadcast packet, VTEP V1 receives this packet and encapsulates it with a VXLAN header. Because the VTEP is able to recognize this as broadcast traffic (DMAC is FFFF.FFFF.FFFF), it employs a destination IP in the outer IP header as the multicast group address. As a result, the broadcast traffic is mapped to the respective VNI's multicast group (239.1.1.1).

The broadcast packet is then forwarded to all VTEPs that have joined the multicast tree for the group 239.1.1.1. VTEP V2 receives the packet, but it silently drops it because it has no interest in the given VNI 30001. Similarly, VTEP V3 receives the same packet that is replicated through the multicast underlay. Because VNI 30001 is configured for VTEP V3, after decapsulation, the broadcast packet is sent out to all local Ethernet interfaces participating in the VLAN mapped to VNI 30001. In this way, the broadcast packet initiated from Host A reaches Host C.

For VNI 30002, the operations are the same because the same multicast group (239.1.1.1) is used across all VTEPs. The BUM traffic is seen on all the VTEPs, but the traffic is dropped if VNI 30002 is not locally configured at that VTEP. Otherwise, the traffic is appropriately forwarded along all the Ethernet interfaces in the VLAN, which is mapped to VNI 30002.

As it is clear from this example, unnecessary BUM traffic can be avoided by employing a different multicast group for VNIs 30001 and 30002. Traffic in VNI 30001 can be scoped to VTEPs V1 and V3, and traffic in VNI 30002 can be scoped to VTEPs V2 and V3. Figure 3-2 provides an example of such a topology to illustrate the concept of a scoped multicast group.

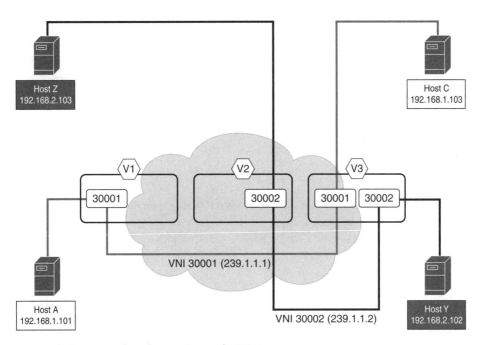

Figure 3-2   *Scoped Multicast Group for VNI*

As before, the three edge devices participating as VTEPs in a given VXLAN-based network are denoted V1 (10.200.200.1), V2 (102.200.200.2), and V3 (10.200.200.3). The Layer 2 VNI 30001 is using the multicast group 239.1.1.1, while the VNI 30002 is using a different multicast group, 239.1.1.2. The VNIs are spread across the various VTEPs, with VNI 30001 on VTEPs V1 and V3 and VNI 30002 on VTEPs V2 and V3. The VTEPs are required to join only the multicast group and the related multicast tree for the locally configured VNIs. When Host A sends out a broadcast, VTEP V1 receives this broadcast packet and encapsulates it with an appropriate VXLAN header. Because the VTEP understands that this is a broadcast packet (DMAC is FFFF.FFFF.FFFF), it uses a destination IP address in the outer header with the multicast group address mapped to the respective VNI (239.1.1.1). This packet is forwarded to VTEP V3 only, which previously joined the multicast tree for the Group 239.1.1.1, where VNI 30001 is configured. VTEP V2 does not receive the packet, as it does not belong to the multicast group because it is not configured with VNI 30001. VTEP V3 receives this packet because it belongs to the multicast group mapped to VNI 30001. It forwards it locally to all member ports that are part of the VLAN that is mapped to VNI 30001. In this way, the broadcast traffic is optimally replicated through the multicast network configured in the underlay.

The same operation occurs in relation to VNI 30002. VNI 30002 is mapped to a different multicast group (239.1.1.2), which is used between VTEPs V2 and V3. The BUM traffic is seen only on the VTEPs participating in VNI 30002—specifically multicast group 239.1.1.2. When broadcast traffic is sent from Host Z, the broadcast is replicated only to VTEPs V2 and V3, resulting in the broadcast traffic being sent to Host Y. VTEP V1 does not see this broadcast traffic as it does not belong to that multicast group. As a result, the number of multicast outgoing interfaces (OIFs) in the underlying network is reduced.

While using a multicast group per VNI seems to work fine in the simple example with three VTEPs and two VNIs, in most practical deployments, a suitable mechanism is required to simplify the assignment of multicast groups to VNIs. There are two popular ways of achieving this:

- VNIs are randomly selected and assigned to multicast groups, thereby resulting in some implicit sharing.

- A multicast group is localized to a set of VTEPs, thereby ensuring that they share the same set of Layer 2 VNIs.

The second option to handling multidestination traffic may sound more efficient than the first, but in practice it may lack the desired flexibility because it limits workload assignments to a set of servers below a set of VTEPs, which is clearly undesirable.

Using Ingress Replication

While multicast configuration in the underlay is straightforward, not everyone is familiar with or willing to use it. Depending on the platform capabilities, a second approach for multidestination traffic is available: leveraging ingress or head-end replication, which is a unicast approach. The terms *ingress replication* (*IR*) and *head-end replication* (*HER*) can be used interchangeably. IR/HER is a unicast-based mode where network-based replication is not employed. The ingress, or source, VTEP makes $N-1$ copies of every BUM packet and sends them as individual unicasts toward the respective $N-1$ VTEPs that have the associated VNI membership. With IR/HER, the replication list is either statically configured or dynamically determined, leveraging the BGP EVPN control plane. Section 7.3 of RFC 7432 (https://tools.ietf.org/html/rfc7432) defines inclusive multicast Ethernet tag (IMET) routing, or Route type 3 (RT-3). To achieve optimal efficiency with IR/HER, best practice is to use the dynamic distribution with BGP EVPN. BGP EVPN provides a Route type 3 (inclusive multicast) option that allows for building a dynamic replication list because IP addresses of every VTEP in a given VNI would be advertised over BGP EVPN. The dynamic replication list has the egress/destination VTEPs that are participants in the same Layer 2 VNI.

Each VTEP advertises a specific route that includes the VNI as well as the next-hop IP address corresponding to its own address. As a result, a dynamic replication list is built. The list is updated when configuration of a VNI at a VTEP occurs. Once the replication list is built, the packet is multiplied at the VTEP whenever BUM traffic reaches the ingress/source VTEP. This results in individual copies being sent toward every VTEP in a VNI across the network. Because network-integrated multicast replication is not used, ingress replication is employed, generating additional network traffic. Figure 3-3 illustrates sample BGP EVPN output with relevant fields highlighted, for a Route type 3 advertisement associated with a given VTEP.

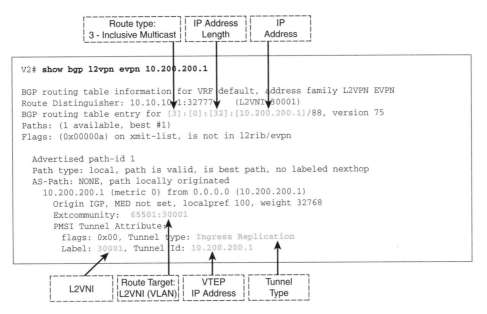

Figure 3-3 *Route type 3: Inclusive Multicast*

When comparing the multicast and unicast modes of operation for BUM traffic, the load for all the multidestination traffic replication needs to be considered. For example, consider a single Layer 2 VNI present on all 256 edge devices hosting a VTEP. Further, assume that a single VLAN exists on all 48 Ethernet interfaces of the edge devices where BUM traffic replication is occurring. Each Ethernet interface of the local edge device receives 0.001% of the nominal interface speed of BUM traffic. For 10G interfaces, this generates 0.0048 Gbps (4.8 Mbps) of BUM traffic at the edge device from the host-facing Ethernet interfaces. In multicast mode, the theoretical speed of BUM traffic remains at this rate. In unicast mode, the replication depends on the amount of egress/destination activity on the VTEP. In the example of 255 neighboring VTEPs, this results in 255 × 0.0048 = ~1.2 Gbps of BUM traffic on the fabric. Even though the example is theoretical, it clearly demonstrates the huge overhead that the unicast mode incurs as the amount of multidestination traffic in the network increases. The efficiency of multicast mode in these cases cannot be understated.

It is important to note that when scoping a multicast group to VNIs, the same multicast group for a given Layer 2 VNI must be configured across the entire VXLAN-based fabric. In addition, all VTEPs have to follow the same multidestination configuration mode for a given Layer 2 domain represented through the Layer 2 VNI. In other words, for a given Layer 2 VNI, all VTEPs have to follow the same unicast or multicast configuration mode. In addition, for the multicast mode, it is important to follow the same multicast protocol (for example, PIM ASM,[4] PIM BiDir[5]) for the corresponding multicast group. Failure to adhere to these requirements results in broken forwarding of multidestination traffic.

VXLAN BGP EVPN Enhancements

The following sections describe some of the feature enhancements that ride on top of the BGP EVPN control plane, further enhancing the forwarding of Layer 2 and Layer 3 traffic in a VXLAN fabric.

ARP Suppression

Address Resolution Protocol (ARP) is responsible for IPv4 address–to–MAC address mapping in IP networks. ARP facilitates obtaining endpoint MAC address information, leveraging the IP address information sent out in an ARP broadcast request. The broadcast request is treated as multidestination traffic that is typically VXLAN encapsulated and sent to every VTEP or edge device that is a member of the corresponding Layer 2 VNI. The response to the ARP request is typically sent as a unicast packet to the requestor. ARP traffic is scoped within the bounds of the broadcast domain represented by the Layer 2 VNI. Correspondingly, IPv6 networks rely on the Neighbor Discovery Protocol (ND) for IPv6 address–to–MAC address resolution. With IPv6, this resolution is triggered via an initial neighbor solicitation (NS) that is multicast through the Layer 2 broadcast domain. A neighbor advertisement (NA) sent in response from the destination completes the neighbor resolution.[6]

When an endpoint needs to resolve the default gateway, which is the exit point of the local IP subnet, it sends out an ARP request to the configured default gateway. The ARP operation allows the local edge device or VTEP to populate IP/MAC mappings of the locally attached endpoints. In addition to the MAC-to-IP table being populated on the edge device, all the MAC information is populated to the BGP EVPN control plane protocol. In addition, for Layer 2, Layer 2 VNI, Route Distinguisher (RD), Route Target (RT), hosting VTEP, and associated IP information is populated, and for Layer 3, Layer 3 VNI, RD, RT, hosting VTEP, and RMAC information is populated. Specifically, this information is populated in a Route type 2 advertisement and distributed to all remote VTEPs, which now have learned about that endpoint.

Typically, all ARP broadcast requests sent out from an endpoint are subject to copy-to-router and forward behavior. The local edge device learns about an endpoint as long as the endpoint sends out some type of ARP request—not necessarily an ARP request for the resolution of the default gateway hosted on the local edge device.

Typically, when an endpoint wants to talk to another endpoint in the same subnet, it sends out an ARP request for determining the IP-to-MAC binding of the destination endpoint. The ARP request is flooded to all the endpoints that are part of that Layer 2 VNI. ARP snooping coupled with the BGP EVPN control plane information can help avoid flooding for known endpoints. By using ARP snooping, all ARP requests from an endpoint are redirected to the locally attached edge device. The edge device then extracts the destination IP address in the ARP payload and determines whether it is a known endpoint. Specifically, a query is done against the known endpoint information from the BGP EVPN control plane.

If the destination is known, the IP-to-MAC binding information is returned. The local edge device then performs an ARP proxy on behalf of the destination endpoint. In other words, it sends out a unicast ARP response toward the requestor with the resolved MAC address of the known destination endpoint. In this way, all ARP requests to known endpoints are terminated at the earliest possible point, which is the locally attached edge device or VTEP or leaf. This is known as *ARP suppression*. ARP suppression is possible because all the information is known on all the VXLAN VTEPs.[7]

Note that ARP suppression is different from the Proxy ARP,[8] in which the edge device or router may serve as a proxy on behalf of the destination endpoint, using its own Router MAC. ARP suppression reduces ARP broadcast traffic by leveraging the BGP EVPN control plane information. ARP suppression is enabled on a per-Layer 2 VNI basis. In this way, for all known endpoints, ARP requests are sent only between the endpoint and the local edge device/VTEP. Figure 3-4 illustrates a scenario where ARP suppression at VTEP V1 results in early ARP termination of a request for a host 192.168.1.102 from a host 192.168.1.101 in Layer 2 VNI 30001. It is important to note that the ARP suppression feature works based on the knob enabled under the Layer 2 VNI, regardless of whether the default gateway is configured on the leafs.

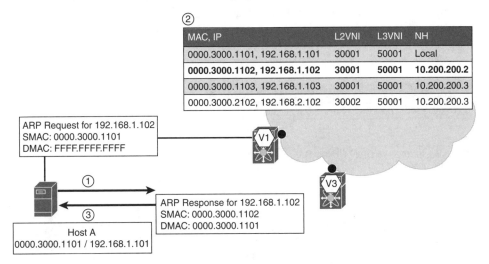

Figure 3-4 *ARP Suppression*

When the destination endpoint is not known to the BGP EVPN control plane (that is, a silent or undiscovered endpoint), the ARP broadcast needs to be sent across the VXLAN network. Recall that ARP snooping intercepts the ARP broadcast request to the locally attached edge device. Because the lookup for the destination endpoint results in a "miss," the edge device re-injects the ARP broadcast request back into the network with appropriate source filtering to ensure that it does not return to the source port from which the ARP request was originally received. The ARP broadcast leverages the multidestination traffic forwarding implementation of the VXLAN fabric.

When the queried endpoint responds to the ARP request, the endpoint generates an ARP response. The unicast ARP response is also subjected to ARP snooping behavior so that it is sent to the remote edge device to which the destination is directly attached.

Consequently, the IP/MAC binding of the destination endpoint is learned by the remote VTEP, resulting in that information being populated into the BGP EVPN control plane. The remote edge device also sends out the ARP response to the original requesting endpoint, thereby completing the end-to-end ARP discovery process. The ARP response is sent via the data plane to ensure that there are no delays in the control plane updates. It is important to note that after the initial miss, all the subsequent ARP requests for the discovered endpoint are handled with local ARP termination, as described earlier.

Figure 3-5 illustrates a scenario involving ARP termination or ARP suppression where a miss occurs in the control plane. Host A and Host B belong to the same IP subnet, corresponding to the Layer 2 VNI 30001. Host A wants to communicate with Host B, but the respective MAC-to-IP mapping is not known in Host A's ARP cache. Therefore, Host A sends an ARP request to determine the MAC-to-IP binding of Host B. The ARP request is snooped by VTEP V1. VTEP V1 uses the target IP address information gleaned from the ARP request payload to look up information about Host B in the BGP EVPN control plane. Since Host B is not yet known in the network, the broadcast ARP request is encapsulated into VXLAN with the destination IP address of a multicast group or a unicast destination IP address. The multicast group is leveraged when multicast is enabled in the underlay. Otherwise, using head-end replication, multiple unicast copies are generated to each remote interested VTEP, as mentioned earlier.

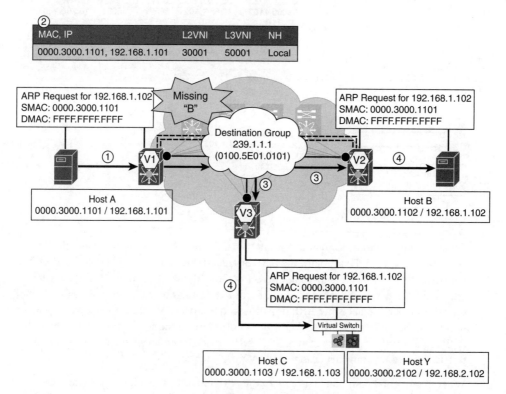

Figure 3-5   *ARP lookup miss with ARP Suppression*

The ARP broadcast sent to VTEP V2 and VTEP V3 is appropriately decapsulated, and the inner broadcast payload is forwarded to all Ethernet ports that are members of VNI 30001. In this way, the ARP request reaches Host B, and Host B answers with a unicast ARP response back to Host A. Once the unicast ARP response hits VTEP V2, the information is snooped, and the control plane is then updated with Host B's IP/MAC address information. At the same time, the ARP response is encapsulated and forwarded across the VXLAN network to VTEP V1. On receiving the ARP response, VTEP V1 decapsulates the VXLAN header and forwards the decapsulated ARP response, based on a Layer 2 lookup, in VNI 30001. Consequently, Host A receives the ARP response and populates its local ARP cache. From this point forward, bidirectional communication between Host A and Host B is enabled because all MAC and IP address information of both hosts is known in the network.

The ARP request and response process between endpoints in a VXLAN BGP EVPN fabric is similar to that in classic Ethernet or any other Flood and Learn (F&L) network. However, the advantage of the control plane and ARP suppression is realized with the BGP EVPN information. A single ARP resolution of an endpoint triggers the control plane to populate that endpoint information across the entire network, at all the VTEPs. Consequently, any subsequent ARP requests to any known endpoint are locally answered instead of being flooded across the entire network.

Because ARP snooping proactively learns the endpoint information to populate the control plane, it certainly helps in reducing unknown unicast traffic. ARP requests really need to be flooded only for the initial period, when an endpoint has yet to be discovered. However, there are other sources of unknown unicast traffic (for example, vanilla Layer 2 non-IP traffic or even regular Layer 2 IP traffic) that may suffer a DMAC lookup miss and the traffic being flooded all across the VXLAN network.

To completely disable any kind of flooding due to unknown unicast traffic toward the VXLAN network, a new feature called *unknown unicast suppression* has been introduced. This independent feature is enabled on a per-Layer 2 VNI basis. With this knob enabled, when any Layer 2 traffic suffers a DMAC lookup miss, traffic is locally flooded, but there is no flooding over VXLAN. Therefore, if no silent or unknown hosts are present, flooding can potentially be minimized in a BGP EVPN VXLAN network.

Next, we consider the third piece of BUM or multidestination traffic, which is called *multicast traffic*. Layer 2 multicast in a VXLAN network is treated as broadcast or unknown unicast traffic because the multicast traffic is flooded across the underlay. Layer 2 multicast flooding leverages the configured multidestination traffic-handling method, whether it exists in unicast mode or multicast mode. Not all platforms can differentiate between the different types of Layer 2 floods, such as multicast or unknown unicast. The IGMP snooping feature presents an optimal way of forwarding Layer 2 multicast traffic if supported by the platform. The Cisco NX-OS default configuration results in behavior that floods Layer 2 multicast traffic both locally and across the VTEP interfaces (see Figure 3-6). This means that all participating VTEPs with the same VNI mapping and all endpoints in that Layer 2 VNI receive this Layer 2 multicast traffic. The multidestination traffic is forwarded to every endpoint in the VNI, regardless of whether that endpoint is an interested receiver.

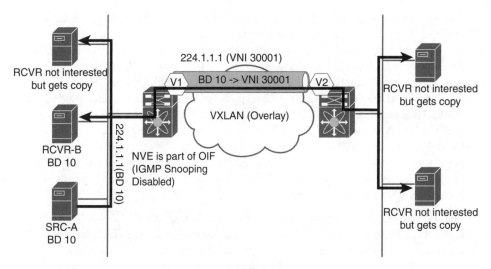

Figure 3-6   *No IGMP Snooping in VLAN/VXLAN*

With VXLAN, the option to implement IGMP snooping in the same way it is implemented in traditional Ethernet-based networks. The main difference is that the VTEP
interface selectively allows Layer 2 multicast forwarding for interested receivers that are
present behind a remote VTEP. If there are no interested receivers behind remote VTEPs,
Layer 2 multicast traffic received from a source endpoint is not sent toward the VXLAN
network. However, as long as there is at least one interested receiver behind some remote
VTEP, Layer 2 multicast traffic is forwarded to all remote VTEPs since they are all part
of the same Layer 2 VNI. The VTEP interface is a multicast router port that participates
in IGMP snooping, thereby allowing Layer 2 multicast forwarding. This is dependent on
the receipt of the IGMP "join" message from an endpoint for a given multicast group in a
Layer 2 VNI.

The received IGMP join report is VXLAN encapsulated and transported to all remote
VTEPs that are members of the corresponding Layer 2 VNI. Note that the multicast
group(s) employed for overlay multicast traffic between endpoints should not be confused with the underlay multicast group that may be associated with the Layer 2 VNI.
Recall that the latter is employed to provide the destination IP address in the outer IP
header for forwarding multidestination traffic in the underlay when using multicast mode.

With IGMP snooping enabled for VXLAN VNIs, the ability to realize the true benefits of
multicast occurs: Traffic is forwarded only to interested receiver endpoints (see Figure 3-7).
In other words, if no interested receivers exist for a given multicast group behind a VTEP
in the same VNI, the Layer 2 multicast traffic is silently dropped and not flooded. After
decapsulation at the remote VTEP, Layer 2 multicast traffic is forwarded based on the
local IGMP snooping state. IGMP join messages are used to selectively enable the
forwarding of certain Layer 2 multicast traffic.

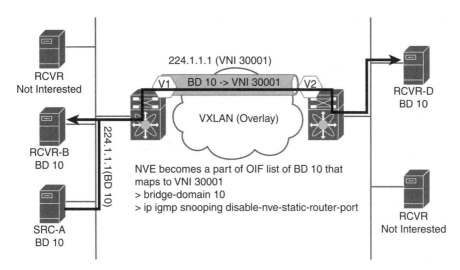

Figure 3-7 *IGMP Snooping in VLAN/VXLAN*

Depending on the platform software support, IGMP snooping for VXLAN-enabled VLANs may not be supported. IGMP snooping is a software feature that does not have any dependencies on the underlying hardware. While this section provided a brief overview, detailed IP multicast flows in a VXLAN BGP EVPN network are presented in Chapter 7 "Multicast Forwarding".

Distributed IP Anycast Gateway

In order for two endpoints in different IP subnets to communicate with each other, a default gateway is required. Traditionally, the default gateway has been implemented centrally at the data center aggregation layer, in a redundant configuration. For an endpoint to reach the centralized default gateway, it has to first traverse a Layer 2 network. The Layer 2 network options include Ethernet, vPC, FabricPath, and even VXLAN F&L. Communication within the same IP subnet is typically bridged without any communication with the centralized default gateway. For routing communication between different IP networks/subnets, the centralized default gateway is reachable over the same Layer 2 network path.

Typically, the network is designed to be redundant as well as highly available. Likewise, the centralized gateway is highly available. First-hop redundancy protocols (FHRP) were designed to support the centralized default gateway with redundancy. Protocols such as HSRP,[9] VRRP,[10] and GLBP[11] are examples of FHRPs. HSRP and VRRP have a single node responsible for responding to ARP requests as well as routing traffic to a different IP network/subnet. When the primary node fails, the FHRP changes the operational state on the backup node to master. A certain amount of time is needed to fail over from one node to another.

FHRPs became more versatile when implemented with virtual PortChannels (vPCs), which allow both nodes to forward routing traffic and permit only the master node to respond to ARP requests. Combining vPC and FHRP significantly enhances resiliency as well as convergence time in case of failures. Enabling ARP synchronization for the FHRP in vPC environments enables ARP synchronization between the vPC primary and the vPC secondary. FabricPath with anycast HSRP[12] increases the number of active gateways from two to four nodes. The FHRP protocol exchange and operational state changes are still present with anycast HSRP. With FHRPs, the default gateway, implemented at the data center aggregation layer, provides a centralized default gateway as well as the Layer 2/ Layer 3 network boundary.

The increasing importance of Layer 2 and Layer 3 operations, especially in a large data center fabric, has demanded additional resiliency in comparison to what has been provided by traditional FHRP protocols. Moving the Layer 2-Layer 3 network boundary to the fabric leaf/ToR switch or the access layer reduces the failure domain (see Figure 3-8). The scale-out approach of the distributed IP anycast gateway dramatically reduces the network and protocol state. The distributed IP anycast gateway implementation at each fabric leaf no longer requires each endpoint to traverse a large Layer 2 domain to reach the default gateway.

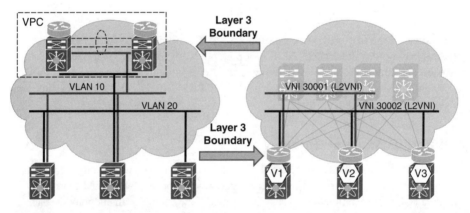

Figure 3-8   *Gateway Placement*

The distributed IP anycast gateway applies the anycast[13] network concept "one to the nearest association." Anycast is a network addressing and routing methodology in which the data traffic from an endpoint is routed topologically to the closest node in a group of gateways that are all identified by the same destination IP address. With the distributed IP anycast gateway (see Figure 3-9), the default gateway is moved closer to the endpoint—specifically to the leaf where each endpoint is physically attached. The anycast gateway is active on each edge device/VTEP across the network fabric, eliminating the requirement to have traditional hello protocols/packets across the network fabric. Consequently, the same gateway for a subnet can exist concurrently at multiple leafs, as needed, without the requirement for any FHRP-like protocols.

Redundant ToRs are reached over a Multi-Chassis Link Aggregation bundle (MC-LAG) technology such as vPC. Port channel hashing selects only one of the two available default gateways, and the "one to the nearest association" rule applies here. The VXLAN BGP EVPN network provides Layer 2 and Layer 3 services, and the default gateway association exists between the local edge device and the endpoint. When the endpoint tries to resolve the default gateway, the locally attached edge device is the only one that traps and resolves that ARP request. In this way, every edge device is responsible for performing default gateway functionality for its directly attached endpoints. The edge device also takes care of tracking the liveliness of its locally attached discovered endpoints by performing periodic ARP refreshes.

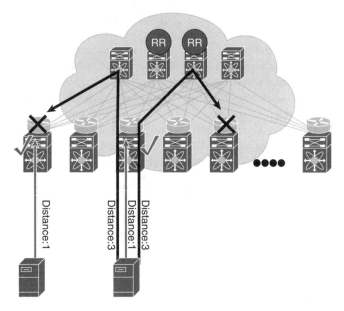

Figure 3-9 *Anycast Gateway Concept*

The scale-out implementation of the distributed anycast gateway provides the default gateway closest to each endpoint. The IP address for the default gateway is shared among all the edge devices, and each edge device is responsible for its respective IP subnet. In addition to the IP address of the default gateway being important, the associated MAC address is equally important. The MAC address is important as each endpoint has a local ARP cache that contains the specific IP-to-MAC binding for the default gateway.

For the host mobility use case, undesirable "black-holing" of traffic may occur if the gateway MAC address changes when a host moves to a server below a different ToR in a different rack even if the default gateway remains the same. To prevent this, the distributed anycast gateways on all the edge devices of the VXLAN EVPN fabric share the same MAC address for the gateway service. This shared MAC address, called the *anycast gateway MAC addresses* (*AGM*), is configured to be the same on all the edge devices. In fact, the same AGM is shared across all the different IP subnets, and each subnet has its own unique default gateway IP. The anycast gateway not only provides the most efficient egress routing but also provides direct routing to the VTEP where a given endpoint is attached, thereby eliminating hair-pinning of traffic.

In a situation where an endpoint is silent or undiscovered, no host route information for that endpoint in known to the BGP EVPN control plane. Without the host route information, the next-best route in the routing table should be used so that the packets destined to that endpoint are not dropped. Having each distributed IP anycast gateway advertise a subnet route from each VTEP where that subnet is locally instantiated allows a "next-best" route to be available in the routing table. A remote VTEP, which does not have that subnet instantiated locally, finds that the subnet prefix is reachable over multiple paths via ECMP. When traffic destined to an unknown/silent endpoint in this subnet is received by this remote VTEP, traffic is forwarded to one of the chosen VTEPs that serve the destination subnet based on the calculated ECMP hash. Once the traffic reaches that VTEP, the subnet prefix route is hit, which in turn points to a glean adjacency. This triggers the VTEP to send out an ARP request to the local-connected Layer 2 network, based on the destination subnet information. The ARP request is also sent to the Layer 3 core encapsulated with the Layer 2 VXLAN VNI associated with the destination subnet. As a result, the ARP request reaches the silent endpoint in the specific subnet. The endpoint responds to the ARP request, which in turn gets consumed at the VTEP that is directly attached to that endpoint. This is because all VTEPs share the same anycast gateway MAC. As a result, the endpoint is discovered, and the endpoint information is distributed by this VTEP into the BGP EVPN control plane.

An alternative to the subnet route advertisement approach is to allow the default route (0.0.0.0/0) to achieve similar results with the disadvantage of centralizing the discovery. However, a distributed approach based on subnet prefix routes scales much better to discover the silent endpoints. Figure 3-10 illustrates the logical realization of a distributed IP anycast gateway in a VXLAN BGP EVPN fabric.

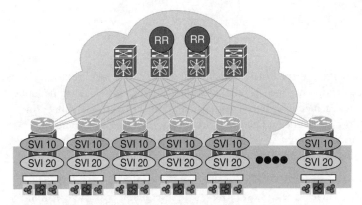

SVI 10, Gateway IP: 192.168.1.1, Gateway MAC: 2020.0000.00AA
SVI 20, Gateway IP: 192.168.2.1, Gateway MAC: 2020.0000.00AA

Figure 3-10 *Subnet Prefix Advertisement for Distributed Anycast Gateway*

With the distributed IP anycast gateway implementation, any VTEP can service any subnet across the entire VXLAN BGP EVPN fabric. Integrated Routing and Bridging (IRB) from the VXLAN BGP EVPN construct provides the capability to efficiently route and bridge traffic. Regardless of the traffic patterns (east–west or north–south), the hairpinning of traffic is completely eliminated. The BGP EVPN control plane knows the identity of an endpoint along with the next-hop (VTEP) information that indicates its location. This leads to optimal forwarding in the network without requiring a large Layer 2 domain.

In summary, the AGM across all edge devices and subnets provides seamless host mobility as no changes to the endpoint ARP cache need to occur. This allows for "hot" workload mobility across the entire VXLAN fabric. The distributed anycast gateway moves the Layer 3 gateway to the leafs, thereby providing reduced failure domains, simplified configuration, optimized routing, and transparent endpoint/workload mobility.

Integrated Route and Bridge (IRB)

VXLAN BGP EVPN follows two different semantics for IRB that are documented and published in the IETF's draft-ietf-bess-evpn-inter-subnet-forwarding (https://tools.ietf.org/html/draft-ietf-bess-evpn-inter-subnet-forwarding).

Asymmetric IRB is the first of the documented first-hop routing operations. It follows a bridge–route–bridge pattern within the local edge device or VTEP. As the name implies, when asymmetric IRB is employed for routing, traffic egressing toward a remote VTEP uses a different VNI than the return traffic from the remote VTEP.

As noted in Figure 3-11, Host A, connected to VTEP V1, wants to communicate to Host X, connected to VTEP V2. Because Host A and Host X belong to different subnets, the asymmetric IRB routing process is used. Post default gateway ARP resolution, Host A sends data traffic toward the default gateway in VLAN 10. From VLAN 10, a routing operation is performed toward VLAN 20, which is mapped to VXLAN VNI 30002. The data traffic is encapsulated into VXLAN with VNI 30002. When the encapsulated traffic arrives on VTEP V2, it is decapsulated and then bridged over toward VLAN 20 because VLAN 20 is also mapped to VNI 30002 on VTEP V2.

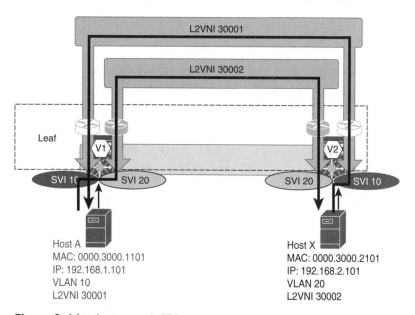

Figure 3-11 *Asymmetric IRB*

Host A–to–Host X communication results in a bridge–route–bridge pattern, with the encapsulated traffic traveling with VNI 30002. For the return traffic, Host X sends data traffic to the default gateway for the local subnet corresponding to VLAN 20. After the routing operation from VLAN 20 to VLAN 10 is performed, the traffic is encapsulated with VXLAN VNI 30001 and bridged toward VTEP V1. Once the traffic arrives at VTEP V1, the data traffic is decapsulated and bridged toward VLAN 10 because VLAN 10 is mapped to VNI 30001. Consequently, for return traffic from Host X to Host A, a bridge–route–bridge operation is performed, with encapsulated traffic traveling with VNI 30001. The end-to-end traffic flow from Host A to Host X uses VNI 30002, and the return traffic from Host X to Host A uses VNI 30001.

The preceding example demonstrates traffic asymmetry with different VNIs used for communication between Host A and Host X with asymmetric IRB. Asymmetric IRB requires consistent VNI configuration across all VXLAN VTEP(s) to prevent traffic from being black-holed. Configuration consistency is required for the second bridge operation in the bridge–route–bridge sequence because the sequence fails if there is a missing bridge-domain/VNI configuration corresponding to the network in which the destination resides. Figure 3-12 illustrates the fact that traffic from Host A and Host Y flows fine, but reverse traffic from Host Y to Host A does not work, due to the absence of the configuration for VNI 30001 at the VTEP attached to Host Y. Traffic between Host A and Host X will be correctly forwarded as both IRB interfaces (SVI 10 and SVI 20) are present on the attached VTEP.

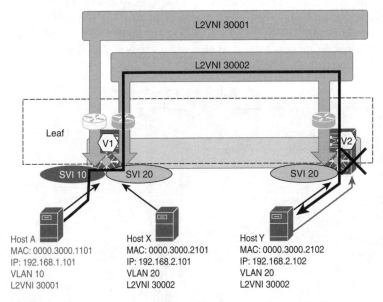

Figure 3-12 *Asymmetric IRB and Inconsistent Provisioning*

In addition to asymmetric IRB, another option for IRB operations is symmetric IRB. Whereas asymmetric IRB follows the bridge–route–bridge mode of operation, symmetric IRB follows the bridge–route–route–bridge mode of operation. Symmetric IRB provides additional use cases that are not possible with asymmetric IRB.

Symmetric IRB uses the same forwarding semantics when routing between IP subnets with VRF Lite or MPLS L3VPNs. With symmetric IRB, all traffic egressing and returning from a VTEP uses the same VNI. Specifically, the same Layer 3 VNI (L3VNI) associated with the VRF is used for all routed traffic. The distinctions between the L2VNI and L3VNI are identified in the BGP EVPN control plane specific to the VXLAN header 24-bit VNI field.

As noted in Figure 3-13, Host A is connected to VTEP V1 and wants to communicate with Host Y, attached to VTEP V2. Host A sends data traffic to the default gateway associated with the local subnet in VLAN 10. From VLAN 10, traffic is routed based on the destination IP lookup. The lookup result indicates which traffic needs to be VXLAN encapsulated and sends traffic toward VTEP V2, below which Host Y resides. The encapsulated VXLAN traffic is sent from VTEP V1 to VTEP V2 in VNI 50001, where 50001 is the Layer 3 VNI associated with the VRF in which Host A and Host Y reside. Once the encapsulated VXLAN traffic arrives at VTEP V2, the traffic is decapsulated and routed within the VRF toward VLAN 20 where Host Y resides. In this way, for traffic from Host A to Host Y, a bridge–route–route–bridge symmetric sequence is performed. Note that the Layer 2 VNIs associated with the networks in which Host A and Host Y reside are not used for the routing operation with the symmetric IRB option.

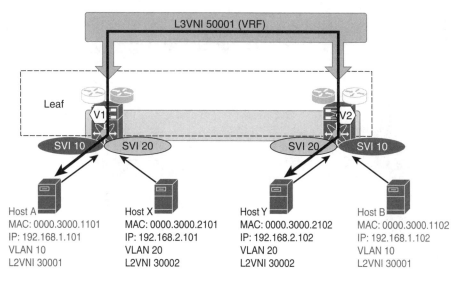

Figure 3-13 *Symmetric IRB*

For the return traffic from Host Y to Host A, the return flow is symmetric, using the same VNI 50001 associated with the VRF. Host Y sends the return traffic to the default gateway associated with its local subnet in VLAN 20. VLAN 20 makes a routing decision toward the VRF and VNI 50001, resulting in the VXLAN-encapsulated traffic being sent to VTEP V1. Once the encapsulated VXLAN traffic arrives at VTEP V1, the traffic is decapsulated and routed toward the VRF and VLAN 10. The return traffic flow from Host Y to Host A follows the same bridge–route–route–bridge sequence, following the same VNI 50001. The traffic from Host A to Host Y and traffic from Host Y to Host A leverage the same VRF VNI 50001, resulting in symmetric traffic flows. In fact, all routed traffic between hosts belonging to different networks within the same VRF employs the same VRF VNI 50001.

Symmetric IRB does not have the requirement of maintaining a consistent configuration across all the edge devices for all the VXLAN networks. In other words, scoped configuration can be implemented when it is not necessary to have all VNIs configured on all the edge devices or VTEPs (see Figure 3-14). However, for a given VRF, the same Layer 3 VNI needs to be configured on all the VTEPs since the VRF enables the sequence of bridge–route–route–bridge operation. For communication between hosts belonging to different VRFs, route leaking is required. For VRF route leaking, an external router or firewall is required to perform VRF-to-VRF communication. It should be noted that support for VRF route leaking requires software support to normalize the control protocol information with the data plane encapsulation. Next to local VRF route leaking, downstream VNI assignment can provide this function for the extranet use cases. These options are discussed further in Chapter 8, "External Connectivity."

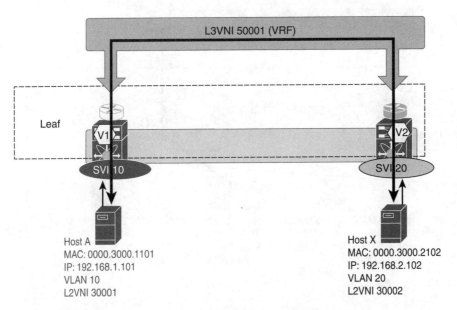

Figure 3-14 *Symmetric IRB and Inconsistent Provisioning*

Both symmetric and asymmetric modes are documented in the IETF draft. The Cisco implementation with NX-OS follows the symmetric IRB mode. The symmetric IRB bridge–route–route–bridge sequence offers flexibility for large-scale multitenant deployments. And the bridge–route–route–bridge sequence follows similar semantics to classic routing across a transit segment. The transit routing segment with VXLAN BGP EVPN is reflected by the Layer 3 VNI associated with the VRF.

Endpoint Mobility

BGP EVPN provides a mechanism to provide endpoint mobility within the fabric. When an endpoint moves, the associated host route prefix is advertised in the control plane through an updated sequence number. The sequence number avoids the need to withdraw and relearn a given prefix during an endpoint move. Instead, an update in the control plane of the new location is performed. Since forwarding in the fabric is always dictated by what is present in the BGP EVPN control plane, traffic is quickly redirected to the updated location of the endpoint that moved, thereby providing a smooth traffic convergence. When an endpoint moves, two host route prefixes for the same endpoint are present in the BGP EVPN control plane. The initial prefix is identified by the original VTEP location, and after the move, the prefix is identified by the new VTEP location.

With two prefixes in the control plane present for the same endpoint, a tiebreaker determines the winner. For this purpose, a BGP extended community called the MAC mobility sequence number is added to the endpoint host route advertisement (specifically Route type 2). The sequence number is updated with every endpoint move. In the event that the sequence number reaches its maximum possible value, the sequence number wraps around and starts over. The MAC mobility sequence number is documented in RFC 7432, which is specific to BGP EVPN.

The endpoint MAC address before the move is learned as a Route type 2 advertisement, and the BGP extended community MAC mobility sequence is set to 0. The value 0 indicates that the MAC address has not had a mobility event, and the endpoint is still at the original location. If a MAC mobility event has been detected, a new Route type 2 (MAC/IP advertisement) is added to the BGP EVPN control plane by the "new" VTEP below which the endpoint moved (its new location). The control plane then sets the MAC mobility sequence number to 1 in the BGP extended community as well as in the new location. There are now two identical MAC/IP advertisements in the BGP EVPN control plane. But only the new advertisement has the MAC mobility sequence number set to a value of 1. All the VTEPs honor this advertisement, thereby sending traffic toward the endpoint at its new location. Figure 3-15 illustrates a sample endpoint mobility use case with the relevant BGP EVPN state where endpoint Host A has moved from VTEP V1 to VTEP V3.

Route type	MAC, IP	L2VNI ("VLAN")	L3VNI ("VRF")	NH	Encap	Seq
2	0000.3000.1101, 192.168.1.101	30001	50001	10.200.200.1	8:VXLAN	0
2	0000.3000.1101, 192.168.1.101	30001	50001	10.200.200.3	8:VXLAN	1

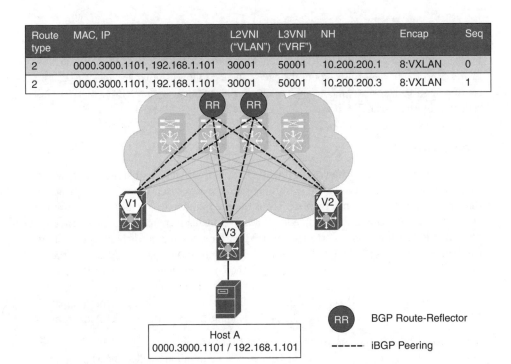

Figure 3-15 *Endpoint Mobility*

An endpoint may move multiple times over the course of its lifetime within a fabric. Every time the endpoint moves, the VTEP that detects its new location increments the sequence number by 1 and then advertises the host prefix for that endpoint into the BGP EVPN control plane. Because the BGP EVPN information is synced across all the VTEPs, every VTEP is aware of whether an endpoint is coming up for the first time or whether it is an endpoint move event based on the previous endpoint reachability information.

An endpoint may be powered off or become unreachable for a variety of reasons. If an endpoint has aged out of the ARP, MAC, and BGP tables, the extended community MAC mobility sequence is 0 as well. If the same endpoint reappears (from the fabric's and BGP EVPN's point of view), this reappearance is treated as a new learn event. In other words, the BGP EVPN control plane is aware of the current active endpoints and their respective locations, but the control plane does not store any history of the previous incarnations of the endpoints.

Whether an endpoint actually moves (a *hot* move) or an endpoint dies and another endpoint assumes its identity (a *cold* move), from the BGP EVPN control plane's point of view, the actions taken are similar. This is because the identity of an endpoint in the BGP EVPN control plane is derived from its MAC and/or IP addresses.

An endpoint move event results in either Reverse ARP (RARP) or Gratuitous ARP (GARP), signaling either by the endpoint or on behalf of the endpoint. In the case of RARP, the hypervisor or virtual switch typically sends out a RARP with the SMAC address set to the endpoint MAC address and the DMAC set to the broadcast MAC (FFFF.FFFF.FFFF). In the case of GARP, both the IP and MAC address of the endpoint are notified at the new location. This results in IP/MAC reachability of the endpoint being updated in the BGP EVPN control plane. On reception of this information at the old location (VTEP), an endpoint verification process is performed to determine whether the endpoint has indeed moved away from the old location. Once this validation occurs successfully, the old prefix with the old sequence number is withdrawn from the BGP EVPN control plane. In addition to the prefix being withdrawn from BGP EVPN, the ARP and/or MAC address tables are also cleared of the old location. Figure 3-16 illustrates a sample BGP EVPN output for a prefix associated with an end host that has moved within the fabric. In the figure, the fields of interest, including the MAC Mobility Sequence Number field, are highlighted.

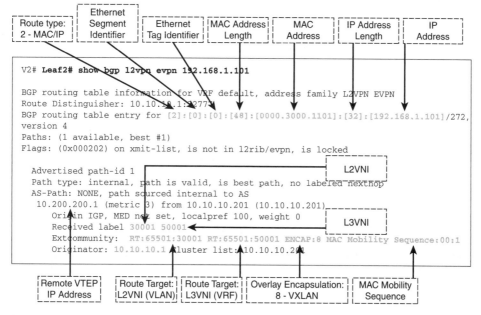

Figure 3-16 *MAC Mobility Sequence*

During the verification procedure, if the endpoint responds at the old location as well, a potential duplicate endpoint is detected since the prefix is being seen at multiple locations. The default detection value for duplicate endpoint detection is "5 moves within

180 seconds." This means after the fifth move within the time frame of 180 seconds, the VTEP starts a "30-second hold" timer before restarting the verification and cleanup process. After the fifth time (5 moves within 180 seconds), the VTEP freezes the duplicate entry. With the Cisco NX-OS BGP EVPN implementation, these default detection values can be modified via user configuration.

By using the MAC mobility sequence numbers carried with the Route type 2 advertisement (MAC/IP advertisement), the BGP EVPN control plane can identify when a potential location change occurs for an endpoint. When a given prefix is determined to still be reachable, the control plane actively verifies whether a given endpoint has actually moved. The control plane provides a tremendous amount of value in not only verifying and cleaning up mobility events but also detecting duplicates within the VXLAN BGP EVPN network.

Virtual PortChannel (vPC) in VXLAN BGP EVPN

The bundling of multiple physical interfaces into a single logical interface between two chassis is referred to as a *port channel*, which is also known as a link aggregation group (LAG). Virtual PortChannel (vPC)[14] is a technology that provides Layer 2 redundancy across two or more physical chassis. Specifically, a single chassis is connected to two other chassis that are configured as a vPC pair. The industry term for this is Multi-Chassis Link Aggregation Group (MC-LAG). Recall that while the underlying transport network for VXLAN is built with a Layer 3 routing protocol leveraging ECMP, the endpoints still connect to the leafs or edge devices via classic Ethernet. It should be noted that the VXLAN BGP EVPN fabric does not mandate that endpoints must have redundant connections to the fabric. However, in most practical deployments, high availability is typically a requirement, and for that purpose, endpoints are connected to the edge devices via port channels.

Several protocols exist to form port channels, including static-unconditional configurations, protocols such as Port Aggregation Protocol (PAgP),[15] and industry standard protocols such as Link Aggregation Control Protocol (LACP).[16]

Port channels can be configured between a single endpoint and a single network switch. When ToR- or switch-level redundancy (as well as link-level redundancy) is a requirement, an MC-LAG is employed to provide the capability to connect an endpoint to multiple network switches.

vPCs allow interfaces of an endpoint to physically connect to two different network switches. From an endpoint perspective, they see a single network switch connected via a single port channel with multiple links. The endpoint connected to the vPC domain can be a switch, a server, or any other networking device that supports the IEEE 802.3 standard and port channels. vPC allows the creation of Layer 2 port channels that span two switches. vPCs consist of two vPC member switches connected by a peer link, with one being the primary and the other being the secondary. The system formed by the network switches is referred to as a *vPC domain* (see Figure 3-17).

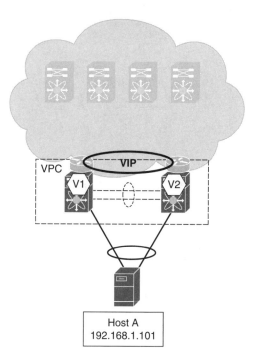

Figure 3-17 *Classic Ethernet vPC Domain*

The vPC primary and secondary members are initially configured as individual edge devices or VTEPs for VXLAN integration. For northbound traffic, the routed interfaces are part of the underlay network to provide reachability to each individual VTEP. Each VTEP is represented by an individual primary IP address (PIP) per VTEP.

With this in mind, the vPC feature first needs to be enabled, followed by the configuration of the vPC domain between the two vPC member network switches. Next, the vPC peer link (PL) and vPC peer keepalive (PKL) need to be connected between the two nodes. The underlay network also needs to be configured on the vPC peer link for both unicast and multicast (if multicast is used) underlay routing purposes.

A single VTEP is configured to represent the vPC domain in the VXLAN BGP EVPN fabric. To achieve the single VTEP, an anycast VTEP is configured with a common virtual IP address (VIP) that is shared across both switches that form the vPC domain. The anycast IP address is used by all the endpoints behind the vPC domain and is represented by a single anycast VTEP for the vPC domain.

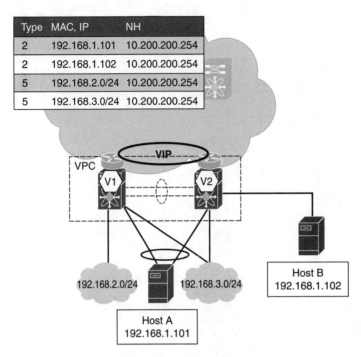

Type	MAC, IP	NH
2	192.168.1.101	10.200.200.254
2	192.168.1.102	10.200.200.254
5	192.168.2.0/24	10.200.200.254
5	192.168.3.0/24	10.200.200.254

Figure 3-18 *vPC with VXLAN BGP EVPN*

A sample vPC domain is shown in Figure 3-18. VTEP V1 has IP address 10.200.200.1/32, and VTEP V2 has IP address 10.200.200.2/32. These are individual physical IP addresses (PIPs) on the NVE interface or the VTEP. A secondary IP address is added to the two VTEPs, which represents the VIP or anycast IP address (specifically 10.200.200.254/32). The secondary address depicts the location of any endpoint that is attached to the vPC pair. This address is the next hop advertised in the BGP EVPN control plane advertisement, representing the location of all local endpoints below a given vPC pair of switches.

The VIP is advertised from both vPC member switches so that both vPC members can receive traffic directly from any locally attached endpoints. Remote VTEPs can reach the VIP advertised by both the vPC member switches via ECMP over the underlay routed network. In this way, dual-attached endpoints can be reached as long as there is at least one path to any one of the vPC member switches or VTEPs.

In a vPC domain, both dual-attached endpoints and single-attached endpoints (typically referred to as orphans) are advertised as being reachable via the VIP associated with the anycast VTEP. Consequently, for orphan endpoints below a vPC member switch, a backup path is set up via the vPC peer link if the reachability to the spines is lost due to uplink failures. Hence, an underlay routing adjacency across the vPC peer link is recommended to address the failure scenarios.

If multicast is enabled on the underlay for carrying multidestination traffic, multicast routing (typically PIM) should also be enabled over the peer link. Of note, by default, the advertisement of an anycast VTEP VIP IP address as the next hop with BGP EVPN applies to the MAC/IP advertisements of Route type 2 as well as the IP prefix routes of Route type 5. In this way, all remote VTEPs can always see all BGP EVPN routes behind a vPC pair as being reachable via a single VTEP represented by the VIP. The VTEP associated with the VIP on the VPC peers of a given VPC domain is sometimes referred to as an anycast VTEP for that domain. If there are N leafs deployed in a VXLAN BGP EVPN fabric and all of them are configured as VPC peers, there are N/2 peers present in the network, represented by the respective anycast VTEPs, one per VPC domain.

The term *anycast VTEP* should not be confused with the *anycast gateway*. Recall that the anycast gateway refers to the distributed IP anycast gateway for a given subnet that is shared by any and all leafs (including those configured as VPC peers) simultaneously with end host reachability information exchanged between the leafs via BGP EVPN. This is referred to as the *gateway* because end hosts within a subnet are configured with the default router set to the corresponding anycast gateway IP. Consequently, from an end host point of view, the default gateway's IP-to-MAC binding should remain the same, regardless of where the end host resides within the fabric. With Cisco NX-OS, all the anycast gateways also share the same globally configured anycast gateway MAC (AGM).

For a given vPC domain, since all ARPs, MACs, and ND entries are synced between the two vPC member switches, both switches are effectively advertising reachability for the same set of prefixes over BGP EVPN. A given vPC member switch thus ignores the BGP EVPN advertisements received from the adjacent vPC member switch since they are part of the same vPC domain because these advertisements are identified by an appropriate site-of-origin extended community attribute that they carry. In this way, only one VTEP or VIP needs to be advertised over BGP EVPN for all endpoints per vPC domain. For a VXLAN BGP EVPN network with N vPC pairs, each remote VTEP needs to know about only N–1 VTEP IPs or VIPs. Even with the presence of only one VIP acting as the anycast VTEP within a given vPC domain, the MP-BGP Route Distinguishers (RDs) are individual identifiers defined on a per-vPC member basis.

However, in some scenarios, IP prefixes may only be advertised by one of the two vPC member switches in a given vPC domain. For example, an individual loopback address may be configured under a VRF on each of the vPC member switches. In this case, because all reachability is advertised into BGP EVPN as being reachable via the anycast VTEP VIP, the traffic destined to a particular vPC member switch may reach its adjacent peer. After decapsulation, the traffic gets black-holed because it will suffer a routing table lookup miss within that VRF.

When IP address information is only advertised by one of the two vPC member switches, such problems may arise. This is because the return traffic needs to reach the correct vPC member switch. Advertising everything from the vPC domain as being reachable via the anycast VTEP IP address does not achieve this. This use case applies to scenarios having southbound IP subnets, orphan-connected IP subnets, individual loopback IP addresses, and/or DHCP relays. With all these use cases, Layer 3 routing adjacency on a per-VRF basis is required to ensure a routing exchange between the vPC domain members. This ensures that even if the packet reaches the incorrect vPC peer, after decapsulation the routing table lookup within the VRF does not suffer a lookup miss.

The configuration of this per-VRF routing adjacency between the vPC member switches may get a bit tedious. However, with BGP EVPN, an elegant solution to achieve similar behavior involves the use of a feature called *advertise-pip*. This feature is globally enabled on a per-switch basis. Recall that every vPC member switch has a unique PIP and a shared VIP address. With the advertise-pip feature enabled, all IP route prefix reachability is advertised from the individual vPC member switches using the PIP as the next hop in Route type 5 messages. Endpoint reachability corresponding to the IP/MAC addresses via Route type 2 messages continues to use the anycast VTEP or VIP as the next hop (see Figure 3-19). This allows per-switch routing advertisement to be individually advertised, allowing the return traffic to reach the respective VTEP in the vPC domain. In this way, a vPC member switch that is part of a given vPC domain also knows about individual IP prefix reachability of its adjacent vPC peer via BGP EVPN Route type 5 advertisements.

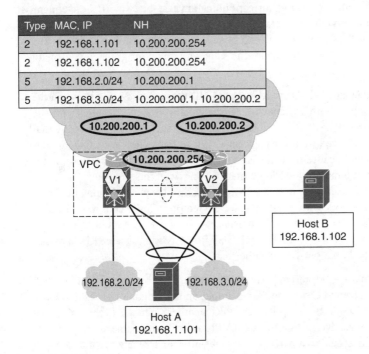

Figure 3-19   *Advertise PIP with vPC*

One additional discussion point pertains to the Router MAC carried in the extended community attributes of the BGP EVPN Route type 2 and Route type 5 messages. With advertise-pip, every vPC switch advertises two VTEPs' IP addresses (one PIP and one VIP). The PIP uses the switch Router MAC, and the VIP uses a locally derived MAC based on the VIP itself. Both of the vPC member switches derive the same MAC because they are each configured with the same shared VIP under the anycast VTEP. Because the Router MAC extended community is nontransitive, and the VIPs are unique within a given VXLAN BGP EVPN fabric, using locally significant router MACs for the VIPs is not a concern.

In summary, by using the advertise-pip feature with VXLAN BGP EVPN, the next-hop IP address of a VTEP is conditionally handled, depending on whether a Route type 2 (MAC/IP advertisement) or a Route type 5 (IP prefix route) is announced. Advertising PIP allows for efficient handling of vPC-attached endpoints as well as IP subnets specific to the use cases for Layer 2 and Layer 3 border connectivity or DHCP relays. Finally, it should be noted that some differences in the way vPC operates with the different Nexus platforms might exist. For an exhaustive list of the configuration required with VPC in VXLAN BGP EVPN environment for Nexus 9000 platform, please refer to Cisco's *Example of VXLAN BGP EVPN (EBGP)*.[17] And for Nexus 7000 and Nexus 5600 platforms, please refer to Cisco's *Forwarding configurations for Cisco Nexus 5600 and 7000 Series switches in the programmable fabric*.[18]

DHCP

Dynamic Host Configuration Protocol (DHCP)[19] is a commonly used protocol that provides IP address and other options for an endpoint. A DHCP server component is responsible for delivering IP address assignments and managing the binding between an endpoint MAC address and the provided IP address. In addition to distributing the IP address (DHCP scope) itself, additional options such as default gateway, DNS server, and various others (DHCP options) can be assigned to the endpoint that serves as a DHCP client. The requester in the case of DHCP is the DHCP client, which sends a discovery message to the DHCP server. The DHCP server then responds to this discover request with an offer message. Once this initial exchange is complete, a DHCP request (from client to server) is followed by a DHCP acknowledgment, and this completes the assignment of the IP address and subsequent information through the DHCP scope options. Figure 3-20 illustrates this DHCP process.

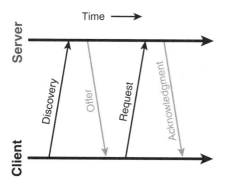

Figure 3-20   *DHCP Process*

Because the DHCP process relies on broadcasts to exchange information between DHCP client and DHCP server, the DHCP server needs to be in the same Layer 2 network in which the DHCP client resides. This is one deployment method for DHCP. In most cases, multiple IP subnets exist, and routers are in the path between a DHCP client and DHCP server. In this case, a DHCP relay agent is required. The DHCP relay agent is a DHCP protocol helper that snoops DHCP broadcasts and forwards these messages (specifically unicasts) to a specified DHCP server.

The DHCP relay is typically configured on the default gateway facing the DHCP client. The DHCP relay agent can support many different use cases for automated IP addressing, depending on whether the DHCP server resides in the same network, the same VRF, or a different VRF compared to the DHCP client. Having a per-tenant or per-VRF DHCP server is common in certain service provider data centers where strict segregation between tenants is a mandatory requirement. On the other hand, in enterprise environments, having a centralized DHCP server in a shared-services VRF is not uncommon. Traffic crosses tenant (VRF) boundaries with the DHCP server and DHCP client in a different VRF(s). In general, we can differentiate between three DHCP server deployment modes:

- **DHCP client and DHCP server within the same Layer 2 segment (VLAN/L2 VNI)**

    - No DHCP relay agent required

    - DHCP discovery from DHCP client is broadcast in the local Layer 2 segment (VLAN/L2 VNI)

    - As DHCP uses broadcasts, multidestination replication is required

- **DHCP client and DHCP server in different IP subnets but in the same tenant (VRF)**

    - DHCP relay agent required

    - DHCP discovery from DHCP client is snooped by the relay agent and directed to the DHCP server

- **DHCP client and DHCP server are in different IP subnets and different tenants (VRF)**

    - DHCP relay agent required with VRF selection

    - DHCP discovered from DHCP client is snooped by the relay agent and directed to the DHCP server into the VRF where the DHCP server resides

Two of the three DHCP server deployment modes relay data with a DHCP relay agent.[20] The DHCP server infrastructure is a shared resource in a multitenant network, and multitenancy support for DHCP services needs to be available. The same DHCP relay agent is responsible for handling the DHCP discovery message and DHCP request message from the DHCP client to the DHCP server and the DHCP offer message and DHCP acknowledgment message from the DHCP server to the requesting DHCP client.

Typically, the DHCP relay agent is configured at the same place where the default gateway IP address is configured for a given subnet. The DHCP relay agent uses the default gateway IP address in the GiAddr field in the DHCP payload for all DHCP messages that are relayed to the DHCP server. The GiAddr field in the relayed DHCP message is used for subnet scope selection so that a free IP address is picked from this subnet at the DHCP server and the respective DCHP options are assigned to the offer that will be returned from the server to the relay agent. The GiAddr field indicates the address to which the DHCP server sends out the response (that is, the DHCP offer or acknowledgment).

Additional considerations need to be taken into account when implementing the DHCP relay agent with the distributed IP anycast gateway in a VXLAN BGP EVPN fabric. This is because the same IP address is shared by all VTEPs that provide Layer 3 service in the form of a default gateway for a given network. Likewise, the same GiAddr field is consequently stamped in DHCP requests relayed by these VTEPs. As a result, the DHCP response from the DHCP server may not reach the same VTEP that had relayed the initial request due to the presence of an anycast IP. In other words, the response may go to any one of the VTEPs servicing the anycast IP, which is clearly undesirable (see Figure 3-21). If a unique IP address per VTEP exists, then that can be used in the GiAddr field, thereby ensuring that the server response is guaranteed to come back to the right VTEP. This is achieved via specification of an **ip dhcp relay source-interface *xxx*** command under the Layer 3 interface configured with the anycast gateway IP.

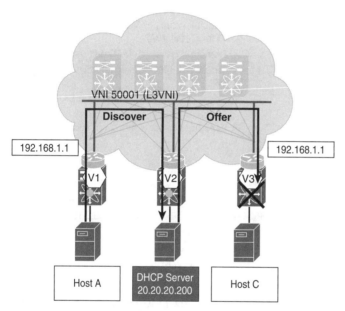

Figure 3-21   *GiAddr Problem with Distributed IP Anycast Gateway*

In this way, the GiAddr field is modified to carry the IP address of the specified source interface. Any given interface on the network switch can be used, as long as the IP address is unique within the network used for reaching the DHCP server. In addition, the IP address must be routable, so that the DHCP server must be able to respond to the individual and unique DHCP relay IP address identified by the GiAddr field. By accomplishing this, the DHCP messages from the client to the server are ensured to travel back and forth through the same network switch or relay agent.

It should be noted that typically the GiAddr field also plays a role in the IP subnet scope selection from which a free IP address is allocated and returned to the DHCP client. Because the GiAddr field has been changed based on the source interface specification, it no longer represents the DHCP scope selection and respective IP address assignment.

As a result, a different way to enable scope selection is required. DHCP option 82 (a vendor-specific option) was designed to put in circuit-specific information, and has been used in different deployments (see Figure 3-22). DHCP option 82 has two suboptions that derive the required IP subnet for the IP address assignment, which provides a different approach for DHCP subnet scope selection.

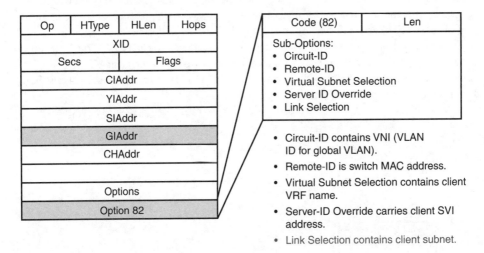

Figure 3-22   *DHCP Option 82*

With DHCP option 82 with the Circuit-ID suboption, the VLAN or VNI information associated with the network in which the client resides is added to the DHCP messages, which provide this information to the DHCP server. The DHCP server needs to support the functionality to select the right DHCP scope, based on the Circuit-ID suboption. DHCP servers that support the DHCP option 82 with the Circuit-ID suboption include Microsoft's Windows 2012 DHCP server, ISC DHCP server (dhcpd), and Cisco Prime Network Registrar (CPNR).

With the second option, which is the preferred option, the DHCP scope selection is performed using the Link Selection suboption of DHCP option 82. Within the Link Selection suboption, the original client subnet is carried, thereby allowing the correct DHCP scope selection. DHCP servers that support the Link Selection suboption include dhcpd, Infoblox's DDI, and CPNR. For an exhaustive list of the DHCP relay configuration required in a VXLAN BGP EVPN network, refer to the vPC VTEP DHCP relay configuration example at Cisco.com.[21]

With the use of the distributed anycast gateway in a VXLAN BGP EVPN fabric and its multitenant capability, centralized DHCP services simplify the ability to provide IP address assignments to endpoints. With a unique source IP address for relaying the DHCP message, and with DHCP option 82, the IP address assignment infrastructure can be centrally provided even across the VRF or tenant boundary.

Summary

This chapter provides an in-depth discussion of the core forwarding capabilities of a VXLAN BGP EVPN fabric. For carrying broadcast, unknown unicast, and multicast (BUM) traffic, the chapter examines both multicast and ingress replication, coupled with the inclusive multicast Route type support with BGP EVPN. It also discusses enhanced forwarding features that allow for reducing ARP and unknown unicast traffic within the fabric. Perhaps the key benefit of a BGP EVPN fabric is the realization of a distributed anycast gateway at the ToR or leaf layer that allows for optimal forwarding of both Layer 2 and Layer 3 traffic within the fabric, using IRB semantics. Efficient handling of endpoint mobility with BGP EVPN is also described, as well as how to handle dual-attached endpoints with vPC-based deployments. Finally, the chapter concludes with a description of how DHCP relay functionality can be implemented in environments with distributed IP anycast gateway.

References

1. Internet Society. *Internet-drafts (I-Ds)*. www.ietf.org/id-info/.

2. Internet Society. *Request for comments (RFC)*. www.ietf.org/rfc.html.

3. Network Working Group. *DHCP relay agent information option*. 2001. tools.ietf.org/html/rfc3046.

4. Network Working Group. *Protocol Independent Multicast–Sparse Mode (PIM-SM) protocol specification (revised)*. 2006. tools.ietf.org/html/rfc4601.

5. Network Working Group. *Bidirectional Protocol Independent Multicast (BIDIR-PIM)*. 2007. tools.ietf.org/html/rfc5015.

6. Network Working Group. *Neighbor discovery for IP version 6 (IPv6)*. 2007. tools.ietf.org/html/rfc4861.

7. Rabadan, J., et al. *Operational aspects of proxy-ARP/ND in EVPN networks*. 2016. www.ietf.org/id/draft-ietf-bess-evpn-proxy-arp-nd-01.txt.

8. Cisco. *Proxy ARP*. 2008. www.cisco.com/c/en/us/support/docs/ip/dynamic-address-allocation-resolution/13718-5.html.

9. Network Working Group. *Cisco's Hot Standby Router Protocol (HSRP)*. 1998. www.ietf.org/rfc/rfc2281.txt.

10. Network Working Group. *Virtual Router Redundancy Protocol (VRRP)*. 2004. tools.ietf.org/html/rfc3768.

11. Cisco. *Cisco GLBP load balancing options*. 1998. www.cisco.com/c/en/us/products/collateral/ios-nx-os-software/ip-services/product_data_sheet0900aecd803a546c.html.

12. Cisco. *Anycast HSRP*. 2016. www.cisco.com/c/en/us/td/docs/switches/datacenter/sw/6_x/nx-os/fabricpath/configuration/guide/b-Cisco-Nexus-7000-Series-NX-OS-FP-Configuration-Guide-6x/b-Cisco-Nexus-7000-Series-NX-OS-FP-Configuration-Guide-6x_chapter_0100.html#concept_910E7F7E592D487F84C8EE81BC6FC14F.

13. Cisco. *VXLAN network with MP-BGP EVPN control plane design guide*. 2015. www.cisco.com/c/en/us/products/collateral/switches/nexus-9000-series-switches/guide-c07-734107.html#_Toc414541688.

14. Cisco. *Cisco NX-OS software Virtual PortChannel: Fundamental concepts 5.0*. 2014. www.cisco.com/c/en/us/products/collateral/switches/nexus-5000-series-switches/design_guide_c07-625857.html.

15. Finn, N. *Port Aggregation Protocol*. 1998. www.ieee802.org/3/trunk_study/april98/finn_042898.pdf.

16. Network Working Group 802.1. *802.1AX-2008—IEEE standard for local and metropolitan area networks—Link aggregation*. 2008. standards.ieee.org/findstds/standard/802.1AX-2008.html.

17. Cisco. *Example of VXLAN BGP EVPN (EBGP)*. 2016. www.cisco.com/c/en/us/td/docs/switches/datacenter/nexus9000/sw/7-x/vxlan/configuration/guide/b_Cisco_Nexus_9000_Series_NX-OS_VXLAN_Configuration_Guide_7x/b_Cisco_Nexus_9000_Series_NX-OS_VXLAN_Configuration_Guide_7x_chapter_0100.html#concept_53AC00F0DE6E40A79979F27990443953.

18. Cisco. *Forwarding configurations for Cisco Nexus 5600 and 7000 Series switches in the programmable fabric*. 2016. www.cisco.com/c/en/us/td/docs/switches/datacenter/pf/configuration/guide/b-pf-configuration/Forwarding-Configurations.html#concept_B54E8C5F82C14C7A9733639B1A560A01.

19. Network Working Group. *Dynamic Host Configuration Protocol*. 1997. www.ietf.org/rfc/rfc2131.txt.

20. Network Working Group. *DHCP relay agent information option*. 2001. tools.ietf.org/html/rfc3046.

21. Cisco. *vPC VTEP DHCP relay configuration example*. 2016. www.cisco.com/c/en/us/td/docs/switches/datacenter/nexus9000/sw/7-x/vxlan/configuration/guide/b_Cisco_Nexus_9000_Series_NX-OS_VXLAN_Configuration_Guide_7x/b_Cisco_Nexus_9000_Series_NX-OS_VXLAN_Configuration_Guide_7x_appendix_0110.html#id_16000.

## Chapter 4

The Underlay

In this chapter, the following topics will be covered:

- The underlay associated with the BGP EVPN VXLAN fabric
- IP address allocation options and MTU considerations for the underlay
- Underlay unicast and multicast routing options

Network virtualization overlays, including Virtual Extensible LAN (VXLAN), require a network over which the overlay-encapsulated traffic can be transported. Several considerations must be made in this regard. With VXLAN being a MAC in IP/UDP overlay, the transport network needs to carry IP traffic from VXLAN Tunnel Endpoints (VTEPs) in an optimal manner. Recall that every overlay adds additional headers on top of the original packet/frame. The transport network, termed the *underlay*, needs to account for the additional bytes incurred by the overlay headers. In the case of VXLAN, typically, the transport network needs to be provisioned for an additional 50 bytes in the maximum transmission unit (MTU). Likewise, the transport network must match the resiliency and convergence requirements of the overlay as well. It is important to consider scalability, resiliency, convergence, and capacity when considering data center fabric designs. With overlay-based data center fabrics, the importance of the underlay cannot be understated. Typically, the overlay's performance is only as good as the underlay transport that carries it. Even for troubleshooting, debugging, and convergence of the overlay traffic, the underlay is the critical piece.

When designing and building the underlay for the fabric, IP address assignment is an important aspect of this process. The IP address assignment is a prerequisite for any kind of routing protocol that provides reachability between the various devices in the fabric. Multiple options are available in assigning these IP addresses, including, among others, a traditional point-to-point (P2P) method or an address-saving option that uses an unnumbered IP addressing scheme. Likewise, it is important to be aware of requirements in addressing the interfaces of the VTEP (also called the Network Virtualization Edge [NVE] interface), the loopback interface over which the multiprotocol BGP session is established, and eventually the multicast rendezvous point, when using a multicast based underlay.

The underlay might be required to not only transport unicast traffic but also provide multicast routing in order to handle broadcast, unknown unicast, and multicast (BUM) traffic in the overlay. All these requirements need to be considered when designing and creating the underlay network for a BGP EVPN VXLAN–based data center fabric.

Underlay Considerations

When building the data center fabric, some upfront considerations regarding the underlay take priority. The first involves defining the anticipated topology to be used for the underlay. Today's data centers have requirements for large amounts of north–south as well as east–west traffic patterns, so the topology must be able to accommodate these different kinds of traffic streams and communication profiles.

North–south data traffic, as illustrated in Figure 4-1, is the traditional communication profile for moving data in and out of the data center. In essence, this profile is utilized if a user in the campus or on the Internet wishes to access data from within a data center. Common examples of north–south traffic are traffic associated with classic web browsing or traffic related to email activities. In each of these cases, an end user has an application on a PC to access data hosted within a data center. This type of north–south traffic is important to efficiently move data between data centers and toward the end user.

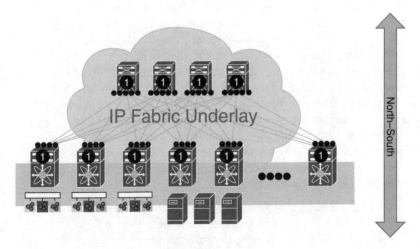

Figure 4-1 *North–South Traffic*

East–west traffic, on the other hand, reflects a slightly different communication profile because this profile describes data communication between servers and/or various applications within the data center (see Figure 4-2). Typically, requests from an end user in a corporate network or in the Internet involve complex preprocessing activities on the underlying data. As a means to demonstrate this need for preprocessing, one example of east–west traffic involves access from a web server (via an app server) to the database. Dynamic rendering of websites and/or business applications often uses a two- or three-tier server architecture, where one tier must communicate with one of the other tiers before delivering the requested data to the end user. When these tiers communicate with one another or need access to data storage or other data residing in the same data center, the term *east–west traffic* is used for this more lateral, or horizontal, traffic profile.

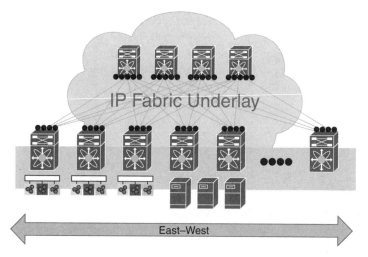

Figure 4-2 *East–West Traffic*

In the early 1950s, when telephone switchboards were manually operated, Charles Clos needed to find a more efficient way to handle call transfers. The switchboards utilized a two-stage network where calls would be transferred by using a single crossbar switch. Unfortunately, frequently calls were blocked because only one path existed, and if another transfer was occupying that path, transfers would fail. Faced with this dilemma, Clos established the best mathematical way for interconnecting two points from an ingress call to an egress one by leveraging multistage fabrics. By having an ingress stage, a middle stage, and an egress stage, calls had multiple path opportunities to reach their transfer destinations. This additional stage created a crossbar matrix of connectivity, and because the resulting networks appeared like woven fibers, the term *crossbar switch* was introduced.

Clos's work and designs, which revolutionized telephone switchboards, also found its way to network switch and data center fabric designs. Most network switches built today are based on Charles Clos's mathematical equations from the 1950s. In a given switch, the front-facing Ethernet ports (first stage) are each interconnected via a network fabric (second stage). As a result of this topology, every front-facing Ethernet port must travel the same distance to every other front-facing Ethernet port (equidistant), thereby ensuring predictable and consistent latency.[1] Figure 4-3 shows the internal architecture of a typical multistage modular network switch.

How does this apply to a data center network or a data center fabric? In applying the Clos fabric concept from the network switch to data center fabric topology, a front-facing Ethernet port is replaced with a top-of-rack (ToR) switch, also known as a *leaf*. The leaf is responsible for providing connectivity to and from servers as well as making forwarding decisions, based on bridging or routing lookups, within the data center fabric. Hundreds of leafs potentially exist, and interconnections among them are needed. A leaf connects to a second stage in the data center fabric, which is composed of a set of spine switches. Depending on the requirements for scale and bandwidth for the fabric, the number of spines can vary between 2 and 32, which is good enough for practical deployments.

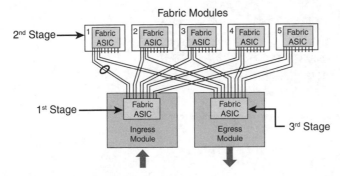

Figure 4-3   *Multistage Network Switch*

Within the data center fabric, a spine is connected to every leaf, thereby providing N paths from every leaf to every other leaf, where N is the number of spines (see Figure 4-4). The spines in turn may connect to another spine layer, termed the super-spine layer, thereby allowing construction of N-stage spine leaf fabrics. Because the spine itself is a connectivity "backbone" in the overlay-based data center fabric, it has no visibility into the user traffic itself because the overlay encapsulation occurs at the leaf. The spine simply ensures that VTEP-to-VTEP communication is done efficiently between different leafs by using the underlay IP network's equal-cost multipath (ECMP) capability provided by the routing protocol. In comparing this to Clos fabric topology concepts, multiple paths are available via the spines, with each offering the same distance and latency between any two endpoints in the data center fabric.

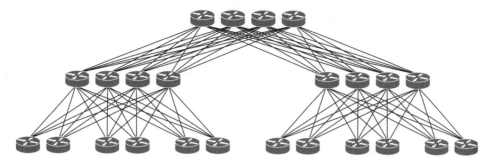

Figure 4-4 *Multistage Clos Network*

MTU Considerations

Recall that VXLAN, as a network virtualization overlay technology, places some additional overhead on the original data frames. This overhead manifests in the form of additional identifier information required for the functioning of VXLAN itself. This helps solve some of the existing deficiencies present in traditional network transport technologies (such as Ethernet). However, due to the overhead, additional considerations need to be taken into account specific to the underlay network design.

As a general rule, fragmentation (splitting of a frame or data packet because it is too large for a transport network) should be avoided. Fragmentation and reassembly put additional burden on the switch resources as well as the server resources, which results in transport inefficiency. Computers, servers, PCs, and other network hardware equipped with Ethernet network interface cards (NICs) have a standard maximum transmission unit (MTU) of 1500 bytes.[2] The total size of the Ethernet frame is 1518 (or 1522, with the additional optional 802.1Q tag), with 6 bytes each for the source and DMAC addresses, 2 bytes for the Ethertype, and 4 bytes for the frame check sequence (FCS). This means that a computer can send a payload of 1500 bytes or less, which includes all header information, from Layer 3 and above. Likewise, a server could potentially send unfragmented data up to an MTU of 1500 bytes as well through its default configuration. However, if VXLAN is employed between the network switches to which the servers are attached, the MTU is reduced to 1450 bytes through its default configuration. This is because VXLAN adds either 50 or 54 bytes of overhead (see Figure 4-5) as part of identifier information.

Employing VXLAN incurs an overhead consisting of a 14-byte outer MAC header, a 20-byte outer IP header, an 8-byte UDP header, and an 8-byte VXLAN header. The 50 or 54 bytes of overhead introduced by VXLAN must be added to the MTU considerations of Ethernet itself. The optional additional 4 bytes that might push the overhead from 50 bytes to 54 bytes would come from preserving the IEEE 802.1Q tag in the original Ethernet frame. In most instances, the 802.1Q tag is mapped to the VNI and stripped off before the VXLAN encapsulation is added to the original frame. However, certain use cases related to Q-in-Q[3] or Q-in-VNI[4] exist (for example, nested hypervisor, Layer 2 tunneling, etc.), that would require the original IEEE 802.1Q tag to be preserved. In any case, these additional bytes of the VXLAN overhead need to be considered as part of the underlay design.

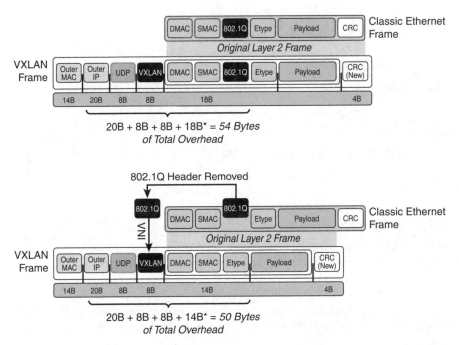

Figure 4-5 *VXLAN Frame Format, Including Byte Count (50/54 Byte Overhead for Comparison)*

In data center networks, efficiency is essential, and therefore, the MTU on the server side is often increased to accommodate jumbo frames (data units that are larger than the traditional 1500 bytes typical of Ethernet frames). Jumbo frames coming from the server side can typically be up to a maximum of 9000 bytes, which most NICs and/or virtual switches offer. With a need to now support MTUs of 9000 bytes from the server side when using jumbo frames, and with the additional bytes from the VXLAN encapsulation, a value around 9050 or 9054 bytes needs to be allowed in order to avoid fragmentation.

Fortunately, most of the network switches from Cisco and other vendors provide a maximum MTU value of 9216 bytes, though some have to reduce this value by 20 to 30 bytes to accommodate a network switch internal service header. Therefore, a jumbo frame MTU of 9000 bytes from the server side can be accommodated by network switches without introducing fragmentation. This is not uncommon because the use of large transmission units is more efficient, and in a high-speed network, using them reduces the number of round trips required over the network. Because MTU configuration is performed at many locales, and because this can potentially affect the overlay during subsequent reconfigurations, an initial consideration regarding the MTU size of the network is critical. The jumbo frame MTU needs to be configured consistently across all points in the network, including the host-facing server interfaces. As an additional safeguard, certain network protocols check to assess whether a neighboring device is using the same MTU value before bringing up the routing adjacency with that neighbor. Thus, while the underlay for VXLAN can accommodate jumbo frame MTU size, specific design considerations remain important.

IP Addressing

IP address allocation and assignment to the various network devices and/or related interfaces (both physical and logical) is important when building a routed network for the underlay. This section focuses on an IPv4-based underlay for a VXLAN-based network. Note that the overlay supports IPv4 as well as IPv6 addresses. Each network switch participating in the underlay for the VXLAN network is uniquely identified by its routing protocol through a router ID, (RID), as demonstrated in Example 4-1.

Example 4-1 *Output from OSPF Showing RID*

```
LEAF11# show ip ospf

Routing Process UNDERLAY with ID 10.10.10.1 VRF default
 Routing Process Instance Number 1
 Stateful High Availability enabled
 Graceful-restart is configured
   Grace period: 60 state: Inactive
   Last graceful restart exit status: None
 Supports only single TOS(TOS0) routes
 Supports opaque LSA
 Administrative distance 110
 Reference Bandwidth is 40000 Mbps
 SPF throttling delay time of 200.000 msecs,
   SPF throttling hold time of 1000.000 msecs,
   SPF throttling maximum wait time of 5000.000 msecs
 LSA throttling start time of 0.000 msecs,
   LSA throttling hold interval of 5000.000 msecs,
   LSA throttling maximum wait time of 5000.000 msecs
 Minimum LSA arrival 1000.000 msec
 LSA group pacing timer 10 secs
 Maximum paths to destination 8
 Number of external LSAs 0, checksum sum 0
 Number of opaque AS LSAs 0, checksum sum 0
 Number of areas is 1, 1 normal, 0 stub, 0 nssa
 Number of active areas is 1, 1 normal, 0 stub, 0 nssa
 Install discard route for summarized external routes.
 Install discard route for summarized internal routes.
```

```
Area BACKBONE(0.0.0.0)
      Area has existed for 5w1d
      Interfaces in this area: 4 Active interfaces: 3
      Passive interfaces: 0  Loopback interfaces: 2
      No authentication available
      SPF calculation has run 86 times
       Last SPF ran for 0.000505s
      Area ranges are
      Number of LSAs: 7, checksum sum 0x25cd5
```

The RID is used in routing protocols to uniquely identify a given neighbor and/or an index to the information received or sent to/from this neighbor in its database. With this in mind, the RID should be always available and accessible, and therefore, it is a good practice to create a loopback interface with an IP address that matches the configured RID. A loopback interface is a logical software interface in a network switch or router that is always up, as there are multiple physical paths to reach the loopback interface(s). Physical interfaces can be unavailable if a neighboring device interface shuts down or disappears (for example, is unplugged). Example 4-2 shows an OSPF configuration that includes loopback interfaces for RID and VTEP.

Example 4-2 *Example Configuration of a Loopback and OSPF*

```
LEAF11# show running-config ospf

feature ospf

router ospf UNDERLAY
  router-id 10.10.10.1

interface loopback0
  ip address 10.200.200.1/32
  ip router ospf UNDERLAY area 0.0.0.0

interface loopback1
  ip address 10.10.10.1/32
  ip router ospf UNDERLAY area 0.0.0.0
```

In addition to the RID, IP addresses are also assigned to the physical interfaces in order to build routing adjacencies. The best way to allocate these IP addresses on the physical interfaces is to establish them as P2P routed interfaces. In the situation shown in Figure 4-6, only the two P2P interfaces each participate in the communication between the spine and leaf with VTEP V1 and the spine and leaf with VTEP V3.

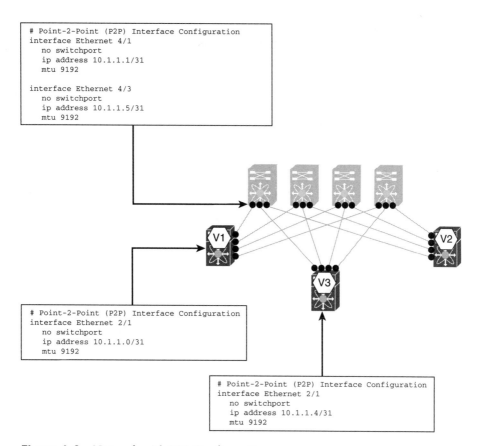

```
# Point-2-Point (P2P) Interface Configuration
interface Ethernet 4/1
   no switchport
   ip address 10.1.1.1/31
   mtu 9192

interface Ethernet 4/3
   no switchport
   ip address 10.1.1.5/31
   mtu 9192
```

```
# Point-2-Point (P2P) Interface Configuration
interface Ethernet 2/1
   no switchport
   ip address 10.1.1.0/31
   mtu 9192
```

```
# Point-2-Point (P2P) Interface Configuration
interface Ethernet 2/1
   no switchport
   ip address 10.1.1.4/31
   mtu 9192
```

Figure 4-6 *Network with P2P Configuration*

IP address subnetting for P2P-routed interfaces offers many ways of assigning netmask or prefix size; however, there are two efficient methods. P2P subnets can use a prefix size of /31 or a prefix size of /30. /30 is the most common prefix size for P2P IP networks. A typical /30 prefix provides one network ID address, two usable IP addresses, and one broadcast ID address. While using this prefix size is an efficient way of assigning IP addresses to P2P networks, note that 50% of the addresses (the network ID address and broadcast ID address) are unusable.

Consider the math for a network with 4 spines and a 40-leaf underlay with a /30 prefix:

4 spines × 40 leafs = 160 P2P links

= 160 links × 4 (/30) = 40 leaf + 4 spines

= 640 IP addresses for P2P links = 44 IP addresses for loopback interfaces

= 684 IP addresses => /22 prefix (1024 IP addresses)

Alternatively, a more efficient option from an IP address assignment perspective would be to use a /31 prefix length. The IP subnet of a /31 prefix consists of only two IP addresses, both capable of being used in the P2P network. With the /30 prefix, the additional two nonusable IP addresses (network ID and broadcast ID) are overloaded due to usage with the two usable IP addresses. However, a /31 prefix provides only two usable IP addresses, without network ID and broadcast ID addresses, and therefore overloading does not occur. By using /31 prefixes instead of /30 prefixes in the underlay network, all the IP addresses in the area of P2P networks are usable.

Consider the match for a network with 4 spines and a 40-leaf underlay with a /31 prefix:

4 spines × 40 leafs = 160 P2P links

= 160 links × 2 (/31) + 40 leafs + 4 spines

= 320 IP addresses for P2P links + 44 IP addresses for loopback interfaces

= 364 IP addresses aggregate required => /23 prefix (512 IP addresses)

An alternative approach for P2P interface addressing is a technique called *IP unnumbered*, which has been available in the networking industry for decades. Essentially, this approach allows for IP processing on a P2P interface without assigning an individual IP address on a per-interface basis, which in turn conserves IP address space in the network. The IP unnumbered option allows reusing the loopback interface created for the RID and "borrow" its IP address for all the physical interfaces. Example 4-3 illustrates a typical IP unnumbered configuration

Example 4-3   *IP Unnumbered Configuration Example*

```
interface loopback1
  ip address 10.10.10.1/32
  ip router ospf UNDERLAY area 0.0.0.0
  ip pim sparse-mode

interface Ethernet2/1
  no switchport
  mtu 9216
  ip unnnumbered loopback 1
  ip ospf network point-to-point
  ip router ospf UNDERLAY area 0.0.0.0
  ip pim sparse-mode
  no shutdown
```

By using this single IP address per network switch, the IP address space is notably saved when compared to the /31 or /30 prefix approaches, and at the same time, the overall address assignment process is simplified.

Consider the math for a network with 4 spines and a 40-leaf underlay with IP unnumbered configured:

    4 spines + 40 leafs = 44 individual devices

    = 44 IP addresses for loopback interfaces (IP unnumbered)

    => /26 prefix (64 IP addresses)

IP unnumbered for Ethernet interfaces (see Figure 4-7) using the OSPF or IS-IS routing protocols is available on most of the Cisco Nexus data center switches.

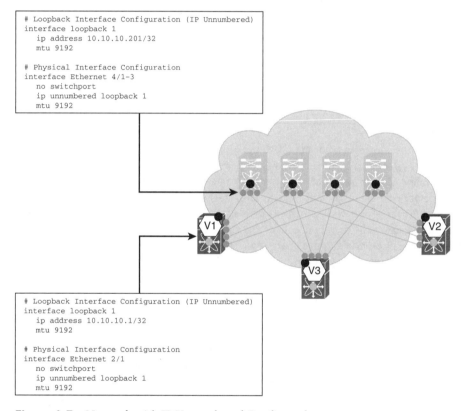

Figure 4-7 *Network with IP Unnumbered Configured*

So far, we have discussed interface addressing options for the underlay. However, one additional function is another essential aspect of the underlay in relation to the overlay network. This involves the VTEP, or NVE, interface. The NVE interface has to derive its IP address from a logical loopback interface, which is always available and accessible much like the RID. The same loopback interface employed for RID can be used for the NVE. This approach avoids configuring additional IP addresses for each NVE interface.

However, from a network design perspective, separating pure underlay functions from overlay functions is desirable. In other words, common best practice is to create a separate loopback interface that is used by the NVE interface, as demonstrated in Example 4-4.

Example 4-4   *Configuration of a Separate Loopback for Routing and NVE*

```
! Loopback0 Interface Configuration (VXLAN VTEP)
interface loopback0
  ip address 10.200.200.1/32
  ip router ospf UNDERLAY area 0.0.0.0
  ip pim sparse-mode

! Loopback1 Interface Configuration (Routing Loopback for Underlay and BGP EVPN)
interface loopback1
  ip address 10.10.10.1/32
  ip router ospf UNDERLAY area 0.0.0.0
  ip pim sparse-mode
```

Note that the addresses associated with both interfaces, Loopback0 and Loopback1, need to be advertised by the underlay interior gateway protocol (IGP) for network reachability. The separation of NVE loopback interface and underlay routing protocols has operational benefits as well. With Cisco NX-OS offering graceful insertion and removal features, a network switch can be isolated from the underlay routing perspective by shutting down the first loopback interface associated with the NVE or VTEP during maintenance or other disruptive operations. This allows troubleshooting of the underlay without necessarily having to turn off both overlay and underlay reachability at the same time. In addition, this also avoids unnecessary traffic disruptions.

Apart from the interface IP assignment inherently necessary to connect the spine–leaf network, additional IP addressing requirements exist on the spine. Typically, a pure spine allows connectivity between the VTEP hosting leafs and does not itself host an NVE interface—and therefore cannot provide VXLAN encapsulation/decapsulation functionality. In this case, a single loopback interface is sufficient on the spine, and it is employed both for the RID associated with the underlay routing protocol and identification of the BGP route reflector. However, the underlay needs to not only support unicast reachability but also be able to transport multidestination traffic.

As mentioned earlier, IP multicast is commonly used in the underlay for this purpose. Support for multicast routing in the underlay, in turn, requires allocation and identification of appropriate multicast rendezvous points (RPs). With a spine–leaf topology, spines are a desirable choice for hosting the RPs. Hence, the spines may need to have additional loopback interfaces that are employed by the RPs.

Various methods exist for addressing RP redundancy. The focus in this discussion only pertains to Anycast RP[5] for PIM Anycast Source Multicast (PIM ASM),[6] and Phantom RP[7] for Bidirectional PIM (PIM BiDir).[8] In order to address RP redundancy and load balancing with these operations, it is necessary to have some IP addresses available to accommodate these services. For PIM ASM, a single additional loopback interface used for Anycast RP addressing is sufficient, and therefore only one single IP address (/32 prefix) is required. For PIM BiDir and Phantom RP, more IP addresses are needed to provide redundancy and load balancing. Therefore, a dedicated subnet of a proportional size is required. Details regarding RP redundancy are provided later in this chapter.

At this point, the need to understand IP addressing requirements for the underlay should be apparent. In order to reduce the size of the routing tables, the creation of aggregate prefixes or aggregates can be considered in relation to these IP addresses. As a best practice, a single IP address aggregate or supernet would be ideal, depending on the number of P2P interfaces in the underlay and the corresponding addressing mode employed. Using this approach, all the /30 or /31 IP subnet prefixes assigned to the various P2P interfaces can be summarized in the single aggregate (first). Likewise, different aggregates (second and third) can be used for the NVE loopback interfaces and the RIDs, respectively, and they can be combined into a single aggregate if desired. In the presence of a Phantom RP, an additional aggregate is necessary. In summary, the aggregate options for the underlay are as follows (see Figure 4-8 for an example):

- A single IP subnet for all P2P interface subnets

- A single IP subnet for all RIDs and NVE interfaces, using individual loopbacks (which can be split into separate IP aggregates if needed or desired)

- A single IP subnet for Phantom RP

P2P Agg: 10.1.1.0/24
RID Agg: 10.10.10.0/24
VTEP Agg: 10.200.200.0/24
RP Agg: 10.254.254.0/24

Figure 4-8   *A Simple Example Showing IP Address Pool Allocation for a Typical Underlay*

IP Unicast Routing

Unicast routing can be achieved with various routing protocols as part of the underlay. Specifically, two types of IGPs have demonstrated efficient functional capabilities within a multistage spine–leaf topology. These fall in the category of link-state and distance-vector protocols. Link-state IGPs are based on Shortest Path First (SPF)[9] algorithms and are suitable for spine–leaf networks. Spines provide multiple equal-cost paths between the leafs, and the SPF-based protocol considers all these links, as well as the respective link speeds, to compute the single best path or multiple equal-cost best paths through the network. As mentioned earlier, equal-cost multipath (ECMP) is one of the biggest advantages an IP-based underlay network provides over the dominant Spanning Tree Protocol (STP) present in Ethernet-based networks (see Figure 4-9).

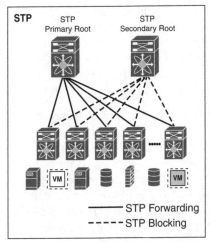 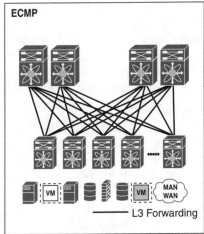

Figure 4-9 *STP Versus ECMP*

While BGP also has valuable merits as an underlay routing protocol, it is a path vector protocol (PVP)[10] and only considers autonomous systems (AS) to calculate paths. However, an experienced network engineer can achieve outcomes with BGP that are comparable to those that are possible with other SPF-based routing protocols.

OSPF as an Underlay

Open Shortest Path First (OSPF) is a widely adopted IGP that has been employed in many LAN, WAN, and data center core network environments.[11] It is widely available in an array of network components throughout the industry (routers, switches, service appliances, etc.), providing strong interoperability in alignment with its IETF background.[12] The OSPF default interface type used for Ethernet interfaces is "broadcast," which inherently results in a designated router (DR) and/or backup designated router (BDR) election, thus reducing control traffic comprising routing updates. While this is appropriate for a multiaccess network such as a shared Ethernet segment, it is unnecessary in a P2P network such as the underlay.

Changing the interface type to **point-to-point** avoids the DR/BDR election process and, therefore, reduces the time required to bring up the OSPF adjacency between the leafs and spines. In addition, with the point-to-point interface mode, there are no type 2 link-state advertisements (LSAs). Only type 1 LSAs are needed, thereby ensuring that the OSPF LSA database remains lean. It also reduces the time needed for the network to converge after a topology change. Example 4-5 shows a typical OSPF configuration employed in the underlay and the corresponding **show** output.

Example 4-5 *OSPF Interface Configuration and Status*

```
interface Ethernet2/1
  no switchport
  mtu 9216
  ip address 10.1.1.0/31
  ip ospf network point-to-point
  ip router ospf UNDERLAY area 0.0.0.0
  ip pim sparse-mode
  no shutdown


LEAF11# show ip ospf interface Ethernet 2/1


Ethernet2/1 is up, line protocol is up
    IP address 10.1.1.0/31, Process ID UNDERLAY VRF default, area 0.0.0.0
    Enabled by interface configuration
    State P2P, Network type P2P, cost 1
    Index 3, Transmit delay 1 sec
    1 Neighbors, flooding to 1, adjacent with 1
    Timer intervals: Hello 10, Dead 40, Wait 40, Retransmit 5
      Hello timer due in 00:00:05
    No authentication
    Number of opaque link LSAs: 0, checksum sum 0
```

A comprehensive understanding of how OSPF operates and the different state machines and transitions related to network triggers would require multiple chapters; the goal of this chapter is to highlight some underlay specifics involved in using OSPF as the IGP. Some additional considerations with OSPF pertain to its behavior when SPF calculations occur and the support of IPv4 as well as IPv6 routing. OSPF is built on IP prefixes, and any change in an IP prefix in an area triggers a full SPF calculation because the respective IP information is advertised in route and network LSAs for the IP prefix itself, as well as for the related topology information (in the same LSA). This means that if an IP address on an interface changes, OSPF is required to send out a router or network LSA, which in turn triggers the full SPF calculation on all routers in the given OSPF area (that is, LSAs are flooded). While this does not necessarily present a critical issue with today's relatively high resources in network switches and routers, it is rather important to understand what happens during these events.

Another consideration pertains to IPv4 and IPv6 support with OSPF. While OSPFv2 only supports IPv4, OSPFv3 is predominantly used for IPv6.[13] In other words, any underlay that wants to use IPv6 requires OSPFv3, and this in turn requires dual-stack configurations and the addition of a second routing protocol.

Thus the key points regarding use of OSPF as an underlay IGP are as follows:

■ Use OSPF with the network type set to **point-to-point.**

■ It is important to understand LSA types used by OSPF and caveats of LSA floods.

■ It is important to understand requirements for OSPFv2 for IPv4 and OSPFv3 for IPv6.

IS-IS as an Underlay

Intermediate System to Intermediate System (IS-IS)[14] is another link-state routing protocol that also uses the SPF algorithm to calculate the shortest and loop-free paths through a network. Unlike OSPF, IS-IS is an ISO standardized routing protocol (ISO/IEC 10589:2002), which the IETF republished as RFC 1195. IS-IS has not yet reached widespread popularity outside service provider networks. A potential reason for this may be that IS-IS does not operate on the IP layer but instead resides at Layer 2, forming adjacencies using a connectionless network service (CLNS). Because of this, IS-IS is independent of the IP addressing used to form respective routing peers, and it can transport any kind of addressing (IPv4 as well as IPv6) over the same routing exchange. However, at the same time, IS-IS requires a different kind of addressing protocol to uniquely identify an intermediate system (a router).

The IS-IS network entity title (IS-IS-NET) is a network-layer address (network service access point [NSAP] address) for CLNS, which identifies a router in a given IS-IS routed network. Three NSAP formats are available in a given router's NET. Example 4-6 shows a sample IS-IS configuration on a Cisco Nexus switch.

Example 4-6   *IS-IS Configuration on a Cisco Nexus Switch*

```
feature isis

router isis UNDERLAY
  net 49.0001.0100.1001.0001.00

interface Ethernet2/1
  no switchport
  mtu 9216
  ip address 10.1.1.0/31
  ip router isis UNDERLAY
  medium p2p
  ip pim sparse-mode
  no shutdown
```

In IS-IS, IP information is carried in a type-length-value (TLV) of a link-state packet (LSP). Because IP prefixes are always considered external, at the end of a shortest path tree calculation in this configuration, running a full SPF is not required when an IP network change occurs. The IS-IS router (node) information, which is necessary for SPF calculation, is individually advertised in IS neighbor or IS reachability TLVs.

This approach separates topology from IP information, allowing partial route calculation. As a result, IS-IS is much less intensive in handling IP routing changes because the topology is unaffected. As in OSPF DR/BDR elections, IS-IS uses a designated intermediate system (DIS) election process. There are significant differences in the details of the election process for multiaccess media between IS-IS and OSPF, but those details are beyond the scope of this chapter.

The key points for IS-IS are as follows:

- IS-IS is based on CLNS and utilizes NSAP addressing.

- IS-IS uses IP-independent routing protocols.

- The topology remains independent from IP route prefixes.

BGP as an Underlay

Border Gateway Protocol (BGP) is a path vector routing protocol that exchanges routing and reachability information among various autonomous systems (AS). BGP functions well in making routing decisions based on paths, network policies, and/or rulesets configured by a network engineer. Thus, it requires greater design and configuration time in a spine–leaf underlay compared to SPF-based routing protocols. While BGP is great for enforcing policies in a network, it was not specifically developed for fast convergence or link-path calculations. Nevertheless, use cases exist,[15] mostly because of operational requirements, where BGP used as an underlay routing protocol provides notable advantages. Note that BGP, as a hard-state protocol, sends out updates only when there is a change in network reachability. Hence, it does not incur the periodic update overhead that link-state protocols like OSPF have in terms of periodic hellos, redundant routing topology updates, etc.

While the initial incarnation of BGP communicated reachability between different AS, now named external BGP (eBGP), the protocol was enhanced to support communication between different peers that are part of the same AS, thereby giving rise to internal BGP (iBGP). iBGP is a popular choice for carrying overlay EVPN reachability information. This is the case when using OSPF or IS-IS for the underlay. However, if eBGP is used for the underlay, and EVPN reachability information must be exchanged for the overlay, some additional considerations come into the picture. Specifically, with a single BGP instance per network switch, when using eBGP in the underlay, the overlay also needs to be configured in eBGP.

With eBGP, the next-hop attribute is always set, which means the neighbor of a route becomes the next hop. In the spine–leaf topology, this would be inappropriate, as the spine would generally not host a VTEP interface and would thereby lack the capability to encapsulate/decapsulate VXLAN traffic. The EVPN advertisement sent out by a leaf, with regard to its locally attached hosts or prefixes, needs to be relayed by the spine to other leafs without a change in the next-hop attribute, which thereby allows VXLAN tunnels to be established end-to-end from leaf to leaf. This is achieved by setting a specific configuration in eBGP where the next-hop attribute is set to **unchanged**. Changing the next hop behavior is related to the overlay portion of the configuration (L2VPN EVPN), as demonstrated in Example 4-7.

Example 4-7   *eBGP:* next-hop unchanged

```
route-map NH-UNCHANGED permit 10
      set ip next-hop unchanged


router bgp 65501
      address-family l2vpn evpn
            nexthop route-map NH-UNCHANGED
neighbor 10.1.1.1 remote-as 65500
      address-family l2vpn evpn
            send-community both
            route-map NH-UNCHANGED out
```

As eBGP is used for the underlay as well as for the overlay, a separate BGP peering for the EVPN address family (that is, overlay) is recommended. The underlay eBGP peering is physical interface to physical interface, while the overlay BGP peering is loopback interface to loopback interface (eBGP multihop).

In addition to this distinction for underlay routing and overlay reachability peering with eBGP, all EVPN information must be reflected to all leafs. In iBGP, the route reflector (RR) provides this functionality, but in eBGP, the role of a route reflector is not necessary. Because an eBGP neighbor only reflects EVPN routes that also have a local instance created, the **retain Route-Target all** knob must be enabled to make the eBGP neighbor act like a route reflector for the EVPN address family. This is not specific to EVPN but is also the case with MPLS VPN or similar MP-BGP VPN approaches. Getting an eBGP neighbor to act like a route reflector for VPN address families is related to the overlay portion of the configuration (L2VPN EVPN), as shown in Example 4-8.

Example 4-8   *eBGP:* retain Route-Target all

```
router bgp 65500
      address-family l2vpn evpn
            retain route-target all
```

Two models for eBGP exist: the two-AS model (see Figure 4-10) and a multi-AS version (see Figure 4-11). The eBGP two-AS model can be described as all spines belonging to one AS and all leafs belonging to a different AS. In the eBGP multi-AS model, all spines belong to one AS, and each leaf (or leaf pair in virtual PortChannel [vPC]) belongs to a unique AS.

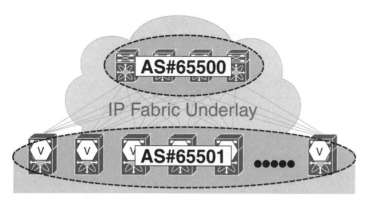

Figure 4-10 *Two-AS Diagram*

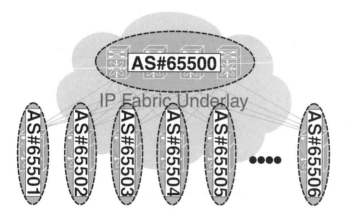

Figure 4-11 *Multi-AS Diagram*

The multi-AS scenario is comparable to the Internet concept where every node in an administrative domain has a unique AS. The configured IP addresses on the physical Layer 3 interfaces that connect the P2P links between the leafs and spines are used for BGP peering. For example, in the case of a four-spine topology, the leaf has to create four different BGP peerings sourced from the four physical interface IP addresses, with a destination of the physical interface IP address of the respective spines. Logical IP interfaces (loopbacks) need to be announced or redistributed by BGP in order to achieve reachability for VTEPs, RPs, and so on.

In the two-AS model, as mentioned earlier, all leafs share one AS, while the spines share another AS. Much as in the multi-AS approach, the BGP peering is established on a per-interface basis, using the IP addresses configured on the point-to-point links. However, in the two-AS mode, some adjustments are needed due to the AS path violation that occurs when the source AS is the same as the destination AS. Fortunately, the Cisco implementation provides all the necessary "hooks and knobs" to make the two-AS approach work with the appropriate configuration. In the case demonstrated in Example 4-9, the peer-

AS check on the spine must be disabled (using the configuration **disable-peer-as-check**) while receiving eBGP updates from a remote router in the same AS as the leaf is permitted (using the configuration **allowas-in**, as demonstrated in Example 4-10).

Example 4-9   *Two-AS Only:* **disable-peer-as-check** *(Spine Only)*

```
router bgp 65500
      router-id 10.10.10.201
neighbor 10.1.1.0 remote-as 65501
            address-family ipv4 unicast
                  send-community both
                  disable-peer-as-check
            address-family l2vpn evpn
                  send-community both
                  disable-peer-as-check
```

Example 4-10   *Two-AS Only:* **allowas-in** *(Leaf Only)*

```
router bgp 65501
      router-id 10.10.10.1
neighbor 10.1.1.1 remote-as 65500
      address-family ipv4 unicast
                  allowas-in
            address-family l2vpn evpn
                  send-community both
                  allowas-in
```

In summary, the key points for eBGP as an underlay option are as follows:

- Two different models exist for BGP: two-AS and multi-AS.

- Some BGP peering configuration work is required.

- It has implications for the overlay control protocol.

IP Unicast Routing Summary

As we have seen, the choice of the underlay protocol can have significant implications on the functioning of the overlay control protocol. By using the same protocol for the underlay and overlay, a clear separation of these two domains can become blurred. Therefore, whenever designing an overlay network, it is a good practice to independently build a transport network, as has been done with MPLS networks for decades. This separation of underlay and overlay control protocol provides a very lean routing domain for the transport network that consists of only loopback and P2P interfaces. At the same time, MAC and IP reachability for the overlay exist in a different protocol—BGP.

This provides a blueprint for a network that is highly scalable due to the separation of the topology address space from the end host reachability address space. It is also noteworthy that IGPs, based on link-state and SPF heuristics, are optimal for an ECMP network, even when a data center fabric involves a few hundred routers. The main advantage of using BGP for both underlay and overlay is having only one routing protocol. However, it requires additional configurations at the leaf and spine switches.

In summary, for a BGP EVPN VXLAN fabric, it is advisable to verify the convergence requirements for the desired overlay service. The underlay convergence should be tested independently of the overlay convergence to make a final decision on which IGP to use for the underlay. It pays to implement a layered approach to measure expectations and assess where results may vary from what is anticipated. Ideally, underlay construction should be done from bottom to top, and individual steps should build on one another. When building network overlays, one of the important guiding principles is to build the underlay, test it thoroughly, and then continue on to build the overlay.

Multidestination Traffic

Multidestination traffic comprises traffic types such as broadcast, unknown unicast, and multicast (BUM). The underlay must provide a way to carry BUM traffic between the edge devices. VXLAN has two different ways of handling BUM traffic:

- Unicast mode, known as *ingress replication,* or *head-end replication*, is one way to create a multicast-independent underlay.

- Multicast mode that employs IP multicast in the underlay is the other option.

The choice of the mode and the associated pros and cons need to be considered when designing and creating the underlay network for a BGP EVPN VXLAN–based data center fabric.

Unicast Mode

In unicast mode, the data packets are replicated by the ingress VTEP and sent to the respective neighboring VTEPs that are part of the same VNI (see Figure 4-12). Because the ingress VTEP has to address all the neighboring VTEPs, it inherently knows about them and has the burden of replicating and sending the BUM traffic to these VTEPs. In other words, if N VTEPs have membership in a given VNI, for every multidestination packet in that VNI, a VTEP has to generate $N-1$ copies of the packet. Each copy is VXLAN encapsulated, with the outer DIP set to that of the destination VTEP to which it must be delivered. From the underlay's as well as the destination VTEP's point of view, this packet is simply treated as a regular VXLAN-encapsulated unicast packet.

In the figure, Host A (192.168.1.101) attached to VTEP V1 sends out an ARP request to resolve the IP-to-MAC binding associated with Host B (192.168.1.102) attached to VTEP V2. Both the hosts belong to the same IP subnet 192.168.1.0/24 associated with VNI 30001. To handle this BUM packet, the figure indicates how VTEP V1 sends out two unicast packets containing this ARP request payload, one destined to VTEP V2 and other one destined to VTEP V3. The important fields of interest in the packet flow are highlighted in the figure.

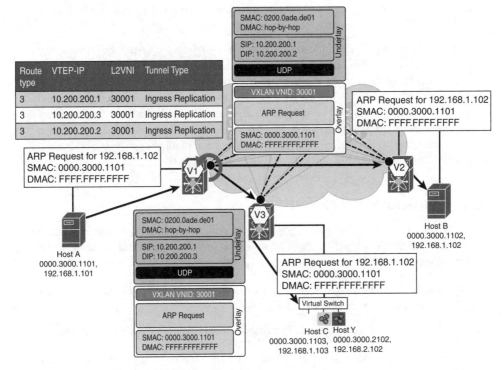

Figure 4-12   *Unicast Mode (aka Ingress Replication)*

There are two configuration options for unicast mode. The first option is *static* where a list of interested VTEPs is configured at each VTEP. The other option is to configure the list *dynamically,* using a control protocol, in this case BGP EVPN, to distribute the interest information within the network. Static configuration reduces scalability because any new VTEP or VNI added to the network requires reconfiguration at each of the neighboring VTEPs (see Example 4-11).

Example 4-11   *Static Ingress Replication Configuration*

```
interface NVE 1
source-interface loopback1
member vni 30001
      ingress-replication protocol static
      peer-ip n.n.n.n
```

BGP EVPN supports unicast mode. For example, in Example 4-12, the BGP EVPN control protocol is leveraged with Route type 3 (inclusive multicast) messages to distribute VTEP and VNI membership information. This does not mean that BGP EVPN is doing the job of ingress replication, but instead it simply distributes the VTEP and VNI membership information over the control protocol. Replication of data traffic is a data plane operation performed by the VTEP. As a result, the ingress or head-end replication operation must be supported by the forwarding functionality that is embedded at the VTEPs.

Example 4-12 *Ingress Replication Configuration with EVPN*

```
interface NVE 1
source-interface loopback1
member vni 30001
      ingress-replication protocol bgp
```

Whether the static or dynamic option is employed with the unicast mode, the data plane operation that requires generation of N copies at a VTEP for every multidestination packet remains the same. With the support of the BGP EVPN control protocol, the discovery of VTEP neighbors is significantly more dynamic. For a given VNI, the receiving VTEP or interested VTEP advertises interest over EVPN, thereby dynamically adding itself to the replication list of a transmitting VTEP. In contrast, with static mode, for a given VNI, as long as the list of peer VTEPs is configured at the sending VTEP, the sending VTEP continues sending a copy to each member in the configured list, regardless of the receiving VTEP's level of known interest. One way to configure static mode is to configure all VTEPs as neighbors so that every time a new VNI is configured, the VTEP list does not have to be manipulated or changed. Only addition or removal of a VTEP results in a change in the VTEP list.

With the disadvantages of the static configuration option, it becomes intuitive that unicast mode for BUM traffic replication in VXLAN is more efficient when using the BGP EVPN control protocol. At the same time, however, it is still less efficient than multicast mode because multicast mode does not require transport of multiple copies of a single packet from the ingress VTEP. Instead, efficient IP multicast on the underlay takes care of transporting the multidestination traffic to the interested VTEPs without putting any additional burden on the VTEPs. Regardless, unicast mode has the advantage of not requiring any additional protocols (such as PIM) or, for that matter, any multicast expertise in maintaining the underlay. In other words, no additional configuration is required in the underlay in order to use unicast mode as long as the network switch hosting the VTEP is capable of supporting the respective unicast mode.

Multicast Mode

When using the multicast mode for transporting multidestination traffic over VXLAN, the multicast routing configured at the VTEP and in the spine–leaf network should be as resilient as that used for unicast routing.

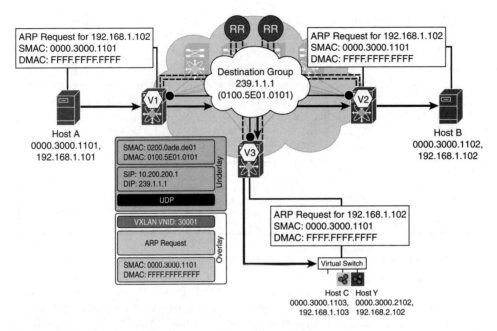

Figure 4-13   *Multicast Mode*

With multicast mode, first the capability of the network switch participating in the underlay comprising the spines and leafs (typically hosting the VTEPs) themselves must be known. This is important because not every type of network switch supports every mode of multicast replication. With Cisco switches, two modes of multicast-enabled underlay are employed. One involves PIM Any Source Multicast (PIM ASM; RFC 7761), sometimes referred to as PIM Sparse Mode (PIM SM). The other mode involves Bidirectional PIM (PIM BiDir; RFC 5015).[16] Depending on the network switch hardware's capability, one or the other would be chosen.

A VXLAN network identified by a Layer 2 VNI or 24-bit identifier is a Layer 2 segment. Any BUM traffic that originated within this network must be sent to all nodes that have membership in this VNI. Typically, the Layer 2 VNI is associated with a multicast group, and the same [VNI, multicast group] configuration is employed on all switches that are part of the same VXLAN network. Even with this symmetric configuration, it is imperative that all the switches be configured to support same PIM multicast mode. For example, in a VXLAN network with four leafs and two spines, if two leafs support only PIM ASM and the other two leafs support only PIM BiDir, multidestination BUM traffic within a VNI cannot be guaranteed to be forwarded appropriately. This is because PIM ASM and BiDir operate in very different ways. Needless to say, in a similar manner, in a VXLAN network, if some leafs support unicast mode and other leafs support multicast mode, the same Layer 2 VNI cannot be stretched among them.

Figure 4-13 depicts how using the multicast underlay, the original ARP request from Host A attached to VTEP V1 will be delivered to all VTEPs that have VNI 30001 locally configured. Since VNI 30001 is mapped to multicast group 239.1.1.1, the original ARP request payload is encapsulated with a VXLAN header with VNI 30001 with the outer Destination IP set to 239.1.1.1. The multicast tree in the underlay will ensure that the packet will be delivered to both VTEPs V2 and V3. Again, as before, the important fields are highlighted in the packet flow depicted in Figure 4-13.

In summary, a common multidestination traffic replication mode is required among the VTEPs sharing the same Layer 2 VNI. Specifically, even if all VTEPs support multicast mode, they need to support the same PIM mode (either ASM or BiDir). Given that a Layer 2 VNI has a consistent replication mode in multicast mode, either multiple Layer 2 VNIs can share a single multicast group (see Figure 4-14), or a single Layer 2 VNI can occupy a single multicast group (see Figure 4-15). A Layer 2 VNI can be freely assigned to a multicast group as long as the requirement for consistent assignment across all VTEPs is respected and as long as they operate within the scale of the respective hardware platform.

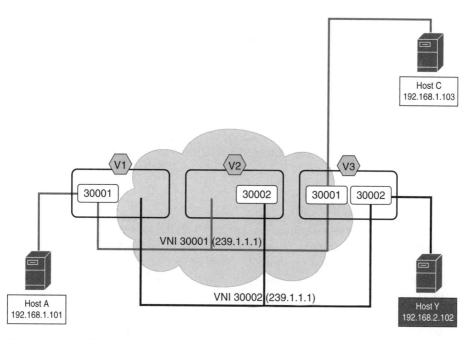

Figure 4-14 *Single Multicast Group VNI Assignment*

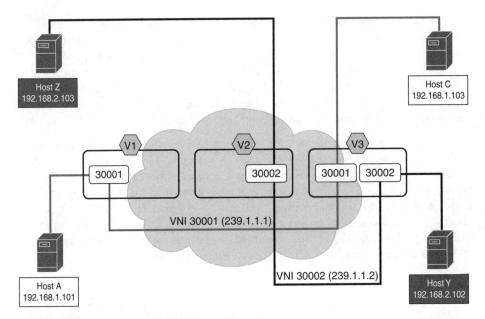

Figure 4-15 *Scoped Multicast Group VNI Assignment*

With multicast mode, because the underlay needs to support multicast routing, there is an inherent dependency on PIM. In multicast networks with PIM ASM or PIM BiDir, a rendezvous point (RP) is required. As mentioned earlier for underlay considerations, the spine serves as a prime location to host the RP because any traffic going between the leafs passes through the spine. The shared multicast tree is rooted at the RP on the spine, and a source tree is formed as needed, which then gets rooted at the respective leaf VTEPs.

PIM Any Source Multicast (ASM)

In PIM ASM, source trees (S,G) are created at the VTEP. Because every VTEP is able to send and receive multicast traffic for a given multicast group, each VTEP is both a source and a receiver. Therefore, multiple source trees can be created, with one sourced at every VTEP participating in a given multicast group. The RP for these various source trees is located at the spine layer. Because multiple spines are available, a significant degree of resiliency and load balancing is available to be exploited.

With PIM ASM, Anycast RP is a means to accommodate an RP being spread across all the available spines while still appearing as a single RP (see Figure 4-16). Anycast RP is available in two different modes: one that uses Multicast Source Discovery Protocol (MSDP)[17] and another that integrates Anycast RP into PIM (see RFC 4610). Because MSDP requires the handling of two protocols (MSDP and PIM), the focus here is on PIM Anycast RP, but this does not, of course, mean that the Anycast RP approach with MSDP is invalid.

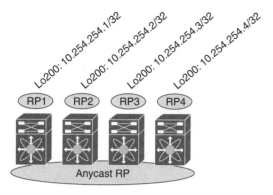

Lo254: 10.254.254.254/32

Figure 4-16 *Anycast RP Conceptual*

With PIM Anycast RP, a common Anycast RP address is selected, and this address is required to be the same across all spines. Among the spines acting as an Anycast RP, PIM Anycast RP peering is configured to allow exchange of state information. Going to back to the four-spine network, Example 4-13 provides a sample Anycast RP configuration from Spine#1.

Example 4-13 *PIM Anycast RP Configuration*

```
! Anycast-RP Configuration on Spine#1
ip pim rp-address 10.254.254.254
ip pim anycast-rp 10.254.254.254 10.254.254.1 (Spine#1 IP)
ip pim anycast-rp 10.254.254.254 10.254.254.2 (Spine#2 IP)
ip pim anycast-rp 10.254.254.254 10.254.254.3 (Spine#3 IP)
ip pim anycast-rp 10.254.254.254 10.254.254.4 (Spine#4 IP)


! Loopback Interface Configuration (RP) on Spine#1
interface loopback 200
 ip address 10.254.254.1/32
 ip pim sparse-mode


! Loopback Interface Configuration (Anycast RP) on Spine#1
interface loopback 254
 ip address 10.254.254.254/32
 ip pim sparse-mode
```

Despite configuring the PIM Anycast RP on the spines with protocol peering to exchange all the necessary information and to act as an Anycast RP, further dynamic assignments in regard to multicast RPs are not necessary. Because all the RPs in the spine are acting as one single RP and are clustered for redundancy and load balancing, dynamic RP assignment on the leaf can be avoided. This said, the configuration on the leaf for

Anycast RP is quite simplified, as it would be for a single RP. An important step entails verifying that multicast peering on the P2P links is enabled and that the RP is defined either globally or on a per-multicast group basis. Once this is accomplished, the multicast network setup for replicating BUM traffic in the VXLAN is established. Thus, the amount of configuration needed for PIM ASM is rather lean except for the additional loopback interface needed in creating the PIM Anycast RP. Example 4-14 provides a sample configuration with a view from any possible leaf.

Example 4-14   *Using Anycast RP*

```
ip pim rp-address 10.254.254.254
```

BiDirectional PIM (PIM BiDir)

PIM BiDir offers a different way of providing multidestination traffic replication in multicast mode. PIM BiDir is quite different from PIM ASM, despite the fact that the interface configurations for the P2P links are exactly the same. As illustrated in Figure 4-17, with PIM BiDir, shared trees or, more specifically, bidirectional shared trees (*,G) are created. These shared trees (*,G) are rooted at the RP, which serves as a routing vector. PIM BiDir is optimized for a many-to-many communication profile. A single bidirectional tree is created, with all the common sources and receivers of a given multicast group as part of that tree. The respective multicast traffic is centered on the RP, which again is optimally placed on the spine. As before, the VTEPs on the leafs act as sources and receivers for BUM traffic.

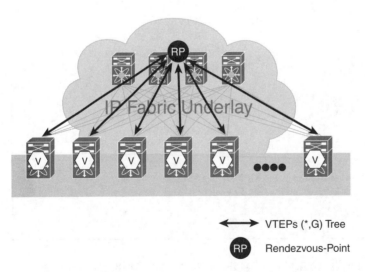

Figure 4-17   *PIM BiDir: Single Tree (*,G)*

The main difference with PIM BiDir is the creation of only a shared-tree (*,G) on a per-multicast group basis instead of creation of a source tree (S,G) per VTEP per multicast group, as is the case with PIM ASM. In PIM BiDir, the RP does not have an actual protocol function. Instead, it acts as a routing vector, to which all the multidestination traffic converges. The same shared tree is used for forwarding the traffic from the source up toward the RP and then down from the RP toward the receivers. Appropriate nodes called *designated forwarders* are elected; they are responsible for forwarding traffic up the shared tree. In addition, the RP has less operational work with regard to tracking the state of individual multicast groups and their respective trees.

To achieve redundancy in a similar way to Anycast RP in PIM ASM, PIM BiDir uses *Phantom RP*.[18] In this case, the RP is configured as an IP address that is not actually assigned to any particular spine (thus the name Phantom RP). The preferred method for providing PIM BiDir RP redundancy is to use logical loopback interfaces with different prefix lengths. This method relies on the unicast routing longest prefix match route lookups to guarantee a consistent path to the RP. The RP address remains a phantom address (one not associated with any physical entity), but it is still necessary to ensure that a route to the RP exists. Loopback interfaces in the primary and secondary routers (spines in this case) are used, and they have different netmask lengths. By advertising different netmasks for the RP route, the primary and secondary routers can be distinguished. Based on a unicast routing longest prefix match lookup result, the primary router is always preferred over the secondary router.

Consider the topology shown in Figure 4-18. In Example 4-15, based on this topology, the primary router advertises the /30 route of the RP, and the secondary router advertises a route with a shorter netmask that corresponds to the /29 route of the RP. As long as both routes are present and both routers are functional and available, unicast routing chooses the longest match and converges to the primary router. The secondary router's advertised route is chosen only when the primary router goes offline or all of its interfaces are not operational.

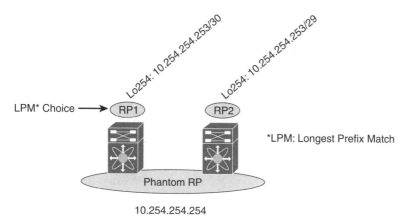

Figure 4-18 *Phantom RP Concept*

Example 4-15 shows a sample configuration from Spine#1.

Example 4-15   *Phantom RP Configuration Spine#1 (Primary)*

```
! Defining Phantom Rendezvous-Point Spine#1
ip pim rp address 10.254.254.254 bidir

! Loopback Interface Configuration (RP) (Redundancy)
interface loopback 254
 ip address 10.254.254.253/30
 ip pim sparse-mode
```

Example 4-16 shows a sample configuration from Spine#2.

Example 4-16   *Phantom RP Configuration Spine#2 (Backup)*

```
! Defining Phantom Rendezvous-Point Spine#2
ip pim rp address 10.254.254.254 bidir

! Loopback Interface Configuration (RP) (Redundancy)
interface loopback 254
 ip address 10.254.254.253/29
 ip pim sparse-mode
```

As mentioned earlier, the Phantom RP simply uses an IP address belonging to a particular subnet (10.254.254.254), but it is not associated with any physical or logical interface on any of the spines. This ensures that the RP address can be reached as long as one of the spines is connected to that subnet and that subnet is operational. The availability of the RP thus relies on the redundancy of the IP routing layer.

Example 4-17 shows a sample configuration with a view from any possible leaf.

Example 4-17   *Using Phantom RP*

```
ip pim rp address 10.254.254.254 bidir
```

In a situation where Phantom RP is used for redundancy only, the configuration on the leaf for the Phantom RP is quite simple: It is the same as it would be for a single RP. As with PIM ASM, multicast peering on the P2P links needs to be enabled, and the RP needs to be either globally configured across all multicast groups or configured on a per-multicast group basis. The keyword **bidir** must be specified at the end of the RP address configuration to indicate that the RP and corresponding groups are going to use PIM BiDir. In cases where Phantom RP is also to be used for load balancing, multiple Phantom RPs can be created, with one for each multicast group slice.

As described earlier, the longest prefix match defines the active spine, which is the Phantom RP for all multicast groups. If load balancing is also desired, the multicast group range can be split into any number of slices (usually powers of 2), such as two or four. When multicast groups are split into two ranges, active Phantom RPs must be created on different spines. For example, if four active Phantom RPs are anticipated, the multicast groups need to be split into four ranges, with each RP becoming the active one for the respective multicast group slice. In order to create two or four Phantom RPs, the same number of loopback interfaces, with appropriate prefix lengths, need to be assigned to a given RP candidate (such as a spine) to achieve the load balancing objective (see Figure 4-19).

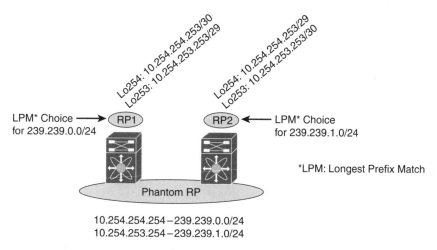

Figure 4-19   *Phantom RP with Load Balancing*

Example 4-18 shows a sample configuration from Spine#1, which hosts the active RP for the multicast group range 239.239.0.0/24. Spine#1 is the active Phantom RP for 10.254.254.254, as per the longest prefix match result provided by the unicast routing lookup.

Example 4-18   *Phantom RP Configuration with Load Balancing of Spine#1*

```
! Defining Phantom Rendezvous-Point Spine#1
ip pim rp address 10.254.254.254 bidir group 239.239.0.0/24
ip pim rp address 10.254.253.254 bidir group 239.239.1.0/24


! Loopback Interface Configuration (RP) (Redundancy)
interface loopback 254
 ip address 10.254.254.253/30
 ip pim sparse-mode


! Loopback Interface Configuration (RP) (Redundancy)
interface loopback 253
 ip address 10.254.253.253/29
 ip pim sparse-mode
```

Example 4-19 shows a sample configuration from Spine#2, which is active for the multicast group range 239.239.1.0/24. As is the case in Example 4-18, here Spine#2 is the active Phantom RP for 10.254.253.254, as per the longest prefix match result provided by the unicast routing lookup.

Example 4-19   *Phantom RP Configuration with Load Balancing of Spine#2*

```
! Defining Phantom Rendezvous-Point Spine#2
ip pim rp address 10.254.254.254 bidir group 239.239.0.0/24
ip pim rp address 10.254.253.254 bidir group 239.239.1.0/24


! Loopback Interface Configuration (RP) (Redundancy)
interface loopback 254
ip address 10.254.254.253/29
ip pim sparse-mode

! Loopback Interface Configuration (RP) (Redundancy)
interface loopback 253
ip address 10.254.253.253/30
ip pim sparse-mode
```

The leaf itself has a split multicast group configuration, where one Phantom RP is defined for a specific multicast group range, and the other multicast group range is assigned to a different Phantom RP. While this sounds a little complex, in essence only classic routing semantics are being used regarding the longest prefix match and the respective best path to a given node. To reiterate, the Phantom RP is a nondefined IP address and requires a subnet route to ensure that the longest prefix match is followed.

Example 4-20 shows a sample configuration from any possible leaf.

Example 4-20   *Using Phantom RP*

```
ip pim rp address 10.254.254.254 bidir group 239.239.0.0/24
ip pim rp address 10.254.253.254 bidir group 239.239.1.0/24
```

In the preceding examples, the longest prefix match points to the active Phantom RP on Spine#1 for all multicast groups in the range 239.239.0.0/24. Likewise, Spine#2 is used as the active Phantom RP for multicast groups in the range 239.239.1.0/24. In a typical situation involving two RPs, load balancing would be achieved based on multicast group assignment to the Layer 2 VNI. If Spine#1 fails, the residing longest prefix route continues to point toward Spine#2, and resiliency is achieved. Therefore, all the failover and load balancing occurs within the unicast routing level (including the function of the Phantom RP itself), with only a minor portion being attributed to the multicast routing level.

In summary, depending on properties desirable for an underlay, multiple choices are available to transport multidestination traffic or BUM traffic in an effective manner. While multicast is the most optimal method for multidestination traffic replication, ingress replication with its unicast mode also presents a viable alternative—albeit with its set of caveats. As a VXLAN network grows, specifically with increasing scale of leafs or VTEPs, the BUM replication must also achieve greater scale. The multicast mode offers the most efficient way of achieving this. If the "performance impact" related to the creation of multiple copies of a single packet of BUM traffic for multiple VTEPs is not an issue, ingress replication can fulfill the job subject to an identified scale limit. However, with the requirement to support tenant multicast traffic over the VXLAN overlay becoming more and more critical, a multicast-in-multicast encapsulation will likely be the preferred option over the unicast mode.

Summary

This chapter describes the BGP EVPN VXLAN fabric underlay that needs to be able to transport both single-destination and multidestination overlay traffic. The underlay needs to provide a set of functionalities and exhibit certain characteristics. The primary objective of the underlay is to provide reachability among the various switches in the fabric. This chapter presents the IP address allocation options for the underlay, using both P2P IP numbered options and the rather attractive IP unnumbered options. This chapter also describes choices of popular IGP routing protocols for unicast routing purposes, such as OSPF, IS-IS, and BGP, along with the salient considerations for each choice. Two primary choices for multidestination traffic replication in the underlay are discussed, namely unicast and multicast modes. While the unicast mode hinges on the hardware VTEP's capability to perform multiple replications, the multicast mode (with either PIM ASM or BiDir) is an attractive option that is likely to become more popular as the requirements for tenant overlay multicast become more stringent.

References

1. Clos, C. A study of non-blocking switching networks. *Bell System Technical Journal*, 32(2):406–424, 1953.

2. Network Working Group. *RFC894: A standard for the transmission of IP datagrams over Ethernet networks*. 1984. tools.ietf.org/html/rfc894.

3. Jeffree, T. *802.1ad—Provider bridges*. 2005. www.ieee802.org/1/pages/802.1ad.html.

4. Cisco. Configuring VXLAN: Configuring Q-in-VNI. *Cisco Nexus 9000 Series NX-OS VXLAN Configuration Guide, Release 7.x*. www.cisco.com/ c/en/us/td/docs/switches/datacenter/nexus9000/sw/7-x/vxlan/configuration/guide/ b_Cisco_Nexus_9000_Series_NX-OS_VXLAN_Configuration_Guide_7x/b_ Cisco_Nexus_9000_Series_NX-OS_VXLAN_Configuration_Guide_7x_ chapter_011.html#task_ED949950FCF0481D9A5E389BAD1FA59B.

5. Network Working Group. *RFC4610: Anycast-RP using Protocol Independent Multicast (PIM)*. 2006. tools.ietf.org/html/rfc4610.

6. Network Working Group. *RFC4601: Protocol Independent Multicast—Sparse Mode (PIM-SM): Protocol specification.* 2006. tools.ietf.org/html/rfc4601.

7. Cisco. *Rendezvous point engineering.* 2009. www.cisco.com/c/en/us/products/collateral/ios-nx-os-software/ip-multicast/whitepaper_c11-508498.html.

8. Network Working Group. *RFC5015: BiDirectional Protocol Independent Multicast (BIDIR-PIM).* 2007. tools.ietf.org/html/rfc5015.

9. Dijkstra, E. W. *A note on two problems in connexion with graphs.* 1959. www-m3.ma.tum.de/foswiki/pub/MN0506/WebHome/dijkstra.pdf.

10. Rexford, J. *Distance-vector and path-vector routing.* 2008. www.cs.princeton.edu/courses/archive/spr08/cos461/slides/14DistVector.ppt.

11. Cisco. *Advance OSPF deployment.* 2004. www.cisco.com/c/dam/en/us/products/collateral/ios-nx-os-software/open-shortest-path-first-ospf/prod_presentation0900aecd80310f6d.pdf.

12. Moy, J. *IETF RFC2328—OSPF Version 2.* 1998. www.ietf.org/rfc/rfc2328.txt.

13. Internet Engineering Task Force. *RFC5838: Support of address families in OSPFv3.* 2010. tools.ietf.org/html/rfc5838.

14. ISO/IEC. Information technology—*Telecommunications and information exchange between systems—Intermediate System to Intermediate System intra-domain routing information exchange protocol for use in conjunction with the protocol for providing the connectionless-mode network service (ISO 8473).* 2002. www.iso.org/iso/iso_catalogue/catalogue_tc/catalogue_detail.htm?csnumber=30932.

15. Lapukhov, P., A. Premji, and J. Mitchell. *RFC7938: Use of BGP for routing in large-scale data centers.* 2016. tools.ietf.org/html/rfc7938.

16. Network Working Group. *RFC5015: BiDirectional Protocol Independent Multicast (BIDIR-PIM). 2007.* tools.ietf.org/html/rfc5015.

17. Fenner, B., and D. Meyer. *IETF RFC3618—Multicast Source Discovery Protocol (MSDP).* 2003. tools.ietf.org/html/rfc3618.

18. Cisco *Rendezvous point engineering.* 2009. www.cisco.com/c/en/us/products/collateral/ios-nx-os-software/ip-multicast/whitepaper_c11-508498.html.

## Chapter 5

Multitenancy

In this chapter, the following topics will be covered:

- Multitenancy concepts
- VLAN-oriented versus bridge domain (BD)–oriented modes of operation for multitenancy
- Layer 2 and Layer 3 multitenancy in VXLAN BGP EVPN networks

Multitenancy is a mode of operation in which multiple independent logical instances (tenants) operate in a shared environment. Each of the logical instances provides a service either at Layer 2 or Layer 3 or both Layer 2 and Layer 3 (the most common deployment scenario. When using multitenancy, the aim is to allow control plane and data plane separation to maintain proper isolation and to prevent unintended cross-communication between tenants. In traditional networks, isolation at Layer 2 is typically achieved using virtual local area networks (VLAN), while isolation at Layer 3 is achieved using virtual routing and forwarding (VRF). In modern cloud-based data centers with overlays, these concepts must be extended to provide similar segregation, while also ensuring that service-level agreements (SLA) are honored.

Multitenancy use cases are present in both enterprise and service provider environments. While service providers transport traffic between customer sites or from customer sites to the Internet, large enterprises typically also have similar requirements. For example, in a large enterprise, due to its hierarchy and organizational structure, every department or business unit needs to be treated as a separate entity, or "customer." In both service provider and enterprise environments, traffic belonging to different entities may be carried over a common infrastructure. In these environments, multitenancy allows transport of traffic with overlapping address space, ensuring separation by Layer 2 and/or Layer 3 multitenancy function.

With network overlays, where the overlay encapsulation and decapsulation are handled at the network edge switches, the separation provided by multitenancy is realized by the ASIC capability located in the hardware of the individual network switches, in conjunction with the software driving that functionality. Certain features related to quality of service (QoS) are typically provided by the hardware because they are applied to traffic flowing at line rate. Other features, such as route leaking across tenants/VRFs, are controlled by software, based on the control plane injection of routing prefixes and appropriate route maps.

Note that both the hardware and software resources on the network switches are shared across various logical instances, and hence these require careful planning and consideration during network design. While the network hardware and software capability might provide the option of supporting thousands of Layer 2 and Layer 3 multitenant services, the network interface transporting this segregated traffic might provide only a limited set of buffers and queues to provide SLA enforcement such as QoS.

In order to provide efficient multitenancy and avoid duplication of required infrastructure services, shared services are a common requirement. Examples of shared services include DHCP, DNS, and others that need to be equally accessible by all tenants without allowing any leakage of information among tenants. Additional enforcement points, such as firewalls, can be employed at the edge of such centralized or shared services to accept and inspect cross-communication between tenants. Various design options are available for providing such centralized services, starting from those that provide simple route "leaking" between tenants to those having multitier fusion routers and firewalls.[1]

Recall that the VXLAN header has a 24-bit identifier called the virtual network identifier (VNI). The VXLAN encapsulation uses this single field to uniquely identify Layer 2 or Layer 3 services. VXLAN with BGP EVPN provides Layer 2 as well as Layer 3 multitenancy, and depending on the type of service under consideration, different terms for the respective VNIs are used. Whenever using a Layer 2 service, which typically means communication within the same subnet or same broadcast domain, the term *Layer 2 VNI (L2VNI)* is used. Whenever using a Layer 3 service like a VRF, the term *Layer 3 VNI (L3VNI)* or *VRF VNI* is used. The separation of Layer 2 and Layer 3 VNIs is solely service dependent and does not attempt to describe a different field in the VXLAN encapsulation itself.

The use cases for multitenancy are very broad, as are the corresponding implementation choices. In order to describe the various available design choices, this chapter provides a basic introduction to multitenancy, with a primary focus on the details of multitenancy services provided by VXLAN BGP EVPN. Likewise, this chapter discusses basic Layer 2 and Layer 3 multitenant services and how they are concurrently realized within the data plane and control plane. Advanced use cases involving integration with services appliances such as firewalls, are described in Chapter 10, "Layer 4-7 Services Integration."

Bridge Domains

A *bridge domain* is a multitenancy service operating at Layer 2 across multiple network technologies. In other words, a bridge domain is a broadcast domain that represents the scope of the Layer 2 network. Using a VLAN is the most common way of providing Layer 2 multitenancy for classic Ethernet deployments with the IEEE 802.1Q (dot1q) header. VXLAN uses a VNI in the header to achieve the same outcome. A bridge domain thus provides a way of stretching a Layer 2 service across multiple encapsulations, or network technologies across Layer 2.

The VLAN namespace provided by the IEEE 802.1Q header is 12 bits and yields 4096 VLANs in a classic Ethernet domain. The VXLAN namespace provides a 24-bit namespace, yielding 16 million segments of VNIs. In this regard, two different namespaces and encapsulations exist, so a mechanism is needed to allow mapping from the VLAN namespace to the VNI namespace and vice versa. This mapping is configured at the edge device, or VTEP, and "stitched" using a bridge domain (see Figure 5-1). Specifically, when the VTEP has a hardware form factor (for example, on a ToR switch), the VLAN and VNI representing the same Layer 2 network are mapped to the same hardware bridge domain. Similarly, when the VTEP has a software form factor (for example, on a virtual switch), the VLAN and VNI for the same Layer 2 network are mapped to the same software bridge domain.

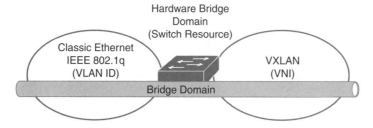

Figure 5-1 *Hardware Bridge Domain*

In summary, in the context of VXLAN, the bridge domain consists of three components:

- The classic Ethernet domain with the VLAN namespace
- The VXLAN domain with the VNI namespace
- The network switch with the hardware/software bridge domain resources

VXLAN yields a much larger namespace, suitable for cloud-scale environments, and the 802.1Q VLAN namespace may not be sufficient for typical deployment use cases in enterprise or service provider environments. The bridge domain concept, in comparing different namespaces and encapsulations, is not specific to VXLAN. It applies equally to other overlay encapsulations such as NVGRE, etc.

VLANs in VXLAN

Most servers or endpoints in a network are connected using classic Ethernet interfaces as described in IEEE 802.1Q.[2] IEEE 802.1Q allows segmentation at Layer 2 and supports multiple VLANs on top of the physical wire. The IEEE 802.1Q (dot1q) standard employs a 12-bit addressing VID field, a 3-bit CoS field, and a 16-bit tag protocol identifier (TPID). While the VID or VLAN identifier is commonly known, the TPID typically carries the value 0x8100 that serves as the Ethertype identifying the dot1q header.

Multiple dot1q tags can be configured back-to-back by using double-tagging (IEEE 802.1ad or q-in-q).[3] When implementing the double-tag 802.1Q header, outer VLANs can be transported in inner VLANs. In order to achieve this, the second TPID used has to identify a second dot1q header and the additional inner VLAN space identifier. The use of q-in-q is common in metro-Ethernet transport cases where the inner VLAN space is assigned to the customer (C-TAG), while the outer VLAN ID is used for the service provider (S-TAG) and has Ethertype 0x88A8. Next to the VLAN ID, the 802.1Q header also carries information for QoS in the Class of Service (CoS) field, which is further documented in the IEEE 802.1p standard.[4]

In a classic Ethernet environment, the VLAN's namespace is globally significant. For a given Layer 2 network, starting from the first switch to the last switch, a single VLAN is used end-to-end as shown in Figure 5-2. This makes the VLAN ID the global identifier in an Ethernet-based network and subsequently provides the 4K VLAN boundary.

VLAN-to-VNI Mapping

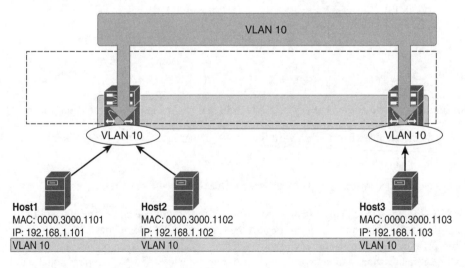

Figure 5-2 *VLAN End-to-End*

With VXLAN, the VLAN becomes locally significant while the global identifier becomes the VXLAN VNI. All endpoints communicating with each other at Layer 2 receive the same L2 VNI (L2VNI) tag when traversing the network switches where the VTEPs reside. As mentioned earlier, endpoints still utilize Ethernet technology to connect to the network switch, which provides a mechanism for mapping a VLAN identifier to a VNI. For example, this would occur with a single VXLAN edge device connected to an endpoint. The local segment to which the server is connected uses a VLAN ID to identify the unique Layer 2 domain where the endpoint resides. The VLAN segment exists from the endpoint all the way to the network switch or edge device and is the local identifier. In most cases, the VLAN becomes a per-switch identifier. On entering the network switch, a translation is performed from the VLAN identifier to the VXLAN VNI (L2VNI), as shown in Figure 5-3. By virtue of having more bits available in the VXLAN VNI than with the dot1q tag, there can be meaningful overlap in choosing the overall numbering scheme for the design.

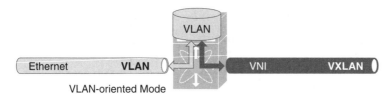

Figure 5-3   *VLAN-to-VXLAN Mapping in an Edge Device*

On a given edge device, this mapping is achieved by configuring the VLAN to the respective VXLAN VNI (**vn-segment**) in a 1:1 relationship, as shown here:

```
vlan 10
 vn-segment 30001
vlan 20
 vn-segment 30002
```

This demonstrates the mapping of a VLAN from the IEEE 802.1Q-defined namespace to an IETF RFC7348-based VXLAN VNI namespace on the ingress edge device.

In this way, the VLAN is the local identifier, and the VNI becomes the global identifier. The VLAN is now significant to that edge device only. In this way, different VLANs on different edge devices can map to the same VNI, as shown in Figure 5-4. Mapping from VLAN to VNI, and eventually back to VLAN, can now be used in a flexible fashion, as long as the VNI is used as the global unique identifier. Example 5-1 provides a sample listing of the configuration on three edge devices for VNIs 30001 and 30002. For consistent mapping, the same source and destination VLAN are mapped to a common VNI (L2VNI). However, some use cases require different source VLANs and destination VLANs.

Per-Switch VLAN-to-VNI Mapping

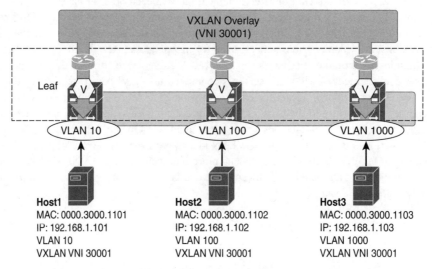

Figure 5-4 *Different-VLAN-to-Same-VNI Mapping*

Example 5-1 *Sample Layer 2 VNI Configuration on Different Edge Devices*

```
Edge-Device #1
vlan 10
 vn-segment 30001
vlan 20
 vn-segment 30002

Edge-Device #2
vlan 100
 vn-segment 30001
vlan 200
 vn-segment 30002

Edge-Device #3
vlan 1000
 vn-segment 30001
vlan 2000
 vn-segment 30002
```

The ability to have switch-local or switch-scoped VLANs permits the scaling of the VLAN namespace across the fabric with VXLAN. It is important to note that the VLAN namespace on a switch is still limited to 4096 VLANs. Moving the VLAN identifier from a per switch basis to a per switch, per port basis, provides a tremendous increase in flexibility. Per-port VLAN uses the VLAN ID arriving on the wire that is stored in the dot1q header. The edge device immediately maps this wire VLAN to an encapsulation-independent identifier without creating this VLAN on the switch. The hardware resources allocated from the network switch provide the stitching capability from the wire VLAN to the respective hardware bridge domain with an encapsulation-independent identifier, which maps the wire VLAN to a VNI. The mapping of a VLAN identifier on a per-port basis thus allows for more flexible use cases compared to the per-switch use cases.

Per-Port VLAN-to-VNI Mapping

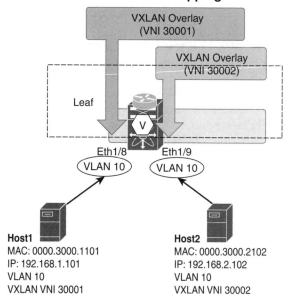

Figure 5-5   *Per-Port VLAN-to-Same VNI Mapping*

Per-port VLAN significance provides the ability to use the full VLAN namespace on a per-port basis and map each (port, VLAN) combination to a unique VXLAN VNI. This allows for an overlapping VLAN use case where same VLANs are mapped to different VXLAN VNIs as long as they belong to different physical switch ports/interfaces. Figure 5-5 depicts a scenario where on a given edge device, the same wire VLAN 10 on two different ports (Ethernet 1/8 and Ethernet 1/9) maps to VNIs 30001 and 30002 respectively. Example 5-2 demonstrates the configuration on the edge device that achieves this typical VLAN translation use case.

Example 5-2 *Sample Layer 2 VNI Configuration with per-Port VLAN Significance*

```
vlan 3501
 vn-segment 30001
vlan 3502
 vn-segment 30002

interface Ethernet 1/8
 switchport mode trunk
 switchport vlan mapping enable
 switchport vlan mapping  10 3501
interface Ethernet 1/9
 switchport mode trunk
 switchport vlan mapping enable
 switchport vlan mapping  10 3502
```

Different CLI implementations exist for creating the hardware bridge domain, depending on the hardware and software platforms. Generally, two modes of operation are available: the VLAN mapping approach and the bridge domain mapping approach. By using the VXLAN VNI as the global identifier, the scaling of the VLAN namespace becomes possible and the flexibility of the Layer 2 multitenancy construct increases. Depending on the network switch platform and software support, a VLAN can be mapped on a per-switch basis or on a per-port basis to a respective VNI. In either case, the mapping from a hardware resource (either VLAN or bridge domain) maintains a 1:1 relationship.

In order to advertise the L2VNI within the BGP-based EVPN address family, configuration of the MAC-based EVPN instance is required, as shown in Example 5-3. The EVPN Layer 2 instance consists of multiprotocol BGP-related requirements to ensure uniqueness and BGP route policy support. In order to uniquely identify the EVPN instance (EVI) within MP-BGP, the instance consists of a VNI (L2VNI) and a Route Distinguisher. In order to support MP-BGP route policies, appropriate Route Targets are defined to ensure that prefixes for the instances are being imported. The values chosen for the EVI are unique for the given instance because they are unique to the L2VNI. The Route Distinguisher is also unique for the Layer 2 EVI, on a per-edge device basis, while the L2VNI and Route Targets have a common value across all the edge devices sharing the same Layer 2 service.

Example 5-3 *Sample Configuration to Advertise Layer 2 VNI Routes into BGP EVPN*

```
evpn
 vni 30001 l2
  rd auto
  route-target import auto
  route-target export auto
 vni 30002 l2
  rd auto
  route-target import auto
  route-target export auto
```

With the Cisco implementation of BGP-EVPN, the Route Distinguisher (RD) and Route Target (RT) values are derived automatically. The RD is generated from the router ID and the internal Layer 2 instance ID as demonstrated in Example 5-4. The RT is derived from the autonomous system number (ASN) of BGP and the Layer 2 VNI (L2VNI). Note that if eBGP is employed for the underlay, the RTs need to be manually configured because the ASN may be different for different edge devices.

Example 5-4 *Sample Output for Route Distinguisher per Layer 2 VNI with Automated Derivation*

```
LEAF1# show bgp l2vpn evpn vni-id 30001 | include "Route Distinguisher"

Route Distinguisher: 10.10.10.1:32777    (L2VNI 30001)
```

Note Automated derivation of the RD uses the type 1 format with RID Loopback IP: internal MAC/IP VRF ID (RD: 10.10.10.1:32777). The internal MAC VRF ID is derived from the VLAN ID (mapped to the L2VNI) plus 32767. For automatic derivation of RTs, the format is ASN: VNI (RT: 65501:30001).

Layer 2 Multitenancy: Mode of Operation

The previous section discussed the significance of VLANs in the context of VXLAN. Likewise, it introduced the concepts of VLANs being the local identifiers and VNIs being the global identifiers. To elaborate on this further, Layer 2 multitenancy in VXLAN allows two modes of operation (see Figure 5-6):

■ VLAN-oriented mode

■ Bridge domain (BD)-oriented mode

While these two modes are conceptually close, the implementation and the corresponding command-line configuration interface are quite different.

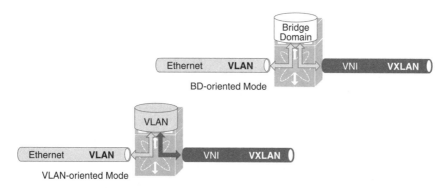

Figure 5-6 *Modes of Operation*

VLAN-Oriented Mode

The VLAN-oriented mode of operation can be described as traditional because the VLAN is the construct that makes the VNI mapping possible. The complete configuration on the edge device also follows VLAN semantics. This includes creating the VLAN and using the Switch Virtual Interface (SVI) for potential Layer 3 services. When operating in the per-switch VLAN mode, the VLAN hosts the respective VNI. The switch then performs the mapping from Ethernet to VXLAN, based on the specified configuration. This case represents a bridge domain spanning from the local Ethernet segment with the VLAN addressing (and the hardware resource within the edge device represented in the VLAN) to the VNI once encapsulation takes place. Figure 5-7 shows the concept of how VLAN, VNI, and switch internal resources are logically used to provide an end-to-end Layer 2 service. The VLAN-oriented mode has been described earlier in this chapter with the VLAN to VNI mapping configured as shown here:

```
vlan 10
 vn-segment 30001
```

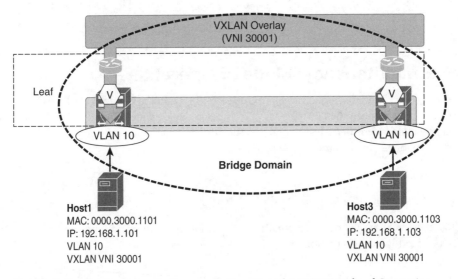

Figure 5-7   *Bridge Domain Span in the per-Switch VLAN Mode of Operation*

In the VLAN-oriented mode, as the name implies, there is a restriction of a maximum possible 4K VLAN-to-VNI mappings on a per-switch basis. Typically, the VLAN mapped to the VNI is also the same one that is received over the local Ethernet port. However, a translation option is also possible, where the wire VLAN is mapped to another translated VLAN that in turn maps to a VNI, as described in the previous section.

BD-Oriented Mode

In the BD-oriented mode of operation, the VLAN resides on the local Ethernet segment, the addressing remains the same, and the encapsulation is specifically determined. With classic Ethernet and VLANs, the encapsulation of dot1q is used to identify the wire VLAN. In contrast, on the global VXLAN segment side (VNI), the encapsulation provides specific naming via the VNI. In this specific construct, an encapsulation profile allows the mapping of a dot1q-based VLAN to a VXLAN-based VNI:

```
encapsulation profile vni from10to30001
  dot1q 10 vni 30001
```

With this approach of using encapsulation mapping profiles, the edge device becomes completely agnostic to tagging, encapsulation numbering, and encapsulation naming used on the wire. Instead, the encapsulation profiles define the mapping from a VLAN to a VNI. It is important to ensure that the correct hardware resources are available to accomplish this and that the encapsulation profile is assigned to the appropriate physical interface. The appropriate interface exists where the local Ethernet segment is attached. In the BD-oriented mode, hardware resources are allocated as a bridge domain. In this way, there is no longer the restriction of a maximum of 4K VNI mappings on a per-switch basis. Instead, in theory, the number of VNIs is restricted to the size of the hardware bridge domain table on the switch, which is typically 16K to 32K. The BD-oriented mode does not have a VLAN-oriented configuration context, even with the existence of Layer 3 service instances. In this situation, the Layer 3 service instances configuration is moved from an SVI to a bridge domain interface (BDI) configuration.

To summarize, the BD-oriented mode has two implementation differences from the VLAN-oriented mode:

- A bridge domain is used instead of a VLAN.

- A bridge domain implements a BDI instead of an SVI.

It is now time to apply the BD concept as it relates to traffic flows. The traffic from a VLAN on the wire reaching an edge device is mapped to a hardware bridge domain at the edge device and assigned a VNI encapsulated toward the VXLAN core. In order to classify the bridge domain to be used for VXLAN encapsulation, the configuration must assign membership of a VNI to the respective bridge domain. As in all the previous modes described, the VNI-to-bridge-domain mapping still maintains a 1:1 relationship, as shown here:

```
vni 30001
bridge-domain 5673
 member vni 30001
```

Once the bridge domain and VNI have been paired, the last task is to configure the interfaces facing the local LAN segment to their respective encapsulation profiles. In order to achieve this, a Virtual Services Instance (VSI) is created for each interface, and the appropriate encapsulation profile is referenced:

```
interface Ethernet 1/8
 no switchport
 service instance 1 vni
  encapsulation profile from10to30001 default
```

The encapsulation profile provides a tremendous amount of flexibility as well as independence from the wire encapsulation while achieving per-port VLAN significance. In the preceding configuration example, there is no relationship between the VLAN identifier, the VNI, or the hardware bridge domain configuration. The identifier can be randomly mapped as long as the encapsulation-specific numbering matches the anticipated addressing. The use of a VSI or an Ethernet Flow Point (EFP) is a common service provider platform approach that allows multi-encapsulation gateways.[5]

In summary, whenever Layer 2 multitenancy is to be achieved using the various modes of operations, the destination VNI to which the service is mapped is always a Layer 2 VNI.

VRF in VXLAN BGP EVPN

Virtual Routing and Forwarding (VRF) is a network switch construct that creates logically separated router instances on top of a single physical device. With VRF, the routing space can be separated in a given physical network while providing path isolation. In addition, if desired, VRF can control communication between these different instances if required. VRF is defined locally on a switch/router; however, technologies exist that can extend local VRF instances across multiple devices. The first method, called *VRF Lite*, is a common approach used to map a VRF to a VLAN identifier.[6] However, scalability and configuration complexity often become challenging when using the VRF Lite approach. With VRF Lite (or Inter-AS Option A), each VRF has its own routing instance and a dedicated routing interface. The configuration must be aligned to the peering/adjacent device.

Example 5-5 shows a typical VRF Lite configuration snippet for two routers that have a VRF instance extended via a Layer 3 subinterface.

Example 5-5   *VRF Lite Configuration Example*

```
Router #1
vrf context VRF-B

interface eth1/10.1002
 encapsulation dot1q 1002
 vrf member VRF-B
 ip address 10.2.2.1/24
 ip router ospf 100 area 0
```

```
router ospf 100
 vrf VRF-B
```

```
Router #2
vrf context VRF-B

interface eth1/10.1002
 encapsulation dot1q 1002
 vrf member VRF-B
 ip address 10.2.2.2/24
 ip router ospf 100 area 0

router ospf 100
    vrf VRF-B
```

Typically, an appropriate IGP is also enabled on these subinterfaces in order to exchange route prefixes between the two peering routers.[7] In Example 5-5, the value **1002** represents the tagged VLAN that will be employed for routing traffic belonging to VRF-B between two routers.

Over the years, VRF Lite has been widely used and deployed; however, as mentioned earlier, for every VRF instance, a dedicated interface is required and a separate peering session between the two involved entities must be present. An appropriate routing protocol is configured over this peering session. In this way, there is a Layer 3 peering session established on a per-VRF instance basis that allows a Layer 3 handoff for stretching a VRF instance across multiple data center pods or sites. In contrast, Multiprotocol Label Switching (MPLS) Layer 3 VPNs offer a scalable solution for Layer 3 multitenancy.[8] Despite the fact that MPLS has Layer 3 multitenancy, flexibility, and scale, the use of MPLS remains rather limited in data centers because data center switches have traditionally not supported MPLS. This pertains to support involving both the control plane as well as the data plane.

Layer 3 VPNs with MPLS are commonly deployed at the data center edge for Layer 3 Data Center Interconnect (DCI) use cases. Another consideration, sometimes forgotten, is the scope of Layer 3 multitenancy. VRF Lite and MPLS L3VPN look at routing information from the perspective of an IP subnet. This means a given IP subnet stays local to a given Provider Edge (PE). A pair of PEs can then provide first-hop redundancy to the connected IP subnet. While the model of centralized routing applies to the traditional data center, with the changing needs and evolution, a more efficient approach is required for first-hop routing due to changing needs and evolution. This can be accomplished with distributed subnets and integrated multitenancy at Layer 2 and Layer 3 with VXLAN BGP EVPN.

Centralized gateways for first-hop routing decisions can be moved to edge devices (ToR switches) with embedded Integrated Routing and Bridging (IRB) functionality. The same gateway can exist simultaneously at multiple edge devices, giving rise to distributed anycast gateway functionality at the edge devices. With the distributed gateway, the first-hop routing scope goes from IP subnet- to IP host-based routing. Furthermore, because the Layer 3 service is now provided at the edge device, Layer 3 multitenancy can be introduced at this level. VRFs can therefore be defined or created for different tenants at the edge device.

MP-BGP EVPN with VXLAN is likewise able to provide enhanced scale functionality for Layer 3 multitenancy compared to that provided by MPLS L3VPNs. Recall that the control plane protocol used by EVPN is based on multiprotocol BGP. The MP-BGP capability assigns a unique Route Distinguisher to each prefix, and transports this information across a single BGP peering session. In addition, appropriate route policies are enforced using import and export of appropriate Route Targets assigned to a given prefix in the BGP control plane. Once a BGP peer receives a Route Target, it verifies whether the Route Target matches its import policy of a given VRF. If there is a match, the route is installed and then used for forwarding.

In MPLS, the L3VPN label is responsible for separating tenant traffic belonging to different VRFs in the data plane. In this situation, the VNI associated with a VRF (Layer 3 VNI [L3VNI]) and carried in the VXLAN header is used to achieve similar results. Notably, the VXLAN header carries only one VNI field. This is the same field that typically carries the L2VNI for achieving Layer 2 multitenancy use cases. With Layer 3 scenarios that involve routing operations, the information carried during Layer 2 services becomes obsolete because source IP information is sufficient to identify the origin. Thus, for Layer 3 routed traffic, the VNI in the VXLAN header is stamped with the VRF VNI.

In summary, Layer 3 multitenancy in VXLAN BGP EVPN uses the power of multiprotocol BGP to exchange the respective information. In addition to the BGP control plane, it works with an IP/UDP-based encapsulation, VXLAN, and the VNI namespace. In addition, with the increased granularity provided with IRB, efficient host-based routing can be achieved with no hair-pinning of traffic between nodes in the same VXLAN-based fabric.

Layer 3 Multitenancy: Mode of Operation

The previous section focused on comparing Layer 3 multitenancy in VXLAN with BGP EVPN and MPLS L3VPNs. Layer 3 VNI (L3VNI) was introduced as the identifier for the VRF in the routing context. Layer 3 multitenancy in VXLAN has a single mode of operation, and some small differences exist when comparing the VLAN- or BD-oriented switch CLIs. Despite this, the overall concept remains the same.

The VRF configuration in VXLAN-based Layer 3 multitenancy deployment consists of the name of the VRF and the respective VNI (L3VNI). All traffic routed within the VRF in a BGP EVPN VXLAN network is always encapsulated with the L3VNI. This is how routed traffic is differentiated from the same subnet, or bridged traffic where the L2VNI is carried in the VXLAN header. While the L3VNI identifies the VRF uniquely across the VXLAN-based network fabric, the name assigned to the VRF itself remains locally significant. However, it is common practice to follow a consistent naming convention for the L3VNI because doing so facilitates network operations and troubleshooting.

As mentioned earlier, in order to make sure a prefix from a given edge device is uniquely identified, each VRF has its unique Route Distinguisher (RD). In addition to the Route Distinguisher, the VRF also contains routing policy values, specifically the Route Targets (RTs). In the extranet case example, the Route Targets are imported and exported by all edge devices that are members of the same VRF. Example 5-6 shows a typical configuration for a VRF on an edge device in a VXLAN BGP EVPN network.

Example 5-6 *Basic VRF Configuration in a VXLAN BGP EVPN Network*

```
vrf context VRF-A
 vni 50001
 rd auto
 address-family ipv4 unicast
  route-target both auto
  route-target both auto evpn
 address-family ipv6 unicast
  route-target both auto
  route-target both auto evpn
```

Much as in the Layer 2 EVPN instance, the VRF construct consists of a Route Distinguisher; this RD is automatically derived from the BGP router ID and the internal VRF identifier (decimal number), provided in Example 5-7. The Route Targets are also automatically derived in the same manner as described in the case involving Layer 2 VNI. Using the BGP ASN together with the L3VNI enables the RT value to be unique for a given VRF. However, the RT value remains the same across all the edge devices in the same VRF.

Example 5-7 *Sample Output for Route Distinguisher per Layer 3 VNI with Automated Derivation*

```
LEAF1# show vrf
VRF-Name                       VRF-ID State   Reason
VRF-A                               3 Up      --
default                             1 Up      --
management                          2 Up      --


LEAF11# show bgp l2vpn evpn vni-id 50001 | include "Route Distinguisher"


Route Distinguisher: 10.10.10.1:3    (L3VNI 50001)
```

Note   Automated derivation of the RD uses the type 1 format with RID Loopback IP: internal MAC/IP VRF ID (RD: 10.10.10.1:3). For automatic derivation of Route Targets, the format is ASN: VNI (RT: 65501:50001).

It is critical to remember that the value of the L2VNI and L3VNI cannot overlap when the Layer 2 or Layer 3 instance is being configured. Specifically, the VNI configuration used for a Layer 2 instance should never be the same as the one used for a Layer 3 instance. This same restriction also applies to the RT configuration. In regard to the Route Distinguisher, it is highly recommended as a best practice to keep the layer configuration segregation as well, but in this case, it is not absolutely mandatory.

For the sake of completeness, it should be noted that RTs cannot be auto-generated in some cases when external BGP (eBGP) is used for the underlay. Specifically, with the eBGP underlay, the autonomous system number may vary on different edge devices. Consequently, the eBGP use case requires manual configuration of the Route Targets, and they must match between the respective edge devices. This is the only situation where manual configuration of Route Targets is required.

In terms of configuration requirements for realizing Layer 3 multitenancy in a VXLAN BGP EVPN network, the VRF context configuration needs to be completed first. Subsequently, the BGP EVPN configuration for the VRF must be enabled. To make the L3VNI associated with the VRF fully active, the following must be present:

- The L3VNI needs to be associated with the VTEP (NVE) interface.

- A core-facing VLAN or bridge domain must be associated with the L3VNI.

- A corresponding Layer 3 interface (SVI or BDI) must be created.

- This L3 interface must be associated with the VRF.

Associating the VRF L3VNI context with the VTEP allows it to be available to VXLAN. Example 5-8 outlines the critical steps required to configure Layer 3 multitenancy for VXLAN.

Example 5-8   *Sample BGP EVPN-Related VRF Configuration for Layer 3 Multitenancy*

```
router bgp 65501
 vrf VRF-A
  address-family ipv4 unicast
   advertise l2vpn evpn

interface nve1
 member vni 50001 associate-vrf
```

VXLAN as an encapsulation requires MAC addresses to be populated in the inner MAC header. This allows the mapping of a Layer 2 bridge domain or a VLAN associated with a Layer 3 VRF. This VLAN or bridge domain model provides the necessary hardware resource for creating the Layer 3 services across the VXLAN encapsulation. Example 5-9 demonstrates a Layer 3 service on top of a Layer 2 encapsulation.

Example 5-9 *VRF-Related VLAN and Bridge Domain Configuration for Layer 3 Multitenancy*

```
VLAN Oriented Command Line Interface
# VLAN for VRF
vlan 2501
  vn-segment 50001


# Layer-3 Interface for VRF
interface Vlan2501
  no shutdown
  mtu 9216
  vrf member VRF-A
  ip forward
```

```
Bridge-Domain Oriented Command Line Interface
# Bridge-Domain for VRF
vni 50001
bridge-domain 2501
  member vni 50001


# Layer-3 Interface for VRF
interface bdi2501
  no shutdown
  mtu 9216
  vrf member VRF-A
  ip forward
```

The VLAN or bridge domain in this case creates the hardware resource in the edge device. The Layer 3 interface provides the semantics of a routing hop, and the VRF membership assigns it uniquely to the VRF. Configuring the MTU ensures that all routed traffic is forwarded, including jumbo frames. Note that there may be some platform-specific commands and nuances for which the appropriate platform release notes and configuration guides must be referenced.

Summary

This chapter describes how multitenancy has become a prime feature for next-generation data centers and how it is accomplished in VXLAN with BGP EVPN. In addition to discussing multitenancy when using VLANs and VXLAN, this chapter covers modes of operation for both Layer 2 and Layer 3 multitenancy. Likewise, it describes the importance of bridge domains in regard to multitenancy in a VXLAN with BGP EVPN network, as well as concepts related to VRF. This chapter thus provides a basic introduction to the main aspects of multitenancy using VXLAN with BGP EVPN.

References

1. Cisco. *Network virtualization: Services edge design guide.* 2008. www.cisco.com/c/en/us/td/docs/solutions/Enterprise/Network_Virtualization/ ServEdge.html.

2. Institute of Electrical and Electronics Engineers. *802.1Q virtual LANs.* 2014. www.ieee802.org/1/pages/802.1Q.html.

3. Institute of Electrical and Electronics Engineers. *802.1ad provider bridges.*" 2009. www.ieee802.org/1/pages/802.1ad.html.

4. Institute of Electrical and Electronics Engineers. *802.1D—1998—IEEE standard for local area network MAC (media access control) bridges.* standards.ieee.org/ findstds/standard/802.1D-1998.html.

5. Cisco. *Cisco CPT configuration guide CTC and documentation release 9.3 and Cisco IOS release 15.1(01)SA.* 2014. www.cisco.com/c/en/us/td/docs/ optical/cpt/r9_3/configuration/guide/cpt93_configuration/ cpt93_configuration_chapter_0100.html.

6. Network Working Group. *RFC4364: Multi-AS backbones.* 2006. tools.ietf.org/ html/rfc4364#section-10.

7. Cisco. *Cisco Nexus 7000 series NX-OS interfaces configuration guide, release 5.x: Subinterfaces.* 2015. www.cisco.com/c/en/us/td/docs/switches/datacenter/ sw/5_x/nx-os/interfaces/configuration/guide/if_cli/if_layer3int.html#48044.

8. Network Working Group. *RFC4364.* 2006. tools.ietf.org/html/rfc4364.

## Chapter 6

Unicast Forwarding

In this chapter, the following topics will be covered:

- Detailed packet flows for bridging in VXLAN BGP EVPN networks with and without early ARP termination

- Detailed packet flows for routing in VXLAN BGP EVPN networks with distributed IP anycast gateway and symmetric Integrated Routing and Bridging

- Handling silent endpoints, dual-homed endpoints, and IPv6 endpoints

This chapter explains the specifics of traffic forwarding across a VXLAN BGP EVPN–based network. It provides a brief description on how unicast forwarding works conceptually in bridging and routing scenarios in a VXLAN BGP EVPN network. This chapter describes how the Layer 2 service in the VXLAN overlay is provided by the Layer 2 Gateway (L2GW); the uses of the BGP EVPN control protocol; and how traffic follows the VLANs and respective Layer 2 virtual network identifier (L2VNI) across the entire bridge domain. It also covers various routing scenarios where the Layer 3 service is provided by the VXLAN Layer 3 Gateway (L3GW), including the use of the distributed IP anycast gateway. Various scenarios are examined involving local routing on the edge device as well as how forwarding is performed with symmetric Integrated Routing and Bridging (IRB) to reach a remote endpoint across the VXLAN overlay. Some specific use cases with non-consistent (scoped) configuration demonstrate how silent endpoints are made reachable within the network. In summarizing these bridging and routing cases, this chapter takes a closer look at dual-homed endpoints and how forwarding takes place in virtual PortChannel (vPC) scenarios. The chapter concludes with a look at IPv6 specifics.

Intra-Subnet Unicast Forwarding (Bridging)

In overlays, a common requirement for the VXLAN data plane encapsulation is to provide a basic Layer 2 service (Layer 2 Gateway or L2GW service). In order to provide this service more efficiently, BGP EVPN control plane–assisted endpoint learning can reduce unnecessary broadcasts that result from ARP processing and unknown unicast traffic.

Typically, bridged traffic is scoped by a VLAN. Learning is based on the SMAC address carried in the packet, and forwarding is based on the DMAC address. With VXLAN, the same semantics apply, but the VLAN is locally significant and scoped to a VTEP only. Consequently, all learning and forwarding is scoped by the Layer 2 VNI (L2VNI) that globally identifies a given Layer 2 network and the broadcast domain it represents. Bridged traffic is transported over VXLAN with the L2VNI, which is mapped from the classic Ethernet VLAN at the ingress VTEP (L2GW). The VLAN is identified from the 12-bit value carried in the IEEE 802.1Q header, and the VNI is identified by a 24-bit VXLAN Network Identifier field in the VXLAN header. At the egress VTEP (L2GW), reverse mapping is performed from the L2VNI to the classic Ethernet VLAN so that traffic can be forwarded out of the appropriate Ethernet port(s).

With VXLAN, functions similar to those in classic Ethernet are superimposed into a network overlay technology. VXLAN, being a MAC-in-IP/UDP data plane encapsulation, determines the forwarding decision based on MAC addressing. When in L2GW mode, VXLAN leverages the ingress VTEP's MAC address table for making the forwarding decision. Typically, a [VLAN, MAC] entry points to a local Ethernet interface, which is common in classic Ethernet network switches. With the introduction of overlays, the [VLAN, MAC] entry in the Layer 2 table can now also point to a remote VTEP's IP address. This signifies that the MAC entry, which identifies a remote endpoint, is reachable over VXLAN. For subsequent explanations regarding conceptual traffic forwarding discussions, please refer to Figure 6-1. VTEPs V1 and V2 are associated with NVE interfaces with IP addresses 10.200.200.1 and 10.200.200.2 respectively.

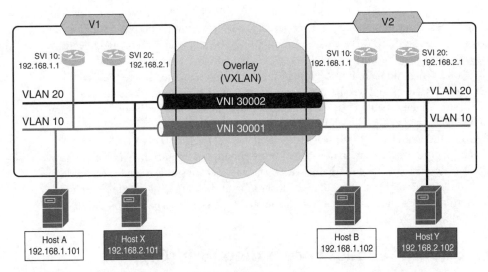

Figure 6-1 *Intra-Subnet Forwarding (Bridging)*

For bridging operations between endpoints connected to the ingress VTEP (V1) and endpoints connected to the egress VTEP (V2), the exchange of Layer 2 MAC address reachability information is required. In classic Ethernet or VXLAN Flood and Learn (F&L) environments, the MAC address reachability information is attained simply through flooding the traffic, which occurs during communication initiation. Specifically, the flooding ensures that all endpoints in the Layer 2 network receive the communication, and this results in Layer 2 learning on the forward path of traffic. Likewise, reverse traffic triggers learning on the return path. With the BGP EVPN control protocol, the locally connected endpoints are learned from a MAC address perspective on the ingress and egress VTEPs. This information is proactively distributed during BGP updates to all neighboring VTEPs. For the scenario shown in Figure 6-1, the BGP EVPN control protocol would carry the information outlined in Table 6-1:

Table 6-1 *BGP EVPN Control Protocol Populated Information (After ARP Discovery)*

MAC, IP	L2VNI	L3VNI	Next Hop
0000.3000.1101, 192.168.1.101	VNI 30001	—	10.200.200.1
0000.3000.1102, 192.168.1.102	VNI 30001	—	10.200.200.2
0000.3000.2101, 192.168.2.101	VNI 30002	—	10.200.200.1
0000.3000.2102, 192.168.2.102	VNI 30002	—	10.200.200.2

The information in Table 6-1 is expected to be present in the BGP EVPN control plane and then installed and used in the VTEP's hardware tables. Cisco NX-OS provides various ways to verify that this information is present. Network administrators typically check BGP tables to determine whether a given prefix is received (see Example 6-1); however, this action only validates reception of this information from a BGP database point of view. It does not validate that the reachability information is installed as a valid forwarding entry in the hardware tables.

Example 6-1   show bgp l2vpn evpn vni-id 30001 *Output (at VTEP V1)*

```
V1# show bgp l2vpn evpn vni-id 30001
BGP routing table information for VRF default, address family L2VPN EVPN
BGP table version is 43, local router ID is 10.10.10.1
Status: s-suppressed, x-deleted, S-stale, d-dampened, h-history, *-valid, >-best
Path type: i-internal, e-external, c-confed, l-local, a-aggregate, r-redist,
  I-injected
Origin codes: i - IGP, e - EGP, ? - incomplete, | - multipath, & - backup

   Network            Next Hop         Metric   LocPrf   Weight Path
Route Distinguisher: 10.10.10.1:32777     (L2VNI 30001)
*>i[2]:[0]:[0]:[48]:[0000.3000.1102]:[0]:[0.0.0.0]/216
                    10.200.200.2                 100          0 i

*>l[2]:[0]:[0]:[48]:[0000.3000.1101]:[0]:[0.0.0.0]/216
                    10.200.200.1                 100      32768 i
```

Because MP-BGP is used with EVPN, if the respective Route Target information does not match the import statement, forwarding does not occur because the entry resides only in BGP. This said, for Layer 2 operations, it is a good practice to verify that the MAC address or MAC/IP prefix (Route type 2) has been received. However, verifying the installation of the prefix is split in two parts. The first part is new and relies on the fact that Layer 2 information is being learned through BGP for forwarding decisions. This information is installed in an EVPN instance, which is also called a *MAC VRF*.

Once the Layer 2 "routing" table has been verified with the appropriate MAC prefixes, as shown in Example 6-2, the next step is to ensure that similar entries should be present in the MAC address table at the VTEP itself, as shown in Example 6-3.

Example 6-2   show l2route evpn mac all *Output at VTEP V1*

```
V1# show l2route evpn mac all
Topology    Mac Address     Prod    Next Hop (s)
----------- --------------- ------  ---------------
10          0000.3000.1102 BGP     10.200.200.2
10          0000.3000.1101 Local   Eth1/5
```

Example 6-3   show mac address-table vlan 10 *Output at VTEP V1*

```
V1# show mac address-table vlan 10
Legend:
        * - primary entry, G - Gateway MAC, (R) - Routed MAC, O - Overlay MAC age -
    seconds since last seen,+ - primary entry using vPC Peer-Link, (T) - True, (F) -
    False
    VLAN    MAC Address     Type      age     Secure NTFY Ports
--------+-----------------+--------+---------+------+----+-----------
*   10      0000.3000.1102  dynamic   0          F      F    nve1(10.200.200.2)
*   10      0000.3000.1101  dynamic   0          F      F    Eth1/5
```

We are focusing on a Layer 2 bridging operation at this time, but the control protocol can be populated with the IP address information in other ways. If at any point an ARP exchange occurs between endpoints connected to the edge devices with the ARP suppression feature explicitly enabled for the L2VNI, the ARP snooping performed on VTEPs V1 and V2 populates the control protocol with this information. Potentially, if VRFs are configured, and first-hop gateways (distributed anycast gateways) are present, the population of the L3VNI would also have taken place.

Next, we walk through a sample use case shown in Figure 6-2, where endpoint Host A (192.168.1.101), which is connected to VTEP V1, wants to communicate with endpoint Host B (192.168.1.102), which is connected to VTEP V2. Both endpoints belong to the same VNI, 30001, and they can represent either virtual or physical hosts. Because Host B belongs to the same IP subnet as Host A, Host A tries to resolve the IP-to-MAC mapping of Host B by first looking up its local ARP cache. If this process results in a miss, Host A initiates an ARP request. The broadcast ARP request is forwarded in VLAN 10, and the request enters the ingress VTEP V1. The MAC address of Host A is learned at VTEP V1 via regular MAC learning, and this information is populated over BGP EVPN to the VTEPs V2 and V3, respectively.

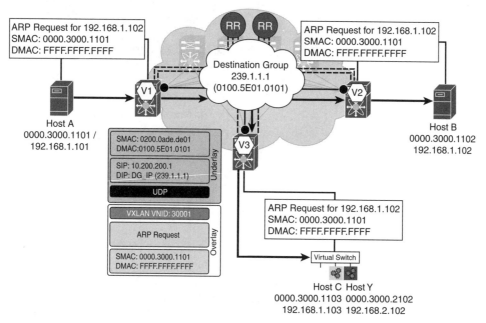

Figure 6-2   *ARP Request, Host A to Host B*

With ARP suppression disabled for VNI 30001 at VTEP V1, the ARP request from endpoint Host A is handled as broadcast, unknown unicast, and multicast (BUM) traffic, encapsulated with Layer 2 VNI 30001, and then forwarded as a multidestination packet. The multidestination traffic can be replicated with multicast or with ingress replication to all VTEPs joining the same multidestination tree. This occurs by using either a multicast group or the ingress replication distribution list. All the viable egress VTEPs receive the respective broadcast and decapsulate and forward the ARP request toward their local Ethernet interfaces participating in VNI 30001. Specifically, at VTEP V2, VNI 30001 is mapped to a local VLAN (namely 10), and subsequently traffic is sent out of the appropriate member classic Ethernet ports encapsulated with the dot1q tag 10. When Host B receives the ARP request, it responds with an ARP reply (unicast), as shown in Figure 6-3.

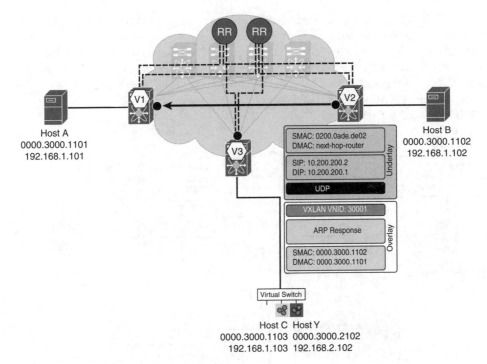

Figure 6-3 *ARP Reply, Host B to Host A*

This response results in regular MAC learning of Host B at VTEP V2, and the BGP EVPN control protocol is populated with Host B's source information. Using the prior reachability information about Host A populated at VTEP V2 over BGP-EVPN, the unicast ARP reply, encapsulated with VNI 30001, is forwarded to VTEP V1. After decapsulation at VTEP V1, the ARP reply is forwarded to Host A. In this way, the ARP cache of both Host A and Host B has been appropriately populated, and they can start sending data traffic to one another using regular bridging semantics.

Optionally, if ARP suppression is enabled on VNI 30001, the initial ARP request from Host A for Host B received at VTEP V1 is subjected to ARP snooping. Consequently, in addition to the MAC address, the IP address of Host A is also populated in the BGP EVPN control plane via Route type 2 messages (see Example 6-4).

Example 6-4 show bgp l2vpn evpn vni-id 30001 *Output at VTEP V1*

```
V1# show bgp l2vpn evpn vni-id 30001
BGP routing table information for VRF default, address family L2VPN EVPN
BGP table version is 43, local router ID is 10.10.10.1
Status: s-suppressed, x-deleted, S-stale, d-dampened, h-history, *-valid, >-best
Path type: i-internal, e-external, c-confed, l-local, a-aggregate, r-redist,
  I-injected
```

```
Origin codes: i - IGP, e - EGP, ? - incomplete, | - multipath, & - backup

   Network            Next Hop          Metric   LocPrf   Weight Path
Route Distinguisher: 10.10.10.1:32777     (L2VNI 30001)
*>i[2]:[0]:[0]:[48]:[0000.3000.1102]:[0]:[0.0.0.0]/216
                     10.200.200.2                100           0 i

*>i[2]:[0]:[0]:[48]:[0000.3000.1102]:[32]:[192.168.1.102]/272
                     10.200.200.2                100           0 i


*>l[2]:[0]:[0]:[48]:[0000.3000.1101]:[0]:[0.0.0.0]/216
                     10.200.200.1                100       32768 i

*>l[2]:[0]:[0]:[48]:[0000.3000.1101]:[32]:[192.168.1.101]/272
                     10.200.200.1                100       32768 i
```

In addition, if Host B is known to the BGP EVPN control plane by MAC and IP, then a unicast ARP response is generated locally by VTEP V1 and returned to endpoint Host A. This results in early ARP termination. The ARP response is generated in the same way that Host B would originate it, with VTEP V1 acting as an ARP proxy for Host B. Because the broadcast ARP request never reached Host B, only Host A's ARP cache is populated with information about Host B, but not the other way around. When data traffic is sent from Host A to Host B, Host B tries to resolve the IP-to-MAC binding for Host A by sending out an ARP request. VTEP V2 then serves as an ARP proxy, thereby appropriately populating the ARP cache of Host B as well.

Figure 6-4 depicts the packet flow for data traffic between Host A and Host B once their ARP caches have been appropriately populated. Host A generates data traffic with a SMAC of 0000.3000.1101 and source IP of 192.168.1.101. The destination information is set to that of Host B, which is MAC 0000.3000.11102 and IP 192.168.1.102, respectively. Once the packet is received at VTEP V1, a destination lookup is performed, based on VLAN 10 mapped VNI 30001 and 0000.3000.1102. This yields the destination VTEP (V2), behind which Host B resides. Subsequently, VXLAN encapsulation is performed with VNI 30001, and the packet is transported to the respective egress VTEP V2. Intuitively, this communication is very similar to the regular bridging operation that occurs in regular LAN environments, where the MAC table lookup drives the result.

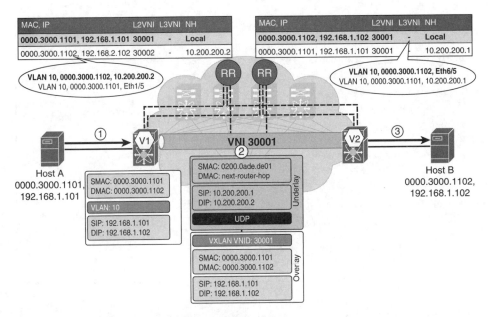

Figure 6-4 *Host A to Host B Forwarding (Bridging)*

In the specific case involving endpoint Host B, the lookup results in a hit based on the prior endpoint discovery and associated control plane population. Table 6-2 shows the details of the respective outer IP, UDP, and VXLAN header fields, as well as the inner MAC and IP header fields for Host-A-to-Host-B data traffic sent from VTEP V1 to VTEP V2.

Table 6-2 *Encapsulated Packet, Including All Headers (as per Table 6-1)*

Outer DIP	Outer SIP	UDP DPort	VXLAN	Inner DMAC	Inner SMAC	Inner DIP	Inner SIP	Payload
10.200. 200.2	10.200. 200.1	4789	VNI 30001	0000.3000. 1102	0000.3000. 1101	192.168. 1.102	192.168. 1.101	—

Once the packet is received at the egress VTEP V2 the packet is decapsulated, and appropriate local mapping is performed from VNI 30001 to VLAN 10, based on the translation table lookup result. The subsequent Layer 2 lookup results in a "hit," based on endpoint Host B's MAC address (specifically [10, 0000.3000.1102]). As a result, the frame is sent toward the Ethernet interface where Host B is connected. In this way, the end-to-end unicast forwarding bridging flow in VNI 30001 is complete. This flow travels from Host A in VLAN 10 behind VTEP V1 to Host B in VLAN 10 behind VTEP V2. VLAN 10 at VTEP V1 and VLAN 10 at VTEP V2 are thus stitched together via a Layer 2 service in VXLAN, identified with the VNI 30001.

Non-IP Forwarding (Bridging)

The previous intra-subnet unicast forwarding case assumes that every endpoint has an IP address assigned to it. Forwarding is still based on the MAC address lookups, classifying the case as a bridging scenario. However, use cases exist where non-IP communication takes place between endpoints (see Figure 6-5), either coordinated by a protocol or an application using an appropriate protocol. Examples include cluster replication and legacy applications. When such non-IP protocols are used, endpoints may be completely devoid of an IP stack. When using non-IP forwarding, the same L2GW functionality is used when providing bridging functionality, as is the case when IP addresses are present.

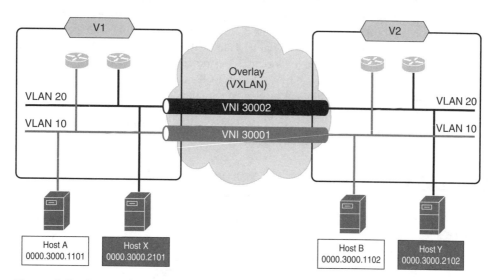

Figure 6-5   *Intra-Subnet Non-IP Forwarding (Bridging)*

In non-IP environments, different Layer 2 to Layer 3 address resolution protocols may be employed, such as the AppleTalk Address Resolution Protocol (AARP). Because BGP EVPN supports only the Layer 3 protocols of IPv4 and IPv6 when IP addressing is absent, BGP EVPN relies on only the MAC information in the control plane to make the forwarding decisions. For the topology depicted in Figure 6-5, the MAC-layer information is populated and distributed within the given VXLAN-enabled network through the BGP EVPN control protocol, as illustrated in Table 6-3.

Table 6-3   *BGP EVPN Control Protocol Populated Information (Non-IP)*

MAC, IP	L2VNI	L3VNI	Next Hop
0000.3000.1101, 0.0.0.0	VNI 30001	—	10.200.200.1
0000.3000.1102, 0.0.0.0	VNI 30001	—	10.200.200.2
0000.3000.2101, 0.0.0.0	VNI 30002	—	10.200.200.1
0000.3000.2102, 0.0.0.0	VNI 30002	—	10.200.200.2

All the information related to the MAC layer is present. For example, the location of a given MAC address identified by the VTEP and the associated Layer 2 VNI where the MAC address resides is included. Because forwarding is based only on the Layer 2 information, the presence of IP addresses or Layer 3 VNIs (L3VNIs) is completely absent. If one of the endpoints begins using IP-based communication, then as soon as the ARP exchange occurs, the IP information also begins appearing in the BGP EVPN control plane, as described in the scenario discussed in the earlier section "Intra-Subnet Unicast Forwarding (Bridging)" of this chapter.

Figure 6-6 describes a sample packet flow for non-IP communication between Host A and Host B. Endpoint Host A generates data traffic with the SMAC address 0000.3000.1101. Host A resides in VLAN 10. The destination information is set to the information associated with endpoint Host B, which is 0000.3000.1102. The higher-layer addressing information is unknown to the VXLAN BGP EVPN network. Once the packet is received at VTEP V1, a destination lookup is performed [30001, 0000.3000.1102]. Based on the information populated via the BGP EVPN control protocol, the lookup result yields the next-hop VTEP (V2) associated with the destination (Host B) as well as the VNI (30001) to be employed for encapsulation. VXLAN encapsulation is then performed, and the packet is sent toward VTEP V2 with the VXLAN VNI 30001.

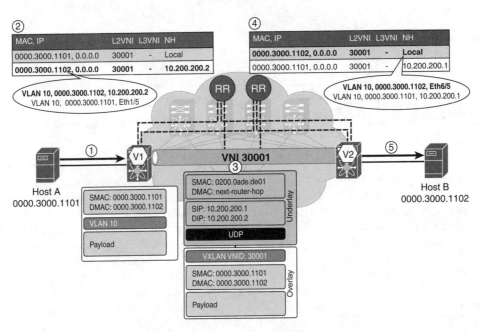

Figure 6-6 *Host A to Host B Forwarding (Non-IP)*

Table 6-4 shows the details of the outer IP, UDP, and VXLAN header fields, as well as the inner MAC fields.

Table 6-4 *Encapsulated Packet, Including All Headers (non-IP)*

Outer DIP	Outer SIP	UDP DPort	VXLAN	Inner DMAC	Inner SMAC	Payload
10.200.200.2	10.200.200.1	4789	VNI 30001	0000.3000.1102	0000.3000.1101	—

From the control protocol perspective, the forwarded packet is considered non-IP (inner or original frame). Everything beyond the inner MAC headers represented in Table 6-4 appears as non-addressing information and is abbreviated with "Payload."

Once the packet is received at the egress VTEP V2, the packet is decapsulated, and a lookup of the forwarding tables occurs. VNI 30001 is mapped to the local VLAN 10, and the Layer 2 lookup is performed as well based on the key [VLAN=10, 0000.3000.1102]. If the lookup results in a hit, the frame is sent toward the Ethernet interface to which Host B is attached. In case of a miss, the frame is flooded out of the local ports having membership in VLAN 10. Consequently, if Host B is behind VTEP V2, it receives the frame. Reverse traffic from Host B to Host A follows a similar flow.

At this stage, the unicast non-IP forwarding from endpoint Host A in VLAN 10 behind VTEP V1 to endpoint Host B in VLAN 10 behind VTEP V2 has been completed. Again, VLAN 10 on VTEP V1 and VLAN 10 on VTEP V2 are stitched together via a Layer 2 service over VXLAN, identified with VNI 30001.

Inter-Subnet Unicast Forwarding (Routing)

Thus far, the bridging packet flows have been discussed in regard to a Layer 2 overlay service using VXLAN as the encapsulation and Layer 2 Gateway (L2GW) as the VTEP function. When considering Layer 3 overlay services provided by VXLAN and the respective Layer 3 Gateway (L3GW) function of the VTEP, a good understanding of how the Layer 2 or bridging operation itself works is crucial. With VXLAN being a MAC-in-IP/UDP header (regardless of Layer 2 or Layer 3 service), the inner payload must have a MAC header. In moving one OSI layer higher to cover Layer 3 operation, it is worthwhile to emphasize this important detail again. Understanding how the encapsulation and forwarding is performed when providing Layer 3 service with VXLAN is essential.

For a BGP EVPN VXLAN network, the function of symmetric Integrated Routing and Bridging (IRB) is used to forward data traffic. With this approach, routed traffic uses the Layer 3 VNI (L3VNI) associated with the VRF within which the routing operation occurs. Every VRF has a unique L3VNI. In a given BGP EVPN VXLAN fabric, the same VRF-to-L3VNI mapping must be present on every edge device or VTEP where that VRF is configured. When multiple VTEPs share the same L3VNI in a given VXLAN-based network, this is referred to as a *routing domain*. The 24-bit VNI used for addressing a VRF or the individual routing domain is the same field in the VXLAN header that is used for carrying the L2VNI for forwarding bridged traffic.

The reason for supporting the coexistence of two different values for a service while only employing a single encapsulation field is related to what happens after a routing operation occurs. With bridging, the MAC addresses have to be end-to-end visible. But in routing, the MAC information changes after the routing operation is completed. Consequently, after routing, the incoming or ingress MAC and VLAN information becomes irrelevant because the Layer 3 IP and VRF information is used for making forwarding decisions. This remains true until the egress VTEP is reached, where a lookup corresponding to [VRF, Destination IP] yields the final DMAC and egress interface on which the packet must be sent. In essence, this procedure for forwarding routed traffic over VXLAN is very similar to routing operations in non-VXLAN environments.

In the subsequent explanations concerning conceptual traffic forwarding, refer to Figure 6-7, which shows four endpoints (Host A, Host B, Host X, Host Y) residing in VRF A associated with L3VNI 50001. As in prior examples, VNI 30001 is associated with IP subnet 192.168.1.0/24, on which endpoints Host A and Host B reside, and VNI 30002 is associated with IP subnet 192.168.2.0/24, on which endpoints Host X and Host Y reside.

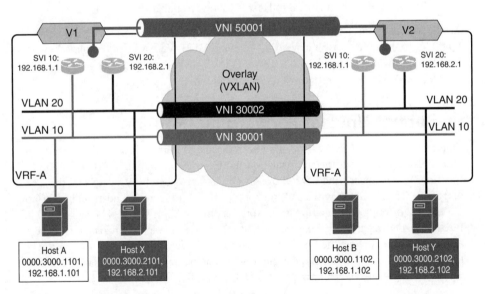

Figure 6-7   *Inter-Subnet Forwarding (Routing)*

For routing operations between endpoints connected to the ingress VTEP V1 and endpoints connected to the egress VTEP V2, the exchange of Layer 3 addressing, IP addresses, and associated IP subnets, has to occur first. With the BGP EVPN control protocol, the information learned about the local endpoints at an ingress VTEP is distributed across BGP updates to all neighboring VTEPs. Specifically, the IP/MAC information about the endpoints is distributed using BGP Route type 2 messages. Likewise, the subnet prefix information is distributed using BGP Route type 5 messages.

For the scenario shown in Figure 6-7, the BGP EVPN control protocol would show the information depicted in Table 6-5.

This information is installed and used in the respective VTEPs' hardware tables if the Route Targets match. When this information is advertised over BGP and received from a VTEP, the portion of information seen as part of the BGP outputs differs from the installed information. As a result, the relationship to the VRF can be achieved only over the VNI detour.

Table 6-5   *BGP EVPN Control Protocol Populated Information (After ARP)*

MAC, IP	L2VNI	L3VNI	Next-Hop
0000.3000.1101, 192.168.1.101	VNI 30001	VNI 50001	10.200.200.1
0000.3000.1102, 192.168.1.102	VNI 30001	VNI 50001	10.200.200.2
0000.3000.2101, 192.168.2.101	VNI 30002	VNI 50001	10.200.200.1
0000.3000.2102, 192.168.2.102	VNI 30002	VNI 50001	10.200.200.2
IP: 192.168.1.0/24	—	VNI 50001	10.200.200.1
			10.200.200.2
IP: 192.168.2.0/24	—	VNI 50001	10.200.200.1
			10.200.200.2

This explanation is not specific to BGP EVPN. It also applies to other MP-BGP VPN–based approaches, such as MVPN or VPNv4/v6 (MPLS L3VPN). Because most network administrators first check the BGP tables to validate whether a given prefix is received, this explanation is needed. MAC routes, IP host routes, and prefix routes are all being carried in BGP EVPN messages. Given that the MAC routes are applicable for MAC VRF identified by the L2VNI, and the IP routes are applicable for the IP VRF identified by the L3VNI, the command **show bgp l2vpn evpn vni-id *XXXXX*** has been introduced to show these routes. The command **show bgp ip unicast vrf *VRF-NAME*** provides the IP prefix information for a given IP VRF.

While it is good practice to verify what BGP prefixes are received for a given IP VRF, it is even more important to verify that the given prefixes are installed, and valid for forwarding. Specifically, the chain of verification at reception should be (a) whether routes have been received and installed in the BGP routing information base (BRIB); (b) whether routes have been installed in the unicast RIB; and (c) whether routes have been installed in the hardware forwarding information base (FIB) tables with the correct adjacency, or next-hop information. Example 6-5 illustrates how the BGP EVPN Layer 2 and Layer 3 information is stored at VTEP V1 with the VNI associated with vrf VRF-A (50001).

Example 6-5   show bgp l2vpn evpn vni-id 50001 *Output at VTEP V1*

```
V1# show bgp l2vpn evpn vni-id 50001
BGP routing table information for VRF default, address family L2VPN EVPN
BGP table version is 43, local router ID is 10.10.10.1
Status: s-suppressed, x-deleted, S-stale, d-dampened, h-history, *-valid, >-best
Path type: i-internal, e-external, c-confed, l-local, a-aggregate, r-redist,
  I-injected
Origin codes: i - IGP, e - EGP, ? - incomplete, | - multipath, & - backup

  Network            Next Hop          Metric   LocPrf   Weight Path
Route Distinguisher: 10.10.10.1:3    (L3VNI 50001)
*>i[2]:[0]:[0]:[48]:[0000.3000.1102]:[32]:[192.168.1.102]/272
                     10.200.200.2               100         0 i
*>i[2]:[0]:[0]:[48]:[0000.3000.2102]:[32]:[192.168.2.102]/272
                     10.200.200.2               100         0 i
* i[5]:[0]:[0]:[24]:[192.168.1.0]:[0.0.0.0]/224
                     10.200.200.2      0        100         0 ?
*>l                  10.200.200.1      0        100     32768 ?
* i[5]:[0]:[0]:[24]:[192.168.2.0]:[0.0.0.0]/224
                     10.200.200.2      0        100         0 ?
*>l                  10.200.200.1      0        100     32768 ?
```

> **Note**   As part of the verification, the EVPN NLRI is being checked with the bit count of the populated fields. This bit count results as a / notation next to the prefix. A MAC-only Route type 2 is represented with a /216 prefix, while a MAC/IP Route type 2 is represented as a /272 prefix (additional bits account for 32 bits for IPv4 address plus 24 bits for L3VNI). When an IPv6 address is carried in Route type 2, it is represented as a /368 prefix (additional bits account for 128 bits for IPv6 address plus 24 bits for L3VNI). A Route type 5 EVPN route carrying an IPv4 prefix is represented by a /224 prefix, and one carrying an IPv6 address is represented by a /416 prefix.

Because MP-BGP is used with EVPN, the IP prefix entry would reside in the BGP RIB only if the respective Route Target information did not match the route import statement under a VRF. As a result, it would never be used for forwarding. It is therefore good practice to verify that the MAC/IP prefix (Route type 2) and IP subnet prefix (Route type 5) have been received for Layer 3 operations. The information retrieved is divided into host routes (/32 for IPv4 or /128 for IPv6) and IP prefix routes. All this information is learned through BGP EVPN and installed in the respective IP VRF, assuming the appropriate Route Targets have been imported. Example 6-6 shows all the IP routes for vrf VRF-A that are installed in the unicast RIB of VTEP V1. This includes both the locally learned and instantiated routes and the routes received via BGP EVPN from remote VTEPs.

Example 6-6   show ip route vrf VRF-A *Output at VTEP V1*

```
V1 show ip route vrf VRF-A
IP Route Table for VRF "VRF-A"
'*' denotes best ucast next-hop
'**' denotes best mcast next-hop
'[x/y]' denotes [preference/metric]
'%<string>' in via output denotes VRF <string>


192.168.1.0/24, ubest/mbest: 1/0, attached
    *via 192.168.1.1, Vlan10, [0/0], 00:16:15, direct, tag 12345
192.168.1.1/32, ubest/mbest: 1/0, attached
    *via 192.168.1.1, Vlan10, [0/0], 00:16:15, local, tag 12345
192.168.1.101/32, ubest/mbest: 1/0, attached
    *via 192.168.1.101, Vlan10, [190/0], 00:12:24, hmm
192.168.1.102/32, ubest/mbest: 1/0
    *via 10.200.200.2%default, [200/0], 00:12:57, bgp-65501, internal, tag 65501
      (evpn) segid: 50001 tunnelid: 0xa64640c encap: VXLAN


192.168.2.0/24, ubest/mbest: 1/0, attached
    *via 192.168.2.1, Vlan20, [0/0], 00:14:24, direct, tag 12345
192.168.2.1/32, ubest/mbest: 1/0, attached
    *via 192.168.2.1, Vlan20, [0/0], 00:14:24, local, tag 12345
192.168.2.101/32, ubest/mbest: 1/0, attached
    *via 192.168.2.101, Vlan20, [190/0], 00:12:24, hmm
192.168.2.102/32, ubest/mbest: 1/0
    *via 10.200.200.2%default, [200/0], 00:11:47, bgp-65501, internal, tag 65501
      (evpn) segid: 50001 tunnelid: 0xa64640d encap: VXLAN
```

Typically, the IP/MAC binding of locally attached endpoints at a VTEP is learned via ARP. As a result, appropriate ARP entries are added to the ARP table, and, in turn, corresponding host routes (/32) are added to the unicast RIB. These host routes are subsequently advertised to remote VTEPs over BGP EVPN using Route type 2 messages. In that sense, validating the ARP tables for a given VRF is a good starting point. Example 6-7 shows the host entries in the ARP table for vrf VRF-A at VTEP V1.

Example 6-7   show ip arp vrf VRF-A *Output at VTEP V1*

```
V1 show ip arp vrf VRF-A


Flags: * - Adjacencies learnt on non-active FHRP router
       + - Adjacencies synced via CFSoE
       # - Adjacencies Throttled for Glean
       D - Static Adjacencies attached to down interface


IP ARP Table for context VRF-A
Total number of entries: 2
Address         Age       MAC Address    Interface
192.168.1.101   00:11:36  0000.3000.1101  Vlan10
192.168.2.101   00:11:16  0000.3000.1102  Vlan20
```

The separation of locally learned information for Layer 3 with ARP, along with the remotely learned Layer 3 information through a routing protocol, is similar to how things operate in traditional routed networks. However, in traditional networks, only the subnet routes are advertised for reachability via an appropriate routing protocol. In contrast, the difference here is the presence of host routes, which are traditionally learned but automatically redistributed into the BGP tables in the appropriate VRF context. With this approach, efficient routing is possible to any endpoint in the same VRF in the VXLAN BGP EVPN network even when the IP subnet is distributed across multiple VTEPs or leafs. Efficient routing occurs because the endpoint's location information is known, as is the VTEP behind which the endpoint resides. With the distributed IP anycast gateway, not only can routing occur at the ingress VTEP, but routing can also be performed efficiently to the correct egress VTEP.

The output in the previous IP- and ARP-related examples assumes that an endpoint has been learned at its directly attached VTEP. This learning occurs by way of the interception of an ARP request from the endpoint. For inter-subnet communications, the endpoint needs to resolve its default gateway, and hence it needs to send out an ARP request. While this is true for an endpoint initiating the inter-subnet communication, in some scenarios, endpoints may be "silent." In other words, these endpoints are not the initiators but are instead responders to communications. Other scenarios where silent hosts could exist could also include the misalignment of a MAC/ARP timer and an unknown behavior of a given endpoint's IP stack. Scenarios involving both non-silent and silent endpoints are covered in this section. And for completeness, the initial ARP resolution process that occurs when non-silent hosts try to resolve their default gateway is discussed as well.

Figure 6-8 shows a scenario where endpoint Host A in VLAN 10 is attached below VTEP V1. Either during endpoint Host A's initialization of its IP stack or whenever it tries to communicate with another endpoint in a different IP subnet, Host A tries to resolve the IP-to-MAC mapping for its default gateway from its local ARP cache. If this process results in a miss, Host A initiates an ARP request for the IP address of its default gateway, which is also the distributed IP anycast gateway configured on VTEP V1. The broadcast

ARP request is forwarded in VLAN 10 and enters VTEP V1. At VTEP V1, the ARP request is then evaluated through ARP snooping, and the retrieved source information is populated in the BGP EVPN control protocol. Host A's MAC 0000.3000.1101 and IP 192.168.1.101 then becomes known as behind VTEP V1.

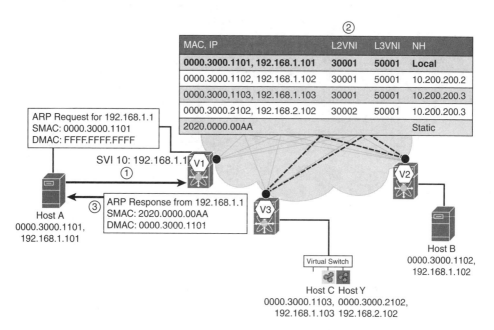

MAC, IP	L2VNI	L3VNI	NH
0000.3000.1101, 192.168.1.101	**30001**	**50001**	**Local**
0000.3000.1102, 192.168.1.102	30001	50001	10.200.200.2
0000.3000,1103, 192.168.1.103	30001	50001	10.200.200.3
0000.3000.2102, 192.168.2.102	30002	50001	10.200.200.3
2020.0000.00AA			Static

Figure 6-8 *ARP Request, Host A to Distributed IP Anycast Gateway*

At the same time, VTEP V1, which is responsible for the queried IP address, responds. The ARP reply sent from the distributed IP anycast gateway is sourced from VTEP V1, and it uses the anycast gateway MAC address (AGM) in the response to endpoint Host A. Once this information is received, Host A updates its ARP cache with the AGM (2020.0000.00AA in this example) mapped to the default gateway IP entry (192.168.1.1). Now, endpoint Host A is ready to communicate with other endpoints in different subnets. With the distributed anycast gateway, the Layer 3 boundary is at the VTEP, which naturally acts as the first-hop gateway for all the directly attached endpoints.

Two major forwarding semantics exist in VXLAN BGP EVPN, along with their respective use of IRB functions. The first relates to the local routing operation that occurs if the source and destination endpoints reside in different subnets in the same VRF and below the same edge device or VTEP. The second relates to forwarding routed traffic to an endpoint behind a remote VTEP, where similar processing occurs, but appropriate VXLAN encapsulation is now required between VTEPs.

In the local routing scenario shown in Figure 6-9, Host A (192.168.1.101) communicates with Host X (192.168.2.101), and both hosts are attached to the same VTEP (V1). Host A generates data traffic with the SMAC address 0000.3000.1101 and source IP address

192.168.1.101. Because the default gateway has already been resolved, the DMAC is set to 2020.0000.00AA. Host A resides in subnet 192.168.1.0/24, which is part of vrf VRF-A, and this subnet is within VLAN 10. The destination information is set to the information of endpoint Host X, which has the destination IP address 192.168.2.101 in the same VRF. Once the packet is received at VTEP V1, a destination lookup is performed for IP 192.168.2.101 in vrf VRF-A, which yields the next hop.

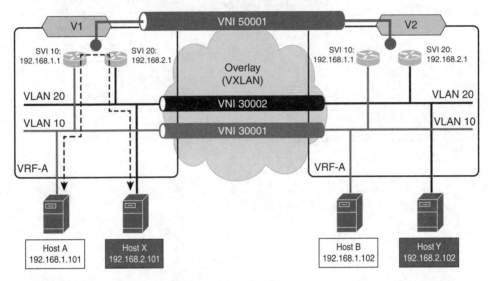

Figure 6-9   *Inter-Subnet Forwarding (Local Routing)*

In the case of local routing, the next hop is a Layer-3 interface in a different VLAN (VLAN 20). The packet is transported to the respective egress VLAN at VTEP V1. Because Host X has already been learned at VTEP V1 based on the prior ARP processing, the longest prefix match entry (the host route 192.168.2.101/32) is hit. Subsequently, the appropriate MAC header rewrites are performed on the packet and the packet is delivered to Host X. Therefore, for local routing, VXLAN encapsulation is not needed. Table 6-6 shows the details of the header fields that are part of the local routing operation.

Table 6-6   *Host A Sourced Packet, Including All Headers*

DMAC	SMAC	Dot1q	Inner DIP	Inner SIP	Payload
2020.0000.00AA	0000.3000.1101	VLAN 10	192.168.2.101	192.168.1.101	—

Once the packet is received at endpoint Host X in a different VLAN and IP subnet, Host X can respond to Host A in a similar manner, thereby completing bidirectional unicast communication through local routing at VTEP V1.

When routing to a destination endpoint behind a remote VTEP, the initial steps for ARP resolution and for reaching the default gateway are identical to that described with local routing. But the routing performed between two different VTEPs needs to be discussed further. In this instance, as shown in Figure 6-10, the source, Host A, is connected to the ingress VTEP V1, while the destination, Host Y, is connected to the egress VTEP V2 in a different IP subnet.

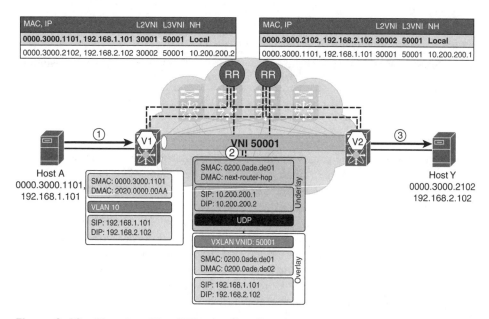

Figure 6-10   *Host-A-to-Host-Y Forwarding (Routing)*

Host A generates data traffic with the SMAC address 0000.3000.1101, the source IP address 192.168.1.101, the DMAC address 2020.0000.00AA, and the destination IP address 192.168.2.102. When the packet is received at VTEP V1, a destination lookup is performed for IP 192.168.2.102 in vrf VRF-A, which results in the next-hop destination VTEP and the VNI to be used for encapsulation. Because the remote host route 192.168.2.102/32 has been learned at VTEP V2, populated over BGP EVPN to VTEP V1, and installed in the hardware FIB tables, the lookup results in a hit. The lookup result yields VTEP V2, L3VNI=50001, corresponding to vrf VRF-A, as well as the appropriate MAC header rewrite information.

Because VXLAN requires an inner MAC header, the source and next-hop MAC address of the involved routers in the overlay have to be present. On the ingress VTEP side, where VTEP V1 encapsulates the packets, the source Router MAC (RMAC) is known because it is owned by VTEP V1. The remote VTEP's RMAC information is encoded in the BGP EVPN NLRI as an extended community. Consequently, whenever a routing lookup is performed at the ingress VTEP for a remote destination IP (host or subnet), the destination RMAC is derived from the BGP EVPN information. Note that intuitively the regular Layer 2/Layer 3 lookup semantics apply here. Because this is a routed case, a Layer 3 lookup is performed, and the lookup result drives the rewrite that must be applied to the packet before it is forwarded out the appropriate egress interface.

Table 6-7 depicts the details of the VXLAN-encapsulated packet sent from VTEP V1 to VTEP V2, including the salient inner and outer header fields. In the table, 0200.0ade.de01 and 0200.0ade.de02 correspond to the RMACs associated with VTEP V1 and VTEP V2, respectively.

Table 6-7 *Encapsulated Packet, Including All Headers*

Outer DIP	Outer SIP	UDP DPort	VXLAN	Inner DMAC	Inner SMAC	Inner DIP	Inner SIP	Payload
10.200. 200.2	10.200. 200.1	4789	VNI 50001	0200.0ade. de02	0200.0ade. de01	192.168. 2.102	192.168. 1.101	—

The VXLAN-encapsulated packet is forwarded using regular Layer 3 lookup as it traverses different routers along the path until it reaches the egress VTEP. Once the packet is received at the VTEP V2, the packet is decapsulated, and the forwarding tables that are responsible for the VNI 50001 mapped vrf VRF-A are consulted. Because endpoint Host Y is known at VTEP V2, the routing lookup results in a lookup hit for 192.168.2.102/32, and the frame is appropriately rewritten and sent toward the Ethernet interface where Host Y is connected. In this way, with symmetric IRB, a bridge–route–route–bridge sequence is performed. In this situation, the packet from Host A is first bridged toward VTEP V1 and then routed on VTEP V1 toward VTEP V2. At VTEP V2, the packet is routed again and subsequently bridged toward Host Y.

At this point, the unicast forwarding from Host A within VLAN 10 behind VTEP V1 to Host Y within VLAN 20 behind VTEP V2 is complete. The subnet (as part of VLAN 10) and the subnet (as part of VLAN 20) are connected together via a Layer 3 service in VXLAN identified with VNI 50001, representing a transit segment between VTEP V1 and VTEP V2.

Routed Traffic to Silent Endpoints

So far the hosts or endpoints have "announced" their presence to their directly attached VTEP via ARP, thereby ensuring efficient routing to these endpoints. This includes both local and remote hosts. These endpoints are different from the silent endpoints introduced earlier, whose presence is not known to the network. In that situation, the silent endpoints are not known at the ingress VTEP or at any of the egress VTEPs.

The Layer 3 forwarding approach with BGP EVPN handles silent endpoints efficiently as well. Sending traffic toward the silent endpoint results in their discovery. Subsequently the endpoint is known to the network and treated like any other known endpoint. Two scenarios for handling silent hosts or silent endpoints in a VXLAN BGP EVPN network are now discussed.

For the scenario depicted in Figure 6-11, the BGP EVPN control protocol shows the information in Table 6-8, where endpoint Host Y is a silent host. Specifically, Host Y's IP address is not known because it has yet to be discovered.

Inter-Subnet Forwarding (Host Y Unknown)

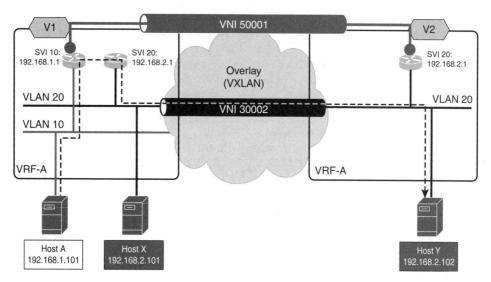

Figure 6-11   *Silent Host Y with L2VNI Present (Router Bridge)*

Table 6-8   *BGP EVPN Control Protocol, VTEP V2 Silent Host*

MAC, IP	L2VNI	L3VNI	Next-Hop
0000.3000.1101, 192.168.1.101	VNI 30001	VNI 50001	10.200.200.1
0000.3000.2101, 192.168.2.101	VNI 30002	VNI 50001	10.200.200.1
0000.3000.2102, 0.0.0.0	VNI 30002		10.200.200.2
IP: 192.168.1.0/24	—	VNI 50001	10.200.200.1
			10.200.200.2
IP: 192.168.2.0/24	—	VNI 50001	10.200.200.1
			10.200.200.2

Assume that Host A wants to communicate with Host Y. As before, Host A generates data traffic with the SMAC address 0000.3000.1101, the source IP address 192.168.1.101, the DMAC address 2020.0000.00AA, and the destination IP address 192.168.2.102. This occurs because the default gateway has already been resolved. Once the packet is received at VTEP V1, a destination lookup is performed for IP 192.168.2.102 in vrf VRF-A. This yields the destination VTEP and the associated VNI (50001 associated with vrf VRF-A) to be employed for VXLAN encapsulation. Given that Host Y is a silent endpoint, the Layer 3 lookup hits the longest prefix match entry. In this case, the prefix corresponding to the subnet 192.168.2.0/24 in which host Y resides, will be the hit.

Because the destination IP subnet is locally known, the direct or connected route is chosen (lowest administrative distance). This subnet prefix entry points to a glean adjacency, and this in turn triggers the generation of an ARP request in the bridge domain associated with VNI 30002. Appropriate BUM forwarding on the underlay ensures that this broadcast ARP request reaches all the other VTEPs participating in VNI 30002. Assume that VNI 30002 is associated with multicast group 239.1.1.1. Table 6-9 shows the details of the header fields involved in this operation.

Table 6-9   *Encapsulated Packet, Including All Headers*

Outer DIP	Outer SIP	UDP DPort	VXLAN	Inner DMAC	Inner SMAC	Inner DIP	Inner SIP	Payload
239.1.1.1	10.200. 200.1	4789	VNI 30002	FFFF.FFFF. FFFF	2020.0000. 00AA	192.168. 2.102	192.168. 2.1	—

Consequently, Host Y also receives the ARP request. Given that the ARP request is sourced from VTEP V1, which hosts the distributed anycast gateway, Host Y responds with a directed ARP reply to the default gateway. The distributed anycast gateway is also hosted on VTEP V2, which captures the ARP response. Based on the ARP response, VTEP V2 learns about the IP-to-MAC binding associated with Host Y. In turn, VTEP V2 advertises this information over the BGP EVPN control protocol. As a result, VTEP V1 learns about the 192.168.2.102/32 address associated with Host Y. Subsequently, traffic is routed over to VTEP V2 and eventually forwarded to Host Y over VLAN 20, which is mapped to VNI 30002.

As with symmetric IRB, routed traffic from VTEP V1 to VTEP V2 is sent out with VXLAN VNI 50001, which is the L3VNI associated with vrf VRF-A. Reverse traffic from Host Y to Host A is also routed from VTEP V2 to VTEP V1, using the same VXLAN VNI 50001, thus providing symmetry. Consequently, with symmetric IRB, VXLAN-routed traffic in either direction uses the same VNI, which is the VNI associated with the VRF.

At this stage, the unicast forwarding scenario is complete, with silent host detection from endpoint Host A (in VLAN 10 behind VTEP V1) to endpoint Host Y (in VLAN 20 connected to VTEP V2). Once the silent host, Host Y is detected, and subsequent forwarding takes place across VNI 50001 (L3VNI). For the scenario shown in Figure 6-12, the BGP EVPN control protocol shows the information in Table 6-10 after silent host discovery.

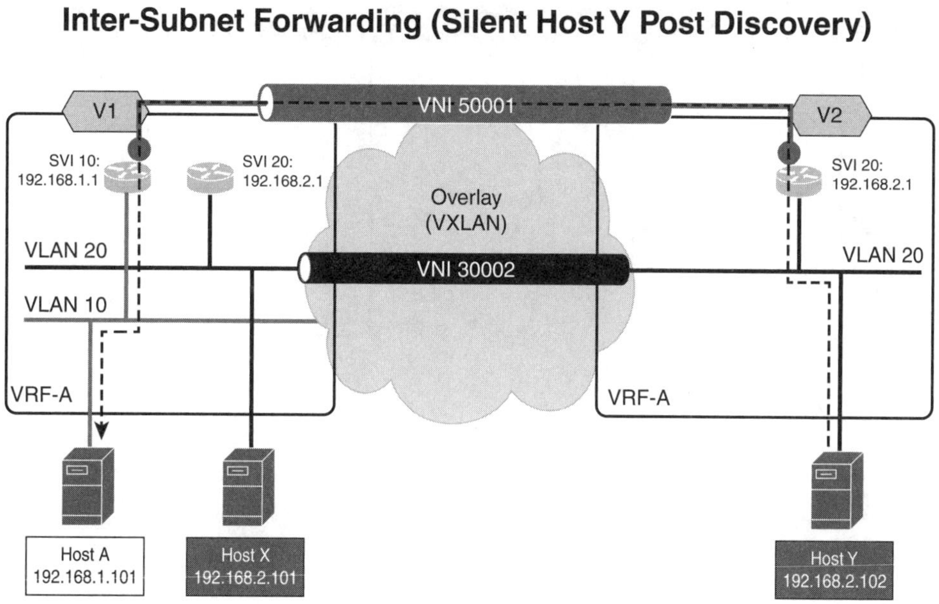

Inter-Subnet Forwarding (Silent Host Y Post Discovery)

Figure 6-12   *Silent Host Y with L2VNI Present (Routing)*

Table 6-10   *BGP EVPN Control Protocol*

MAC, IP	L2VNI	L3VNI	Next Hop
0000.3000.1101, 192.168.1.101	VNI 30001	VNI 50001	10.200.200.1
0000.3000.2101, 192.168.2.101	VNI 30002	VNI 50001	10.200.200.1
0000.3000.2102, 192.168.2.102	VNI 30002	VNI 50001	10.200.200.2
IP: 192.168.1.0/24	-	VNI 50001	10.200.200.1
			10.200.200.2
IP: 192.168.2.0/24	-	VNI 50001	10.200.200.1
			10.200.200.2

The previous scenario discusses silent host detection where the bridge domain of the destination endpoint is local to the ingress VTEP. Because this is not always the case, silent host detection has to also work in cases where no Layer 2 extension is present. In such a situation, the destination IP subnet prefix is chosen to forward data traffic toward the destination endpoint. Subsequently, one of the VTEPs hosting the destination subnet is chosen as the candidate to discover the silent endpoint via ARP.

For the scenario depicted in Figure 6-13, the BGP EVPN control protocol has the information shown in Table 6-11.

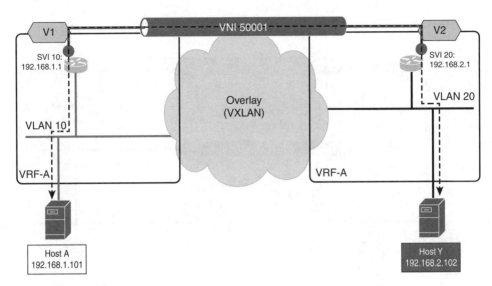

Figure 6-13 *Silent Host Y (Routing Only)*

Table 6-11 *BGP EVPN Control Protocol information at VTEP V1*

MAC, IP	L2VNI	L3VNI	Next Hop
0000.3000.1101, 192.168.1.101	VNI 30001	VNI 50001	10.200.200.1
IP: 192.168.1.0/24	—	VNI 50001	10.200.200.1
IP: 192.168.2.0/24	—	VNI 50001	10.200.200.2

As in prior examples, here Host A with IP 192.168.1.101 wants to communicate with Host Y with IP 192.168.2.102. After ARP resolution of the default gateway, Host A generates data traffic with the SMAC address 0000.3000.1101, the source IP address 192.168.1.101, the DMAC address 2020.0000.00AA, and the destination IP address 192.168.2.102. Once the packet is received at VTEP V1, a destination lookup is performed for IP 192.168.2.102 in vrf VRF-A, which results in a hit for the subnet prefix 192.168.2.0/24. Because this subnet prefix is advertised by VTEP V2, traffic is VXLAN-encapsulated with the VRF-A VNI 50001 and sent toward VTEP V2 using the symmetric IRB function at VTEP V1. Once again, the inner SMAC is rewritten with the information of VTEP V1, and the inner DMAC is rewritten to the RMAC associated with VTEP V2, which was advertised over BGP EVPN using the Router-mac extended community. Table 6-12 shows the details of the outer IP, UDP, and VXLAN header fields, as well as the inner MAC and IP header fields for this operation.

Table 6-12 *Encapsulated Packet, Including All Headers*

Outer DIP	Outer SIP	UDP DPort	VXLAN	Inner DMAC	Inner SMAC	Inner DIP	Inner SIP	Payload
10.200. 200.2	10.200. 200.1	4789	VNI 50001	0200.0ade. de02	0200.0ade. de01	192.168. 2.102	192.168. 1.101	—

When the traffic reaches VTEP V2, it is decapsulated, and the subsequent destination IP lookup in vrf VRF-A, which is mapped from VNI 50001, results in the 192.168.2.0/24 subnet prefix entry being hit. Because Host Y is silent, its /32 route has not yet been discovered at VTEP V2. The glean adjacency associated with the local subnet 192.168.2.0/24 is hit, and, in turn, VTEP V2 injects an ARP request in VLAN 20, associated with this subnet. The broadcast ARP request flooded in VNI 30002 mapped from VLAN 20, also reaches Host Y. The ARP response from Host Y is then directed to the default gateway (specifically the distributed anycast gateway), which is hosted on VTEP V2.

As in earlier examples, Host Y is discovered, its address information is injected into the BGP EVPN control plane, and distributed to all remote VTEPs, including VTEP V1. In this way, subsequent data traffic is forwarded from Host A to Host Y via routing from VTEP V1 to VTEP V2, using the symmetric IRB bridge–route–route–bridge operation. For the scenario shown in Figure 6-13, the BGP EVPN control protocol shows the information in Table 6-13 after silent host discovery:

Table 6-13   *BGP EVPN Control Protocol Information After Silent Host Discovery of Host Y*

MAC, IP	L2VNI	L3VNI	Next Hop
0000.3000.1101, 192.168.1.101	VNI 30001	VNI 50001	10.200.200.1
0000.3000.2102, 192.168.2.102	VNI 30002	VNI 50001	10.200.200.2
IP: 192.168.1.0/24	—	VNI 50001	10.200.200.1
IP: 192.168.2.0/24	—	VNI 50001	10.200.200.2

Note that the announcement of the IP subnet route of a given L3GW instance (SVI or BDI) has to be performed manually via an appropriate configuration. Chapter 2, "VXLAN BGP EVPN Basics," explains this approach and the merits of this redistribution. Example 6-8 shows a simple configuration with this in mind.

Example 6-8   show run vrf VRF-A *Output (at VTEP V1)*

```
interface Vlan10
  vrf member VRF-A
  ip address 192.168.1.1/24 tag 12345
  fabric forwarding mode anycast-gateway

route-map FABRIC-RMAP-REDIST-SUBNET permit 10
  match tag 12345

router bgp 65501
  vrf X
    address-family ipv4 unicast
      advertise l2vpn evpn
      redistribute direct route-map FABRIC-RMAP-REDIST-SUBNET
```

Forwarding with Dual-Homed Endpoint

Virtual PortChannel (vPC) is a technology used in forwarding traffic to dual-homed endpoints attached to a pair of switches. From a VXLAN perspective, the vPC domain represents a common VTEP within the VXLAN network and is referred to as the *anycast VTEP*. This section explains vPC-based forwarding and its use with VXLAN BGP EVPN and the distributed IP anycast gateway. By default, the location of every endpoint connected to a vPC domain is represented by the corresponding anycast VTEP IP address.

For the scenario depicted in Figure 6-14, VTEP V1 and VTEP V2 form a vPC domain represented with the anycast VTEP (VIP) with the IP address 10.200.200.12. Once Host A intends to send traffic toward Host B, port channel hashing decides whether Host A should choose VTEP V1 or VTEP V2 as an ingress VTEP for VXLAN encapsulation and forwarding. Once the hashing decision has been made between the endpoint and the VTEPs for transporting the traffic across the port channel, the same semantics described in previous sections related to intra-subnet (bridging) or inter-subnet (routing) forwarding are used. Figure 6-14 shows the end-to-end bridging scenario from a dual-attached endpoint (Host A) to a single attached endpoint (Host B). Whether the traffic ingresses VTEP V1 or VTEP V2, the outer source IP address is always set to that of the anycast VTEP, in this case, 10.200.200.12. This holds true for both routed and bridged traffic sent out from the vPC domain toward the VXLAN network.

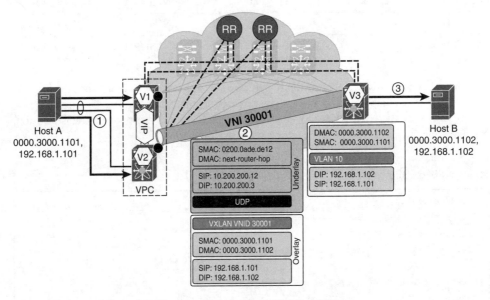

Figure 6-14 *Endpoint Behind Ingress Anycast VTEP (vPC)*

In the opposite direction, where traffic is directed to an endpoint connected to a vPC domain (represented by the anycast VTEP in VXLAN), additional details should be taken into consideration. For the scenario depicted in Figure 6-15, traffic from Host B toward Host A is VXLAN encapsulated and sent out with the outer destination IP address set to the anycast VTEP IP address 10.200.200.12. Both VTEP V1 and VTEP V2 are part of the same vPC domain and are configured with this anycast VTEP. Consequently, they both advertise reachability of 10.200.200.12 over the IP underlay.

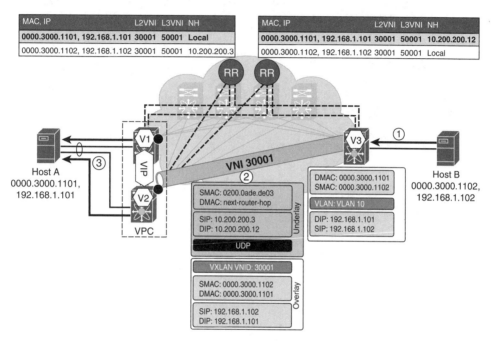

Figure 6-15 *Endpoint Behind Egress Anycast VTEP (vPC)*

Traffic directed toward 10.200.200.12 is forwarded either toward VTEP V1 or VTEP V2 by the underlay, based on equal-cost multipath (ECMP). Depending on the hashing used in the underlying transport network, an egress VTEP hidden behind the anycast VIP, is chosen. In this way, traffic reaches either VTEP V1 or VTEP V2. Likewise, the same semantics are used for intra-subnet (bridging) or inter-subnet (routing) forwarding, as described in the previous sections. Figure 6-15 shows the end-to-end bridging scenario from a non-VPC attached endpoint (Host B) to a vPC-attached endpoint (Host A). Only one of the two VTEPs, V1 or V2 will receive the traffic, decapsulate it and forward it toward Host A over the port channel.

With vPC-enabled edge devices, orphan endpoints are still present. An orphan endpoint, by definition, is connected to only one of the two vPC member switches that are part of the vPC domain. For an orphan endpoint, traffic destined to that endpoint might need to travel the vPC peer link because the endpoint information is always announced over BGP EVPN with the anycast VTEP being the next hop. This is also true for dual-homed endpoints that may become singly attached due to link/port failures.

Figure 6-16 shows an orphan endpoint Host A that is only attached to VTEP V1. As before, VTEP V1 and VTEP V2 form a vPC domain with the same anycast VTEP VIP advertised from the vPC domain. When traffic is ingressing from a remote VTEP and is destined to Host A, there is a chance that traffic directed toward VIP will be sent to VTEP V2, based on the ECMP hashing in the underlay network. After VXLAN decapsulation at VTEP V2, traffic is bridged across the vPC peer link toward VTEP V1. Subsequently, VTEP V1 forwards it on the orphan port where Host A is attached.

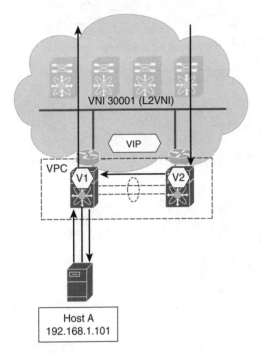

Figure 6-16 *Orphan Endpoints*

For routed traffic received at VTEP V2 that is destined for Host A, the routing lookup and rewrite occur on VTEP V2. Subsequently, the rewritten packet is bridged toward VTEP V1 over the vPC peer link. In the opposite direction, for traffic from Host A traveling toward any remote endpoint, VTEP V1 is used for both bridging and routing decisions. This is because Host A is connected only to this specific VTEP.

For a local bridging operation within a vPC domain in a VXLAN BGP EVPN network containing orphan endpoints, forwarding occurs in a manner similar to what happens with a traditional vPC deployment. Figure 6-17 shows a scenario with two orphan hosts, Host A and Host B, connected to VTEPs V1 and V2 respectively. Since Host A and Host B belong to the same L2VNI 30001, traffic from Host A is received at VTEP V1 and forwarded across the vPC peer link toward VTEP V2. Once traffic reaches VTEP V2, the traffic is forwarded toward the orphan port where Host B is attached. In general, this operation does not involve any VXLAN encapsulation, but certain platform limitations may still require traffic to be VXLAN-encapsulated across the vPC peer link.

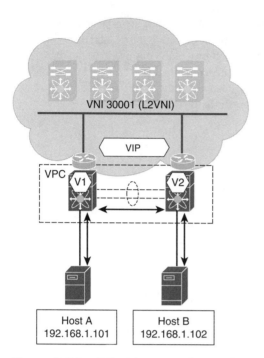

Figure 6-17 *vPC with two Orphan Endpoints*

Notably, all bridged and routed traffic within a vPC domain is announced with a next hop as the anycast VTEP associated with that domain. When routing through a vPC domain, the egress VTEP receiving the traffic needs to have the routing information in order to make further decisions. If the traffic reaches VTEP V1, but further egress routing has to happen from VTEP V2, a routing exchange must occur between VTEP V1 and VTEP V2. This can be achieved between vPC peers through either full-mesh external routing connectivity or VRF Lite across the vPC peer link. Regarding VRF Lite across the vPC peer link, a dedicated interface is required for establishing the routing adjacency. This restriction can be lifted by advertising routing information (Route type 5) with the individual IP address of the VTEPs rather than the anycast VTEP IP.

IPv6

VXLAN-based overlays using the BGP EVPN control protocol support IPv4- as well as IPv6-based Layer 2 and Layer 3 services. The distributed IP anycast gateway hosted at the VTEPs can act as a first-hop gateway for either IPv4 or IPv6, as well as in dual-stack mode. Just as with IPv4, all the VTEPs can share the same distributed anycast gateway IPv6 address with global addressing for a given IPv6 subnet. The anycast gateway MAC (AGM) is shared between IPv4 and IPv6. The overlay services are fully supported with both IPv4 and IPv6 addressing; however, the underlying transport network is presently only available with IPv4 addressing. Underlay transport based on IPv6 addressing will be supported in the future.

Figure 6-18 shows a sample topology where two IPv6 endpoints are attached to different VTEPs in a VXLAN BGP EVPN fabric. For endpoint detection, move, and deletion events with IPv6 endpoints, Neighbor Discovery Protocol (ND) is used instead of ARP. The locally learned IPv6 entries at a VTEP are subsequently advertised over the BGP EVPN control plane, using the same MP-BGP channel. In this way, the locations of all known IPv6 endpoints are learned everywhere in the BGP EVPN network.

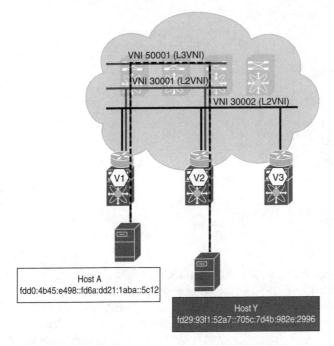

Figure 6-18   *IPv6 Endpoints in a BGP EVPN VXLAN Network*

With IPv6, the BGP EVPN NLRI is populated in a similar way as with IPv4 (see Figure 6-19). The differences are obvious, given that IPv6 addresses are 128 bits compared to 32 bits for IPv4. The **show** commands use hex notation for IPv6 addresses, but the rest of the BGP EVPN NLRI and extended community fields are equally applicable to IPv6 and IPv4. Recall that an appropriate routing protocol is responsible for populating the VTEP-to-VTEP reachability in the underlay. MP-BGP as the overlay reachability protocol employs the VTEP IP addresses as next-hop information associated with the BGP EVPN route advertisements. While the end host information can be MAC, IPv4, and/or IPv6 and only associates with the overlay, the next hop always follows the underlay. Consequently, even in the case of IPv6-based communication in the overlay network, the next hop is still a VTEP with an IPv4 address, as shown in Figure 6-19.

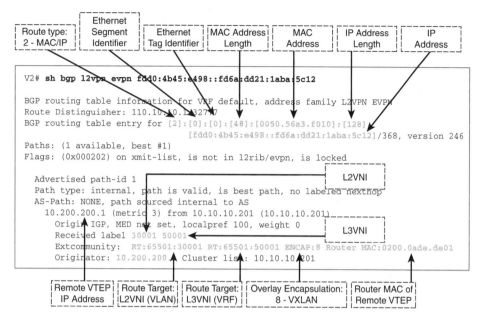

Figure 6-19 *Sample BGP EVPN Advertisement with IPv6 Endpoints*

Summary

This chapter provides a set of sample packet flows that indicate how bridging and routing operations occur in a VXLAN BGP EVPN network. Critical concepts related to IRB functionality, symmetric IRB, and distributed IP anycast gateway that are introduced in earlier chapters are described here in action for real-world traffic flows. This chapter pays special attention to scenarios with silent hosts as well as to dual-homed endpoints.

## Chapter 7

Multicast Forwarding

In this chapter, the following topics will be covered:

- How Intra-Subnet Multicast traffic is forwarded in a VXLAN BGP EVPN network

- Optimized multicast forwarding over VXLAN with IGMP snooping enhancements

- Intra-Subnet multicast forwarding to dual-homed and orphan endpoints

This chapter discusses multicast forwarding in a VXLAN BGP EVPN–based network. Previous chapters discuss multidestination traffic for the overlay and underlay. This chapter focuses on the handling of multicast traffic in the overlay. It also explains Intra-Subnet Multicast forwarding, including specific enhancements to IGMP snooping for optimized forwarding. This chapter also covers single-homed Intra-Subnet Multicast forwarding, followed by dual-homed deployments in virtual PortChannel (vPC) environments. Finally, this chapter briefly discusses Inter-Subnet Multicast forwarding or Routed Multicast in a VXLAN BGP EVPN overlay. Note that Layer 2 Multicast and Intra-Subnet Multicast are used interchangeably and Layer 3 Multicast and Inter-Subnet Multicast or Routed Multicast are also used interchangeably in the chapter.

Layer 2 Multicast Forwarding

VXLAN, as a MAC-in-IP/UDP data plane encapsulation, does not have any particular dependence on multicast; however, in order to forward overlay multidestination traffic (typically referred to as broadcast, unknown unicast, and multicast [BUM]), some mechanism is needed in the underlay transport. For this reason, the underlying transport network employs either the unicast mode of ingress/head-end replication or IP multicast. While both methods work well, they both also have advantages and disadvantages. Note that Layer 2 multicast refers to multicast traffic between a multicast source and receivers within the same broadcast domain or VXLAN VNI in this case. Ideally, Layer 2 multicast traffic should be sent from the source to only the interested receivers.

Unicast mode works well in environments with a small amount of multidestination traffic (for example, that associated with ARP, ND, DHCP, and so on) and with a small number of Virtual Tunnel Endpoints (VTEPs). Unicast mode works well for small deployments in most cases because a VTEP has to create multiple replicas for multidestination traffic, one for each neighboring VTEP. Multicast in the underlay is a better fit, however, when multicast applications are present and when a higher-bandwidth demand for BUM traffic is anticipated for the overlay. Clearly, with multicast traffic in the overlay, a definite advantage exists in employing multicast in the underlay. When the scale increases, using multicast is the preferred method of handling multidestination traffic in the underlay (see Figure 7-1).

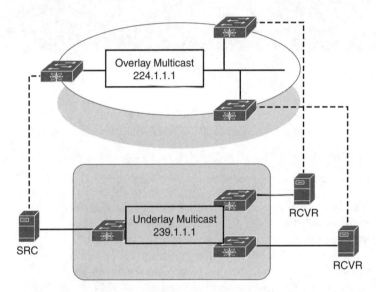

Figure 7-1   *Multicast-in-Multicast*

When the unicast mode is used for handling multidestination traffic, the VTEPs require a mechanism to know which other VTEPs are interested in receiving the multidestination traffic. As discussed in the previous chapters, this is facilitated via a BGP EVPN Route type 3 message that advertises VTEP membership interest in the Layer 2 VXLAN VNI (L2VNI). With multicast mode, the native IP multicast mechanism in the underlay is enough to create a multicast tree with the interested VTEPs because *an L2VNI is mapped to a specific multicast group*. This configuration is done symmetrically at all the VTEPs where that L2VNI is instantiated. Consequently, with a multicast-enabled underlay, no requirement exists for exchange of any BGP EVPN messages to signal the (L2VNI, VTEP) membership. From this point onward, unless otherwise mentioned, it is assumed that multicast is employed in the underlay.

When a multicast packet from an endpoint connected to a VTEP is to be transported over VXLAN, specific outer header fields need to reflect the change from unicast to multicast forwarding. The change in the fields triggers the correct forwarding behavior in the underlay. With multicast, the outer DMAC as well as the outer destination IP is set to a multicast address. For Layer 2 multicast traffic, the multicast address is set to be that of the Layer 2 VXLAN VNI's mapped IP multicast group. The multicast outer DMAC uses the well-known multicast group MAC address derived from the outer IP destination multicast address. The multicast group information in the original payload (received from the endpoint) is placed in the inner MAC and IP header and becomes invisible to the underlay (see Figure 7-2).

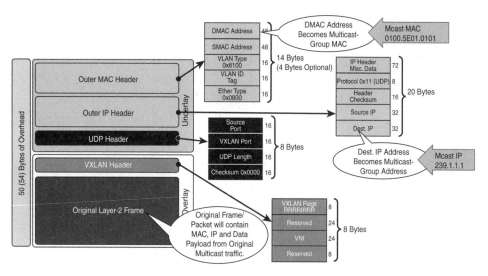

Figure 7-2 *Multicast-in-VXLAN*

In order to provide overlay multicast service, the same semantics as with classic Ethernet apply. In other words, Layer 2 multicast forwarding is dependent on the bridge domain's capability to forward multicast traffic. In a VXLAN network, multicast traffic starts from the classic Ethernet VLAN namespace and moves toward the VXLAN VNI namespace.

With the advent of VXLAN as a standard network virtualization overlay, most initial implementations supported Layer 2 multicast in VXLAN without IGMP snooping. In other words, IGMP snooping is disabled for VLANs that are extended over VXLAN; however, this is not specific to the VXLAN VNI. IGMP snooping is also disabled for the VLAN(s) where the endpoints are attached. As a result, Layer 2 multicast traffic in VXLAN is treated the same way as broadcast and unknown unicast traffic. In other words, Layer 2 multicast traffic is flooded across the network to wherever that Layer 2 VNI extends.

The local bridge domain is represented by a VLAN without IGMP snooping. Also, the corresponding VTEP on which the Layer 2 VNI is enabled is unconditionally part of the same flood tree as that associated with the multicast group. This common flood tree results in traffic being sent to all other VTEP(s) that are part of the same L2VNI or multicast group.

By consuming additional resources from the classic Ethernet segments, as well as from the VXLAN portion of the network, inefficiency exists because Layer 2 multicast traffic is seen everywhere; however, despite this inefficiency, the requirement to forward Layer 2 multicast within a VXLAN VNI is satisfied. With this forwarding approach, even endpoints that are not interested in a specific multicast stream, receive the traffic. This behavior is not specific to VXLAN Flood and Learn (F&L) environments but is also present in VXLAN BGP EVPN networks.

Because one of the primary goals of BGP EVPN was to provide efficient unicast forwarding and flooding reduction, forwarding Layer 2 multicast traffic in an efficient manner became necessary. As a result, enhancements to IGMP snooping for VXLAN were required. Before detailing these enhancements, we provide a look at how multicast without IGMP snooping works in a VXLAN BGP EVPN network.

IGMP in VXLAN BGP EVPN Networks

Figure 7-3 shows a sample network with three VTEPs, each configured with VNI 30001, that is mapped to multicast group 239.1.1.1.

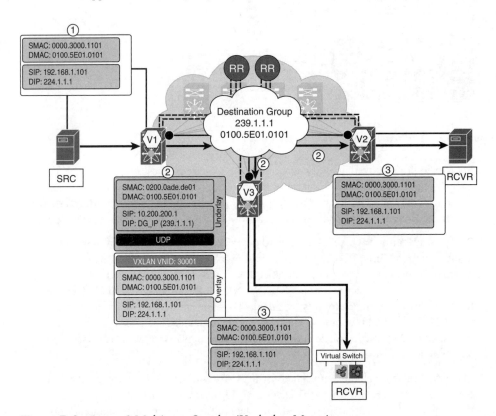

Figure 7-3 *Layer 2 Multicast: Overlay/Underlay Mapping*

Consequently, the three VTEPs V1, V2, V3 join the corresponding multicast tree in the underlay. The steps labeled 1, 2, 3, in the figure highlight the salient packet fields as the multicast traffic is forwarded from the source attached to VTEP V1 to receivers attached to

VTEPs V2 and V3 respectively. Here, we specifically concentrate on how multicast traffic is forwarded between VTEPs V1 and V2, in the example topology depicted in Figure 7-4. Multicast Source A provides a multicast stream destined to the group 224.1.1.1. Endpoints in the same bridge domain (10) as Source A unconditionally receive the multicast stream, regardless of their interest. This occurs because IGMP snooping is disabled in that bridge domain. Because bridge domain 10 is extended across VXLAN VNI 30001, packets that are sent to the multicast group 224.1.1.1 are also encapsulated across the VXLAN fabric. This occurs because all the VTEPs that are members of the L2VNI 30001 are configured with the same mapping between L2VNI to underlay multicast group 239.1.1.1. The same behavior that is seen in the local VLAN segment (BD 10) for traffic destined to multicast group 224.1.1.1 is also seen by all remote bridge domains that are mapped to the VXLAN VNI 30001. This occurs even if no interested receivers are present for the multicast traffic.

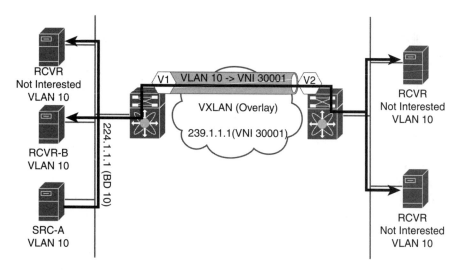

Figure 7-4 *Layer 2 Multicast (No IGMP)*

Having IGMP snooping enabled for both local and remote LAN segments (and coexisting with VXLAN) optimizes multicast traffic forwarding. As a result, endpoints that are not interested in the multicast traffic or that failed to send an IGMP join message for a particular multicast stream do not get the traffic. IGMP snooping enhancements on the Cisco Nexus platforms allow differentiation of the logical VTEP interface on a per-VNI basis. With "standard" IGMP snooping enabled, the VTEP interface is unconditionally added as an outgoing interface (OIF) for multicast traffic. In other words, even if no interested receiver(s) behind a remote LAN segment are present, the traffic is still forwarded across the VXLAN network and then dropped. This is true for all edge devices that have a VTEP responsible for a given L2VNI.

With IGMP snooping enabled in the local and remote LAN segments, the data provided by multicast Source A with group of 224.1.1.1 is seen only if the endpoint-connected interface is added based on IGMP signaling (see Figure 7-5). Endpoints in the same bridge domain (10) as Source A receive the multicast stream only if the interested receiver signals that interest through IGMP reports (IGMP join). As before, packets that are sent to the multicast group 224.1.1.1 are also forwarded across the VXLAN fabric because bridge domain 10 is extended across VXLAN with VNI 30001.

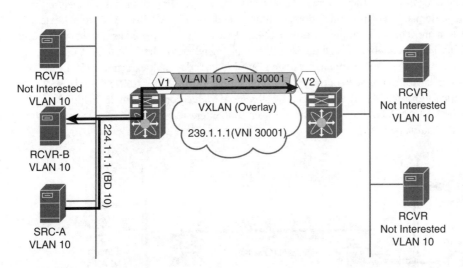

Figure 7-5 *Layer 2 Multicast with IGMP Snooping (Classic Ethernet Only)*

To reiterate, VTEP V1 is unconditionally added to the multicast outgoing interface list for group 224.1.1.1 for VNI 30001 even if there are no interested receivers behind the remote VTEPs (in this case VTEP V2). The behavior seen at the local LAN segment (BD 10) at VTEP V1 for multicast group 224.1.1.1 is also seen by all remote VTEPs participating in VXLAN VNI 30001. This occurs because only endpoint-connected interfaces on which IGMP join reports are received, get the multicast stream destined to 224.1.1.1.

Even with the enhancements of IGMP snooping enabled on the classic Ethernet segment side, traffic is still flooded unconditionally across the VXLAN network as long as remote VTEPs have membership in a given VNI. Additional enhancements have been added to control the addition of the VTEP interfaces on a per-VNI basis. These enhancements prevent the unnecessary flooding of multicast data traffic across the VXLAN fabric. Notably, IGMP member reports are still flooded as control packets across the VXLAN network. This flooding triggers the addition of the VTEP interface to the outgoing interface list for Layer 2 multicast traffic forwarding.

With IGMP snooping-enabled LAN segments, the conditional addition of the VTEP interface to the multicast outgoing interface list for a given VNI and overlay multicast group is achieved via the configuration **ip igmp snooping disable-nve-static-router-port** under the bridge domain. As shown in Figure 7-6, multicast data traffic from source A to group 224.1.1.1 is not sent over VXLAN to VTEP V2 because no interested receivers behind VTEP V2 exist. As in the previous example, VNI 30001 extends across both VTEPs V1 and V2. Multicast traffic is forwarded only to interested receivers behind VTEP V1 based on IGMP join reports (specifically receiver B).

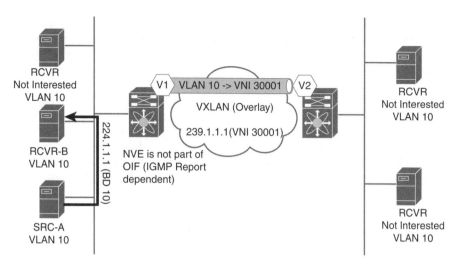

Figure 7-6 *Layer 2 Multicast with IGMP Snooping Enhancements for VXLAN with no remote interested receivers*

If receiver D behind VTEP V2, which is part of VNI 30001 (see Figure 7-7), sends out an IGMP join message for multicast group 224.1.1.1, the IGMP join message is received by VTEP V2 and forwarded to VTEP V1 over the overlay. This triggers the addition of VTEP V1 to the multicast outgoing interface list for VNI 30001 and the multicast group 224.1.1.1. The control for forwarding traffic in multicast group 224.1.1.1 occurs at the ingress VTEP V1, which is closest to the source. In this way, every remote VTEP serving VNI 30001 receives the multicast traffic once a receiver on any remote VTEP has sent an IGMP join message across the VXLAN fabric. This behavior occurs because of the mapping between the Layer 2 VNI (L2VNI) and the underlay multicast group. The same behavior occurs even if ingress replication is used for forwarding multidestination traffic in the underlay.

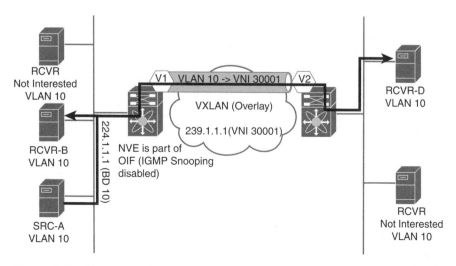

Figure 7-7 *Layer 2 Multicast with IGMP Snooping Enhancements for VXLAN with at least one remote interested receiver*

As in classic Ethernet IGMP snooping, only interested receivers see the multicast data traffic, even if the VTEP receives it. Multicast copies are forwarded toward the endpoint-connected interfaces only if an interested receiver is present because of standard IGMP snooping behavior.

Note: IGMP snooping enhancements for VXLAN are available on Cisco Nexus 7000/7700 switches with the F3 linecard module starting with NX-OS version 7.2.[1] These enhancements are also supported on Cisco Nexus 9000 switches starting with NX-OS version 7.0(3)I5(1).[2] In the future, other Cisco Nexus platforms will inherit similar functions. Please consult the Cisco NX-OS software release notes for the current status.

Layer 2 Multicast Forwarding in vPC

With the introduction of vPC with VXLAN and the anycast VTEP concept, there's a need to elect roles for encapsulation and descapsulation in a vPC domain. If the election is not maintained correctly, multicast traffic is duplicated and has a negative impact on the network.

With vPC, one of the two peers that are part of the vPC domain is elected as the designated forwarder (DF) or encapper/decapper. The DF is responsible for VXLAN encapsulation and forwarding of the encapsulated traffic over the underlay. As described previously for multidestination traffic, the outer destination IP address is set to that of the multicast group associated with the corresponding L2VNI. Typically, the DF and encapsulating node also combine the decapsulating node function for the vPC domain (see Figure 7-8), although this is not mandatory. For example, with Cisco Nexus 9000 switches, the decapsulating node is elected to be the one of the two vPC peers that offers the least cost to the rendezvous point (RP). When the cost for each vPC peer is the same, the vPC primary node is elected as the decapsulating node.

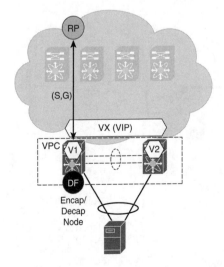

Figure 7-8 *vPC Designated Forwarder*

In the DF election process in a vPC domain, both vPC members send a PIM join message (null registration) toward the RP, as shown in Figure 7-9. The PIM join message is sourced from the anycast VTEP IP address shared by both vPC member nodes (secondary IP address on the VTEP). The RP responds with a PIM join message, which is forwarded toward the anycast VTEP IP address. Only one PIM join message is sent by the RP, and the respective PIM join message is hashed toward one of the two vPC peers participating in the vPC domain.

The vPC peer that has the (S,G) entry toward the RP becomes the DF; the source (S) is the anycast VTEP IP address, and the group (G) is the multicast group assigned to the VNI. In practical deployments with BGP VXLAN EVPN fabrics that have PIM ASM employed in the underlay, anycast RP is employed both for redundancy and load balancing. The DF election procedure previously described remains the same because both vPC peers source a PIM join message toward the anycast RP. This, in turn, goes to one of the RPs.

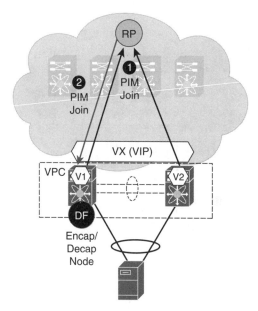

Figure 7-9   *vPC Designated Forwarder Election*

The next example involves a scenario where a Layer 2 multicast stream is sent from a remote source to a dual-homed receiver behind a vPC domain and is destined to group 224.1.1.1 (see Figure 7-10). Specifically, VTEP V3 sees Layer 2 multicast traffic from the directly attached multicast source (SRC). If IGMP snooping is enabled, and the VTEP is not unconditionally forwarding multicast traffic with the **ip igmp snooping disable-nve-static-router-port** command, multicast traffic is seen only between the source (SRC) and the edge device (V3).

Once the dual-homed receiver (RCVR) behind anycast VTEP VX becomes interested in multicast group 224.1.1.1, an IGMP join message is sent. The IGMP join message is flooded across the VXLAN network and reaches VTEP V3. Consequently, VTEP V3 in VNI 30001 is added to the outgoing interface list for the Layer 2 multicast entry associated with group 224.1.1.1.

The multicast receiver (RCVR) is within the vPC domain and is represented by the anycast VTEP IP address. Multicast data traffic destined to group 224.1.1.1 reaches the DF (assuming that it is the decapsulation node as well) in the vPC domain. After decapsulation, the Layer 2 multicast traffic is forwarded toward the receiver (RCVR) on the locally attached classic Ethernet interface. Notably, the regular PIM operation of transitioning from a (*,G) to a (S,G) tree stills occur. The details regarding this transition are not described in detail and follow the well known transition from (*, G) to (S,G). Figure 7-10 shows the packet fields of interest for the multicast traffic flow forwarded from multicast SRC attached to VTEP V3 to the dual-homed receiver RCVR attached to anycast VTEP VX, over VXLAN in VNI 30001.

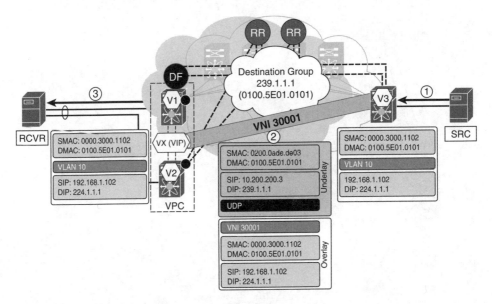

Figure 7-10   *Layer 2 Multicast with vPC*

Not all endpoints in a vPC domain are dual attached, that is, attached to both of the vPC peers. Some endpoints may be attached to only one of the two vPC peers, and these are typically called *orphan endpoints* or *orphans*. Even when multicast receivers are attached to orphan ports or become singly attached (when one vPC leg goes down), multicast traffic must be forwarded appropriately to these receivers. Because only one of the two vPC peers in a vPC domain is responsible for decapsulation, traffic may need to traverse the vPC peer link in order to reach an orphan endpoint attached to the adjacent peer after decapsulation.

Figure 7-11 illustrates how Layer 2 multicast traffic is sent and received from an orphan endpoint behind a vPC domain. As before, VTEPs V1 and V2 form a vPC pair where

VTEP V1 is elected to be the DF responsible for both encapsulation and decapsulation of multicast traffic for the given vPC domain. The orphan endpoint sends multicast (or any BUM traffic) within its local LAN segment. The edge device, vPC member node V2, receives the traffic and evaluates the forwarding decision. Because V2 is not the DF for the vPC domain, the multicast traffic is forwarded across the vPC peer link to VTEP V1. Once the multicast traffic is received at VTEP V1 (DF), the data traffic is encapsulated and forwarded toward the VXLAN network. This procedure remains the same if the underlay transport for forwarding multidestination traffic uses either multicast or ingress replication.

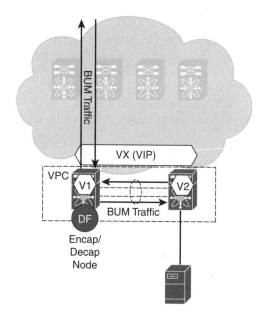

Figure 7-11 *vPC Layer 2 Multicast with an Orphan Endpoint*

The same behavior occurs in the reverse direction when a remote VTEP (not shown in Figure 7-11) wants to send multicast traffic toward the orphan endpoint connected to VTEP V2. Because VTEP V1 is responsible for decapsulating the VXLAN-encapsulated multidestination traffic for the vPC domain, decapsulated traffic is sent to the orphan endpoint across the vPC peer link connected to VTEP V2. Because VTEP V2 is not the DF, traffic is not sent toward the VXLAN core but forwarded only toward the classic Ethernet interfaces attached to orphan endpoints.

All the explanation thus far has assumed that PIM ASM is employed in the VXLAN underlay when using multicast for forwarding multidestination traffic. While conceptually only one of the two nodes should be responsible for encapsulation and decapsulation with vPC to avoid duplication, the exact mechanism employed may vary slightly when PIM BiDir is employed in the underlay. The main difference with PIM BiDir is the presence of (*,G) entries instead of (S,G) entries for forwarding multidestination traffic in the underlay.

Layer 3 Multicast Forwarding

When providing Layer 3 multicast services in the overlay, also known as *routed multicast*, extending a bridge domain over VXLAN is insufficient. A control plane protocol is required to advertise information of multicast sources and receivers existing in different IP subnets thereby facilitating appropriate forwarding of routed IP multicast traffic. In F&L deployments, VXLAN VNIs provide similar Layer 2 semantics as classic Ethernet VLANs. For forwarding routed multicast traffic in VXLAN F&L environments, per-tenant PIM peering is established, much as unicast routing is used with VRF Lite. However, this per-tenant multicast peering is extremely inefficient in regard to the configuration as well as the state that must be maintained.

This section discusses the integrated approach for Layer 3 overlay multicast with regard to VXLAN BGP EVPN. While the Layer 3 overlay multicast forwarding feature (*tenant-routed multicast*) is due to be released on Cisco Nexus switches in the middle of 2017, the goal here is to provide guidance for current solutions as well as look at how it will be integrated in upcoming releases. Several IETF draft proposals exist for handling Layer 3 multicast traffic in VXLAN BGP EVPN networks,[3] and one of the proposals will eventually emerge as the *de facto* standard.

When tenant-routed multicast support is required, VXLAN BGP EVPN provides a centralized design that leverages external PIM routers attached to the VXLAN network (see Figure 7-12). The VXLAN header is removed before the multicast traffic is forwarded toward the external PIM routers. This approach allows the Layer 2 multicast in a given bridge domain to be extended from the local classic Ethernet VLAN segment, across the VXLAN VNI segment, and to the externally attached PIM routers. The external PIM routers are required to participate in the multicast bridge domain.

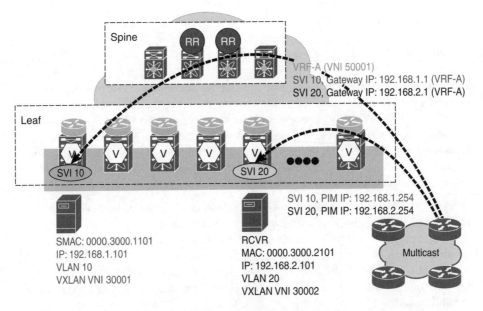

Figure 7-12 *Layer 3 Multicast (Centralized)*

In order to provide multicast routing between the bridge domain and the respective IP subnets, a PIM router must be enabled in all the bridge domains that require multicast routing. The IP address on the PIM-enabled interface on the external PIM router does not need to be that of the default gateway of the associated IP subnet. This allows the VXLAN BGP EVPN fabric to continue provide the support for the distributed IP anycast gateway.

Only the multicast-designated router port is presented through the external router with the IP PIM interface. The external PIM routers can peer with other multicast routers, as is the case currently with traditional networks where multicast routing is enabled. Notably, in order to be able to pass multicast reverse path forwarding (RPF), the external PIM routers need to know about source IP addresses associated with the multicast sources. Appropriate route peering from the VXLAN EVPN fabric to the external PIM routers can advertise all the source information. At the PIM routers, the source address will be found in the RIB, and the outgoing interface is determined. If the outgoing interface found in the RIB is the same as the interface the multicast packet was received on, the packet passes the RPF check. Multicast packets that fail the RPF check are dropped because the incoming interface is not on the shortest path back to the source. This behavior on the PIM routers is the same as what exists in traditional networks today.

With this centralized approach, dedicated external PIM routers are required for supporting Layer 3 IP multicast services in the VXLAN overlay network. Enhancements to integrate the external router into a pair of edge devices or VTEPs native to the VXLAN network are present.

In the future, a more distributed multicast forwarding approach will be available as standards and implementations evolve. These standards are determining the functional attributes required, such as a fully distributed multicast router at the distributed IP anycast gateway, as well as the associated integration required with the BGP EVPN control protocol (see Figure 7-13).

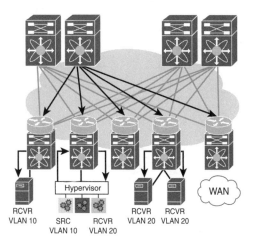

Figure 7-13 *Distributed Layer 3 Multicast (Tenant-Routed Multicast)*

Additional enhancements that will require only a single copy of the multicast traffic in the VXLAN core with multistage replication are also under consideration. Finally, structured handoff approaches to external networks with PIM, LISP, and/or MVPN are additional options being considered with such a design. With the availability of a true Layer 3 multicast approach where each edge device with distributed anycast gateway will become a multicast router, the requirement for Layer 2 multicast can be reduced or completely eliminated.

Summary

This chapter provides details of forwarding multicast data traffic in a VXLAN BGP EVPN network. It discusses vanilla Layer 2 multicast traffic forwarding over VXLAN as well as its evolution, with enhancements in IGMP snooping. Special considerations are also presented for dual-homed and orphan multicast endpoints behind a vPC domain. The chapter concludes with a discussion of the current and future support of overlay Layer 3 multicast traffic in VXLAN BGP EVPN networks.

References

1. Nexus 7000 reference http://www.cisco.com/c/en/us/td/docs/switches/ datacenter/sw/7_x/nx-os/release/notes/72_nx-os_release_note.html.

2. Nexus 9000 reference http://www.cisco.com/c/en/us/td/docs/switches/ datacenter/nexus9000/sw/7-x/release/notes/70351_nxos_rn.html.

3. Internet Engineering Task Force (IETF). *IGMP and MLD proxy for EVPN.* 2015. tools.ietf.org/html/draft-sajassi-bess-evpn-igmp-mld-proxy.

## Chapter 8

External Connectivity

In this chapter, the following topics will be covered:

- Border node connectivity options in a VXLAN BGP EVPN network

- External Layer 3 connectivity options using VRF Lite, LISP, and MPLS L3VPN

- External Layer 2 connectivity options with virtual PortChannel (vPC)

- VRF routing leaking using downstream VNI assignment

Data centers host data and applications for users, where the users are typically external to the data center. This chapter focuses on the design options for external connectivity. It describes different placement options for external connectivity as well as various interconnectivity options. This chapter includes a discussion of Layer 3 connectivity options, including VRF Lite, LISP, and MPLS integration, as well as Layer 2 connectivity options. For the applications that do not support IP and communicate via Layer 2, this chapter covers a couple of design recommendations, including the use of single-homed as well as dual-homed (vPC) classic Ethernet options.

External Connectivity Placement

When discussing external connectivity in a spine–leaf topology, the external interconnection point is called the *border node* (see Figure 8-1). The border node can provide external connectivity for both Layer 2 and Layer 3 traffic to the VXLAN BGP EVPN–based spine–leaf topology or network fabric. The border node itself is a VXLAN edge device that hosts the VTEP to encapsulate and decapsulate external VXLAN traffic originating from or destined to endpoints below edge devices in the data center fabric.

The border node is a fully functioning edge device in the network fabric with a different focus than other edge devices. The generic edge device with a leaf role provides connectivity to endpoints and the first-hop routing service. The border node, on the other hand, is a transit node. The border node is responsible for forwarding north–south traffic—that is, traffic destined from within the data center to outside or vice versa.

Recall that this is different from east–west traffic, which is server-to-server traffic within the data center that is optimally forwarded between leaf switches and doesn't traverse the border node. East–west traffic flows in a VXLAN BGP EVPN network are covered in detail in Chapter 6, "Unicast Forwarding"; the focus of this chapter is north–south traffic flows.

A main difference between a border node and a generic leaf is that the border node does not typically have any directly attached endpoints. Separating roles simplifies operations, thereby preventing overload of too many functions on a set of special-purpose edge devices, namely the border nodes.

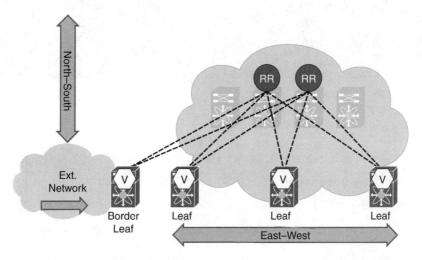

Figure 8-1 *The Border Node*

In order to make the decision on the proper border node placement, it is important to understand the placement options available in a spine–leaf topology. The two options available are the *border spine* and the *border leaf* (see Figure 8-2). Several considerations are critical in selecting the right border node location for the services required in a VXLAN BGP EVPN–based network fabric.

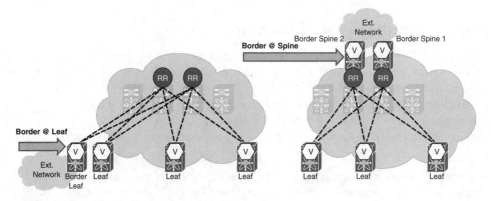

Figure 8-2 *Border Node Placement*

Placing the border node at the spine provides efficiency with respect to the north–south traffic flows (see Figure 8-3). With the border node placed at the spine, all traffic from the endpoints attached to the leaf is one hop away when destined to reach the external networks outside the fabric. Note that this is different from the typical east–west traffic flows, which go from leaf (source) to spine to leaf (destination). The placement of the border node at the spine is common for situations when most of the traffic flows in the data center fabric are north–south.

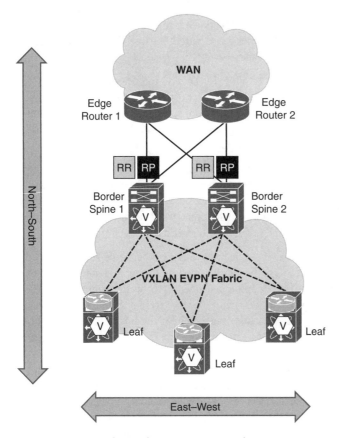

Figure 8-3   *Border node at Spine or Border Spine*

Whenever the spine and border node placement is combined, the transport for both north–south and east–west traffic is combined as well. In addition to the traffic flows, the border spine becomes a VXLAN edge device configured as a VTEP that encapsulates and decapsulates VXLAN traffic for north–south flows. Recall that for east–west flows, the spine continues to provide underlay functionality by routing traffic between the edge devices based on the outer IP header.

Having a VTEP configured on the border spine is not an issue. The VTEP is specifically called out as capacity planning needs must be considered to accommodate all the north–south and east–west traffic flows. A major benefit of the spine–leaf architecture and function separation is the allowance for a scale-out approach where additional spines can be added to provide more bandwidth and resiliency.

Scaling the spine with the border node also requires increasing the external connectivity interfaces and adjacencies to provide the ability to have consistent reachability information for all available network paths. For the applications requiring Layer 2 external connectivity, additional considerations need to be taken into account with the border spine, specifically when more than two spines are required because the spines need to be deployed in pairs, with Layer 2 redundancy.

The pair deployment recommendation is to allow for Layer 2 multihoming with vPC. Instead of creating multiple vPC pairs at the spine layer for Layer 2 connectivity, one spine pair could be configured for Layer 2 external connectivity, which would yield uniform reachability for Layer 2 traffic. Alternatively, external Layer 2 connectivity could be built redundantly in pairs (dual homing with vPC).

Additional services can also be enabled on the border spines. The spine typically hosts the BGP route reflector (RR) as well as the multicast rendezvous point (RP). These additional functions need to be considered for the border spine. In summary, the border spine provides external connectivity, VTEP support, RR support, RP support, and the baseline functionality to transport east–west and north–south traffic for the fabric.

The next option, as illustrated in Figure 8-4, is to have the border node functionality at a special leaf called the *border leaf*. The border leaf decouples north–south and east–west traffic flows. In the previous border spine placement, the border spine served as a transit node for leaf-to-leaf traffic (east–west) and for the external connectivity (north–south). With border node functionality placement at the border leaf, the role of the spine changes because it no longer performs any encapsulation or decapsulation for VXLAN traffic. In fact, a VTEP is not required on the spines in this scenario. The border leaf hosts a VTEP and is responsible for the encapsulation/decapsulation of traffic that provides external connectivity. In other words, the border leaf is responsible for all north–south traffic. This option reduces the requirement for capacity planning for the border leaf from an intra-DC perspective. Capacity planning is required only for the north–south traffic flows. An additional hop for north–south traffic with a border leaf deployment may be considered less than desirable. However, a clean separation is a major advantage of this deployment, and uniform reachability from the entire fabric is another benefit.

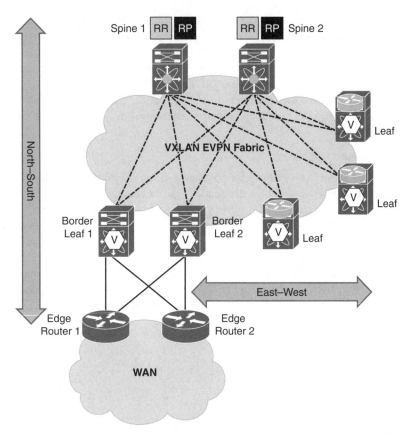

Figure 8-4 *Border node at Leaf or Border Leaf*

For applications that require Layer 2 connectivity and dual-homing with vPC, the same considerations as discussed in the case of the border spine are important. The reduced amount of functionality on the border leaf compared to the border spine simplifies the design and reflects a key difference. At worst, using the border leaf design has the same effect as scaling out the border spine design. However, the border leaf is less likely to host the BGP RR or multicast RP because this would be inefficient in a spine–leaf topology, where the spine is clearly a much better option for the RR and RP placement.

In summary, the border leaf topology provides specific functions such as external connectivity, and VTEP support for north–south traffic flows for a fabric at a single location.

External Layer 3 Connectivity

With placement of external connectivity at the border spine or border leaf, the connection of the VXLAN BGP EVPN fabric to the external network can be considered. External networks could involve the Internet, WAN, branch, other data centers, or the campus network. All these external networks require a common set of protocols for communication.

The following sections look at popular Layer 3 handoff options from a VXLAN BGP EVPN fabric. Note that a *handoff* causes the VXLAN encapsulation to be terminated at the border node, and then an appropriate translation occurs to carry the traffic externally while still retaining the context of the unique VRF or tenant that originated that traffic. Various handoff options are possible, including VRF Lite, LISP, and MPLS L3VPN. Before diving into the handoff options, a brief introduction of the different physical connectivity choices between the border and the external network will be discussed.

U-Shaped and Full-Mesh Models

This section describes the primary options for physically wiring the border nodes to the external networks. Regardless of the external connectivity placement—at the border leaf or border spine—two major wiring or connectivity models are available for redundant border nodes. The most common and recommended model is the full-mesh connectivity model. In this approach, each of the border nodes is connected to each of the edge routers (see Figure 8-5). For example, with two border nodes and two edge routers, four links are used to build a highly resilient external connectivity deployment. When using a full-mesh connectivity model, links between the border nodes are not required. The full-mesh connectivity model provides any-to-any connectivity, and thus the exchange of the routing information is synchronized.

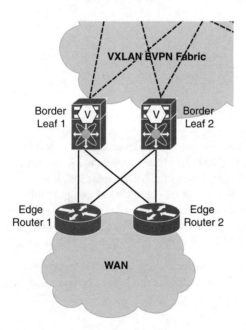

Figure 8-5 *Full-Mesh Border Nodes*

From a routing perspective, full-mesh connectivity appears a bit messy, but this model is the easiest and most resilient option. Notably, the full-mesh model does not require any additional synchronization between the border nodes. Likewise, a big advantage of the full-mesh model is that black-holing of traffic is impossible in the event of a single link failure. Only when all the links on one border node are lost, is 50% of the traffic potentially black-holed.

An alternative to the full-mesh model for connecting the border nodes to the edge routers is the U-shaped model (see Figure 8-6). This is a more resilient evolution of the straight-through model. The straight-through model is commonly seen when a single border node is connected to one edge router, and it is a nonredundant way of connecting the fabric to external networks. It is therefore generally not recommended.

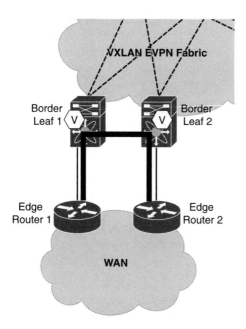

Figure 8-6   *U-Shaped Border Nodes*

With the U-shaped model, two border nodes and two edge devices are connected using the straight-through connectivity model. If a single link or node fails, 50% of the traffic will potentially be black-holed. To prevent this black-holing of traffic, a cross-link between the border nodes is required and recommended. The route peering session is established between the border nodes over this cross-link, which provides a redirection path in case the straight-through uplink between border node and edge router fails. The cross-link provides an additional network traffic path, without the need for a full-mesh wiring model. The cross-link makes the straight-through connection between border nodes and edge routers look like a "U"—hence the name *U-shaped model*. Conditional advertisement is not needed in the U-shaped model. Traffic from inside the VXLAN BGP

EVPN fabric can still reach both border nodes and can then be forwarded outside the fabric either directly or via the additional cross-link for external connectivity.

The full-mesh and U-shaped models both provide the necessary resiliency for external connectivity. While the full-mesh model provides extensive redundancy in most failure scenarios, the U-shaped provides just enough redundancy to avoid traffic black-holing in basic situations. Both models are widely adopted and deployed in the field. In summary, the full-mesh connectivity model is superior and the most optimal traffic-forwarding model in the event of failure scenarios.

VRF Lite/Inter-AS Option A

The BGP EVPN control plane integrates Layer 3 multitenancy. MP-BGP has capabilities to transport information for multiple virtual routing and forwarding (VRF) instances across the VXLAN network on a single BGP session. Different options are available to carry VRF or VPN information from VPN-based address family (L2VPN EVPN) networks to non-EVPN networks. The simplest option is to use VRF Lite or Inter-AS Option A.[1]

With VRF Lite, the border node has all VRF instances and sends the associated Layer 3 prefix information from the EVPN network into individual VRF-specific routing tables toward the edge router. The routing information can be exchanged with the external router via an appropriate routing protocol (control plane).

In addition to static route support on a per-VRF basis, dynamic routing protocols also have per-VRF isolation. This results in a routing protocol on a per-VRF basis. The routing protocol has its own routing instance and address family support, and it can be used to create individual route peering sessions to the external router. While this is the simplest of the Inter-AS options, it is also the least scalable as it requires a Layer 3 interface and a peering session on a per-VRF basis.

Several routing protocol options are available. Because the fabric already implements BGP, reusing the same routing protocol (eBGP) provides benefits, such as the presence of embedded advertisements that do not require any explicit protocol redistribution. BGP provides clear separation of autonomous systems, and this enables a structured handoff between the VXLAN BGP EVPN fabric and the external routing domain, be it WAN, campus, or other external networks. BGP also provides an option to configure an extensive set of routing policies that can manipulate received or announced network reachability information. A network administrator therefore has the option to create custom routing policies suited to particular domains. Enforcement of the routing policies can be configured on a per-neighbor basis since each neighbor will be associated with a specific autonomous system number (ASN).

While BGP is certainly a good choice for external connectivity, other dynamic routing protocols, such as OSPF, EIGRP, IS-IS, and simple static routing work as well.

Because none of these protocols have a direct interaction with the intra-fabric overlay control protocol (BGP), redistribution must be configured in order to have the proper IP prefix information exchange.

Each dynamic routing protocol has individual needs and requirements for how reachability information is redistributed from the external world into the VXLAN BGP EVPN–based network and vice versa. For example, when redistributing IP prefix information between IGPs (that is, OSPF to EIGRP), the process of redistribution is very different when compared with the redistribution from iBGP to other IGPs. Because all iBGP routes are tagged as internal routes by default, they are not advertised to IGPs.

Redistributing all iBGP IP prefix information into IS-IS, OSPF, or EIGRP requires additional configuration. Specific to NX-OS, a route map is required to match the iBGP internal routes. Example 8-1 demonstrates how iBGP routes can be redistributed into an IGP such as OSPF. Note that this only redistributes routes originated in BGP; routes redistributed into BGP from another routing protocol are not in turn redistributed.

Example 8-1 *Advertise iBGP Routes to OSPF*

```
route-map RM_iBGP_ALLOW permit 10
  match route-type internal

router ospf EXTERNAL
  vrf VRF-A
     redistribute bgp 65001 route-map RM_iBGP_ALLOW
```

When iBGP IP prefixes are advertised into the external network via an appropriate routing protocol, additional considerations apply with regard to summarizing the entire internal IP prefix space. Coverage of host routes (/32 or /128) needs to be available for the external network either by summary routes and specific routes, summary routes only, or an overarching supernet summary route. In addition to BGP, IGP routing protocols also have filtering capabilities. Appropriate route filtering options should be considered when external connectivity is required.

In addition to having the routing protocols to exchange the VRF information with external networks, and thus having the ability to provide control plane separation, the data plane also needs to keep the different VRF data traffic separated and isolated when leaving the border node. When using a single physical link between the border node and the external router, per-VRF segregation can be achieved using IEEE 802.1Q tags, with a unique tag allocated per VRF, as shown in Figure 8-7. Recall that with a 12-bit VLAN field, a maximum of 4K tags can be allocated on a per-physical interface basis. Leveraging individual VLAN tags for the individual VRFs ensures that separation occurs not only at the control plane level but also at the data plane level. This provides the capability to transport VRF-specific traffic that is isolated from the other traffic.

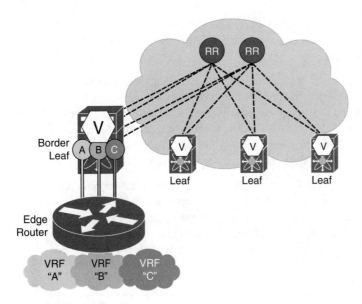

Figure 8-7 *VRF Lite*

Two methods are available for implementing VRF Lite between the border node and the external router. The first method is to configure Layer 3 VLAN interfaces (switch virtual interfaces [SVI]), and the second method is to configure subinterfaces on the physical routed interface.

The first method requires the physical interface to be configured as an IEEE 802.1Q (dot1q) trunk port. The SVI initiates the routing protocol peering on a per-VRF basis, and it also serves as the next hop for routing. Configuring a dot1q trunk between the border node and the external router allows the use of Layer 2 transport for Layer 3 routing and forwarding. This approach does not allow any Layer 2 control plane information exchange to occur between the two network domains of the border node and the external router.

The second option involves implementation of subinterfaces on the physical interface (**no switchport**) between the border node and the external router. Subinterfaces only require dot1q tagging for marking the traffic belonging to a specific VRF. Layer 2 capabilities are automatically disabled on the physical interface. The subinterface is used for the routing protocol peering as well as next-hop reachability. The subinterface has a direct interface-to-IP relationship, which results in additional signaling when the interface is brought down, thereby bringing down the routing protocol peering session and resulting in traffic converging onto an alternate path. In the SVI-based approach, the physical interface down detection needs to ensure that the SVI goes down as well, thereby bringing down the associated routing protocol peering session.

The subinterface signaling detection is a simple approach that implements Bidirectional Forwarding Detection (BFD). BFD also enhances the failover detection of routing protocols that are enabled on the corresponding routed interface (subinterface in this case).

If a requirement for external Layer 2 connectivity exists (for example, for Data Center Interconnect [DCI]) or for Layer 4 to 7 services, the connectivity can be combined with the VRF Lite/subinterface approach by using dedicated interfaces for the Layer 2 connectivity. The additional interfaces would operate in Layer 2–only mode and would be configured as a dot1q trunk port. For Layer 2 redundancy, it is recommended to use vPC. Example 8-2 demonstrates VRF Lite with BGP using subinterfaces.

Example 8-2   *VRF Lite with BGP Using Subinterfaces on the Border Node*

```
# Subinterface Configuration
interface Ethernet1/10
  no switchport
interface Ethernet1/10.1002
  mtu 9216
  encapsulation dot1q 1002
  vrf member VRF-B
  ip address 10.2.2.1/30
  no shutdown

# eBGP Configuration
router bgp 65501
  vrf VRF-B
    address-family ipv4 unicast
      advertise l2vpn evpn
      aggregate-address 192.168.0.0/16 summary-only
    neighbor 10.2.2.2 remote-as 65599
      update-source Ethernet1/10.1002
      address-family ipv4 unicast
```

Customers often ask for best-practice recommendations for VRF Lite–based external connectivity. The use of subinterfaces is recommended for Layer 3 connectivity and route peering, as shown in Example 8-2.

For the routing protocol, eBGP between the border node and external router is the recommended option. If a Layer 2 external connectivity requirement is present, implementing vPC for Layer 2 connectivity, multihoming, and high availability is recommended. Operationally and technically, pros and cons exist with the VRF-Lite option, depending on the environment as well as the trade-offs related to greenfield designs versus brownfield integration.

LISP

Similarly to VRF Lite, Locator/ID Separation Protocol (LISP) provides external connectivity, extending Layer 3 multitenancy from the VXLAN fabric to the rest of the enterprise. While VRF Lite and LISP both provide multitenancy, LISP exchanges reachability information and transports the multitenant traffic in a different way. The LISP data plane encapsulation is agnostic to the underlying network transport and therefore provides simplified operations over traditional Layer 2 requirements (for example, Ethernet, FabricPath) and label-switching technologies (such as MPLS).

In addition, the LISP architecture implements a pull-based approach to exchange reachability information, whereas traditional routing protocols use a push-based model. Before going into the details regarding LISP integration with the VXLAN BGP EVPN fabric, this section provides a brief introduction to LISP, with an emphasis on the different features of LISP that make it inherently scalable.

LISP is a next-generation routing architecture. It is based on a topology-independent addressing mechanism and an on-demand (pull-based) lookup approach for forwarding decisions. LISP also provides its own reachability protocol, based on a mapping database. In addition, LISP has its own data plane encapsulation. The LISP data plane encapsulation is very similar to the VXLAN data plane format (see Figure 8-8). The main difference between the LISP and VXLAN headers is that VXLAN is a MAC-in-IP/UDP encapsulation, while LISP is an IP-in-IP/UDP encapsulation.

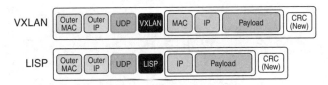

Figure 8-8   *VXLAN/LISP Encapsulation*

To provide the details on how LISP achieves the separation of location (locator) and endpoints (ID), a comparison to traditional routing protocols is a good first step; see Figure 8-9.

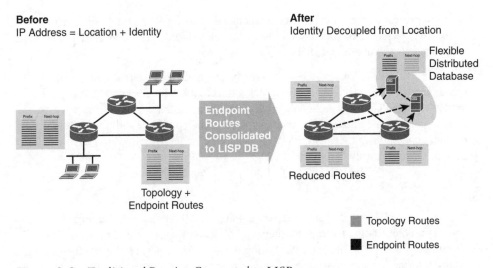

Figure 8-9   *Traditional Routing Compared to LISP*

With traditional routing protocols, the operating model is such that the endpoints are bound to a specific location. The approach in traditional routing protocols leverages hierarchical addressing, where the endpoint (Host IP address) is bound to the IP subnet. This naturally associates an endpoint to the location of the router where the IP subnet itself is configured or defined.

Traditionally, routing protocols were only required to work with IP subnet prefixes, while host IP addresses were summarized. As a result, the routing tables and the resource consumption in the forwarding tables of the routers were manageable. In addition, the mobility of endpoints was deployed at Layer 2, which means the location of the router hosting the IP subnet did not change.

Even the possibility of extracting a single endpoint address (/32 in IPv4 or /128 in IPv6) from the IP subnet from a new location presented challenges in scaling the routing entries for traditional routing protocols. Host-based routing became a requirement because deployments began moving toward a complete Layer 3 model. Advertising all host IP addresses over traditional routing protocols would result in an exhaustion of the hardware routing table resources.

With LISP, the identity of an endpoint is decoupled from its location, and the respective relation of these two attributes is stored in a mapping system. This way, the infrastructure responsible for providing reachability between the locations (routing locator [RLOC]) is kept very lean and scalable. Only the information of the topology is required because the endpoint information is imposed onto the LISP overlay.

Traditional routing protocols are optimized to provide the endpoint location within the RLOC space or topology. With the endpoint address information moved onto the overlay, any requirement for RLOC space to know this information is eliminated. As a result, a level of abstraction is achieved. With this abstraction, the ingress LISP tunnel router (iTR) queries the LISP mapping server that holds the respective information of the endpoints (identity) and their respective RLOCs (location). Based on the lookup result, the iTR adds the LISP header with the respective destination ID and RLOC.

Unaware of the endpoint information, the rest of the infrastructure simply forwards the LISP-encapsulated packet toward the destination RLOC. The packet is subsequently decapsulated and sent toward the destination endpoint. The same process happens on the egress tunnel router (eTR) for the return traffic.

The inherent pull-based or on-demand model of LISP has some advantages over the push-based model used by traditional routing protocols (see Figure 8-10).

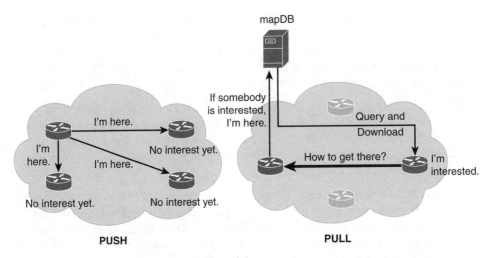

Figure 8-10 *Routing Push and Pull Models*

With traditional routing protocols, whenever information is learned on a router for a given routing domain, the respective information is immediately sent to all other routers participating in that routing domain. Even if interest in a given route at that time is not present, the routers still receive this information, process it, and install it in the hardware tables if local policy specifies a permit action. This consumes CPU and memory resources for routing path computation, storage space in the routing information base (RIB), and costly ternary content addressable memory (TCAM) as well as forwarding information base (FIB) resources.

The large table state in both the RIB and FIB has direct implications on scalability and convergence times. LISP introduces a different behavior that is more graceful to computation and resource usage/consumption. When a new IP subnet or endpoint is learned, the directly associated LISP tunnel router populates this information to the LISP mapping system. Only the router responsible for the origin of the information and the LISP mapper are involved.

If communication between two endpoints is initiated, as mentioned earlier, only the source of the communication (the iTR) consults the LISP mapper to download the required routing information on demand. The lookup provides the location of the egress tunnel router (eTR), which contains the RLOC's IP address.

Only the iTR and eTR are involved in the routing operation. Route demand (pull) and path computation operations only happen between the iTR and eTR. As a result, CPU and memory consumption only occurs on the communicating nodes. In addition, the resource consumption in TCAM and FIB is localized to the participating nodes, resulting in more efficient use of hardware resources in the overall view of the routing domain.

To summarize, the IP addresses in the routing tables with LISP only have the location information (RLOC), and the identities (EID) stored in the mapping system. In case of endpoint mobility, the identity is mapped to a new location in the LISP overlay only.

The identity and location are only known in the LISP mapping system and by the ingress and egress LISP tunnel routers participating in the conversation (forwarding).

LISP provides many capabilities, benefits, and options for network overlay approaches, including mobility, scalability, security, and support options for DCI. As a result, LISP provides significant advantages compared to other overlay approaches.

Looking specifically at the mobility use case, LISP provides IP prefix address family portability for both IPv4 and IPv6. Its on-demand (or pull approach) provides scalability so that the IP prefix portability can be specific to each endpoint. The combined LISP mobility and scalability features provide endpoint mobility, and only consume hardware resources for conversations that are required (on demand).

The security part of LISP is encompassed in a tenant ID (instance ID) for segmentation. This provides end-to-end Layer 3 multitenancy. The three elements of LISP (mobility, scalability, and security) enable data center interconnect use cases that support high-scale IP mobility in a secure way. When an endpoint (ID) is moved between data centers, the tenant isolation needs to remain intact, and traffic should be optimally forwarded to the proper destination (location) to which the endpoint (ID) has moved. The decoupling of the location and endpoint address spaces in LISP allows for ingress routing optimization, which is an inherent advantage for DCI use cases.

LISP is integrated with the VXLAN EVPN fabric, thereby providing the capability to exchange all the reachability information from the BGP EVPN control protocol into the LISP-based mapping database. With LISP integration, the border node provides the multi-encapsulation gateway function. A set of border nodes is implemented to route from a VXLAN BGP EVPN infrastructure to a LISP transport network.

In the integrated external connectivity approach, the border node also becomes the LISP tunnel router (xTR), as shown in Figure 8-11. This allows the combination of two different encapsulation and control plane protocols with a "single-box" solution instead of having a "two-box" solution approach, as in the VRF Lite use case.

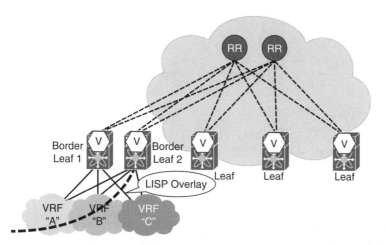

Figure 8-11 *LISP Border Node*

In addition to the single-box solution, LISP offers several advantages for external connectivity. One advantage involves the manner with which LISP installs reachability information into a network node (on-demand, or pull). With LISP, the need or requirement to hide the endpoints' IP information (/32 in IPv4 or /128 in IPv6) no longer exists. LISP also provides on-demand, or pull, semantics to accommodate the scale of the endpoint reachability information. This results in using fewer resources for all the participating network nodes.

Another advantage with LISP is that all the endpoint reachability information is registered with the LISP database. This allows for optimal ingress path selection without consuming expensive network hardware resources. Example 8-3 provides a snippet of a relevant LISP configuration on a border node in a VXLAN BGP EVPN fabric.

Example 8-3   *LISP Extension from VXLAN BGP EVPN*

```
# LISP Configuration
feature lisp

ip lisp itr-etr
ip lisp itr map-resolver
ip lisp etr map-server 10.8.12.9 key MY_MS_KEY

# VRF Configuration
vrf context VRF-A
  list instance-id 10
  ip lisp locator-vrf default
  lisp dynamic-eid MY_LISP_SUBNETS
    database-mapping 192.168.0.0/16 10.8.2.46 priority 1 weight 50
    register-route-notification tag 65501

# BGP Configuration
router bgp 65501
  vrf VRF-A
    address-family ipv4 unicast
      advertise l2vpn evpn
```

MPLS Layer 3 VPN (L3VPN)

Similarly to both VRF Lite and LISP, Multiprotocol Label Switching Layer 3 Virtual Private Network (MPLS L3VPN) provides external connectivity by keeping intact the Layer 3 multitenancy in the VXLAN EVPN network. Reachability information is exchanged in MPLS L3VPNs much the way it is in BGP EVPN—based on multiprotocol BGP.

MPLS L3VPN uses label switching in the data plane to separate the tenants on the wire using a VPN label in addition to a per-hop label. The difference between the VXLAN and MPLS implementations involves the use of the respective Network Layer Reachability

Information (NLRI), which is specific to the different address families. VXLAN EVPN uses the L2VPN EVPN address family, while MPLS L3VPN leverages the VPNv4 address family for IPv4 and the VPNv6 address family for IPv6.

VXLAN BGP EVPN–to–MPLS L3VPN internetworking enables an integrated approach to exchanging Layer 3 reachability information between the EVPN address family and the VPNv4/VPNv6 address family. This approach leverages the location of the border node to provide the multi-encapsulation gateway function. The MPLS L3VPN border nodes route from a VXLAN BGP EVPN infrastructure to a MPLS L3VPN–based transport network.

With this integrated external connectivity approach, the VXLAN BGP EVPN border node also becomes a MPLS L3VPN provider edge (PE), resulting in a role called a BorderPE (see Figure 8-12). This approach allows the combination of two different encapsulations and address families, using a "single-box" solution instead of a "two-box" approach/solution, as is used in traditional service provider CE–PE routing deployments.

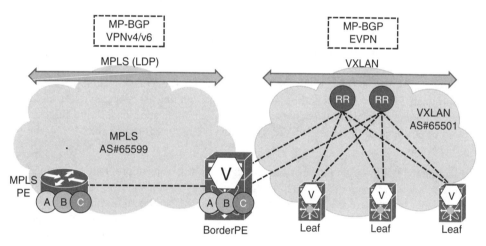

Figure 8-12   *Border Node with MPLS (BorderPE)*

The BorderPE at the edge of a VXLAN network performs the internetworking between the control and data planes to achieve separation and tenant isolation. The BorderPE model keeps iBGP within the VXLAN fabric, while the external peering with the MPLS PE occurs via eBGP. This results in the implementation of a different BGP autonomous system within the data center, thereby leveraging the existing WAN or DCI MPLS autonomous system configuration. This approach of Inter-AS allows eBGP to be used from the BorderPE by any other MPLS L3VPN PE or BGP route reflector.

The VXLAN BGP EVPN fabric announces Route type 5 for IP subnet prefixes and Route type 2 for host IP addresses (/32 in IPv4 or /128 in IPv6) from the respective VTEPs. The routing information is specific to each VRF or Layer 3 VNI from each leaf switch. The border node receives this information over EVPN and reoriginates it toward the L3VPN address families (VPNv4/VPNv6). This re-origination (see Figure 8-13) from EVPN to VPNv4/VPNv6 is achieved with a single command that imports the EVPN-related prefixes into the L3VPN format: **import l2vpn evpn reoriginate**.

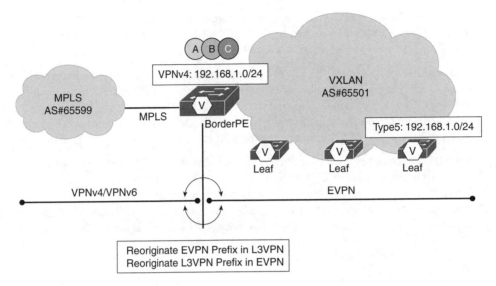

Figure 8-13 *BorderPE Reoriginate*

A similar approach exists in the reverse direction, where the VPNv*x*-related prefixes are re-originated into the EVPN address family (**import vpn unicast reoriginate**). In addition to the reoriginate-related BGP address family configuration, additional Route Targets need to be added to the extended VRFs to match those configured on the MPLS L3VPN side.

Aligning the Route Target information is straightforward, using appropriate import and export statements from the MPLS L3VPN autonomous system and using the EVPN autonomous system to drive label imposition. This is comparable to traditional implementations, where MPLS labels are driven through the MP-BGP control plane. In exactly the same way, the BorderPE performs integrations through control plane learning and the respective data plane actions. Example 8-4 provides a sample configuration of the relevant sections of a typical BorderPE node in a VXLAN BGP EVPN network.

Example 8-4 *MPLS Extension from VXLAN BGP EVPN*

```
# VRF Configuration
vrf context VRF-A
  vni 50001
  rd auto
  address-family ipv4 unicast
    route-target both 65599:50001
    route-target both auto
    route-target both auto evpn
```

```
# BGP Configuration
router bgp 65501
  neighbor 10.2.2.2 remote-as 65599
    update-source loopback254
    address-family vpnv4 unicast
      import l2vpn evpn reoriginate
  neighbor 10.10.10.201 remote-as 65501
    address-family l2vpn evpn
      import vpn unicast reoriginate
  vrf VRF-A
    address-family ipv4 unicast
      advertise l2vpn evpn

# Interface Configuration
interface ethernet 1/10
  ip address 10.2.2.1/30
  mpls ip
```

By announcing the host and subnet prefix information from EVPN toward L3VPN, it is always a best practice to summarize and/or filter unnecessary routing information. In the case of EVPN, this involves announcing the IP subnet routes and suppressing the host routes (/32 in IPv4 or /128 in IPv6).

Even with the end host route information being suppressed, silent host detection is supported in the EVPN network. External traffic reaching the border node hits the appropriate IP subnet route entry and is forwarded over ECMP to one of the leafs that serve that IP subnet. At that leaf, the subnet prefix route is also hit, but the result is a glean adjacency. An ARP/ND-triggered detection of the silent endpoint from this leaf occurs so that the endpoint is detected behind its directly attached leaf. Once this silent host is detected, the host route is advertised over EVPN to the border node, which can directly send traffic to the corresponding egress VTEP.

With the reorigination of the control protocol information and the related data plane actions, BorderPE provides an integrated MPLS L3VPN approach to a VXLAN BGP EVPN network. Simplified multitenancy transport can be achieved across a label switch transport for WAN connectivity or DCI.

External Layer 2 Connectivity

External connectivity is commonly achieved at Layer 3, and it has been the main focus so far in this chapter. Nevertheless, if certain bridging communication is required, structured communication at Layer 2 also becomes necessary. Common use cases that require Layer 2 connectivity between two data centers include non-IP communication and special application needs.

One of the most commonly seen requirements for external Layer 2 connectivity is related to endpoint mobility use cases. These use cases require specific signaling for move operations through the transport of Reverse ARP (RARP) messages. RARP inherently requires Layer 2 connectivity; RARP is a non-IP packet with Ethertype 0x8035.

Additional use cases arise when a spanning-tree-based classic Ethernet network needs to be integrated into a VXLAN BGP EVPN network. For these use cases, certain considerations need to be discussed for proper interconnectivity, integration, multihoming, and loop avoidance. It is also important to note that in a VXLAN BGP EVPN fabric, Layer 4 through 7 services (such as firewall, IDS/IPS, and load balancers) often require certain Layer 2 connectivity with classic Ethernet. These scenarios are described in greater detail in other chapters.

For all the cases mentioned, single-attached classic Ethernet connectivity is not desirable due to the lack of redundancy and fault tolerance. Consequently, for Layer 2 connectivity, dual-homing or multihoming technology needs to be implemented. With VXLAN BGP EVPN, dual-homing options are available with virtual PortChannel (vPC) and with the extension of the EVPN control protocol for multihoming support. This latter option occurs without the tight pairing of two network switches and also achieves more than dual homing. While vPC support with EVPN is available on all the Nexus platforms, checking the respective platform release notes to assess which platforms have EVPN multihoming support, is recommended.

Layer 2 connectivity at the border node (see Figure 8-14) is similar to the "two-box" approach with VRF Lite. The border node provides Layer 2 dual homing or multihoming toward the VXLAN BGP EVPN network as well as Layer 2 classic Ethernet services. The classic Ethernet services leverage IEEE 802.1Q capability used by any external connected service such as Layer 2 DCI, legacy spanning-tree-based networks, or Layer 4 through 7 services.

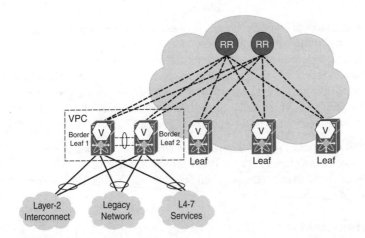

Figure 8-14 *Layer 2 Connectivity*

Classic Ethernet and vPC

Classic Ethernet and virtual PortChannel (vPC) implement the same configuration as with traditional endpoint-facing interfaces. With vPC, the participating vPC peer devices share a common virtual VTEP IP address termed as the anycast VTEP IP address. This allows both devices to handle the forwarding and receipt of Layer 2 traffic.

When vPC peers learn MAC address reachability information for endpoints via classic Ethernet, they propagate the information into the EVPN control protocol while associating that information with a VIP or anycast VTEP IP address as the respective next hop. Note that vPC is only responsible for synchronizing the Layer 2 information within its vPC domain. Therefore, when using vPC in conjunction with Layer 3, additional synchronization is required between the routing table and the vPC peers. Similarly, the host or endpoint IP addresses (IPv4 or IPv6) associated with the endpoint MAC address below a vPC pair are advertised over the Route type 2 with the anycast VTEP IP address as the respective next hop.

An alternative approach could be to specifically announce the IP subnet prefix information (Route type 5) with the individual border nodes' IP addresses (**advertise pip** option). It is important to keep routing and bridging information in sync between the vPC peers, especially when operating within a Layer 2 / Layer 3 border node construct. vPC and routing were discussed in earlier chapters, and STP-based classic Ethernet networks and their integration with the VXLAN BGP EVPN fabric, is the focus here.

VXLAN does not natively integrate with STP, and this results in a VXLAN-enabled bridge domain (VLAN/L2VNI) that is always in forwarding state. Because BPDUs are not transported over the point-to-multipoint VXLAN network, the southbound classic Ethernet connectivity is required to be loop-free.

If a classic Ethernet switch is connected downstream to two different VTEPs, the VLANs toward them are put in forwarding state. Since the BPDU exchange is not sent over the VXLAN encapsulation, the downstream classic Ethernet network is unaware of a redundant link, which results in a classic Layer 2 loop (see Figure 8-15).

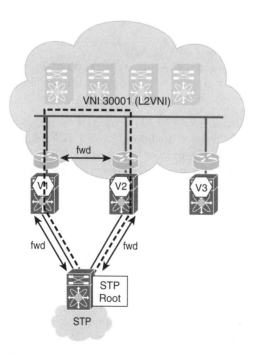

Figure 8-15 *Layer 2 Loop*

There are ways to block ports from a dual-connected classic Ethernet network towards VXLAN. However, the best practice for multihoming an STP-based classic Ethernet network to VXLAN is to implement vPC (see Figure 8-16).

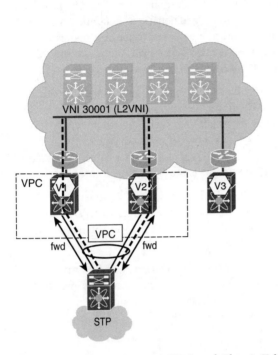

Figure 8-16 *VXLAN with VPC and Classic Ethernet*

Interconnecting classic Ethernet–based networks and VXLAN-based networks while leveraging vPC enables the implementation of a logical loop-free topology. This can also be achieved leveraging EVPN multihoming.

In addition to the specific connectivity requirements for VXLAN, protecting the network boundary is also important and a recommended practice. Traditional Layer 2 tools such as BPDU guard, root guard, or storm control provide protection at any classic Ethernet edge port. These tools allow for a clean and protected demarcation, which prevents undesirable failure propagation. As a result, desired network stability is ensured.

Extranet and Shared Services

In many cases, there is a requirement to deploy services that are shared by different tenants aka VRFs. Examples include services such as DHCP and DNS. The shared services may be deployed or attached to certain leafs within a fabric in a "shared" VRF. Consequently, there may be a need to allow communication between the tenant VRF and the shared VRF. This is achieved via route leaking, as described in this section. The same mechanism is also employed for deploying extranet services.

Local/Distributed VRF Route Leaking

Virtual routing and forwarding (VRF) provides the ability to have multiple virtual routing and forwarding instances in a single network router/switch. Typically, each VRF is associated with a unique VPN identifier. VRF route leaking allows leaking of prefix information between multiple VRF instances within the same network router (see Figure 8-17).

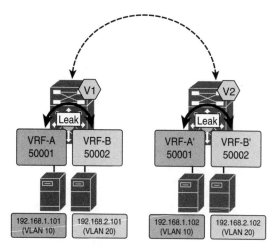

Figure 8-17 *VRF Route Leaking*

With this approach, there is no requirement to interconnect the leaked VRFs via an external routing instance using a loopback cable. Use cases specific to VRF route leaking are common for the Internet access VRF, the shared services VRF, and the centralized services VRF.

In general, VRF route leaking is a native function of MP-BGP, together with the VRFs and related Route Targets, as shown in Example 8-5.

Example 8-5 *VRF Route-Leaking Concept*

```
# VRF Configuration at Ingress VTEP (V1)
vrf context VRF-A
 vni 50001
 rd auto
  address-family ipv4 unicast
    route-target both auto
    route-target both auto evpn
    route-target import 65501:50002
    route-target import 65501:50002 evpn
```

```
vrf context VRF-B
 vni 50002
 rd auto
  address-family ipv4 unicast
    route-target both auto
    route-target both auto evpn
    route-target import 65501:50001
    route-target import 65501:50001 evpn

# VRF Configuration at Egress VTEP (V2)
vrf context VRF-A
 vni 50001
 rd auto
  address-family ipv4 unicast
    route-target both auto
    route-target both auto evpn
    route-target import 65501:50002
    route-target import 65501:50002 evpn

vrf context VRF-B
 vni 50002
 rd auto
  address-family ipv4 unicast
    route-target both auto
    route-target both auto evpn
    route-target import 65501:50001
    route-target import 65501:50001 evpn
```

Functionality in the data plane has to be present to allow correct forwarding beyond the local network switch. This requires the exchange of control protocol information, as well as the correct origination of the encapsulation header when traffic is destined to a given prefix.

With VXLAN BGP EVPN, the attributes of the prefix also carry the associated VNI information, but from an encapsulation perspective, the configured value of the VRF is honored. In other words, even if the correct VNI is associated with the destination VRF, the VXLAN encapsulation uses the VNI associated with the source VRF for remote traffic.

The previous configuration example demonstrates how VRF route leaking can be achieved in a VXLAN BGP EVPN fabric. With this approach, the functionality of VRF route leaking is present, but it requires the source and destination VRFs to be configured everywhere leaking is necessary. This requirement is solely bound to the fact that route leaking happens in the control protocol on the ingress VTEP, while the data plane operation happens on the egress VTEP.

To explain this concept better, the topology in Figure 8-18 shows two VTEPs, V1 and V2, both having VRF-A and VRF-B locally configured on them. This example demonstrates VRF route leaking between two endpoints in different VRFs.

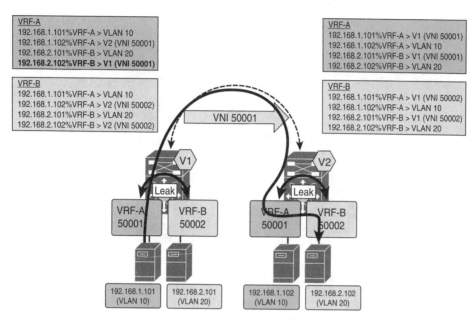

Figure 8-18 *VRF Route Leaking: Flow shows 192.168.1.101 (VRF-A) to 192.168.2.102 (VRF-B)*

The endpoint with IP 192.168.1.101 (VRF-A) connected to VTEP V1 wants to communicate with the endpoint with IP 192.168.2.102 (VRF-B) connected to VTEP V2. On ingress VTEP V1, the IP address 192.168.2.102 is seen in VRF-A as the information is leaked between the VRFs by the respective Route Target import configuration. From a forwarding perspective, remote traffic destined to 192.168.2.102 is encapsulated on ingress VTEP V1 with VNI 50001 toward the egress VTEP V2. Once traffic arrives on VTEP V2, VNI 50001 is evaluated in VRF-A, and a lookup for 192.168.2.102 results in the traffic being locally leaked over to VRF-B. In turn, this traffic is sent to the destination endpoint.

It is important to understand that the encapsulation occurs with the VNI of the VRF where the source endpoint is connected. Therefore, the source VRF and VNI must be configured in the destination system. Consequently, this mechanism is termed local/distributed VRF route leaking.

Because route leaking is configured locally, on all participating ingress VTEPs, the data plane leaking always happens locally on the egress VTEP. With this route leaking approach, the related forwarding results have a certain asymmetry, depending on the forwarding direction.

In the opposite direction (see Figure 8-19), the endpoint with IP 192.168.2.102 in VRF-B can reach endpoint 192.168.1.101 in VRF-A. On ingress VTEP V2, the IP address 192.168.1.101 is seen in VRF-B because the information is leaked between the VRFs by the appropriate Route Target import configuration. This time, traffic destined to 192.168.1.101 from VTEP V2 to VTEP V1 is encapsulated with VNI 50002, which is the VNI associated with VRF-B. As before, traffic is leaked over to VRF-A at the egress VTEP V1 and finally sent to the destination.

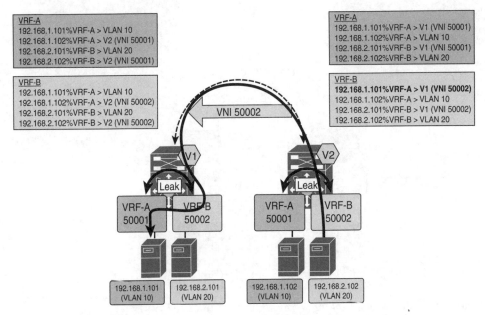

Figure 8-19   *VRF Route Leaking: Flow shows 192.168.2.102 (VRF-B) to 192.168.1.101 (VRF-A)*

This route leaking approach requires additional configuration, and it impacts scalability by forcing consistent configuration on all the VTEPs where either of the leaking VRFs is present. Traffic is always sent toward the remote VTEP with the VRF VNI associated with the source VRF even though the traffic is destined to an endpoint in the destination VRF. This asymmetric behavior has similar disadvantages as prescribed for asymmetric IRB as described in Chapter 3, "VXLAN/EVPN Forwarding Characteristics." Alternative approaches, such as downstream VNI, are available for more scalable cross-VRF communication that uses the control protocol to drive the VNI used within the data plane encapsulation.

Downstream VNI Assignment

For traditional VRF route leaking, the downstream VNI assignment scheme uses a similar approach to that used by MPLS L3VPN. In this instance, the upstream device (egress node) dictates the label to be used for the VPN to the ingress node. In VXLAN, a slightly different approach is used since the label (aka VNI in the case of VXLAN) is not dynamically assigned but is statically configured.

With downstream VNI assignment for a given VRF, in addition to the locally assigned VNI (configured L3VNI), a VTEP can use different VNI assignments but still achieve communication. This is similar to a generic route leaking case. With downstream VNI, specifically, the egress VTEP advertises its local VRF VNI in the MP-BGP EVPN route update. This VNI information is part of the EVPN NLRI and present in Route type 2 and Route type 5 messages.

Upon reception of a route update on the ingress VTEP, BGP pushes the route update into the hardware tables with the VNI advertised from the egress VTEP. As a result, the egress VTEP dictates the VNI to be used by the ingress VTEP with downstream VNI assignment via the control protocol. Clearly, to support this function, both the egress and ingress VTEPs should support this functionality because a per-VNI per-VTEP association has to be stored within the forwarding information base (FIB).

This instantiation and storing of information is needed because the right VNI has to be chosen to reach the prefix advertised by the egress VTEP during the encapsulation process at the ingress VTEP. Downstream VNI assignment offers various optimizations to reduce the VNI range and corresponding peer VTEPs. With this approach, downstream VNI is less configuration-intensive.

For the same topology employed for the VRF route leaking use case between VRF-A and VRF-B, the downstream VNI assignment scheme operation can now be considered, as shown in Figure 8-20. As before, the endpoint with IP 192.168.1.101 in VRF-A wants to reach endpoint with IP 192.168.2.102 in VRF-B. On ingress VTEP V1, the IP address 192.168.2.102 is seen with the VNI of VRF-B (50002), as advertised from VTEP V2 via MP-BGP EVPN.

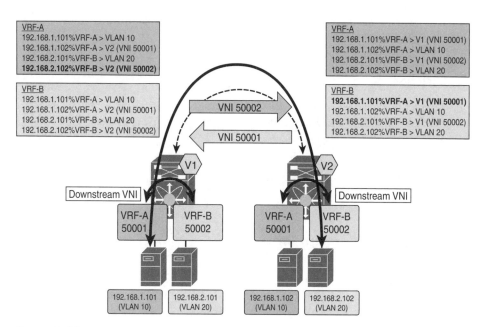

Figure 8-20 *Downstream VNI Assignment*

From a forwarding perspective, traffic is encapsulated on ingress VTEP V1 with VNI 50002 toward egress VTEP V2. On reception at VTEP V2, VNI 50002 is evaluated in VRF-B, and traffic is ultimately forwarded to endpoint 192.168.2.102 in VRF-B.

It is important to understand that the VNI to be used for encapsulation is determined by the destination VTEP and, in turn, the destination endpoint. This means that VTEP V2 announces the VNI downstream to VTEP V1 for the ensuing encapsulation operation. This is where this scheme, *downstream VNI assignment*, gets its name.

While downstream VNI assignment can operate within a large-scale VXLAN BGP EVPN fabric, the amount of per-VTEP, per-VNI information required may explode if every VTEP starts using a different VNI for every VRF. This can result in additional requirements for operations personnel as well as for the hardware table scale, and it may become a significant problem. Reasonable use of this feature in the use case of common Internet VRF or the centralized shared services use case is therefore recommended, thereby leveraging the resulting simplification most effectively.

Summary

This chapter presents external connectivity options with a VXLAN BGP EVPN fabric. After introducing the border leaf and border spine options, this chapter provides details on the options for external Layer 3 connectivity using VRF Lite, LISP, and MPLS L3VPN. This chapter also covers Layer 2 external connectivity options, with an emphasis on vPC. Finally, this chapter discusses how VRF route leaking can be implemented in the fabric using local leaking. The use of downstream VNI assignment for VRF route leaking scenarios provides a more elegant solution.

Reference

1. Internet Engineering Task Force (IETF). *BGP/MPLS IP virtual private networks (VPNs)—Multi-AS backbones*. 2006. tools.ietf.org/html/rfc4364#page-32.

## Chapter 9

Multi-Pod, Multifabric, and Data Center Interconnect (DCI)

In this chapter, the following topics will be covered:

- OTV and VXLAN technologies

- Multi-pod and multifabric options with VXLAN BGP EVPN deployments

- Interconnection options that can be deployed between multiple VXLAN BGP EVPN fabrics

Data centers are expected to function 24 hours a day, 365 days a year. With such a high demand for availability, a disaster recovery plan is almost always in place. Depending on the size of the organization, data center deployments may be spread across multiple geographic sites. In some cases, multiple data center pods are deployed at the same site. Data center fabrics are often constructed in multiple rooms, halls, or sites, and interconnectivity is mandatory. This chapter focuses on interconnecting multiple pods, or fabrics (sites), to one another. It leverages many concepts described in earlier chapters.

This chapter describes various considerations involving the deployment of VXLAN EVPN in multi-pod and multisite environments. Overlay Transport Virtualization (OTV) is often discussed for providing Layer 2 DCI functionality and is commonly mentioned in the same sentence with VXLAN. Therefore, this chapter discusses Layer 2 DCI and the difference between OTV and VXLAN. It also dives into various options for DCI and for splitting VXLAN BGP EVPN networks in multiple-pods, or fabrics. Experience has shown that a single large fabric is difficult to operate and maintain. As discussed at the end of this chapter, approaches to scale a network by separating administrative and operational boundaries are congruent with interconnecting data centers.

Contrasting OTV and VXLAN

Is it possible to use VXLAN with EVPN instead of OTV for DCI? Answering this question requires exploration of the world of Data Center Interconnect (DCI) to evaluate architectural considerations and potential solutions. If VXLAN is only considered as an encapsulation with EVPN as a control protocol, and if this combination is acknowledged as a DCI solution, it would be unfair and limited in considering OTV and its functionality. In an effort to limit the discussion of Ethernet or label-switched DCI solutions such as Wavelength-Division Multiplexing (WDM)[1,2] or Virtual Private LAN Service (VPLS),[3,4] this section focuses on comparing two transport-agnostic IP-based solutions, namely OTV and VXLAN.

OTV employs a control protocol for peer auto-discovery and for the exchange of unicast and multicast reachability information. In addition, OTV provides a data plane that transports data traffic from one site to another site or to multiple sites.[5] OTV uses IS-IS[6] as a control protocol; it uses the generic extensions to IS-IS to transport Layer 2 information.[7] In addition, specific IS-IS protocol extensions have been added for OTV.[8]

On the data plane side, OTV was first produced with a combination of GRE[9] and EoMPLS[10] in order to provide the desired functionality with existing hardware. This was in contrast to the documented data plane encapsulation stated in the IETF's OTV draft. The second version of OTV more accurately followed the IETF draft. In comparing the OTV data plane encapsulation and the VXLAN frame format, significant similarities exist, with notable differences in the specific fields and their associated nomenclature (see Figure 9-1). This has resulted in some speculation about the similarities between these two different data plane encapsulations. However, significant differences exist, and this section explains why the question between OTV versus VXLAN arises.

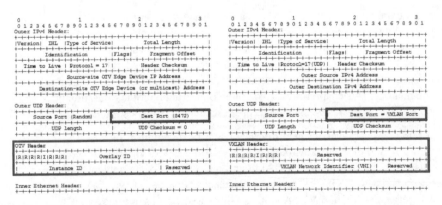

Figure 9-1   *OTV and VXLAN (Frame Format)*

Initially, VXLAN was primarily proposed as a MAC-in-IP/UDP data plane encapsulation, with an associated Flood and Learn (F&L) learning mechanism. This is the first difference between VXLAN and OTV: OTV provides an integrated control protocol for exchanging peer and Layer 2 address information in order to avoid F&L. Once OTV has been configured with its approximately 5–10 commands, all the necessary control protocol and data plane functions are enabled. With VXLAN control protocols, namely BGP EVPN, a similar functionality is available, but EVPN itself is not integrated in a true sense. VXLAN and BGP EVPN have to be separately configured, and VXLAN must be instructed to use that control protocol. Having described the specifics of the OTV data plane encapsulation and its control protocol, solution differences can now be discussed between those provided by OTV and by VXLAN (or, more specifically, VXLAN with BGP EVPN).

Because the service to be provided relies on resiliency, redundancy for DCI is important. Various ways to provide all-active paths in Layer 3 exist—for example, with equal-cost multipath (ECMP). When moving to Layer 2, however, the number of options to accomplish this becomes limited. OTV provides redundancy via multihoming based on a designated forwarder (authoritative edge device [AED]) election on a per-VLAN basis. Enabling OTV multihoming functionality does not require any specific configuration other than defining the devices that share the same site. Also, OTV does not require any method of multihoming, as is the case with virtual PortChannel (vPC).

In contrast, VXLAN does not provide any integrated multihoming; however, with the addition of vPC, Layer 2 redundancy for VXLAN and classic Ethernet traffic is available for edge devices. Whether using VXLAN or VXLAN EVPN, vPC is an available multihoming solution in which VTEPs can be paired to ensure Layer 2 redundancy. Endpoints can be dually attached to a pair of VTEPs that are part of a vPC domain.

EVPN multihoming capabilities will soon become available and will allow the use of native multihoming for Layer 2 redundancy. With the control protocol–related approach, no additional technology, such as vPC or Multi-Chassis Link Aggregation Group (MC-LAG), is required, and more than two devices can provide Layer 2 redundancy in an integrated way. When EVPN multihoming for VXLAN becomes available, in this specific area, the difference between OTV and VXLAN EVPN will become negligible.

When extending networks at the level of Layer 2, loops are perhaps the most serious threat that can undermine the entire network. To prevent possible situations such as a backdoor link introducing a loop, the OTV site VLAN continuously probes for potential OTV edge devices (EDs) on the classic Ethernet side. If another OTV ED is detected, the site identifier is compared. If these are found to be different, the overlay extension is disabled. All this is done to ensure that no Layer 2 loops occur through the OTV overlay or through the backdoor link (see Figure 9-2).

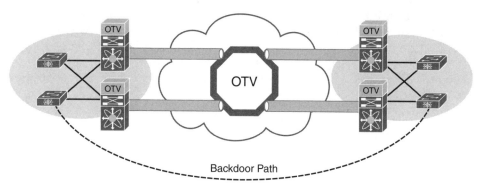

Figure 9-2 *Backdoor Path*

VXLAN, with or without BGP EVPN, has no ability to detect a southbound loop introduced by a backdoor link. This doesn't necessarily make VXLAN more exposed to Layer 2 loops; however, additional measures have to be taken for loop prevention. A good practice is to protect the classic Ethernet interfaces in VXLAN with bridge protocol data unit (BPDU) guards[11] and storm control to ensure that a loop is prevented in the event of an accidental backdoor link. Also, whenever a need to connect a classic Ethernet environment to the VXLAN edge device or VTEP exists, building a vPC domain and connecting the classic Ethernet network with a port channel to this vPC-only domain is a consideration.

These kinds of measures are beneficial as long as there is no classic Ethernet switch connected to the VXLAN edge devices or VTEP. When southbound classic Ethernet connectivity to STP-based network switches is required, the BPDU guard has to be removed, and STP has to perform loop protection as a non-VXLAN integrated technology. The VTEPs participate in the root bridge election as regular switches. Because VXLAN itself doesn't forward BPDUs, and therefore doesn't understand the difference between forwarding and blocking ports, the VXLAN "tunnel" is considered an "always-forwarding" link.

OTV, on the other hand, does have some integration abilities with spanning tree. The OTV edge device acts as a classic Ethernet Layer 2 network switch. This means it participates in STP if the site has been configured to use it. However, there is no forwarding of BPDUs over the OTV overlay interface, which is comparable to the way VXLAN handles this. The differences with OTV in regard to STP handling are related to topology change notifications (TCN).[12] Upon reception of a TCN, OTV performs typical actions such as the clearing of the MAC address table for the given VLAN. Also, OTV evaluates TCNs if an OTV topology change occurs. This ensures accuracy in terms of the reachability of an endpoint.

With OTV, the STP root continues to reside at the location where it was placed before the integration of OTV. If deemed beneficial, the spanning tree root can be moved to the OTV edge device; however, it is important to understand that spanning tree domains are kept localized on an OTV site. The same considerations apply when using VXLAN to interconnect classic Ethernet sites.

Multidestination traffic can be handled with OTV and with VXLAN with BGP EVPN. When interconnecting data centers or network fabrics, fault containment is mandatory most of the time. This can be achieved by reducing or eliminating unnecessary network traffic in the overlay. An optimal way of accomplishing this is with ARP suppression, which reduces unnecessary ARP broadcast traffic over the network. Such ARP broadcasts can be answered locally once seen as broadcasts. This functionality is available with VXLAN BGP EVPN as well as with OTV.

Unknown unicast is another kind of network traffic that is a legacy from the classic Ethernet times. The need for unknown unicast flooding may be required in cases of silent host detection on Layer 2 or during some endpoint failover scenarios. In modern networks, attempts to prevent such traffic are desirable because that traffic can introduce network storms. OTV implicitly does not forward any unknown unicast traffic. If a DMAC address is not known, the traffic is simply dropped. In the event that a specific MAC address should be allowed to generate unknown unicast flooding, the MAC address can explicitly be allowed to perform this function on a per-VLAN basis.

VXLAN with BGP EVPN prevents unknown unicast traffic. As is the case with active control protocol learning, an unknown MAC should not exist. However, VXLAN does not stop unknown unicast forwarding by default. Some implementations of VXLAN with EVPN have a feature by which unknown unicast forwarding can be disabled on a per-Layer 2 VNI basis. But once disabled, options to selectively enable the flooding for a single MAC do not exist. However, the need for unknown unicast forwarding is infrequently required.

When multicast forwarding is necessary in the same Layer 2 domain, the interaction with IGMP messages and IGMP snooping allows the forwarding of multicast in the most optimal way. The OTV edge device receives and evaluates these IGMP reports to optimally forward multicast traffic across the overlay. For multicast forwarding, OTV uses data groups that are based on PIM source-specific multicast (SSM)[13] learning and forwarding semantics. With PIM SSM, the source for a group is always known, and overlay multicast traffic can be forwarded in the most efficient way.

OTV also has the ability to separate the data groups used for multicast traffic from the ones used for broadcast traffic. This can allow further fine-tuning for the traffic and is like having a "rate-limiter" for broadcast traffic only. In VXLAN, all broadcast, unknown unicast, and multicast (BUM) traffic is handled in the same way and is forwarded by the multicast group or ingress replication method assigned to the Layer 2 VNI. The capability to specifically differentiate between the different BUM traffic types is not implicitly available. Nevertheless, optimization of multicast in the same VLAN/L2VNI can be achieved through the availability of IGMP snooping. Chapter 7, "Multicast Forwarding," elaborates on the mechanics of IGMP when used together with VXLAN. In summary, OTV provides active control protocol and data plane integration for multicast traffic, while VXLAN only partly offers such granularity.

Table 9-1 highlights the differences between OTV and VXLAN discussed in this section. The applicability of VXLAN with BGP EVPN evolves as the control protocol and the related optimizations evolve. Also, VXLAN was notably built as an extension to LANs, with the primary focus of having it not be an extension over WANs. Previously, VXLAN was just another encapsulation that imposed F&L on top of a Layer 3 network and required multicast. However, VXLAN now, with BGP EVPN, has applicability for deployment of large-scale networks that traverse multiple data center sites.

Table 9-1 *VXLAN and OTV Functions*

	Data Plane	Control Plane	Multihoming	Loop Prevention	Fault Containment	Multicast Optimization
OTV	1.0 (EoMPLSoGRE)	IS-IS	Native	Block BPDU STP integration (for example, TCN handling)	Stop unknown unicast Selective unicast flooding ARP suppression	IGMP snooping
	2.5 (UDP, VXLAN)	IS-IS	Native	Block BPDU STP integration (for example, TCN handling)	Stop unknown unicast Selective unicast flooding ARP suppression	IGMP snooping
VXLAN	VXLAN	F&L	vPC	Block BPDU	—	IGMP snooping
	VXLAN	BGP EVPN	vPC	Block BPDU	Minimize unknown unicast ARP suppression Unknown Unicast suppression	IGMP snooping

In terms of data center networks, active peer discovery and learning of Layer 2 and Layer 3 information over BGP EVPN provides the capability to scale well beyond the capacity of F&L networks. In the near future, VXLAN with BGP EVPN will prove its capability for being a full-featured DCI solution, through enhancements related to multihoming, fault containment, and loop protection. Likewise, the additional gains in efficiency using multicast forwarding will support this claim as well, once VXLAN with BGP EVPN is maturely developed.

After comparing OTV with VXLAN EVPN, the following sections will discuss design considerations for the inter-pod connectivity and DCI.

Multi-Pod

Overlay networks inspire "flat" network designs. This might be a good approach for scaling out the network and removing unnecessary layers. However, with respect to operational simplicity, the practices involving hierarchical network design also apply to overlay networks deployed on top of spine–leaf topologies. Spine–leaf topologies are introduced in Chapter 1, "Introduction to Programmable Fabric," but there are many more variations to this approach than are discussed in that chapter. Significant flexibility exists that goes beyond a single tier of spine and leaf, in the ability to scale out horizontally.

The leaf layer provides endpoint connectivity, and additional southbound tiers probably do not exist other than virtual switches, FEX (Fabric Extender/Nexus 2000),[14] Cisco UCS FI (Unified Computing System Fabric Interconnect),[15] or switches in a blade-server enclosure. This does not mean that the connection of network service functions (for example, firewall, load-balancer, router, other service appliances) is not a feasible option. However, the connection of additional southbound switch tiers for endpoint connectivity and cascaded access is not considered in this discussion.

In general, connection of a full-fledged Layer 2 network below the leafs requires special considerations for STP, such as root placement, TCN handling, and loop prevention. This is a very common problem, especially because overlay technologies such as VXLAN do not transport BPDUs or TCNs today.

With the leaf being responsible for hosting the VTEP, the traditional spine is a simple IP/UDP traffic forwarder (see Figure 9-3). In that sense, the spines are unaware of the endpoint addresses, and their forwarding tables only need to scale in the order of the number of leafs and not in the order of the number of endpoints. By scaling out the spine in the same stage, in addition to increasing its bandwidth and resiliency, advantages listed earlier related to scale and operational simplicity still apply.

The optimal number of spines is defined by the available uplink interfaces on the leafs, at least when the symmetrical connectivity of the spine–leaf topology is assumed. For example, in a topology where a leaf has 6 × 40G interfaces, the optimal number of spines would be between 4 and 6. This takes into consideration vPC-based deployments where some 40G links may be employed for the vPC peer link.

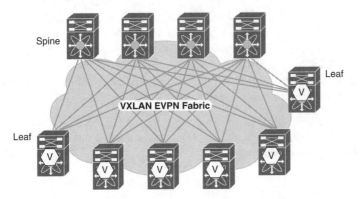

Figure 9-3   *Two-Tier Spine–Leaf Topology*

It is not always possible to provide the needed interface density for a spine layer at the beginning of a buildout. Initially, a standard two-tier spine–leaf topology that typically contains two spines and *N* leafs may be used. As the demands of the data center grow, more leafs and spines may be required. At some point, a new pod is added, with an additional set of spines serving at the same tier level as the initially deployed one. The new pod includes a new set of leafs as well.

Because some leafs connect to some spines and other leafs connect to other spines, it is important that these different pods are interconnected. A multi-pod design is simplified by introducing a super-spine layer (see Figure 9-4). All the spines at Tier 1 connect to all the super-spines. This way, instead of a two-tier spine–leaf topology, the fabric becomes an *n*-stage topology, where *n* represents the number of spine levels. The value of *n* can be increased as much as required to accommodate the network design. For most practical deployments, having one super-spine layer is usually sufficient.

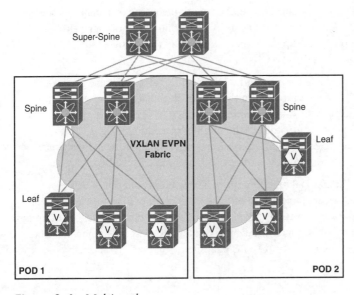

Figure 9-4   *Multi-pod*

The MP-BGP EVPN control protocol needs to be part of the design considerations in an *n*-stage fabric. The exchange of reachability information across all the available stages is required even if only the VTEPs need this information for making forwarding decisions. The spines or super-spines are used as BGP route reflectors (RRs) for distributing this reachability information in an efficient way (see Figure 9-5). In addition to the placement of BGP RRs, the overall design also needs to consider the appropriate placement of rendezvous points (RPs) if multicast is being used for forwarding BUM traffic.

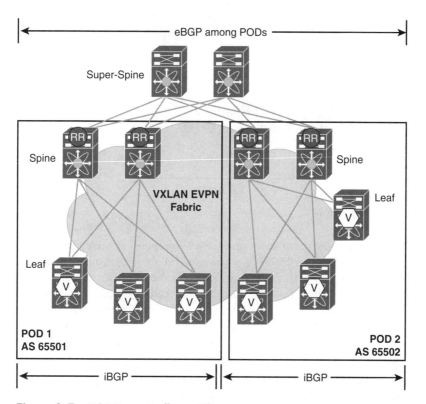

Figure 9-5 *BGP Route Reflector Placement*

In relation to the use of multicast and RPs in an *n*-stage or multistage fabric, another advantage also exists, involving scaling the output interfaces (OIFs) for multicast. Once the OIF limit is reached for the number of leafs in a given pod, an upstream super-spine can help increase that scale by extending the multicast tree to other spines (see Figure 9-6). This can subsequently increase the scale of the OIF limit for the fabric.

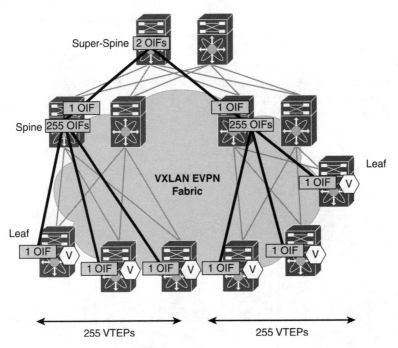

Figure 9-6 *Multicast OIF Scaling*

With a simple multi-pod topology as shown in Figure 9-6, a spine can serve up to 256 OIFs and can represent as many as 256 leafs, which would allow a single multicast tree between the 256 leafs and the spine acting as the RP. To further increase the scale, the pod would need to be split before the maximum OIF scale could be reached at the spine layer. Assuming that this split is created upon reaching 255 leafs, the spine is allowed to have 255 southbound OIFs toward the leafs and one northbound OIF toward the super-spine. At that point, if the super-spine also allowed scaling to 256 OIFs, 256 spines could be served by a single set of super-spines.

With this type of multi-pod design having 256 spines multiplied by 255 leafs, theoretically the number of leafs would expand to 65K from an OIF perspective. While this demonstrates how OIFs can be scaled to higher numbers by using an *n*-stage spine–leaf topology, the overall scale in terms of the number of VTEPs and prefixes (MAC and IP) also needs to be considered.

In the case of a multi-pod design where any-to-any reachability is required across all the leafs across all the VNIs, the maximum scale is defined by the least common denominator. By using a fabric approach, and by employing the notion of moving intelligence to the leaf layer with a scale-out property, it might not be necessary to have all VNIs configured everywhere. If this is the case, configurations can be constructed only where needed at the leaf layer, and the scale potentially achieved is far beyond what current Layer 2 networks can provide. With this approach, the theoretical maximal number of 65K leafs may seem attractive. However, it is impractical, especially with the operational complexity associated with deploying, managing, and maintaining such a large network.

When having such multitier or multistage spine layers, the placement of the RP is also important. To achieve some independence between the different pods, the use of a single PIM Anycast RP per pod is a reasonable approach. Because multiple pods exist, and BUM traffic needs to flow between these pods when Layer 2 VNIs are extended, additional considerations need to be taken into account for interconnecting the different pods.

One way to expand the PIM Anycast RP approach across each of the different pods is to use the same RP address and provide a full-mesh neighbor relationship. Configuring the anycast IP address on the spine ensures that multicast traffic that always uses the shortest path to reach the RP, stays within the pod. In a pod where pod-local RPs must be used, different sets of PIM Anycast RPs along with Multicast Source Discovery Protocol (MSDP)[16] can be used to ensure that the multicast source and receiver group information is exchanged between the pods (see Figure 9-7). In this way, the independence of the pods is increased from a multicast perspective.

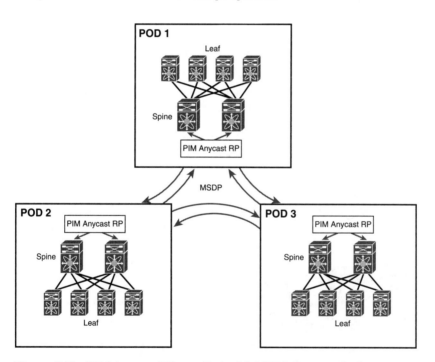

Figure 9-7 *PIM Anycast RPs per Pod with MSDP Between Pods*

The use of multicast forwarding for BUM traffic is a potentially superior alternative to the use of ingress replication. This may be especially true as the amount of BUM traffic grows. When multicast is employed for forwarding BUM traffic, an efficient single packet per link for a given BUM packet would result because the traffic is forwarded along the multicast tree. When using ingress replication, this is notably different because BUM traffic alone can result in a significant amount of traffic in the multi-pod environment.

With ingress replication, a single BUM packet is replicated to each of the peer VTEPs that host the same Layer 2 VNI. Therefore, with 256 VTEPs in a VXLAN domain, a

VTEP has to replicate a single packet 255 times. With 64-byte packets, the uplink from the VTEP where the packet originates sees the transport of $255 \times 64 = 16{,}320$ bytes, or about 16KB.

If a couple of southbound interfaces from this VTEP toward locally attached endpoints were considered instead of a single packet, the negative impact of ingress replication in a worst-case scenario could easily be appreciated. Consider one VTEP with 20 active endpoints, with each of them creating 1Kb/s (kilobit per second) of BUM traffic. This would result in 20Kb/s ingressing the VTEP. Assuming once again that the number of remote VTEPs are 255, this would result in 5100Kb/s (255×20Kb/s), or 637.5KB/s.

Because the feasibility of only one VTEP having active endpoints sending BUM traffic is not likely, other endpoints below other VTEPs are also producers as well as consumers of BUM traffic. As a result, the amount of traffic in the network for handling BUM packets when using ingress replication can grow from megabits per second to gigabits per second. Therefore, at the design phase, it is important to consider the type and volume of application traffic that will be transported over the multi-pod topology. This consideration facilitates making the correct decisions regarding the underlay technology employed for forwarding BUM traffic.

Finally, in a VXLAN BGP EVPN fabric, not all leafs are expected to provide the same Layer 2 and/or Layer 3 service for all tenants. In other words, sets of leafs may be divided into clusters, also called *mobility domains*. Leafs within a mobility domain are configured with the same set of Layer 2 and Layer 3 VNIs (see Figure 9-8). As a result, a cluster with common spines may be converted into a pod that resides in a room or hall in a single physical data center location.

Some use cases also exist where pods are separated across a few close-quarter data centers that are providing limited separation for a high-availability set. This use case would apply to some metro data center approaches where failure propagation is not a primary concern because a disaster recovery site is always available.

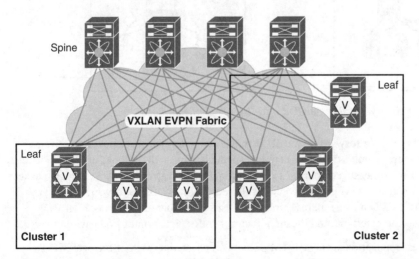

Figure 9-8 *Leaf Cluster (Mobility Domain)*

As previously described, one of the main advantages of a VXLAN BGP EVPN network compared to traditional networks related to the overlay is the distributed IP anycast gateway. With the default gateway being spread across all the available leafs or VTEPs, any concerns regarding the impact on first-hop gateway decisions becomes limited to the endpoints connected to a particular leaf. In this way, operational tasks become much simpler because a pair of critical switches holding the majority of the network functions no longer exists as is the case with the aggregation or distribution-layer switches in a traditional three-tier (access/aggregation/core) topology.

Because the distributed anycast gateway is available at the leaf layer in every pod, special localization configuration is not required. This is not the case for FHRP protocols in traditional deployments. Also, with the distributed anycast gateway, optimal one-hop forwarding between endpoints on any VTEP in any pod in a multi-pod fabric deployment is possible.

With all these different design options, the existence of multiple pods has several operational benefits. Having multiple pods minimizes the impact of one pod on other pods. For example, if some maintenance needs to be performed on one of the pods while all other pods continue to carry production traffic, the maintenance at the one pod might impact the overlay connectivity toward that pod, but all the other pods would continue to operate independently, without any impact. This is substantially different from what happens in a large expanded two-tier spine–leaf topology (see Figure 9-9), where the underlay change on one leaf could impact the entire underlay routing domain and, in turn, may impact the overlay as well.

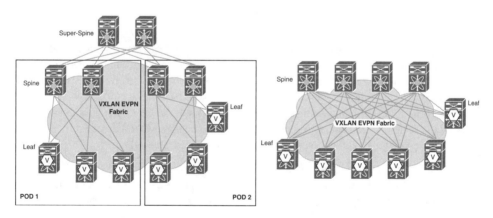

Figure 9-9   *Multi-pod Versus Two-Tier Spine–Leaf Topology*

The underlay routing design in multi-pod environments requires special considerations as well. The underlay routing has to be able to exchange reachability information for the VTEP, BGP RR, multicast RP, and other addresses used for building and maintaining the pods. Since full visibility of the VTEP addresses (/32 in IPv4 or /128 in IPv6) is required, and no summary should be used, the routing domain could benefit from separation. When using an interior gateway protocol (IGP) in a multi-pod environment, area separation for the different pods should be considered. While this provides a certain separation into what LSAs are sent between pods (for example, with OSPF), the complete underlay routing can be affected if the link-state database is compromised with faulty information (such as a duplicate router ID).

There are other ways to achieve separation in multi-pod deployments, such as using stub areas and only injecting the default route between the pods. However, this approach has a significant impact on the convergence of the overlay control protocol because the VTEPs are no longer individually visible. If a VTEP fails in a remote area, the default route toward the exit of the area still exists. Therefore, traffic may potentially black-hole until the dead timer removes the prefix from the control protocol. In such a case, the benefits of simplicity versus complexity must be weighed.

It is possible to achieve strong separation between the pods by using BGP to interconnect the pods from an underlay perspective. But with this approach, implications involving the overlay control protocol exist because the underlay and overlay control protocols merge (using BGP).

Today, multi-pod designs provide the option of hierarchical network design in the underlay and potentially in the overlay control plane. As a result, a single data plane domain remains. In other words, the VXLAN tunnels always begin and terminate at the leafs, regardless of whether the traffic is being forwarded between endpoints in the same pod or across pods. This means the same consistent configuration of Layer 2 and Layer 3 services is required across all pods. This approach also allows virtual machine mobility across multiple pods in a multi-pod environment.

Overlay control plane separation in the different pods can be achieved by using different BGP autonomous system (AS) numbers in each pod. However, the separation only involves the handling functions within the control protocol provided by the BGP EVPN feature set. As a result, the prefix scale per MAC and IP becomes a global consideration in the entire multi-pod environment. As previously noted, intelligent network design can allow the scale requirements at the individual leafs to be somewhat amortized by not requiring every Layer 2 and Layer 3 VNI to be configured everywhere.

In considering a multi-pod design, a residing point remains in regard to the available physical connectivity. Because many existing infrastructure cablings were designed to accommodate the classic hierarchical three-tier topologies, additional factors must be considered with spine–leaf and n-tier spine–leaf fabrics. In cases where sufficient cabling for symmetrical connectivity is available, the single-tier spine–leaf approach may be sufficient. Once an n-tier deployment is required, the super-spine helps interconnect rooms, halls, or sites with a minimal amount of cabling. As an alternative to using an additional spine tier to interconnect pods, the option of using the interconnection at the leaf layer also exists. Determining when to use spine versus leaf approaches involves multiple considerations, as discussed in the next section.

Interconnection at the Spine Layer

When only two pods exist, adding a super-spine layer or a third tier may not be necessary. Simply interconnecting the spines may suffice in such instances (see Figure 9-10). Apart from the BGP RR and multicast RP placement, the spine only acts as an IP/UDP forwarder or router for unicast and multicast forwarding in the underlay. If a third pod needs to be introduced in the future, this design could become a bit cumbersome because full-mesh connectivity between the pods would require additional links and configurations. In such scenarios, having a super-spine layer offers notable advantages, as previously discussed.

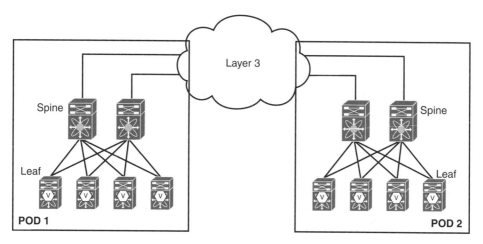

Figure 9-10   *Interconnection at the Spine, Back-to-Back*

With the direct spine back-to-back interconnection specifically, the spine configuration may become quite loaded, which goes against the principle of having lean spines. If an interconnection between two pods at the spine layer is truly needed, it serves to contrast the complexity versus simplicity to determine how much separation is needed. Because the overlay is end-to-end, and the overlay control protocol has all information stored across the pods, this configuration may be satisfactory. Once an additional spine layer, aka super-spine, is introduced, an underlay routing protocol change can be performed. This might be accomplished through an eBGP approach. The super-spine can be kept lean with BGP as the only routing protocol. Likewise, the spines stay within their IGP domain with redistribution of the information into BGP for inter-pod exchange.

Interconnection at the Leaf Layer

Much like using the back-to-back interconnection at the spine layer, employing an interconnection at the leaf layer is also a feasible way to connect pods (see Figure 9-11). It is possible to add another layer south of the leaf. However, multiple pods interconnected at the leaf layer might appear a bit cumbersome in a data center. The interconnection at the leaf layer is advantageous when a degree of geographic separation is needed and when the same nodes are used for multi-pod and external connectivity.

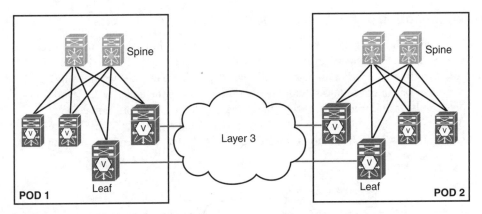

Figure 9-11 *Interconnection at the Leaf, Back-to-Back*

The same options available for interconnecting multiple pods at the spine layer are also available at the leaf layer. The main difference between these interconnection approaches resides in the available connectivity between pods. In addition, consider that the leaf might also act as a VTEP and become burdened with a heavy load of functionality. For example, if the interconnecting leaf is a default gateway for a given network, part of a vPC domain, and also provides Layer 2 interconnectivity, a fair amount of complexity, from an operational perspective, occurs. Because these leafs need to be highly available to ensure cross-pod connectivity, reducing complexity may be preferred, and an approach allowing the interconnection point to be as lean as possible may be ideal when dealing with multi-pod deployments.

Multifabric

While multi-pod deployments follow the concept of multiple control protocol domains in the underlay as well as in the overlay, a single data plane that extends end to end across all the pods exists. Therefore, a multi-pod environment is considered a single fabric. In a multifabric deployment, complete segregation at the control plane level typically occurs, as does segregation at the data plane level. In other words, a single VXLAN BGP EVPN fabric can consist of its own underlay, its own overlay control protocol, and related data plane encapsulation.

The advantage of such a multifabric design not only involves the option of having true separation of the traffic but also benefits from an administrative domain perspective. In regard to the administrative domain, benefits relate to the BGP autonomous system as well as the numbering of VNIs, multicast groups, and other components that are completely independent between different fabrics. This means an individual fabric can use any numbering model desired without being dependent on any of the other fabrics numbering models. In addition, with respect to BUM traffic forwarding, one fabric can use multicast and another fabric can use ingress replication. The capability to have this degree of independence is not possible in multi-pod environments.

Because things are truly localized within a fabric, traffic egressing needs to be terminated at the border of the fabric. Specifically, the VXLAN encapsulation needs to be terminated, and an appropriate Layer 2 or Layer 3 handoff needs to occur. This provides the option of interconnecting multiple fabrics where VNIs can be independently stitched together via a different technology (for example, by using OTV with VLANs). This separation or normalization allows the introduction of demarcations and the option of an enforcement point at the border of the fabric.

In summary, the main difference in multi-pod versus multifabric deployments (see Figure 9-12) lies solely in the structuring and the applicability of hierarchical network design principles. Key aspects of this discussion therefore focus on the notion of building multiple data center networks and achieving the necessary separation between them.

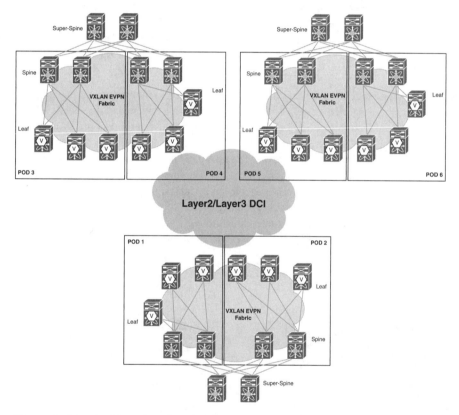

Figure 9-12 *Multi-pod and Multifabric*

In the past, Layer 2 DCI was a hot topic of discussion because virtual machine mobility required the stretch of Layer 2 networks between data centers. As the stretching of such networks across multiple data centers raised concerns about failure propagation, solutions such as OTV came to the forefront. OTV-like solutions offered the desired feature set to address the requirements. With the spine–leaf fabric evolution in the data center, however, the need for Layer 2 DCI remains a primary requirement.

There is a common misconception that virtual machine mobility can now be achieved via Layer 3 networks. This would imply that Layer 2 DCI may not be required. But while the transport network over which the VMs are moved can be routed or Layer 3, the specific network segment on which the endpoint or virtual machine resides still requires a Layer 2 extension. This is because the virtual machine typically retains its IP and MAC addresses after a VM move. Consequently, a Layer 2 or bridge service between data centers is required.

Note that using approaches such as those prescribed by LISP, where routing is employed for within-subnet communications, it may be possible to get away from the Layer 2 DCI requirement; however, such deployments are not common.

With a Layer 2 stretch, the clean separation of multiple fabrics must be ensured. Separating the data plane from the source fabric and the destination fabric with a technology in between allows protection in case of a "storm" in one fabric. This is a critical requirement. This separation helps avoid propagation of any unnecessary traffic to the other fabric in case of faults. This failure containment is one of the many features a DCI solution must provide.

Interconnecting data centers requires a Layer 2 extension, and in many deployments, a Layer 3 extension is needed as well. The extension of such a Layer 3 service needs to have simple availability for routing between subnets, and it also requires optimization so that traffic is always forwarded to the right fabric without hair-pinning. Architectures that use functionality such as LISP provide the option of integration with VXLAN BGP EVPN fabrics, thereby allowing efficient steering of the ingress traffic to the right data center (see Figure 9-13). The same can be achieved by advertising host routes outside the data center fabric (/32 in IPv4 or /128 in IPv6). However, this approach is much less scalable compared to approaches that introduce indirection at the control protocol level. The advantages of LISP in regard to external connectivity are discussed in other chapters.

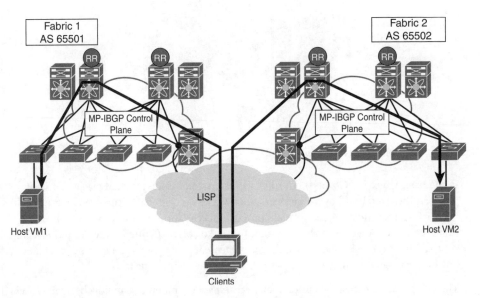

Figure 9-13 *Multifabric and Ingress Traffic Optimization*

In summary, there are many ways to construct multiple fabrics and interconnect them. It is important to understand the difference between a multi-pod design and the use of multiple individual fabrics. While multi-pod designs provide a hierarchical structure for individual pods, the multifabric approach adds an additional level of hierarchy to the multi-pod design for true data center separation.

Inter-pod/Interfabric

Often it is suggested that separation of the underlay and overlay control protocols between pods is sufficient network segregation for failure containment. Unfortunately, this is one of the most significant misconceptions in the world of overlay networking. While structuring has some scale and operational advantages, a broadcast storm in the overlay can be propagated throughout the whole multi-pod network if the Layer 2 service is expanded across all pods. One approach to address such failure propagation is to use multicast storm control in the underlay. However, this approach also affects the transport of legitimate BUM traffic. Because it is very difficult to limit these kinds of "storms" once they exist in the overlay, it is critical to have enforcement points available in the network. With multi-pod networks, the VXLAN encapsulation is end-to-end between different pods. Therefore, enforcement points between the pods are not present. This is where multifabric designs offer an advantage, thereby limiting failure propagation.

Currently, the enforcement point for filtering traffic is only available through the termination of the VXLAN encapsulation at the border of the fabric. After decapsulation, traffic is carried across classic Ethernet over the DCI domain and then re-encapsulated at the ingress of the remote fabric.

When the need for a classic Ethernet segment between decapsulation and encapsulation becomes obsolete, more scalable multi-pods can be constructed with better segregation features to prevent failure propagation (also known as *multisite*). Currently, the only way to achieve such separation of individual fabrics is through DCI solutions such as OTV (see Figure 9-14). The following sections discuss different interconnectivity options available for multifabric or multi-pod deployments.

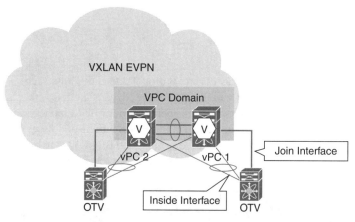

Figure 9-14 *OTV Hand-off through Ethernet.*

Interfabric Option 1: Multi-Pod

Interfabric Option 1 basically follows the model of a multi-pod design (see Figure 9-15). It is listed here for the sake of completeness.

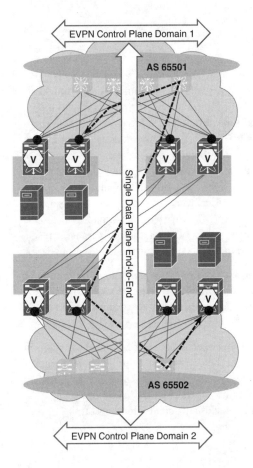

--- VXLAN Encapsulation

Figure 9-15 *Interfabric Option 1 (Multi-pod)*

As with multi-pod designs, independent overlay control protocol domains within each fabric exist, but a single data plane is present end-to-end. All the MAC/IP prefixes are distributed to all the participating VTEPs, and the same mechanism for BUM replication must be employed in all the fabrics. Interfabric Option 1 is more of a multi-pod design and not a real interfabric connectivity option per se. Nevertheless, this option may be sufficient for certain implementations to have such an end-to-end approach. However, it is important to clearly understand the disadvantages, such as failure propagation and separation of the individual pods. Interfabric Option 1 should not be expected to be the primary solution for interconnecting fabrics together in the context of DCI.

Interfabric Option 2: Multifabric

Interfabric Option 2 follows the model of classic DCI by employing classic Ethernet at the border of the fabric. The DCI network between the fabrics is cleanly separated from the fabrics themselves. This is basically the multifabric approach described earlier in this chapter.

In this interconnectivity model, independent overlay control protocol domains as well as individual overlay data planes are present in the different fabrics (see Figure 9-16). By having these two overlay control protocol domains interconnected, the exchange of all reachability information happens non-uniformly. This means that all prefix (MAC and IP) information is not spread across all the participating VTEPs. Therefore, a much better scale results with this option than with interfabric Option 1.

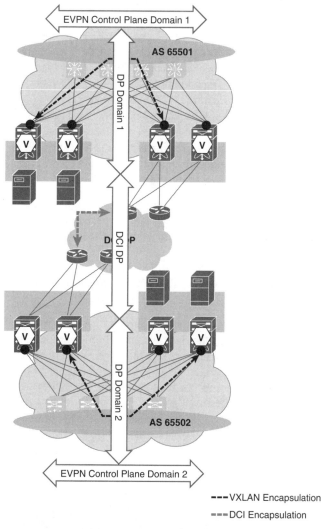

Figure 9-16 *Interfabric Option 2 (Multifabric)*

Because neither the reachability information nor the data plane is extended end-to-end, the option of having an enforcement point is achieved, allowing clean separation between the different fabrics. By having separation from an overlay perspective, the underlay can also be completely separated. As a result, the need for a VTEP from one fabric to connect to the VTEP in the other fabric does not occur. End-to-end reachability between endpoints in the two fabrics is achieved via the DCI domain between the fabrics.

This also means that the underlay-related information, such as the VTEP information and the multicast tree, does not need to exist end-to-end and can be constrained within a fabric. As a result, one fabric could use multicast for BUM traffic handling, while the other fabric uses ingress replication. Also, the DCI domain in the middle can completely and independently replicate BUM traffic, depending on its capability.

The handoff from a fabric toward the DCI domain is achieved by terminating the VXLAN encapsulation at the border of that fabric and by employing classic Ethernet to transport the necessary information to the DCI domain. The use of VRF Lite[17] and IEEE 802.1Q trunks provides the ability to normalize the VXLAN-related information and transport the data within the respective segmentation context (Layer 2 or Layer 3) across the DCI domain. With VRF Lite, an eBGP session per VRF is typically established to carry the IP prefix information from the fabric to the DCI domain from a control plane point of view. Similarly, for every Layer 2 VNI or Layer 2 network that needs to be extended between the fabrics, a VLAN is employed between the fabric and the DCI domain for Layer 2 purposes. Once traffic reaches the remote fabric, the forwarding decision is evaluated based on data plane contents. Subsequently, the traffic is encapsulated over VXLAN toward the remote leaf below which the destination endpoint is attached in that fabric.

At the point where the handoff from VXLAN to classic Ethernet occurs, enforcement points such as QoS, rate limiters, and other storm control functions can be applied. With all these features, it is possible to separate unnecessary traffic and stop failures from propagating to the remote fabric. Also, with the use of OTV in the DCI domain, data traffic can be efficiently transported between the fabrics. This helps leverage the additional benefits that OTV provides as a DCI solution.

Interfabric Option 2 provides much better separation between fabrics than Option 1, but it requires the termination of the VXLAN encapsulation at the fabric border, followed by normalization using classic Ethernet constructs. This approach might become a potential scale bottleneck because the use of VLAN IDs on the wire for segmentation separation at the VRF or network level occurs with this normalization. Because the VLAN IDs are used only on the Ethernet interface toward the DCI domain, the number of VLANs can potentially be scaled through the per-port VLAN significance feature. This requires additional configuration and alignment between the fabric border and the DCI nodes. This could become operationally complex. However, automation for the classic Ethernet normalization with IEEE 802.1Q trunks and VRF Lite can significantly ease this operational burden.

Interfabric Option 3 (Multisite for Layer 3)

Interfabric Option 3 (see Figure 9-17) involves integrated DCI handoff for Layer 3
services. This scalable interconnectivity approach for handling interfabric routed
traffic involves segmentation-related functions that lack the drawbacks of the VRF
Lite approach (interfabric Option 2). Option 3 basically employs the same multifabric
concept described earlier but with an option that allows reorigination of Layer 3 routing
information. For interfabric Option 3, only the integrated Layer 3 interconnections are
considered; the Layer 2 components are discussed in interfabric Option 4.

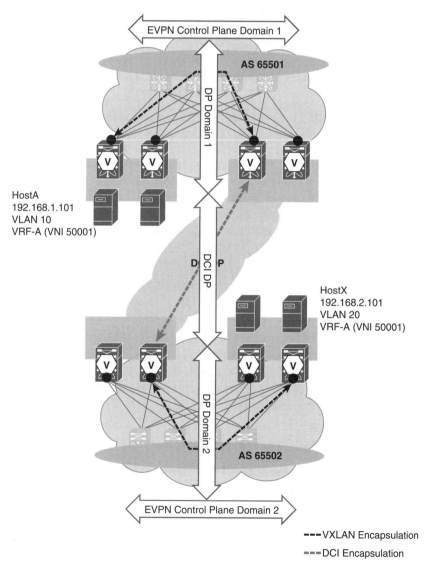

Figure 9-17   *Interfabric Option 3 (Multisite for Layer 3)*

All the considerations related to the overlay and underlay described with Option 2 apply to Option 3 as well. The handoff from one fabric toward the DCI domain is achieved by terminating the VXLAN encapsulation at the border of one fabric and through an integrated reorigination approach for Layer 3 routing to transport the necessary information across the DCI domain. The integrated handoff approach using LISP[18] or MPLS Layer 3 VPN (L3VPN)[19] is employed in this situation. In addition to the approaches mentioned earlier in this chapter, a VXLAN BGP EVPN integrated multisite solution is planned.[20]

With MPLS L3VPN, a VRF is identified by a VPN label. Recall that a Layer 3 VNI identifies a VRF in the VXLAN header. Using MP-BGP with the L3VPN address family, the EVPN prefix routes are reoriginated as VPNv4/v6 routes, and advertised by the border node toward the DCI domain. From a data plane point of view, the VXLAN header is removed, and the border node stamps a VPNv4 label and a MPLS label for interfabric Layer 3 traffic. This permits the forwarding of the packet over the MPLS core toward the remote fabric.

A similar approach is used with LISP, where the VXLAN header is removed and an appropriate LISP header identifying the VRF is stamped by the border node. The integrated handoff approach provides the ability to normalize the VXLAN-related information and transport the data in the respective segmentation context (Layer 2 or Layer 3) across the DCI domain. When the MPLS- or LISP-encapsulated traffic reaches the remote fabric, the reverse operation is performed at the border node. In other words, the LISP/MPLS header is stripped off, and traffic is again VXLAN-encapsulated, based on the Layer 3 lookup, and dispatched toward the destination VTEP in that fabric. Where Layer 2 connectivity to remote fabrics is needed, interfabric Option 2 can also be incorporated.

For routed traffic, Layer 2 enforcement points are not needed; however, protection against routing loops may still be needed. This may be the case in instances where route leaking is employed for enabling inter-VRF communication either directly at the border node or by way of a fusion router.[21]

Interfabric Option 3 retains all the advantages of Option 2, and this option also provides a simplified and scalable multitenant Layer 3 DCI alternative. Using a separate data plane to encapsulate Layer 3 traffic and using a control protocol for information exchange allows true segregation without normalization to classic Ethernet.

Interfabric Option 4 (Multisite for Layer 2)

Interfabric Option 4 follows a similar model as Option 3, with an integrated DCI handoff. While Option 3 covers Layer 3 services, Option 4 provides a similar approach for Layer 2 services (see Figure 9-18). This integrated interconnectivity approach for Layer 2 extensions enables a scalable approach for a bridging service by keeping the segmentation-related information intact.

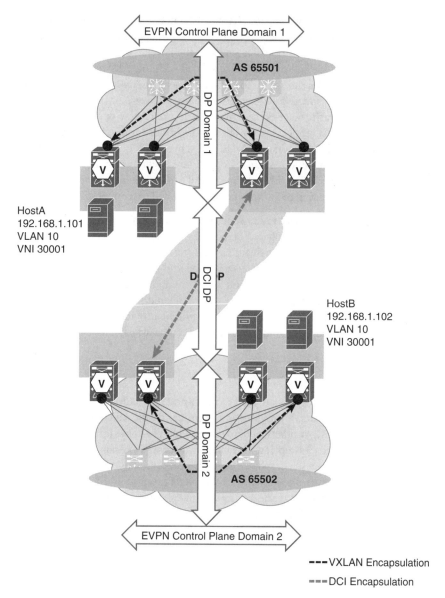

HostA
192.168.1.101
VLAN 10
VNI 30001

HostB
192.168.1.102
VLAN 10
VNI 30001

---VXLAN Encapsulation
===DCI Encapsulation

Figure 9-18   *Interfabric Option 4 (Multisite for Layer 2)*

All the considerations related to the overlay and underlay described for Option 2 apply
here as well. The handoff from one fabric toward the DCI domain is achieved by terminating the VXLAN encapsulation at the border of one fabric. Likewise, an integrated
reorigination approach for Layer 2 bridging to transport the necessary information across
the DCI domain is also present. Whereas IEEE 802.1Q trunks are employed for this
approach with Option 2, an integrated handoff approach to OTV (or EVPN in the future)
is prescribed with Option 4.

A Layer 2 network is represented by a specific Layer 2 VNI in one fabric. With a VNI-to-VNI stitching feature, VXLAN-encapsulated bridged traffic is mapped from one VNI to another VNI and sent toward the DCI domain. Similarly, the Layer 2 VXLAN traffic can be terminated at the border node and directly encapsulated with the OTV header. The integrated handoff approach provides the ability to normalize the VXLAN-related information and transport the data in the respective segmentation context (Layer 2 or Layer 3) across the DCI domain. When the traffic reaches the remote fabric, the reverse operation is performed so that the Layer 2 DCI header is removed, and the bridged traffic is encapsulated into VXLAN and sent toward the destination VTEP. The Layer 2 DCI handoff point at the border node allows enforcement actions such as stopping unknown unicast, applying appropriate QoS, enforcing rate-limiting, or other storm control functions. localizing the failures to a given fabric, thereby preventing them from being propagated to a remote fabric.

Interfabric Option 4 provides a much better separation than Option 1, and it provides greater simplification for multitenant Layer 2 deployments as compared to Option 2. The use of a separate data plane to encapsulate Layer 2 traffic, and the use of a control protocol for information exchange allows true separation without normalization to classic Ethernet. In combination with interfabric Option 3, Layer 3 and Layer 2 extensions can be provided in an integrated, scalable, and secure way compared to with Options 1 and 2. The combination of interfabric Option 3 and Option 4 will be provided in a VXLAN with BGP EVPN-integrated multisite solution that will become available in 2017.[22]

Summary

This chapter describes various concepts related to multi-pod and multifabric options with VXLAN BGP EVPN deployments. It provides a brief primer on the salient distinctions between OTV and VXLAN. Most practical deployments require some form of interconnection between different pods, or fabrics. This chapter discusses various considerations involved in making a decision on when to use the multi-pod option and when to use the multifabric option. These include underlay protocols, overlay protocols, the placement of route reflectors, the placement of rendezvous points, vPC considerations, and others. The chapter concludes with an exhaustive list of interconnection options that can be employed between multiple VXLAN BGP EVPN fabrics.

References

1. International Telecommunication Union. *G.694.2: Spectral grids for WDM applications: CWDM wavelength grid.* 2003. www.itu.int/rec/ T-REC-G.694.2-200312-I.

2. International Telecommunication Union. *G.694.1: Spectral grids for WDM applications: DWDM frequency grid.* 2012. www.itu.int/rec/T-REC-G.694.1/en.

3. IETF Network Working Group. *Virtual Private LAN Service (VPLS) using Label Distribution Protocol (LDP) signaling.* 2007. www.ietf.org/rfc/rfc4762.txt.

4. IETF Network Working Group. *Virtual Private LAN Service (VPLS) using BGP for auto-discovery and signaling.* 2007. www.ietf.org/rfc/rfc4761.txt.

5. IETF Network Working Group. *Overlay transport virtualization draft-hasmit-otv-04*. 2013. tools.ietf.org/html/draft-hasmit-otv-04.

6. IETF Network Working Group. *OSI IS-IS intra-domain routing protocol*. 1990. tools.ietf.org/html/rfc1142.

7. IETF. *Extensions to IS-IS for Layer 2 systems*. 2011. tools.ietf.org/html/rfc6165.

8. IETF Network Working Group. *IS-IS extensions to support OTV draft-drao-isis-otv-00*. 2011. tools.ietf.org/html/draft-drao-isis-otv-00.

9. IETF Network Working Group. *Generic Routing Encapsulation (GRE)*. 2000. tools.ietf.org/html/rfc2784.

10. IETF Network Working Group. *Encapsulation methods for transport of Ethernet over MPLS networks*. 2006. tools.ietf.org/html/rfc4448.

11. Cisco. *Configuring spanning tree protocol*. 2007. www.cisco.com/c/en/us/td/docs/wireless/access_point/1300/12-2_15_JA/configuration/guide/o13span.html.

12. Cisco. *Understanding Spanning-Tree Protocol topography changes*. 2016. www.cisco.com/c/en/us/support/docs/lan-switching/spanning-tree-protocol/12013-17.html.

13. IETF Network Working Group. *Source specific multicast for IP*. 2006. tools.ietf.org/html/rfc4607.

14. Cisco. *Cisco Nexus 2000 series fabric extenders*. www.cisco.com/c/en/us/products/switches/nexus-2000-series-fabric-extenders/index.html.

15. Cisco. *Cisco UCS 6300 series fabric interconnects*. www.cisco.com/c/en/us/products/servers-unified-computing/ucs-6300-series-fabric-interconnects/index.html.

16. IETF Network Working Group. *Multicast Source Discovery Protocol (MSDP)*. 2003. tools.ietf.org/html/rfc3618.

17. IETF Network Working Group. *How PEs learn routes from CEs*. 2006. tools.ietf.org/html/rfc4364#section-7.

18. Cisco. *Optimizing ingress routing with LISP across multiple VXLAN/EVPN sites*. 2015. www.cisco.com/c/en/us/products/collateral/switches/nexus-7000-series-switches/white-paper-c11-734843.html.

19. Cisco. *Configure the Cisco fabric border provider edge feature for VXLAN EVPN fabric*. 2016. www.cisco.com/c/dam/en/us/products/collateral/switches/nexus-7000-series-switches/white-paper-c11-737109.pdf.

20. IETF Network Working Group. *Multi-site EVPN-based VXLAN using border gateways*. 2016. tools.ietf.org/html/draft-sharma-multi-site-evpn.

21. Cisco. *Network virtualization—Services edge design guide*. 2008. www.cisco.com/c/en/us/td/docs/solutions/Enterprise/Network_Virtualization/ServEdge.html.

22. IETF Network Working Group. *Multi-site EVPN based VXLAN using border gateways*. 2016. tools.ietf.org/html/draft-sharma-multi-site-evpn.

Chapter 10

Layer 4–7 Services Integration

In this chapter, the following topics will be covered:

- Layer 4–7 services deployment in a VXLAN BGP EVPN network
- Intra-tenant and inter-tenant firewall deployment in transparent and routed modes
- Load balancer deployment in single-arm routed mode
- A sample service-chaining deployment with a firewall and a load balancer

This chapter discusses the integration of Layer 4–7 services into a VXLAN BGP EVPN–based network and highlights how such a setup works with the distributed IP anycast gateway. The chapter covers the process of securing the tenant edge and how traffic leaves a given VPN or IP VRF serviced by EVPN and traverses the tenant-edge service node. Tenant-edge services designs are reviewed, which are often used to make inter-tenant communication possible. The chapter also looks at some scenarios for intra-tenant traffic where endpoints in different IP subnets in a given VRF need to be protected from one other. This chapter also examines how policy-based routing (PBR) is used in this environment, in conjunction with Layer 4–7 services.

Other popular Layer 4–7 services are also covered, such as application delivery controllers (ADCs) and load balancers. This includes a combination of a load balancer and firewall deployment together in a service chaining example. Additional services are available in the Layer 4–7 space other than firewall and ADCs, and this chapter provides the groundwork necessary to derive many other deployment use cases. Overall, this chapter covers how to successfully integrate different Layer 4–7 services in a VXLAN BGP EVPN network.

Firewalls in a VXLAN BGP EVPN Network

The most popular service appliance in use in networks today is the firewall. When organizations require some kind of security or segregation between different networks, the deployment of one or more firewalls invariably satisfies this requirement. Most network switches or routers today can satisfy firewall rules based on Layer 3–4 headers via regular security access control lists (ACLs); however, when visibility is required into the application payload, and when security rules need to be set based on that, a dedicated appliance (either virtual or physical) is typically required.

Modern firewalls allow quite a bit of flexibility in enforcing policies and inspecting traffic. While several different types of firewalls can be deployed, depending on the specialized functionality they offer, they all have some basic functionality by which an inside network can be protected from an outside network (see Figure 10-1).

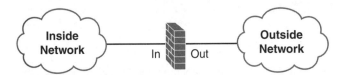

Figure 10-1 *Firewall*

A firewall typically has at least two interfaces: an "IN" interface directed interiorly, toward the network for which it provides protection, and an "OUT" interface directed toward the untrusted or unprotected network. These interfaces may be logical or physical in nature. Firewalls may be deployed within a network in either Layer 3 or routed mode, or in Layer 2 or bridged mode (also sometimes called transparent mode). The following sections discuss these deployment modes in greater detail, with emphasis on nuances associated with their deployment in a VXLAN BGP EVPN network.

Routing Mode

In routing mode, a firewall protects routed or inter-subnet traffic. Currently, a firewall can be deployed as a router, and forwarding decisions can be performed based on IP routing. The simplest option when operating in routed mode is to have the firewall act as the default gateway for the endpoints. The firewall performs all inter-subnet operations, while the network behind the interfaces provides only Layer 2, or bridging, functionality (see Figure 10-2).

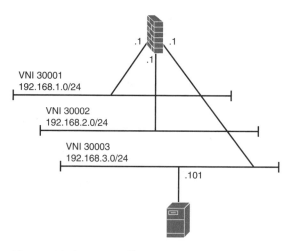

Figure 10-2   *Firewall as a Default Gateway*

Figure 10-2 shows three networks, depicted as Layer 2 VNIs 30001, 30002, and 30003. These networks map to subnets 192.168.1.0/24, 192.168.2.0/24, and 192.168.3.0/24, respectively. The firewall is configured with the default gateway IP address for these networks (specifically 192.168.1.1, 192.168.2.1, and 192.168.3.1). In many enterprise networks, PCIE compliance demands that all inter-subnet traffic must go through a firewall to provide strict control on which endpoint can talk to another endpoint.

Traffic to and from the endpoints flows through the firewall because it serves as the default gateway; however, the firewall is also able to perform forwarding decisions based on static or dynamic routing, just like a regular router. In static routing, the IP subnet protected by the firewall (and its location behind the firewall's IN interface) is defined statically through its configuration at the upstream router. On the firewall itself, a default route configured (0/0) typically exists that points to the next-hop router reachable via the OUT interface.

With dynamic routing, routing protocols come into the picture, and routing adjacencies are established between the firewall and other routers/switches in the network. New networks can be added and protected by the firewall without requiring any additional network configuration. Depending on the firewall vendor and software versions, various IGP protocols or even BGP may be supported for dynamic routing. These are often supplemented with Bidirectional Forwarding Detection (BFD)[1] to help with fast failure detection and fast convergence.

With dynamic routing, routing adjacencies are established between the network and the firewall, thereby allowing the firewall to advertise all subnets being protected to the network. Similarly, from the network side, either a default route or more specific external routes may be advertised to the firewall. This approach allows greater flexibility in learning the respective network location with regard to an IP subnet's location.

All higher-level functions of the firewall, such as network address translation (NAT),[2] packet inspection, and application inspection, should be configured as usual. Even if the forwarding rules on the firewall are properly configured to allow the transport of packets, the additional functions of the firewall might still prevent traffic from being forwarded. With this approach, security integrity can still be kept intact, while the forwarding decisions are based on dynamically learned information. This allows segregation of duty from network and security perspectives.

Additional aspects of routing mode need to be considered when the firewall operates in high-availability mode for both dynamic and static routing. Depending on the firewall vendor appliance and the associated software version, routing tables may not be synchronized between the active and standby instances. In these cases, especially with dynamic routing, the standby device does not learn any of the routes learned through dynamic routing, nor does it establish a routing adjacency.

In case of a failover event, the standby firewall becomes active and is required to first establish routing adjacency with the network. Then the routing information should be learned. Only then the standby firewall is ready to handle traffic forwarding. In this instance, despite the simplicity of learning new networks, dynamic routing with a firewall becomes less feasible because the reconvergence after a failure or failover event could take several seconds.

Bridging Mode

Firewalls have the option to operate in a bridging, or transparent, mode. In this mode, a firewall does not learn IP routes or carry any static or dynamic routing information. Instead, the firewall acts as a security enforcement point from a forwarding perspective, representing a "bump on the wire." The biggest advantage of deploying a firewall in transparent mode is that no changes are required to the network configuration with respect to IP addressing.

Depending on where the firewall is located, there are different ways to force traffic through the inspection or enforcement device. One option is to place the firewall in the transparent mode between the endpoints and the default gateway. Here, the default gateway resides in a different bridge domain (or typically VLAN) from the endpoints, and the firewall transparently stitches these two bridge domains together.

Figure 10-3 shows a typical transparent firewall deployment where the two legs of the firewall are associated with VLAN 10 and VLAN 100 respectively. In this case, every endpoint for external communication must pass firewall inspection in order to reach the default gateway. Similarly, all traffic toward the protected endpoints must also be inspected by the firewall. In this particular deployment option, the MAC address table of the firewall dictates the forwarding decision, just as a typical network switch would normally operate. The endpoints are separated from the default gateway through the firewall. As a result, multiple bridge domains or VLANs have to be used for each IP subnet to force the traffic through the firewall. This approach is therefore often referred to as *VLAN stitching*.

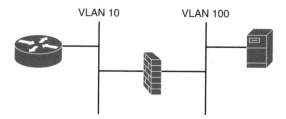

Figure 10-3   *Transparent Firewall with VLAN/L2 VNI Stitching*

In cases where more scalable solutions are required, and a services edge design is anticipated, a routing sandwich can be created. The transparent firewall is placed between two routers (logical or physical), and the two routers form routing adjacencies through the transparent firewall and exchange all necessary routing information for the protected and unprotected networks.

In order to create this routing or VRF sandwich, each router must advertise an individual, unique MAC address over the peering interface. Otherwise, the firewall will not be able to forward traffic correctly since the source and DMAC would be the same. This would naturally create some network issues. The reason for mentioning this is that many smaller switching platforms commonly work with a single MAC address shared across all routed interfaces (physical and logical). This would make it impractical to deploy such a transparent firewall using a router sandwich approach.

Firewall Redundancy with Static Routing

When a firewall is deployed as a high-availability pair (HA pair) in routed mode, some considerations regarding the attachment of the HA pair to the VXLAN BGP EVPN network are noteworthy. If both firewall instances are attached to the same leaf or leaf pair with vPC, special considerations for a failover case are not necessary. From a routing and forwarding perspective, the VTEP IP address serving the firewalls does not change on an HA event.

If the firewalls are attached to different leafs or leaf pairs (with or without vPC), the VTEP IP address for reaching the firewall changes on an HA event. In these cases, only the VTEP hosting the active firewall instance should be considered for forwarding, and the most efficient path toward this VTEP should be selected.

To elaborate further on the redundancy designs with firewalls, the firewall IP address is assumed to persist as the active firewall node. Typically, the standby firewall node is dormant and continuously monitors the health of the active firewall node. It can take over in case of a failure to ensure minimal disruption. Therefore, in such a network, only the VTEP attached to the active firewall node should advertise reachability for the firewall into the BGP EVPN network.

When using a static route on a given VTEP attached to the active firewall (which points to the local connected firewall as the next hop), the static route becomes active. This is because the next-hop IP address for the static route is the firewall, and the firewall IP address is locally resolved through ARP. In the Cisco BGP EVPN implementation on

Nexus switches, this information is populated into the local routing table through a component called the *host mobility manager (HMM)*.

So far, the static route configured where the active firewall is connected works perfectly, and no special considerations have to be made. But this changes once firewall high availability is present. In this scenario, the firewall HA pair is assumed to be distributed, and the standby firewall is located behind a different leaf or pair of leafs (with vPC) from the current active firewall (see Figure 10-4). This assumption is made so that comprehensive background information can be provided for the configuration of a routing entry at a given location in the network.

Most of these considerations are required when firewalls are distributed. But in today's world of virtual services appliances and scale-out extensions, it is best to consider any possible design and failure option to meet the requirements.

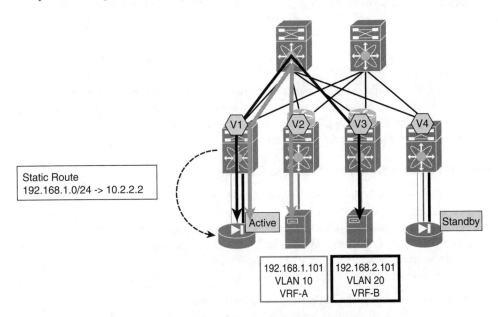

Figure 10-4 *Firewall Failover with Static Routing (Steady State)*

With the standby firewall located behind a different VTEP on an HA event, the physical location associated with the active firewall changes. Even with the location change, the previously configured static route at the location of the former active firewall still remains active. As a result, it steers traffic toward the firewall, to the old VTEP location. This is because the next hop (aka the firewall's IP address) for the static route is still present in the routing table or RIB.

On the HA event, the new VTEP learns the firewall's IP address through ARP, creates an IP address entry in the local routing table, and then distributes it as an IP prefix via BGP EVPN. All remote VTEPs, including the VTEP attached to the formerly active firewall, receive this information and install/update that entry in the RIB. Consequently, having this entry present allows the former VTEP to still keep the static route active.

In the best-case scenario, roughly 50% of the traffic directed to the firewall is suboptimally forwarded. In the worst-case scenario, this traffic is black-holed, resulting in traffic impairment caused by a redundancy event.

In Figure 10-4, the firewall with the cluster IP address 10.2.2.2 is connected to VTEP V1. Behind the firewall, a protected subnet has prefix 192.168.1.0/24. The firewall's IP address is learned locally on VTEP V1 through ARP resolution and propagated into the routing table via HMM. On VTEP V1, the static IP route is configured such that 192.168.1.0/24 is reachable via 10.2.2.2. In order to make this route available to the whole VXLAN BGP EVPN network, this static route is redistributed to all VTEPs in the network.

In this steady state, when an endpoint in a different network (VLAN 20) intends to reach an endpoint in the protected IP subnet 192.168.1.0/24 (VLAN 10), it follows the redistributed route toward VTEP V1. Subsequently, it then follows through the active firewall and eventually reaches the protected IP subnet.

Say that an event occurs that requires the active firewall to fail over to the standby firewall located behind VTEP V4 (see Figure 10-5). With this event, the cluster IP address of the firewall, 10.2.2.2, has moved from VTEP V1 to VTEP V4. The firewall's IP address is now learned locally on VTEP V4 through ARP resolution and propagated into the routing table via the HMM.

As the cluster IP address is distributed through BGP EVPN from VTEP V4, VTEP V1 still has a valid next hop for the static route. In this failover state, when an endpoint in a different network intends to reach an endpoint in the protected IP subnet 192.168.1.0/24, the traffic follows the redistributed route toward VTEP V1. It then follows to VTEP V4 and finally through the firewall to reach the protected IP subnet.

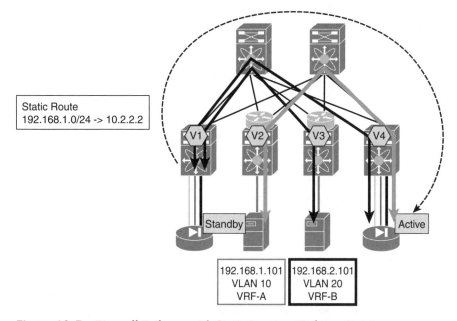

Figure 10-5 *Firewall Failover with Static Routing (Failover State)*

Given the previous explanation, it might be more feasible for all VTEPs hosting the firewall to have this static route present. In this instance, the traffic flow is partly optimal and partly suboptimal. This is the case not only in the failover state but also in the steady state. The following sections discuss two recommended approaches for preventing this suboptimal forwarding.

Static Route Tracking at a Service Leaf

Whenever an endpoint, a firewall, or any other device is attached to a leaf hosting the distributed IP anycast gateway in a VXLAN BGP EVPN network, the IP address is learned via ARP through the HMM in the local routing table and subsequently distributed into BGP EVPN. In this approach, a route-tracking condition is added to this particular route when adding the static route for the protected IP subnet behind the firewall.

The static route configured on the service leaf (leaf attached to the firewall) is allowed to become active only if the route is being learned through the HMM. This prevents the configured static route from remaining active if the next hop is learned through anything other than HMM. Alternatively, if the next hop for the route is learned through BGP, the static route becomes inactive. As a result, the static route is only active on the VTEP where the active firewall is present.

The following special configuration is required on the leaf where the firewalls are attached so that the firewall's cluster IP can be tracked (10.2.2.2 in this case) and learned via HMM only:

```
track 5 ip route 10.2.2.2/32 reachability hmm
ip route 192.168.1.0/24 10.2.2.2 track 5
```

Static Routing at a Remote Leaf

An alternative approach to configuring route tracking by HMM is to employ static route resolution at the remote leafs. In other words, a static route can be configured at all the remote leafs having endpoints that need to reach the protected subnet behind the firewall. This occurs as follows:

```
ip route 192.168.1.0/24 10.2.2.2
```

This is simply a regular static route configuration for a remote route. Notably, this requires remote leafs to support recursive route resolution when the next hop is behind a remote VTEP. The active firewall's IP address is learned at the service leaf and advertised over BGP EVPN unconditionally to all remote leafs, just like any other endpoint. When an HA event occurs, and the standby firewall takes over, it typically sends out a Gratuitous Address Resolution Protocol (GARP) or ARP request to announce its "takeover" to the network. The leaf attached to the standby firewall learns the firewall's IP address as a local entry. After a rapid EVPN sequence number–assisted mobility convergence event, traffic is directed to the VTEP attached to the new active firewall. In this way, the HA event for the firewall is treated just like any other endpoint move event from the BGP EVPN network's point of view.

Physical Connectivity

There are many ways to connect a firewall to a leaf or pair of leafs. Options vary from a single attached interface to using a local port channel to using a virtual PortChannel (vPC). The cases for using a single interface or a port channel attached to a single VTEP are not really different. Options for both Layer 2 and Layer 3 connectivity are available, and no special implications for routing protocols are present.

In case of static routing, the use of a Layer 2 interface or port channel is most commonly chosen when using a switch virtual interface (SVI) on the VTEP side, while the firewall provides its option of a logical interface. Between the VTEP and the firewall, VLAN IDs are used to separate the different logical firewall interfaces, if this approach is in compliance with the deployment. Alternatively, if a stronger separation than VLANs is required, separate physical or port channel interfaces can be used. However, this may require the use of VLANs within the separate interfaces in order to address the logical interfaces within the VTEP or firewall.

In cases where a firewall is connected to only one leaf, the redundancy is achieved by the firewall's high-availability capability. Here, it is assumed that one VTEP serves a firewall of the HA pair, while a different independent VTEP serves the respective HA partner. In these specific instances, the firewall provides the device redundancy, while the network takes care of providing the path redundancy.

From an operational perspective, this is the simplest way to deploy firewalls into networks because there is no "fate sharing" between the responsible network switches. Firewall redundancy is provided by two firewalls, network redundancy is provided by two network switches, and link redundancy is provided by two interfaces in a local port channel.

For deployments requiring further redundancy, vPC can provide some additional network options. vPC enables the use of dynamic routing protocols, but the choice here needs to be evaluated carefully. Support for dynamic routing protocols over vPC is available on some hardware platforms and software releases, but even with this feature, certain constraints exist. Whenever the use of vPC is required, it is important to consult the appropriate release notes and configuration guides for applicability.

When vPC is required for redundancy, consider attaching each firewall to individual vPC domains and the associated switch pairs. This implementation provides common fate sharing in a vPC domain; it is recommended to keep additional network redundancy requirements intact. Both firewalls in the HA pair can also be connected to a single vPC domain, but the operational tasks of a vPC domain have to be included in the overall redundancy consideration.

In discussing the deployment models, mode, and connectivity, it is important to consider the location of the firewall or firewall HA pair. Once the location is defined in the physical network, it is also important to think about the logical insertion of the firewall in regard to VRFs, distributed anycast gateway, and VNIs. As initially mentioned, a firewall can be placed anywhere in a VXLAN BGP EVPN network. However, the network switch where the firewall is connected is required to have the ability to encapsulate and decapsulate VXLAN traffic and serve as a VTEP. In most common spine–leaf deployments, the leaf provides this VTEP service. When a border exists, the firewall may be attached to the border node.

Inter-Tenant/Tenant-Edge Firewall

An inter-tenant, or tenant-edge, firewall is a security enforcement point placed at the edge or exit of a given tenant. The term *tenant* can have multiple definitions, but in this case it is used interchangeably with *VRF* and *VPN*. The tenant-edge firewall allows access to and from a given VRF. The method used for this approach is often referred to as *VRF stitching* because a service device—in this case a firewall—stitches an inside or protected VRF from an outside VRF. The outside VRF may even directly lead to the Internet. In a VXLAN BGP EVPN data center network, the inside VRF is a VPN and may comprise multiple IP subnets. Likewise, the VPN or VRF may exist at many different locations (leaf switches) in the overall network.

Figure 10-6 depicts a logical flow with a tenant-edge firewall where Tenant 1 has a single VRF-A with three networks (192.168.1.0/24, 192.168.2.0/24, and 192.168.3.0/24). Hosts within these networks (Host A, Host X, and Host R) need to traverse the tenant-edge firewall whenever they need to send traffic to a destination outside the VRF. Similarly, external traffic destined to the hosts needs to first traverse the tenant-edge firewall. This traffic is allowed to enter VRF-A only if appropriate permit rules are configured. In this way, whenever traffic from an endpoint within this VRF at any given leaf wants to exit this tenant, it follows the respective network path toward the exit, where a firewall controls that exit.

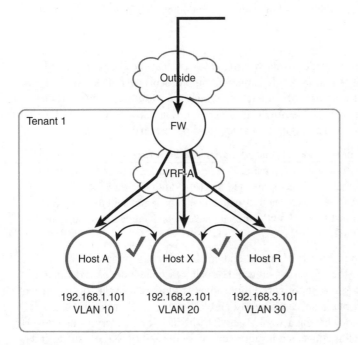

Figure 10-6   *Inter-tenant Firewall*

Just as the endpoints can be located anywhere within the VXLAN BGP EVPN fabric, the firewall can also be located behind any leaf. The best practices for deployment place the tenant-edge firewall at the service leaf or border leaf. In the case of the border leaf, the given tenant-edge firewall is generally in control of external access. Once traffic has entered the tenant, VRF, or VPN, the tenant-edge firewall does not enforce any further control. This means that data traffic between various IP subnets in the given tenant is not enforced through the tenant-edge firewall.

Once traffic is allowed to enter the VRF, based on the configured policy rules, it is free to communicate within the boundaries of the VRF. In summary, the tenant-edge firewall is the gatekeeper for traffic entering or leaving a given tenant, VRF, or VPN construct.

Figure 10-7 shows a tenant-edge firewall HA pair connected to the border in a VXLAN BGP EVPN fabric. The connectivity of the firewall to the border can happen individually as well as in association with a vPC domain. The leaf attached to endpoint 192.168.1.101 has subnet 192.168.1.0/24 in VRF-A locally configured. Similarly, the leaf attached to endpoint 192.168.2.102 has subnet 192.168.2.0/24 in VRF-B locally instantiated. The networks in VRF-A and VRF-B need to be protected. VRF-C is the unprotected network where the Internet or WAN is connected. VRF-A, VRF-B, and VRF-C are instantiated on the border to which the tenant-edge firewall is attached.

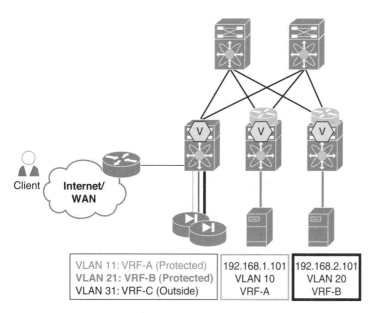

Figure 10-7   *Deployment of Tenant-Edge Firewall at Border Leaf*

If an external client wants to connect to the endpoint 192.168.1.101, the traffic from the client needs to enter the VXLAN BGP EVPN network through the external router and reach the border leaf in the unprotected VRF-C. Based on routing information in VRF-C, the traffic is directed toward the firewall HA pair (specifically the active firewall node) and inspected.

The active firewall applies the appropriate security policies to the traffic, and if the traffic is permitted, the firewall makes a forwarding decision based on the routing table, determining the appropriate interface through which the traffic should exit in order to reach the border leaf protected by VRF-A. Once in VRF-A on the border leaf, the traffic is VXLAN encapsulated and sent toward the leaf hosting endpoint 192.168.1.101 in the most efficient way. Recall that because this is routed traffic, the VXLAN VNI carried in the header corresponds to the Layer 3 VNI associated with VRF-A.

If endpoint 192.168.1.101 wants to connect to the WAN/Internet, the traffic from the endpoint flows toward its default gateway, which is the distributed IP anycast gateway on the connected leaf. Once the leaf is reached, a routing lookup is performed that hits the default route leading to the exit point (the tenant edge) of VRF-A. The default route in VRF-A is advertised by the border leaf. Based on the routing table lookup, the traffic is encapsulated in VXLAN with the VNI associated with VRF-A and sent toward the border leaf.

At the border leaf, the default route to exit the VXLAN BGP EVPN network is set to point toward the firewall HA pair. After the firewall is reached, its local routing table is consulted, and traffic is forwarded toward the appropriate next hop. In this case, the lookup hits the default-route match, which points to the border leaf in VRF-C. Once in VRF-C, external routing provides the exit by a learned default route, and in following this path, traffic reaches the external world, the WAN, or the Internet.

Some variations exist in the connection between the tenant-edge firewall and the unprotected network VRF-C on the external router. One option is to provide a Layer 2 network where the firewall can directly build Layer 3 adjacency with the external router (see Figure 10-8). This option sounds rather simple but might raise some complexity issues if multiple routers and multiple firewalls are present.

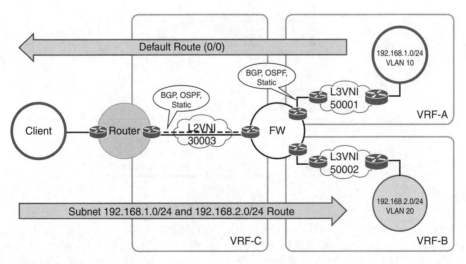

Figure 10-8 *Logical Diagram for Tenant-Edge Firewall Connectivity (Bridge Unprotected)*

Alternatively, the VXLAN BGP EVPN network can become the routing neighbor to the external router or routers as well as to the firewalls. In this case, the routers and firewall build local routing adjacency to the leaf where they are connected (see Figure 10-9). All this information is then redistributed into the BGP EVPN control protocol. With this approach, it is important to understand that the routing adjacency can occur with either a physical or logical interface.

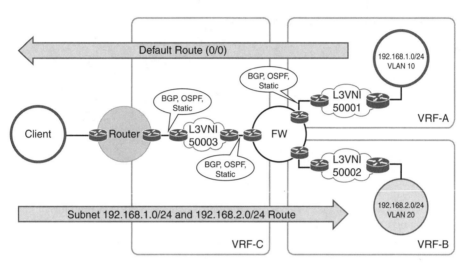

Figure 10-9 *Logical Diagram for Tenant-Edge Firewall Connectivity (Routed Unprotected)*

In the case of a logical interface or an SVI, the interface should not be a distributed IP anycast gateway. There are many reasons for this. First, such an interface would result in the existence of multiple overlapping router IDs because every leaf would have the same IP for respective peering. Furthermore, a logical interface is not required because a physical interface can provide additional advantages in terms of convergence. Likewise, a logical interface might need additional protocols such as BFD (if available).

When the firewall is deployed in the bridged or transparent mode, the exchange of IP information must be achieved between the logical router instances of the protected (VRF-A/VRF-B) and the unprotected networks (VRF-C), as shown in Figure 10-10. As a result, a logical or physical interface on the protected network side of the firewall must be present for each network as one side of the routing adjacency. Also, an additional logical or physical interface is needed on the unprotected side of the firewall. As discussed previously in describing firewall deployment in bridged mode, it is imperative that interfaces have individual MAC addresses. The firewall creates its bridging table based on these addresses, and if the MAC addresses are all the same, the firewall sees no need to forward anything.

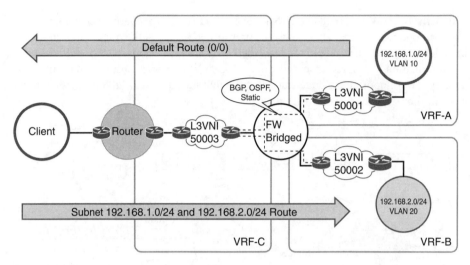

Figure 10-10   *Logical Diagram for Tenant-Edge Firewall Connectivity (Bridged Firewall)*

In this model, the firewall only acts as a security enforcement and potential address translation point. All forwarding is in a pure bridged mode on the firewall, while the logical routers or VRFs ensure that traffic from a given protected network can flow to the unprotected side and vice versa.

Services-Edge Design

Various white papers, design guides, and books cover services-edge design.[3,4] With network virtualization, such deployments are simpler because the multitenancy constructs are already reflected. With VXLAN BGP EVPN, the construct of VRFs or VPNs is inherently available, which simplifies the transport of segmentation through the network.

When normalization to the firewall or other service tiers becomes necessary, traditional approaches are considered, such as those described in connection with external connectivity. Data center networks using VXLAN BGP EVPN enable multitenancy and allow integration with various services-edge deployment designs.

Intra-Tenant Firewalls

An intra-tenant or east-west firewall is a security enforcement point placed between networks in a given tenant or VRF. The terms *network*, *VLAN*, and *IP subnet* are used interchangeably in this section. An intra-tenant firewall allows access control between networks. In regard to a VXLAN BGP EVPN data center fabric, the network is a Layer 2 VNI, and it refers to a single IP subnet within this fabric at any location (that is, leaf).

Whenever an endpoint at any given leaf in the network wants to reach an endpoint in a different network, traffic follows the network path toward the exit, which is controlled by a firewall. Just as endpoints can exist at any location in the VXLAN fabric, the firewall can also be located behind any and every possible leaf. However, firewalls are most commonly attached to a set of service leafs or border leafs.

As noted in the discussion regarding tenant-edge firewalls, once traffic has entered the tenant, VRF, or VPN, the tenant-edge firewall does not enforce any further control. This enforcement is the responsibility of the intra-tenant, or east–west, firewall. In other words, control of data traffic between various IP subnets within a given tenant is enforced through the intra-tenant firewall.

The east–west firewall inspects the communications and enforces the configured policy set for east–west communication when the endpoints in one network want to communicate with endpoints in a different network. Figure 10-11 shows a sample intra-tenant firewall deployment where three VLANs in Tenant 1 are protected by an east–west firewall. Specifically, the three VLANs (VLAN 10, VLAN 20, and VLAN 30) map to three unique Layer 2 VNIs (VNI 30001, VNI 30002, and VNI 30003), each associated with a different subnet (192.168.1.0/24, 192.168.2.0/24, and 192.168.3.0/24). The policies configured at the firewall ensure that traffic between hosts in different subnets is denied.

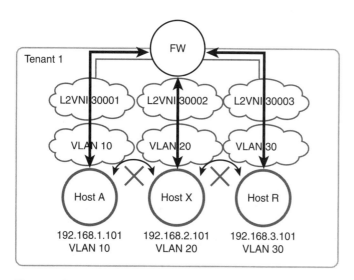

Figure 10-11 *Intra-Tenant/East–West Firewall*

An intra-tenant firewall can be deployed in a VXLAN BGP EVPN network in different ways. One option is to integrate the firewall in routed mode and provide the default gateway for the networks on the firewall. This implementation method requires that the VXLAN network only operate in Layer 2 mode, while the distributed IP anycast gateway and VRFs are not configured. In this case, the endpoints communicate via a VXLAN Layer 2 VNI toward the default gateway configured on the firewall, and all first-hop routing is performed at the firewall, as shown in Figure 10-12. In the figure, VLAN 10 maps to VNI 30001, which in turn terminates on the firewall in the protected leg where the default gateway for that subnet resides. Similarly, VLAN 20 maps to VNI 30002. The unprotected leg of the firewall maps to VNI 30003, over which appropriate route prefixes are exchanged to allow for reachability from an endpoint in the protected subnet to an endpoint in any other subnet and vice versa. In this scenario, the intra-tenant firewall is deployed in routed mode.

The Cisco implementation of VXLAN BGP EVPN provides the option to operate the network in Layer 2–only mode. The control protocol is only leveraged for MAC prefix distribution and for ARP suppression. In this case, the east–west firewall provides a centralized default gateway-like functionality, which is seen in many classic non-fabric approaches.

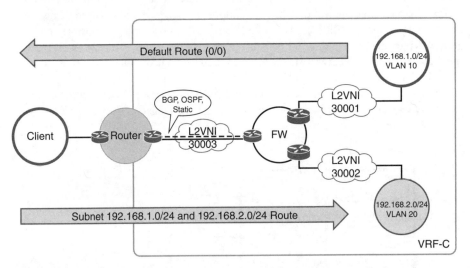

Figure 10-12 *Intra-Tenant/East–West Firewall as the Default Gateway*

When deploying the firewall in transparent mode, a slightly different option becomes available, as shown in Figure 10-13. VLANs 10, 20, and 30 are all part of the 192.168.1.0/24 subnet. Endpoints in VLAN 10 and 20 need to be protected by the firewall. In this situation, the distributed IP anycast gateway of the VXLAN BGP EVPN network can still be leveraged, in conjunction with a Layer 2 approach. The firewall is connected to a VTEP that serves the distributed IP anycast gateway for a given network. The network represented by VLAN 30 in the figure is available in the whole VXLAN BGP EVPN fabric and represents the unprotected side. Endpoints can be connected to this network in VLAN 30, but traffic toward these endpoints from other networks is directly routed without any enforcement via the transparent firewall.

The connectivity between the VTEP hosting the distributed IP anycast gateway and the firewall is a classic Ethernet trunk, which feeds the unprotected network and the default gateway toward the firewall. The firewall operates in transparent mode and enforces the respective security policies for all passing traffic.

Because the firewall is like a bump in the wire, the protected side is represented with a different VLAN ID from the unprotected side. Specifically, as shown in Figure 10-13, VLANs 10 and 20 represent the protected side. The protected VLANs are fed back to the VTEP and get mapped to Layer 2 VNIs, making these protected networks available throughout the VXLAN BGP EVPN network. With this approach, the distributed IP anycast gateway can be better leveraged. Note that all endpoints in VLANs 10, 20, and 30 share the same default gateway IP because they are part of the same subnet, 192.168.1.0/24. However, the default gateway IP is only provisioned in VLAN 30 that maps to VNI 30003.

The advantage of this transparent firewall deployment is that protected and unprotected bridge domains can be used throughout the VXLAN BGP EVPN network. This allows flexibility and also enables the firewall, the distributed IP anycast gateway, and Layer 2 and Layer 3 VNIs to coexist, which is not possible when a firewall is deployed in routed mode as a default gateway. Also, this implementation allows simple integration with vPC because Layer 3 operations toward the firewall are not especially needed.

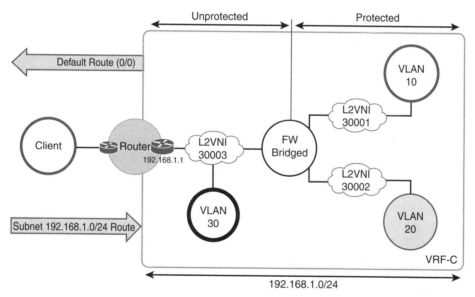

Figure 10-13   *Intra-Tenant/East–West Firewall - Transparent Mode*

When using the VXLAN BGP EVPN network to provide Layer 2 and Layer 3 function with the distributed IP anycast gateway, additional considerations are needed, particularly if the firewall is to be part of the routing path.

For example, when an endpoint (192.168.1.101) wants to connect to an endpoint (192.168.2.101) in a different subnet, the traffic must be inspected by the east–west firewall. In a VXLAN BGP EVPN network, where a distributed IP anycast gateway is being used, the firewall participates in routing and also in the network itself. This means the firewall announces the IP subnets intended to be protected by it. Because these IP subnet prefix routes are less specific than host routes (/32 in case of IPv4), the routes announced by the firewall might not be considered. When inter-subnet traffic from the endpoint 192.168.1.101 reaches its distributed IP anycast gateway, it performs a lookup for the destination endpoint, 192.168.2.101. Because both IP subnets belong to the same VRF, an LPM lookup match hits the 192.168.2.101/32 host route. This results in the next hop being the egress VTEP, which is the VTEP where the destination endpoint resides.

Consequently, the IP subnet route advertised by the firewall is ignored. Therefore, the requirement of inspecting the traffic between the two endpoints is not fulfilled. As previously described, not only does the distributed IP anycast gateway provide the first-hop routing functionality for an endpoint, it is also responsible for advertising the endpoint location from a MAC and IP perspective. With this approach, shortest-path routing is achieved in the overlay directly from the ingress VTEP to the egress VTEP.

When inspection through a firewall is required, the previously described approach must be overridden. As explained, the advertisement of an IP subnet does not help in this case. If the firewall announces host routes, the best possible outcome would be a destination lookup that yields an ECMP path with the next hop being the firewall and the egress VTEP. However, this would still not satisfy the requirement that *all* inter-subnet traffic must be inspected via the intra-tenant firewall.

Because classic destination-based routing is insufficient in the case of east–west firewalls with networks in the same VRF, different approaches have to be selected. One option would be to set one network to Layer 2–only mode and use the firewall as the default gateway for that network. In this way, the use of the distributed IP anycast gateway would be removed for that network, but it would still be available for use by the other network. Nevertheless, this approach would be quite restrictive if more than just two networks were present and if firewall enforcement were required. In this situation, only one single network would be able to use the distributed IP anycast gateway, while all the others would use the firewall as a default gateway. Because the use of the distributed IP anycast gateway offers a significant advantage in the VXLAN BGP EVPN network, using it together with east–west traffic enforcement is desirable when the protected and unprotected networks reside in the same VRF.

With policy-based routing (PBR), routing decisions can be overridden based on different classification match criteria. Specifically, PBR classified traffic can be directed and forwarded recursively to a specific firewall (see Figure 10-14). This means that if traffic from IP subnet 192.168.1.0/24 wants to reach IP subnet 192.168.2.0/24, traffic is classified and directed to a firewall. This firewall can be on the same VTEP where the PBR rule is configured or somewhere else in the VXLAN BGP EVPN network.

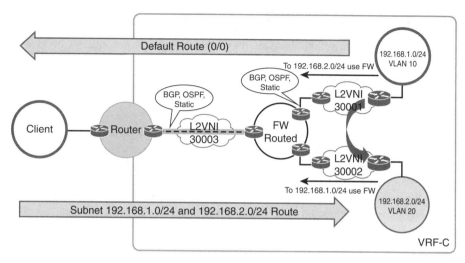

Figure 10-14   *Intra-Tenant/East–West Firewall—Policy-Based Routing*

The PBR match result can point to a next hop, which requires recursive lookups and is reachable over VXLAN. This is possible as long as the next hop is known and reachable. Because it is assumed that traffic from endpoint 192.168.1.101 to 192.168.2.101 must be sent to the firewall and return traffic must also go through the firewall, the PBR rule must also be configured on the VTEP serving endpoint 192.168.2.101. Now if every endpoint within the 192.168.1.0/24 subnet needs to be protected while communicating with endpoints in the 192.168.2.0/24 subnet, the PBR rule must be installed on all VTEPs servicing either of these subnets. With the presence of the distributed IP anycast gateway, and endpoints spread across the fabric, this could potentially mean PBR rules being configured on all leafs under the IRB interfaces associated with the subnets. The PBR rule sets could quickly become unwieldy if the number of subnets in the VRF that need protection also goes up. The complexity in managing these rules and the corresponding maintenance may make the use of PBR impractical if the number of networks within a VRF becomes even a handful. In addition, the ACL table scale for installing the PBR rules becomes a concern.

With the PBR-based approach, IP subnet traffic for endpoint-to-endpoint protection can be enforced, and this traffic can bypass the firewall during certain communications for performance reasons. While Network Services Header (NSH),[5] Segment Routing (SR),[6] and LISP[7] are presently valid standards related to services redirection, the ability to influence and control traffic forwarding with PBR in a VXLAN BGP EVPN network on a hop-by-hop basis also exists. The following section looks at a combination of VXLAN with the technologies previously mentioned so simplification of existing traffic direction rules for VXLAN BGP EVPN networks can be achieved.

Mixing Intra-Tenant and Inter-Tenant Firewalls

Data center networks are not uniform, and therefore the requirement for east–west as well as north–south security policy enforcement has to be accommodated simultaneously. The previous sections explain in detail approaches used for firewall insertion in a VXLAN BGP EVPN network. These approaches are not mutually exclusive as long as operations are in the same mode (routed or transparent).

A firewall can operate at a tenant edge with routing protocols configured, and a different interface can act as the default gateway for an intra-tenant segment. The question arises, however, whether it is permissible to mix the slightly different modes and positions in the network on a given firewall. Often, organizations require the separation of the different stages in a network layer by layer. To support these separation requirements, modern firewalls allow virtualization and the creation of multiple contexts with dedicated or shared interfaces. This helps achieve a more logical separation than is provided by VLANs or VRFs.

Regardless of whether one or multiple firewalls are used to build an infrastructure, the placement, function, and integration approach should be flexible enough to accommodate the required deployment permutations.

Figure 10-15 depicts a sample deployment with both inter-tenant and intra-tenant firewalls for VRF-A. The logical topology also depicts a service leaf to which the firewalls are attached, and a regular leaf(s) to which various endpoints may be attached. The intra-tenant networks 192.168.1.0/24 and 192.168.2.0/24 are part of the same VRF (VRF-A) connected to the same VTEP (Leaf 1), as shown in Figure 10-15.

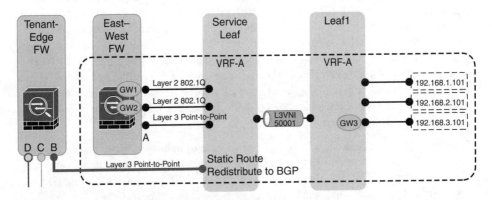

Figure 10-15 *Inter-Tenant and Intra-Tenant Firewalls*

Because the east–west firewall becomes the default gateway for these networks, they are extended as Layer 2 only across the VXLAN BGP EVPN fabric toward the service leaf. On the service leaf, IEEE 802.1Q trunks are used to extend the Layer 2 VNI via VLANs toward the firewall. On the firewall, logical interfaces (similar to SVIs) provide the Layer 3 first-hop function (default gateway) to the endpoints in intra-tenant networks namely, 192.168.1.101 and 192.168.2.101.

Layer 3 point-to-point peering is set up between the east–west firewall and the service leaf over which the 192.168.1.0/24 and 192.168.2.0/24 subnet prefixes are advertised from the firewall to the service leaf. This enables them to be redistributed into the BGP EVPN network. The third network 192.168.3.0/24 uses the distributed IP anycast gateway of the fabric and is therefore routed immediately to the leaf for different IP subnet forwarding. This is accomplished by using the Layer 3 VNI associated with the VRF (VRF-A).

If an endpoint in 192.168.1.101 wants to reach an endpoint in 192.168.2.101, traffic is forwarded via Layer 2 across the VXLAN BGP EVPN network. At the service leaf, the traffic is decapsulated and mapped from the Layer 2 VNI to a VLAN, where it is forwarded to the east–west firewall. The firewall performs security policy enforcement and first-hop routing toward the network where the destination endpoint resides (192.168.2.101).

Leaving the firewall, the traffic is IEEE 802.1Q tagged on egress, depending on the destination determined by the firewall. The service leaf maps the traffic, and adds a VXLAN header according to the configured VLAN–to–Layer 2 VNI mapping. The encapsulated traffic is then forwarded toward the leaf where the destination endpoint 192.168.2.101 resides.

The VXLAN BGP EVPN fabric thus operates in Layer 2–only mode. In other words, a distributed IP anycast gateway is not configured for the two networks (192.168.1.0/24 and 192.168.2.0/24) within the fabric. Instead, the default gateway resides on the east–west firewall.

For communication from an endpoint in the network 192.168.1.101 or 192.168.2.101 toward an endpoint in the network 192.168.3.101, the flow begins in a similar fashion. Traffic is forwarded via Layer 2 across the VXLAN BGP EVPN network. At the service leaf, the traffic is decapsulated and mapped from the Layer 2 VNI to a VLAN, where it is forwarded to the firewall. The firewall then performs security policy enforcement and first-hop routing toward the network where the destination endpoint resides (192.168.3.101).

Leaving the firewall, the traffic is routed based on the firewall's routing tables. The egress interface is determined based on the destination identified by the firewall. The service leaf takes the routed traffic, performs a lookup, and encapsulates traffic according to the locally configured VRF-to-Layer-3 VNI mapping. The Layer 3 lookup in the VRF (VRF-A) also provides the next hop behind which the endpoint 192.168.3.101 resides.

The VXLAN BGP EVPN fabric operates in Layer 3 mode, which means the distributed IP anycast gateway is configured for the network 192.168.3.0/24 on the leaf. The default gateway sits on the leaf for all endpoints in the network 192.168.3.0/24. For communication from the endpoint 192.168.3.101 toward any other network in the same VRF, the distributed IP anycast gateway on the leaf is employed.

As shown in Figure 10-15, a separate tenant-edge firewall is connected in the same VRF where the endpoints reside, in order to provide external connectivity. A static default route 0/0 may be configured in the tenant VRF on the service leaf pointing to the tenant-edge firewall. In turn, the default route is distributed within the BGP EVPN fabric so that all traffic that needs to leave the VRF is directed toward the service leaf and then to the tenant-edge firewall, where the appropriate policies may be applied.

As an alternative, the east–west firewall can be connected to the tenant-edge firewall to perform external connectivity in a two-staged approach. Many valid alternative approaches also apply in this case, but some common cases are discussed in the following section to provide an overview on the subject.

Application Delivery Controller (ADC) and Load Balancer in a VXLAN BGP EVPN Network

Thus far, this chapter has provided a lot of information regarding the use of firewalls as Layer 4–7 service nodes. Other than firewalls, the most commonly deployed service appliances are load balancers. Load balancing is often seen as a service provided by multiple real servers, but a load balancer also allows the distribution of load based on specific criteria.

This section does not provide details of the mechanics of load balancers, but it is important to realize that these are stateful[8] devices, just as firewalls are. *Stateful* implies that data traffic, which creates sessions on the load balancer, must flow through the same Layer 4–7 device in both forward and reverse directions. This ensures that the server applications behind the load balancer can be addressed from a request perspective, and it also ensures that the return traffic stays valid within this communication. This is similar to the behavior of a firewall, where traffic must not only be validated but also allowed.

The same considerations described for firewall placement and connectivity also apply for the load balancer service appliances. Specifically, the classic integration approaches with VLAN or VRF stitching apply in exactly the same way. In contrast to the approaches already covered, the following sections focus on some of the different connectivity models a load balancer allows (for example, the one-armed source-NAT approach).

Note In one load balancing approach, called Direct Server Return (DSR), the reverse traffic from the servers sitting behind the load balancer is sent directly back to the client, without traversing the load balancer. This method is generally not the preferred deployment mode with load balancers and hence is not discussed here.

One-Armed Source-NAT

In the one-armed source-NAT mode, the load balancer is connected with a single link or port channel to the leaf. A single port channel can include the use of vPC to achieve connectivity redundancy across a pair of leafs. With a load balancer deployment, client-side and server-side parts typically exist. The client side represents requests for a service, which maps to a virtual IP (VIP) address configured on the load balancer. The VIP may be allocated from the same subnet associated with a directly attached interface of the load balancer. Alternatively, it may be allocated from a completely separate subnet.

The server side comprises the set of server IP addresses that provide the service advertised by the VIP. This section describes both the client side and the server side.

Direct VIP Subnet Approach

Figure 10-16 shows a sample VXLAN BGP EVPN deployment with a service leaf attached to a load balancer. The load balancer is configured with VIP (192.168.200.200) being part of the subnet (192.168.200.0/24) and associated with the load balancer's physical interface (192.168.200.254). This is called the *direct VIP subnet approach*. The default gateway for the subnet is configured on the directly attached leaf (192.168.200.1). The servers serving the VIP are in subnet 192.168.1.0/24; 192.168.1.101 is the IP address of one such server attached to the leaf with VTEP V3. The client endpoint is attached outside the VXLAN BGP EVPN fabric behind the border node hosting VTEP V1.

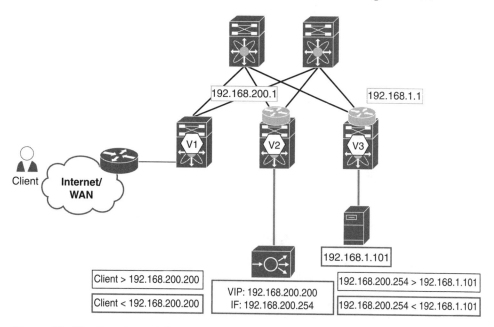

Figure 10-16   *One-Armed Source-NAT: Direct VIP Subnet*

In this connectivity option, the load balancer and its VIP act like an endpoint that has multiple IP addresses on its interface and is recognized in this way by the VXLAN BGP EVPN network. The VIP is learned on the directly attached leaf via ARP resolution, and the associated IP and MAC binding is advertised in a Route type 2 BGP EVPN message to all the remote leafs. This means the VIP is immediately available for client connections. In this way, 192.168.200.200/32 and 192.168.200.254/32 are advertised as reachable from VTEP V2 associated with the service leaf. Similarly, 192.168.1.101/32 is advertised from VTEP V3. Forward traffic from the client enters the fabric via the border leaf hosting VTEP V1. The forwarding lookup based on the destination IP address corresponding to the VIP, results in traffic being VXLAN encapsulated and sent toward VTEP V2 and in turn to the load balancer.

If the load balancer disappears or fails over to standby, the standby load balancer takes over, and the announcement of the VIP is performed "just in time." Such a failover event is handled in a similar manner as a virtual machine mobility event, where GARP- or Reverse ARP (RARP)–based signalization of the moved endpoint is employed. The direct connectivity model to the leaf switch also allows the use of VLAN tagging and the presence of multiple IP subnets with VIPs present.

Indirect VIP Subnet Approach

As an alternative to having the VIP subnet being the same as the one on which the load balancer interface resides, a dedicated IP subnet(s) for the VIP space can also be defined, as shown in Figure 10-17. This is termed the *indirect VIP subnet approach*. In this case, the VIPs are behind the physical interface of the load balancer, and routing is required to reach the corresponding IP subnet (10.10.10.0/24).

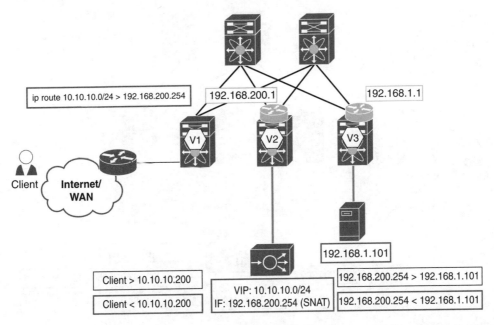

Figure 10-17 *One-Armed Source-NAT: Indirect IP Subnet*

Unlike with the *direct VIP subnet approach*, the specific IP address for the VIP is not learned via ARP resolution. Instead, the VIP-associated IP subnet (10.10.10.0/24) is either configured statically or advertised using a dynamic routing protocol at the leaf. In turn, it is then redistributed into BGP EVPN as a Route type 5 prefix so that it is known throughout the network. In case of a failover event, the VIP subnet is still reachable via the active load balancer.

Just as in the firewall case previously described with static routes, the same options are available to ensure that VIP-directed traffic is always forwarded to the leaf attached to the active load balancer. These options include static route configuration on the leafs where the endpoints are connected (except for the service leaf, where the load balancer is attached), and also static route configuration on the service leaf with HMM tracking enabled.

In both the direct and indirect VIP subnet approaches, the VIP is advertised only if the load balancer is available. This can help when a multiple-load-balancer cluster or HA pair is available. The VIP used depends on the routing metric; this approach can help handle either failure or load distribution scenarios.

Return Traffic

Thus far, the client-side details have been described with traffic following the regular forwarding path from the client to the VIP advertised by the load balancer. The server side is less spectacular, since the major requirement involves a request from the client via the load balancer that is forwarded to the chosen destination server. The load balancer must have a valid forwarding path toward the server endpoints participating in the server farm for the load balancer service.

Typically, load balancers monitor the health of each of these servers and the services they are hosting, so that requests are only forwarded to healthy servers. Also, because a load balancer is a stateful device, the return traffic from the servers must go through a load balancer before going back to the client. This is specifically important because the load balancer does not alter the client IP address under normal circumstances. As a result, the servers participating in the server farm try to use the best path toward the requesting client IP.

Because the load balancer is not located in the physical path between the client and server, source-NAT is employed. For all requests from the client reaching the load balancer, the source IP address is modified to one that is owned by the load balancer. The destination IP address then directs traffic to the selected server endpoint. In this way, with the source-NAT feature, the individual client IP addresses are hidden behind a set of IP addresses owned by the load balancer. This way, return traffic from the servers within the server farm is always sent to the load balancer, and, in turn, the load balancer sends the traffic back to the client based on its stateful NAT tables.

One disadvantage of this deployment scenario is that the original client IP address is hidden behind the load balancers' source-NAT pool. As a result, servers in the server farm see only the load balancers' information. This can have some implications in deployments where certain compliance regulations are in place. Nevertheless, client credentials are often transported in the application-layer payload, and this can help bypass the requirement of providing them redundantly in the network layer.

Figure 10-18 shows a sample load balancer deployment with the direct subnet VIP option and source-NAT feature. As before, the client wants to reach an application or service hosted on the server endpoint (192.168.1.101). This server endpoint is serviced by a VIP (192.168.200.200) configured on the load balancer with interface IP 192.168.200.254. The request from the client travels through the VXLAN BGP EVPN network to reach the VIP (client > 192.168.200.200). The VIP is advertised into the network via either static or dynamic routing options. Recall that the VIP is advertised to the remote VTEPs using a Route type 2 advertisement since it is learned on the service leaf as a regular ARP entry. Because the client and load balancer reside in the same VRF, the request is transported over VXLAN with the VNI set to the Layer 3 VNI associated with the corresponding VRF.

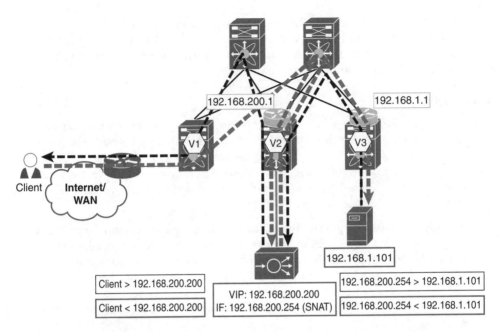

Figure 10-18 *Source-NAT*

Once the request has reached the load balancer, a session is created, and the destination server endpoint is selected based on the server farm, the load balancing algorithm, and other decision criteria configured on the load balancer. The client-side request is terminated, and a new server-side request is initiated toward the selected server endpoint (192.168.1.101) with the source IP address of the load balancer (192.168.200.254). Because the load balancer and the server endpoint reside in different subnets, the new server-side request from the load balancer reaches the service leaf where it is routed over VXLAN to VTEP V3. The VNI will be set to the L3 VNI associated with the VRF in which the load balancer and server resides. After decapsulation at VTEP V3, the request will undergo a routing lookup and finally be forwarded to 192.168.1.101. After processing, the response from the server is directed to the load balancer's source-NAT IP address (192.168.1.101 > 192.168.200.254). Again, given this is inter-subnet communication, the response will be routed over to the service leaf and delivered to the load balancer.

The server-side response is terminated on the load balancer, and a new client-side response is initiated toward the client. The VIP address is used as the source IP address, and the client IP address is used as the destination address for the response (192.168.200.200 > client). The response is routed over the VXLAN network to VTEP V1, where the client is attached. In this example, the VIP and the IP address for the source-NAT pool are different. Depending on the load balancer vendor and software version, the IP address for VIP and source-NAT pool may be different or may be the same.

Service Chaining: Firewall and Load Balancer

Service chaining is an extensive topic involving the chaining of multiple Layer 4–7 services so that data traffic can be inspected for security purpose and so that load balancing can occur for traffic distribution. Individual integration of the VXLAN BGP EVPN fabric with firewalls and load balancers has been discussed thus far. Building on the integration story, additional deployment scenarios will be covered by adding a service-chain to include firewall as well as a load-balancer.

From a placement perspective, some additional considerations are warranted as the two types of services are traversed sequentially. One involves the unnecessary passing of switches and respective encapsulation/decapsulation passes, and the second relates to flooding the VXLAN BGP EVPN network with "transit" segments.

Consider a deployment scenario in which the firewall is attached at the border leaf, and the load balancer is attached at a service leaf in the fabric. Depending on the source of the traffic generated from within the fabric, traffic first reaches the border node, is decapsulated, is sent through the firewall, and then is once again encapsulated. Subsequently, the traffic is sent to the service leaf, is decapsulated again, then sent to the load balancer, then encapsulated again, and finally reaches the endpoint on a different leaf in the server farm.

While this scenario can be easily supported with a VXLAN BGP EVPN fabric, traffic flows should traverse service chains as local as possible to avoid the need for additional forwarding hops through the switches. In addition, the VXLAN BGP EVPN network need not be aware of the transit segments between the firewall and the load balancer. Only the leaf that participates in the service chain needs the transit information for forwarding and failover purposes.

In an optimal deployment, a client request from outside first enters the VXLAN BGP EVPN fabric through the border leaf. Before allowing traffic to reach the protected IP subnet, the traffic is inspected by a tenant-edge firewall, which is typically attached to the border leaf. From there, traffic is sent to the load balancer attached to the border leaf. Alternatively, the traffic can enter the VXLAN BGP EVPN fabric pre-inspected and reach the service leaf where the east–west firewall and the load balancer are attached. In both cases, the traffic is encapsulated only once to pass through the service chain (firewall and load balancer) in order to reach the endpoint on any given leaf in the VXLAN BGP EVPN fabric.

Additional stages can be easily integrated into the service chain if required. For example, if a requirement for a firewall sandwich exists with a load balancer and IDS/IPS (intrusion detection system/intrusion prevention system[9]) in between, this can be integrated into the service chain. Service chains can therefore begin in a very simple manner and develop into very sophisticated sets of service steps before reaching the final endpoint.

With the different ways of integrating firewalls and load balancers, two main use cases need to be covered. One involves the firewall and load balancer being physically in path. This means a client request has to first flow through the firewall before being allowed to access the load balancer. The other involves the firewall and load balancer not being physically in path but instead having the load balancer deployed in a single-armed mode.

In the latter situation, the firewall and load balancer can be deployed in either routed or transparent mode. The main difference between these choices involves the use of Layer 2 or Layer 3 segments for the respective transit segments. Figure 10-19 shows a sample logical topology with an in-path firewall and load balancer service chain deployment.

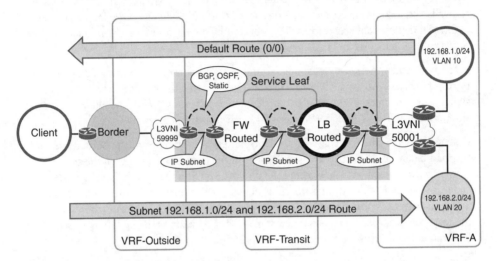

Figure 10-19 *Routed Service Chain*

Deploying a service chain in routed mode, the transit segment between the unprotected router, the firewall, the load balancer, and the protected router are IP subnets in the same switch or vPC domain. In order to ensure that the transit segment between the protected and unprotected VRF is not leaked and that traffic is forced from firewall to load balancer, a dedicated VRF is created in between.

The segment before the firewall is the unprotected network (VRF-Outside), which operates in Layer 3 mode toward the firewall. At the point where the unprotected VRF segment toward the firewall is presented, a Layer 3 interface for routing exchange is present. At this point, the routing configuration can be either static or dynamic. This eases the announcement of the IP subnets in the protected VRF (VRF-A). As a result, a similar interconnection point exists in the secured or protected portion of the service chain. Between the firewall and load balancer, the routing information for forwarding is passed along, and in order to provide isolation, a service leaf local VRF (VRF-Transit) is employed.

Traffic initiated from the client enters the VXLAN BGP EVPN network through the border leaf. The traffic is then destined to the VIP configured on the load balancer, which is advertised through the firewall into VRF-Outside. The routing lookup on the border leaf forwards the traffic, encapsulated with the Layer 3 VNI of VRF-Outside toward the service leaf where the firewall is attached. At the service leaf, the egress interface is determined based on a local routing lookup, and traffic is sent into the firewall through its OUT or unprotected interface.

At that stage, the firewall performs its inspection duties, and upon a permit result, traffic is forwarded toward the interface over which the VIP can be reached. The load balancer VIP is known via routing (static or dynamic) between the load balancer and the firewall. Once traffic reaches the load balancer, the application-layer function is performed, and the destination server endpoint is determined from the configured server farm.

Based on routing lookup, the egress interface is determined, and the traffic is forwarded toward the protected VRF (VRF-A). In this way, traffic enters the service leaf on an ingress interface associated with VRF-A. The destination lookup in VRF-A toward the endpoint in either in network 192.168.1.0/24 or 192.168.2.0/24 yields the leaf behind which the former resides. Traffic is appropriately VXLAN-encapsulated with the Layer 3 VNI associated with VRF-A and sent toward the destination leaf. In turn, it is then decapsulated and sent toward the destination. The reverse traffic from the destination to the client follows a similar path but in the opposite direction.

In the service chaining example described so far, the option to deploy the load balancer in the one-armed source-NAT mode exists instead of deploying the load balancer in two-armed mode. In this situation, it is not necessary to create a transit VRF between the load balancer and the firewall since the load balancer is positioned virtually in path by using source-NAT. The service chain scenario with a tenant-edge firewall and a one-armed load balancer is discussed next.

Figure 10-20 shows a logical topology with a firewall and one-armed load balancer service chain in routed mode. The source-NAT feature is enabled on the load balancer. The single arm or leg of the load balancer resides in the protected VRF (VRF-A). In addition, the IN, or protected leg of the firewall resides in a segment or subnet that is part of VRF-A. The OUT leg of the firewall resides in a subnet in the unprotected VRF, namely VRF-Outside, and the corresponding segment operates in Layer 3 mode.

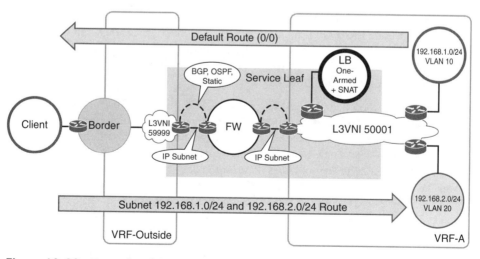

Figure 10-20 *Routed and One-Armed Source-NAT Service Chain*

At the point where the unprotected VRF segment toward the firewall is presented, a Layer 3 interface for routing exchange is present with either a static or dynamic routing configuration. The protected network (VRF-A) also has a dedicated interface toward the firewall to facilitate routing exchange of the protected network into the unprotected network. This eases the announcement of all protected IP subnets toward the client. The VIP network for the load balancer participates in the VXLAN BGP EVPN fabric in a similar way to the endpoint networks within the protected VRF-A.

Because the load balancer is in one-armed source-NAT deployment mode, the traffic from the endpoints in network VLAN A or B always returns to the originator, whether it is the client directly or the load balancer. With this deployment mode, only load-balanced traffic is required to flow bidirectionally through the load balancer. Other traffic, however, can bypass the load balancer. This advantage allows scaling of the load balancer with more services because only a portion of the traffic is transported through it. This is not the case when the load balancer is physically in path. In such a situation, all traffic has to be forwarded by the load balancer, and this can impact the overall scale. Recall that with source-NAT, an inherent disadvantage exists because the original client IP address is hidden behind the load balancer source-NAT pool when client requests are sent to the servers in the server farm. However, as mentioned before, client credentials are often transported in the application layer, circumventing this problem to a large extent.

Next, the flow of traffic from the client to the server endpoints is described for the topology shown in Figure 10-20. As before, traffic initiated from the client enters the VXLAN BGP EVPN network through the border leaf. The destination IP address is the VIP, which has been configured and advertised by the load balancer (via the service leaf) and by the firewall into the unprotected VRF-Outside. Traffic is thus VXLAN-encapsulated with the Layer 3 VNI associated with VRF-Outside, and sent toward the service leaf to which the firewall is attached.

At the service leaf after decapsulation, the routing lookup sends the traffic toward the firewall, ingressing via its OUT interface. After inspection, traffic is then sent out of the firewall over its IN interface, which is the VIP-reaching interface. In this way, traffic ingresses the service leaf in the protected VRF-A, goes through a regular routing lookup based on the VIP, and is sent toward the load balancer.

Once traffic hits the load balancer, the application-layer function is performed, and an appropriate destination server endpoint is determined. Based on routing lookup, the egress interface is decided, and the traffic is again forwarded toward the protected VRF-A after it has had a new source IP address applied via NAT. On the service leaf in the protected VRF, a further lookup is done for the destination endpoint in either network 192.168.1.0/24 or 192.168.2.0/24. Traffic is appropriately VXLAN-encapsulated with the Layer 3 VNI associated with VRF-A and sent toward the leaf where the destination endpoint is attached. Finally, after decapsulation at the destination leaf, traffic is sent out toward the server endpoint.

The return traffic from the endpoint is sent to the load balancer source-NAT pool–selected IP address. In this way, only load balanced return traffic is sent to the load balancer before it traverses the tenant-edge firewall and returns to the client, thereby ensuring stateful behavior.

The two deployment approaches with service chains presented in this section indicate how they can be integrated into a VXLAN BGP EVPN network. Various permutations and combinations exist, but this section provides a good idea of how the deployment of choice can be derived by extension.

In conclusion, the tenant-edge service insertion with VXLAN BGP EVPN networks has a similar implementation as in traditional networks. For intra-tenant firewall deployment, there are some changes because of the presence of the distributed IP anycast gateway in the fabric. For load balancer deployments, the injection of the VIP as a host route and automatic handling of that advertisement even in case of a move or failure scenario provides for a simple, elegant, and optimized deployment in the fabric.

Summary

This chapter provides details on how Layer 4–7 services can be integrated into a VXLAN BGP EVPN network. Deployments with intra-tenant and inter-tenant firewalls are covered as these services can be deployed in both transparent and routed modes. The chapter also describes a common deployment scenario with a load balancer. Finally, the chapter presents two commonly deployed service-chaining scenarios involving a firewall and a load balancer. While this chapter certainly does not provide an exhaustive list of all possible service deployments in a VXLAN BGP EVPN fabric, it presents adequate details to potentially allow any desired deployment to be realized.

References

1. Internet Engineering Task Force (IETF). *Bidirectional Forwarding Detection (BFD)*. 2010. tools.ietf.org/html/rfc5880.

2. Cisco. *Network address translation (NAT) FAQ*. 2014. www.cisco.com/c/en/us/support/docs/ip/network-address-translation-nat/26704-nat-faq-00.html.

3. Cisco. *Network virtualization—Services edge design guide*. 2009. www.ciscopress.com/store/network-virtualization-9781587052484.

4. Cisco. *Network virtualization*. Indianapolis, IN: Cisco Press, 2006.

5. Internet Engineering Task Force (IETF). *Network service header*. 2016. www.ietf.org/id/draft-ietf-sfc-nsh-09.txt.

6. Internet Engineering Task Force (IETF). *Segment router*. http://www.segment-routing.net/

7. Internet Engineering Task Force (IETF). *The Locator/ID Separation Protocol (LISP)*. 2013. tools.ietf.org/html/rfc6830.

8. Wikipedia. *Stateful devices*. 2016. en.wikipedia.org/wiki/Stateful_firewall.

9. Wikipedia. *Intrusion detection system*. 2016. en.wikipedia.org/wiki/Intrusion_detection_system.

## Chapter 11

Introduction to Fabric Management

In this chapter, the following topics will be covered:

- Day-0 operations that involve touchless device provisioning of the VXLAN BGP EVPN fabric using POAP

- Day-1 operations that involve Layer 2 and Layer 3 overlay service provisioning in the fabric based on active endpoints

- Day-2 operations for continuous monitoring and visibility in the fabric

- VXLAN OAM and troubleshooting for overlay-based fabrics

Operating the fabric in a VXLAN BGP EVPN–based network requires more than just control plane and data plane forwarding. In the world of automation, orchestration, and controllers, simply having the network operationalized is no longer sufficient. Instead, the elements of the switches, routers, and endpoints need to be managed and set up according to business and security requirements. To complement the content presented in the other chapters so far, in this chapter, a brief overview will be provided on the management, orchestration, and automation aspects of the data center fabric. Figure 11-1 depicts the typical elements involved in a fabric management framework.

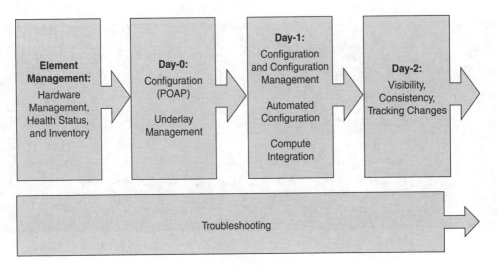

Figure 11-1 *Fabric Management Framework*

The first step involves setting up the individual network components and building the fabric. The build-out of the fabric is referred to as *day-0 operations*. This includes a model of the network configuration for the initial setup as well as the cabling plan layout of the fabric. Zero-touch provisioning options such as Power On Auto Provisioning (POAP)[1] can help achieve these tasks autonomously.

Once the initial cabling of the fabric has been completed for Layer 1 connectivity between the spines and leafs, additional configurations for each network and each tenant are required. This is referred to as *day-1 operations* of the fabric. The overlay services instantiate the necessary configurations on the fabric devices to ensure that the fabric is ready to carry traffic to and from the endpoints when they are brought into their respective network/tenant. Day-1 configuration can be done via the CLI at one extreme or can be completely automated with close integration with compute orchestrators, at the other extreme.

Certain use cases add an incremental step between the day-0 initial setup and the day-1 operations. In such situations, the endpoints (servers, firewalls, and so on) are added and connected for the first time. An order of operation for specific automation tasks exists. For example, it is important to understand that endpoint interfaces (trunk or access) need to be configured before the network (VLAN, VRF, SVI, etc.). The order of operation is thus important for specific interface configuration management; it is referred to as *day-0.5 operations*.

Once the network is set up and the endpoints are connected, the overlay provides the necessary multitenant communication capabilities. At this point in the life cycle, the focus turns to operation: monitoring, visibility, and troubleshooting. *Day-2 operations* for the life cycle management of the data center network with VXLAN BGP EVPN provide insight into current functioning of the data center fabric.

While having visibility of the overlay is important, having visibility into the underlay—including performance and element management—is also important. The ability to correlate events in the underlay to services in the overlay provides a holistic view of the data center fabric. This entails health and inventory management of every individual hardware device that is part of the network.

Troubleshooting spans the entire life cycle of the data center fabric. It begins with day-0 provisioning operations and extends through the life cycle until the last network component has been decommissioned. In addition to preliminary troubleshooting, comprehensive sets of dedicated references are also available for troubleshooting a VXLAN BGP EVPN network as an entire entity.[2]

This chapter briefly describes details of each of the elements of the fabric management framework: day-0, day-0.5, day-1, and day-2 operations.

Day-0 Operations: Automatic Fabric Bring-Up

Zero-touch provisioning allows the automation of the fabric "bring-up" to enable day-0 configuration. This is an easy and automated way to unbox, cable, and power on the switching infrastructure that results in a consistently configured data center network.

NX-OS has a feature called Power On Auto Provisioning (POAP),[3] which enables the day-0 operational model. POAP allows for unattended switching configuration, and it also achieves consistent configuration and software deployment across the entire data center fabric.

Before unpacking, cabling, and powering up the switching infrastructure, some preparation tasks must be completed for the infrastructure to receive the configuration. For example, the devices need to be assigned roles in the DC fabric, depending on their intended functionality (such as leaf, spine, or border). This allows them to be appropriately wired and configured.

Cisco's POAP leverages DHCP and specific DHCP options to tell the switch where the boot-up instructions are to be received. The boot-up instruction set can be transported via various protocols, such as Hypertext Transfer Protocol (HTTP)[4] or Trivial File Transfer Protocol (TFTP). The choice of the protocol used is defined in the DHCP options.

The boot-up instructions are transported in a Tcl[5] or Python[6] script that tells the switch exactly which steps to perform during the POAP process. It is recommended to only have the boot-up script hosted on the TFTP server. The actual network configuration, which is more sensitive, is recommended to leverage secure protocols such as Secure Copy (SCP) or Secure File Transfer Protocol (SFTP)[7] to transfer the entire configuration to the appropriate network switch during the POAP process.

The Python/Tcl script instructs the device to implement SCP or SFTP transfers. Likewise, it also has precise instructions to retrieve configurations specific to the booting switch identified by the serial number and/or MAC address associated with that switch. Note that other switch identification parameters can also be incorporated into the Python/Tcl script for use during the POAP process.

The infrastructure required for the POAP process includes a DHCP server, a TFTP/HTTP server for the Python/Tcl script download, and a SCP/SFTP server for the device configuration file and software image, if desired. Several options exist for products that provide POAP server functionality. Some recommendations include the following:

- Leverage Cisco's Data Center Network Manager (DCNM),[8] which can also perform the tasks needed for all Cisco NX-OS–based hardware switches

- Leverage Cisco's Nexus Fabric Manager (NFM)[9] for relevant Nexus switching platforms

- Leverage Cisco's project Ignite at the open source github repository[10]

In-Band Versus Out-of-Band POAP

POAP is a simple process and can be implemented using two different methods:

- Out-of-band POAP

- In-band POAP

The out-of-band method is the most common method for implementation, and uses the "Management0" (mgmt0) interface of the network switch for the POAP process. With the out-of-band method (see Figure 11-2), the network switch boots up without any configuration. The mgmt0 interface requests an IP address, leveraging DHCP. The DHCP server, which is either embedded separately or resides in a POAP service's engine, responds with an IP address as well as the specific DHCP scope options needed to retrieve the Python or Tcl script via TFTP or HTTP.

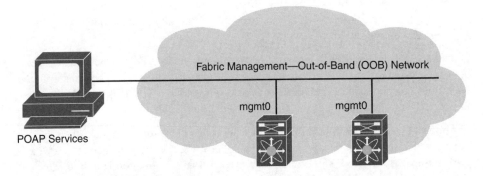

Figure 11-2 *Out-of-Band POAP*

The network switch retrieves the specific NX-OS image as well as the specific configuration mapped to its identity (such as the serial number or MAC address). The steps are defined within the script, and the ability to detect reboot requests during configuration playback is also supported.

Cisco provides predefined Python scripts with these tasks via the NX-OS image download, for example, with DCNM. Once all the tasks defined in the script have been successfully completed, the network switch boots into operation with the respective configuration. In the event that NX-OS licensing is required for enabling specific configurations or feature sets, software license installation can be achieved through the POAP process with appropriate modifications to the script.

The in-band method for POAP (see Figure 11-3), on the other hand, leverages switch interfaces, which are also known as "front panel ports," as opposed to the mgmt0 interface. DHCP requests are sent out on all front-panel ports. Once a DHCP response is received, the Integrated Routing and Bridging (IRB) interface, or switch virtual interface (SVI) associated with VLAN 1, is assigned the DHCP-offered IP address. Note that SVI 1 is always present on all Nexus switches. Subsequently, SVI 1 is the routed interface on which all the POAP steps are executed, including download and execution of the appropriate Python-/Tcl-based POAP script, which in turn triggers appropriate system image download, startup configuration download, optional license download and installation, and so on. In a sense, SVI 1 is comparable to the mgmt0 interface used for POAP with the out-of-band method.

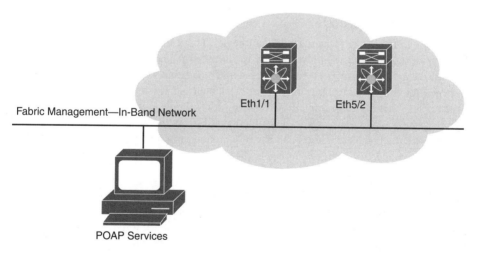

Figure 11-3   *In-Band POAP*

The choice of out-of-band versus in-band POAP requires careful consideration. With the out-of-band option, POAP services such as DHCP, TFTP, and SCP need to be reachable from the mgmt0 interface of every switch. The services could be Layer 2 or Layer 3 adjacent. If the management network is implemented as a flat Layer 2 domain, the services are all part of the same broadcast domain or VLAN. There may be scale issues if the number of switches goes up; consequently, sufficient bandwidth must be provisioned in the management network to accommodate these scenarios. A more scalable option is to have the services be reachable via routing. If the DHCP server is Layer 3 adjacent, a DHCP relay needs to be configured to allow the DHCP packets from the switch to reach the DHCP server and vice versa.

As with the out-of-band option, with the in-band option, the POAP services should be reachable via the front-panel interfaces. For a VXLAN BGP EVPN fabric, a seed switch (or a pair, for redundancy) provides this reachability. Once the seed switch (typically a leaf) comes up via POAP, the next switch to come up is one of the spines. Recall that because the underlay is a routed network, all interfaces between the leafs and spines are configured as routed ports. DHCP requests coming in from a new spine are blocked at the neighboring uplink interfaces of the seed switch (aka leaf). To overcome this limitation, a DHCP relay needs to be configured on the leaf interfaces toward the new spine switch being added to the fabric. The same holds true for any new leaf coming up where DHCP relay needs to be configured on appropriate spine interfaces.

Today, the mgmt0 interface on most Nexus switches is a 1G port, while the front-panel ports can be 10G, 25G, 40G, and 100G. Clearly, with the in-band option using the front-panel interface, there is plenty of bandwidth available for expansion, which is one of its major advantages. However, with the in-band option, the leaf and spine switches need to come up in a certain order during the bootstrap phase. On the other hand, with the out-of-band option, because every switch has independent reachability to the POAP services, there is no order dependency in terms of which switches need to come up before others.

Other Day-0 Considerations

In addition to the POAP process itself, and the dependencies of the SCP, TFTP, and Python/Tcl script requirements, the ability to generate the respective startup configuration for the network switches is the next essential piece. Previously, the configurations were generated by hand or by a creative scripting method. The use of an integrated template approach that is present in DCNM can improve, simplify, and scale configurations significantly. It allows templates to be defined in a flexible and customizable fashion, with the desired parameterization and use of common programming constructs such as iterative loops and **IF-ELSE** statements. In this way, the same template can be applied to multiple devices for efficient use and maintenance.

Tools such as Ignite, NFM, and DCNM provide the capability to set the management IP address on a network switch as well as the capability to generate full feature configuration for VXLAN BGP EVPN. NFM has an embedded capability to push the necessary configuration down to the network switches as a turnkey solution. This allows minimal attention to be given to the day-0 configuration.

DCNM behaves slightly differently from Ignite and NFM. The POAP definitions are not only defined for VXLAN BGP EVPN networks, but the DCNM templates are flexible enough to handle all kind of configurations through POAP. Within the template, sections and fields can be defined for all configurations through a GUI-based framework. DCNM can be used to provision multiple devices at once by entering multiple serial numbers and IP address pools. Much like NFM, DCNM provides a fabric setup wizard to create the VXLAN BGP EVPN fabric in a workflow.

While an overlap may appear to be present between Cisco NFM and DCNM, some key differences are important to mention. NFM assigns an IP address to the switch from the beginning and keeps the same IP address through the entire life cycle of the switch.

In contrast, DCNM uses a temporary IP address for the switch for the POAP process initially, and subsequently, it replaces that IP address with the one defined in the configuration after POAP. This may not appear to be a major difference, but the scope of the hardware platforms supported with NFM is somewhat limited. (Refer to the latest release notes for current information.) It is also important to mention that DCNM supports the POAP setup of any Cisco Nexus hardware platform with extensive templates for VXLAN, Cisco FabricPath, and classic Ethernet. DCNM also has additional templates to support virtual PortChannel (vPC), Fibre Channel/Fibre Channel over Ethernet (FC/FCoE), and Overlay Transport Virtualization (OTV) deployments.

Loading the NX-OS image along with the configuration for the device(s) including feature sets and licensing during the POAP process, promotes consistent output to the console for real-time troubleshooting. The information sent to the console is also collected in a log file and stored on the network switches' local storage (bootflash).

Building the in-band or out-of-band network is a one-time task that may not appear to be an attractive investment for an automation setup. It might seem as though the overall preparation work, investment, and modeling of the network is too time intensive. However, there are significant benefits to setting this up correctly, such as saving operational expenses for troubleshooting and preventing inconsistent configuration. This is especially beneficial during device return merchandise authorization (RMA).

When managing the configuration manually across multiple devices, a high percentage of errors can occur, resulting in mismatched configuration across the data center infrastructure. To prevent manual and inconsistent device configuration, the template-based approach with day-0 automation allows for consistency across the data center. For the hardware failure use case, the stored day-0 configurations can be quickly reapplied to the new device(s).

Once the new switch is unboxed, cabled, and powered on, the specific configuration related to the device role and identity is applied without requiring manual configuration. Day-0 automation provides tremendous value for unattended network device setup. As a result, the operational process is simplified for the life cycle of the data center infrastructure.

Day-0.5 Operations: Incremental Changes

After the day-0 automation, incremental changes may be required for new requirements or for the addition of other servers or compute nodes over time. These day-0.5 operations could be specific to the configuration of additional virtual port channels for host-facing interfaces. While all these configuration additions can be placed in the POAP configuration, this information is not available during day-0 bring-up of the network switch in most practical scenarios. Therefore, requirements for day-0.5 operations are quite common. Depending on the tools, software, and operational model used, the interface configuration might be embedded directly in the day-1 process when the overlay services are configured.

With a Clos-based spine–leaf fabric, an important step is validation of the connectivity between the various switches. The cable plan that serves as a blueprint for which interface on which switch should be connected to which interface on which other switch, requires validation so that the actual connectivity matches the intended design. This can be done in a brute-force manner, with the CDP or LLDP outputs on every switch cross-checked against the cable plan. This is not a one-time process and requires continuous monitoring as connectivity may be inadvertently changed, or misconnections may occur during the lifetime of a fabric. The idea is to have an assurance model where the actual device connectivity is continuously monitored and matched against an intended blueprint, with appropriate notifications and alerts being pushed out when inconsistencies are detected.

Typically, a graph-based network topological visualization can greatly aid in this process. Cisco Nexus switches have a cable-management feature[11] that can be used independently or in conjunction with DCNM to greatly ease the connectivity validation burden. The idea is that a network administrator can come up with a "golden" connectivity cable plan that is then imported on the switches. Each switch independently validates its current physical connections against that specified in the golden plan, and if there are discrepancies or inconsistencies, appropriate actions can be taken, such as bringing down a port. (Please check the release notes for updates on which Nexus platforms support this feature.)

Day-1 Operations: Overlay Services Management

The VXLAN BGP EVPN overlay requires additional configuration steps to be considered. In addition to the traditional VLAN configuration, VXLAN VNIs needs to be configured so the bridge domain can be extended across the VXLAN overlay. Additional services that need to be configured specific to the BGP EVPN control plane include distributed IP anycast gateway, VRFs, Layer 3 VNIs, and Layer 3 SVIs.

Generic services also need to be configured for the VXLAN BGP EVPN, such as NVE interfaces (VTEP), multicast groups, EVPN instances (EVI), and the associated BGP configuration. Several configuration components need to be aligned for the VXLAN EVPN fabric. Aligning all of the Layer 2 and Layer 3 configurations requires overlay services management to achieve consistent, correct, and efficient configuration.

In addition to the entire configuration itself, the management and operation of the different namespaces (VLANs, VNIs, and IP subnets) are critical to ensuring reusability of local resources while ensuring that global resources do not overlap. All the participating entities such as the VXLAN VTEPs participating in the overlay, need to be visible and managed to complete the overlay services management.

The ability to discover all the devices participating as VXLAN VTEPs is a critical requirement for importing all the capabilities into the overlay services management. Discovery and configuration not only apply to the VXLAN BGP EVPN network but extend to the external connectivity and the Data Center Interconnect (DCI) components.

Discovery includes learning different device roles and functions to gain complete knowledge of all available resources. Such a discovery allows better visibility of the overlay topology and also a comprehensive understanding of the physical components. The end-to-end discovery, visibility, and operation are important to call out since the boundaries between network and compute operations typically serve as an impediment to providing the necessary visibility. The overlay services management and controllers require the ability to understand the physical and logical infrastructure in conjunction with virtual machine managers and virtual switch VTEPs.

Proving end-to-end visibility and monitoring of the underlay and overlay allows resources to be placed, configured, and provisioned on specific underutilized segments. The placement of these resources can be triggered on notifications received from compute managers of endpoints such as virtual machines or containers via a northbound API. Manual configuration triggered by the administrator via an appropriate GUI or some scripts or even CLIs is also an option.

The most common use case involves the agility to provision the network at the same time an endpoint is attached. The requirement to automate the overlay provisioning service gives the operations teams a couple of options:

- Push model

- Pull model

A push model pushes a configuration snippet (configlet) to the appropriate network devices. The configuration push sends individual CLI commands. When using deletion via CLI, simply adding **no** in front of every command in the configlet that created the initial configuration works in certain situations, but subcommands below a parent command or other subcommands require some intelligent handling.

When the push approach is not desired, Cisco permits a second method, a pull model. In a pull model, the network device (or, in a VXLAN BGP EVPN fabric, the VTEP) is responsible for downloading the required configuration. The switch or VTEP uses a trigger to detect an endpoint and in turn sends a query to fetch the relevant configuration required for that endpoint. The download or pull request is serviced on the overlay services manager, where the desired configuration is stored in the configuration repository.

The push model needs to know exactly where to send the configuration. One advantage of this model is that minimal requirements on the network switch are present; however, from a scalability point of view, the push model is inherently centralized and may not be desirable because it has to manage every network switch individually. For a large network, this may become a performance bottleneck; however, the push model, being inherently centralized, has the advantage of a single point of configuration push and easy tracking.

With the pull model, more requirements for the network switch exist, but the location is not important because the network device is the source of the requests when triggered. This results in not having a real-time topology, but instead having a dependency on the configuration repository. With the pull model, the load is distributed among all the leaf switches so that they manage the endpoints below them. This provides a more scalable option. The individual switches manage both configuration provisioning and cleanup services in a distributed manner.

While so far the discussion on overlay provisioning has considered CLI as the primary option, a more modern approach that leverages API calls can be used to perform the same task. It is crucial to add overlay configuration for specific Layer 2 or Layer 3 services, and it is equally critical to provide deletion and modification options. Compared to the CLI option, API calls are more efficient and flexible.

Virtual Topology System (VTS)

The Cisco Virtual Topology System (VTS)[12] is a service-oriented tool that focuses exclusively on provisioning the overlay services. VTS uses a push model leveraging NX-API.[13] With the efforts in the IETF for EVPN service models such as Layer 2 VPN: L2SM and Layer 3 VPN: L3SM,[14] Cisco will continue to expand the capabilities of NX-API and orient it from the CLI[15] to the model-driven NX-API REST.[16] VTS's tight compute integration—for example, with OpenStack and VMware vCenter—allows for endpoint location awareness to enable the provisioning of Layer 2 or Layer 3 overlay services on the relevant switches, including the relevant VXLAN BGP EVPN configuration.

In addition to the VXLAN VTEP provisioning on Cisco Nexus switches, VTS also provides the software Virtual Topology Forwarder (VTF).[17] The VTF resides on the compute servers and functions as a virtual VTEP, performing host-based VXLAN overlays. The VTF is provisioned by the VTS, using appropriate RESTCONF/NETCONF interfaces and is supported in hypervisor environments such as VMware ESXi and KVM. VTS has an integrated controller for VTF functionality that allows seamless integration of physical and virtual VTEPs. In addition to physical and virtual overlay automation, VTS also provides external connectivity (DCI) and Layer 4–7 services stitching automation. VTS relies on a tool like DCNM to enable provisioning and automation of the underlay network.

VTS is also able to integrate with the model-based Cisco Network Services Orchestrator (NSO), which is powered by Tail-f Systems.[18] VTS includes management for Cisco Nexus 9000, Cisco Nexus 5600, and Cisco Nexus 7000/7700. In addition, the Cisco ASR 9000 series routers can be provisioned from the VTS for the external connectivity use case.[19]

Nexus Fabric Manager (NFM)

The Cisco Nexus Fabric Manager (NFM)[20] provides a turnkey solution for deploying VXLAN BGP EVPN networks. NFM's integrated approach enables a simple point-and-click interface for creating Layer 2 and Layer 3 overlay services for the VXLAN BGP EVPN network. NFM has a fabric-aware control engine that understands current configurations. This feature allows NFM to react to potential misconfigurations entered through the CLI.

NFM not only provides overlay services management but also provides the initial setup of the fabric with Auto Fabric Provisioning (AFP). At the present time, NFM exclusively manages and configures the Nexus 9000 series of switches. For specific hardware platform support, consult the NFM software release information.[21]

Data Center Network Manager (DCNM)

Much like NFM, DCNM provides underlay and overlay management, while VTS only provides overlay services management. Cisco DCNM was initially built to be a data center element manager, but it has been significantly enhanced to provide overlay services management as well automated instantiation of the underlay. In addition to the Ethernet and IP capabilities, DCNM also manages storage area networks (SANs). DCNM leverages POAP services to provide a turnkey, automated underlay network.

The DCNM-integrated services such as DHCP, TFTP, and SCP are complemented with a template-driven workflow to enable provisioning of the VXLAN BGP EVPN network. The templates required for automated network deployment are included with the DCNM image. Additional templates can also be downloaded from cisco.com.

DCNM provides integrated template and profile deployment capabilities that allow the configlets to be pushed to Cisco NX-OS-based network switches. The network switches can also use the same configuration repository used for storing the push-based configlets to pull the configuration. As a result, DCNM supports both the push-based and pull-based models for overlay services management. With the extensibility of using CLI configuration-based templates and profiles, any configuration can be applied to a network switch managed through DCNM.

With regard to VXLAN BGP EVPN networks in particular, external connectivity is critical for making applications and data center resources accessible. As discussed for VTS, Cisco DCNM also integrates the border leaf and external routers with VRF Lite, MPLS L3VPN (BorderPE), and LISP. All the configurations are driven through CLI-like template and profiles. Layer 4–7 services can also be easily integrated and automated with DCNM. Likewise, DCNM supports and manages all Cisco NX-OS-based switches, including the Cisco MDS SAN platforms.[22]

In addition to the commercial products provided by Cisco, open source tools are available for configuration of overlay services. IT automation tools such as Puppet, Chef, and Ansible provide a framework to create a manifests to deploy VXLAN BGP EVPN networks. While many of the open source automation tools provide options for VXLAN Flood and Learn, Ansible[23] and Puppet[24] provide a VXLAN BGP EVPN option for Cisco NX-OS. While these are the current options available, extension of Chef and other IT automation tools are expected in the future. For automation integrated to the CLI shell within the Cisco NX-OS-based network switches, Python[25] can also be used to automate the configuration of VXLAN BGP EVPN.

Compute Integration

Compute integration for network automation can be implemented in multiple ways. For the use case in which a controller takes ownership and triggers a specific configuration to the network switches, the integration is performed in a top-down manner. In other words, the orchestration layer uses APIs or registered callbacks to drive configuration requests to the overlay services manager. These triggers are based on the endpoints coming up or going down to the respective compute nodes.

Using the existing topology mapping between the compute nodes and the network switches, decisions on where and what needs to be instantiated can be performed. Either the northbound orchestrator provides specific instructions on endpoint placement or a horizontal integration between the compute manager and overlay services manager needs to exist.

With OpenStack[26] and Cisco UCS Director (UCSD),[27] such an approach is performed in the absence of an overlay services manager. Therefore, the capabilities are limited to only the information that OpenStack or UCSD can tell the network. By exposing the overlay services and allowing OpenStack or UCSD to drive the intent through an overlay services manager, a more flexible configuration can be achieved in the network layer. OpenStack/UCSD[28] combined with DCNM provides these benefits.

With the resource management available, the intent-based request can be completed and extended, and this in turn provides comprehensive network deployments in a VXLAN BGP EVPN network. While OpenStack or UCSD have been mentioned as examples, many orchestration options are capable of driving network-related requests via an API. These other options also support the top-down approach to overlay service instantiation (see Figure 11-4).

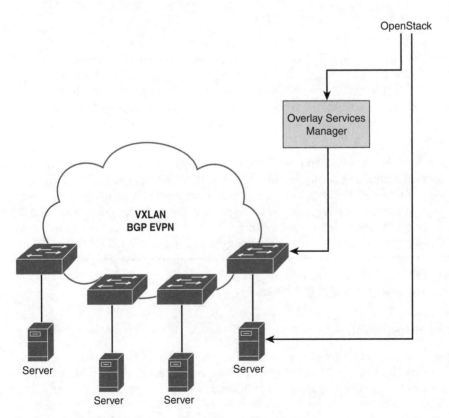

Figure 11-4   *Top-Down Overlay Service Instantiation*

Alternative approaches involve the integration of the network switch with the compute manager. In this model, the network switch is combined with the virtual machine manager (VMM) to allow an exchange of information. Based on specific actions occurring in the virtual machine layer, the associated information is directly sent to the network switches registered with the VMM.

A network switch decides if the message is relevant, based on whether the message is related to a virtual machine below a compute node that is directly attached to that switch. If the message is relevant, the network switch acts on it, triggering the appropriate configuration for that virtual machine. With Cisco's VM Tracker[29] feature, communication between the VMM (specifically VMware vCenter) and the network switch can be achieved. In turn, the provisioning/deprovisioning of the appropriate network configuration is enabled.

The integration of VM Tracker with the overlay services manager[30] enables extensive configuration that starts with basic Layer 2 configuration and extends all the way to complete VXLAN BGP EVPN configuration and Layer 3 services. The VM Tracker integration uses a pull-based model for overlay configuration provisioning, with DCNM as the overlay services controller (see Figure 11-5).

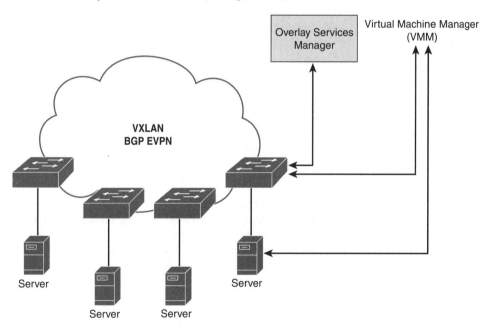

Figure 11-5 *Bottom-Up Overlay Service Instantiation*

Day-2 Operations: Monitoring and Visibility

The VXLAN BGP EVPN fabric is composed of two key elements:

- VXLAN data plane encapsulation
- BGP-based EVPN control protocol

Because many components are involved in the overall solution, it is important to understand where specific information is derived and how that information can be validated. Network operators typically verify BGP functionality first because this is an important verification step in showing relevant reachability information.

Monitoring and retrieving the correct information for visibility are important for all troubleshooting exercises. This section focuses on the operational aspects on how information can be retrieved from a VXLAN BGP EVPN network. It also includes troubleshooting approaches.

VXLAN BGP EVPN provides Layer 2 and Layer 3 services in the overlay network. Verification of the learning of Layer 2 MAC address information and Layer 3 IP address information is a great place to start. This process also verifies whether certain endpoints are being learned locally.

When verifying the classic Ethernet side, initially the local MAC address table is verified to ensure that it has learned the endpoint(s). This initial procedure verifies the mapping between the endpoint, the connected interface, and the associated VLAN, as demonstrated in Example 11-1.

Example 11-1   *MAC Table Output at Leaf*

```
L11# show mac address-table
Legend:
        * - primary entry, G - Gateway MAC, (R) - Routed MAC, O - overlay MAC
        age - seconds since last seen,+ - primary entry using vPC Peer-Link,
        (T) - True, (F) - False
   VLAN     MAC Address      Type      age     Secure NTFY Ports
---------+-----------------+--------+---------+------+----+------------------
* 100      0011.0100.0001   dynamic  0         F      F    Eth2/1
```

Example 11-1 verifies that the MAC address 0011.0100.0001 is learnt on interface Ethernet 2/1 on VLAN 100. When this happens, local MAC learning on the network switch is verified. The same MAC address is advertised to BGP EVPN, into the appropriate MAC-VRF or EVPN instance (EVI) by the Layer 2 Routing Information Base (L2RIB) component on the switch. This can be validated by using the **show l2route evpn mac all** command, as demonstrated in Example 11-2.

Example 11-2   *MAC Entries Advertised Over BGP-EVPN at Leaf*

```
L11# show l2route evpn mac all
Topology    Mac Address    Prod    Next Hop (s)
----------- -------------- ------ ----------------
100         0011.0100.0001 Local   Eth2/1
```

The output in Example 11-2 shows the presence of the locally learned MAC address in topology 100, where topology 100 maps to the VLAN ID. Based on the information present, it is not possible to derive the Layer 2 VNI from the given outputs. Verifying the VLAN to the segment mapping retrieves the respective L2VNI used for topology 100 and EVI 100, as demonstrated in Example 11-3.

Example 11- 3 *VLAN to Layer 2 VNI Mapping at Leaf*

```
L11# show vlan id 100 vn-segment


VLAN Segment-id
---- -----------
100  30000
```

The MAC is verified in the local address table as well as in the L2RIB table. Now it is possible to verify and determine whether the respective MAC address has been sent to the BGP EVPN address family for further advertisement, as shown in Example 11-4.

Example 11-4 *BGP EVPN Route type 2 Entries at Leaf*

```
L11# show bgp l2vpn evpn vni-id 30000
BGP routing table information for VRF default, address family L2VPN EVPN
BGP table version is 1670, local router ID is 10.100.100.11
Status: s-suppressed, x-deleted, S-stale, d-dampened, h-history, *-valid, >-best
Path type: i-internal, e-external, c-confed, l-local, a-aggregate, r-redist,
  I-injected
Origin codes: i - IGP, e - EGP, ? - incomplete, | - multipath, & - backup
   network          Next Hop          Metric     LocPrf     Weight Path


Route Distinguisher: 10.100.100.11:32867    (L2VNI 30000)
*>l[2]:[0]:[0]:[48]:[0011.0100.0001]:[0]:[0.0.0.0]/216
                    10.200.200.11                    100        32768 i
*>l[2]:[0]:[0]:[48]:[0011.0100.0001]:[32]:[192.168.100.200]/272
                    10.200.200.11                    100        32768 i
```

Based on the BGP output for the Layer 2 VNI 30000, the MAC address previously observed in the local MAC address and L2RIB table has been advertised to BGP. The output includes two Route type 2 entries, with one containing the MAC address and the other containing the MAC address and the IP address. In order to verify that the local advertisement matches the configured attributes and to assess whether the appropriate prefix is received on the remote site, the **show bgp** command with the relevant MAC address is executed on the local and remote leafs. Example 11-5 depicts the output from the **show bgp l2vpn evpn** command on a local leaf, and Example 11-6 depicts the output from the **show bgp l2vpn evpn** command on a remote leaf.

Example 11-5   *Details of a Particular BGP EVPN Route type 2 Advertisement at a Leaf*

```
L11# show bgp l2vpn evpn 0011.0100.0001
BGP routing table information for VRF default, address family L2VPN EVPN
Route Distinguisher: 10.100.100.11:32867    (L2VNI 30000)
BGP routing table entry for [2]:[0]:[0]:[48]:[0011.0100.0001]:[0]:[0.0.0.0]/216,
  version 1540
Paths: (1 available, best #1)
Flags: (0x00010a) on xmit-list, is not in l2rib/evpn


  Advertised path-id 1
  Path type: local, path is valid, is best path, no labeled nexthop
  AS-Path: NONE, path locally originated
    10.200.200.11 (metric 0) from 0.0.0.0 (10.100.100.11)
      Origin IGP, MED not set, localpref 100, weight 32768
      Received label 30000
      Extcommunity:  RT:65501:30000


  Path-id 1 advertised to peers:
    10.100.100.201    10.100.100.202
BGP routing table entry for [2]:[0]:[0]:[48]:[0011.0100.0001]:[32]:[192.168.100.200]
  /272, version 1550
Paths: (1 available, best #1)
Flags: (0x00010a) on xmit-list, is not in l2rib/evpn


  Advertised path-id 1
  Path type: local, path is valid, is best path, no labeled nexthop
  AS-Path: NONE, path locally originated
    10.200.200.11 (metric 0) from 0.0.0.0 (10.100.100.11)
      Origin IGP, MED not set, localpref 100, weight 32768
      Received label 30000 50000
      Extcommunity:  RT:65501:30000 RT:65501:50000


  Path-id 1 advertised to peers:
    10.100.100.201    10.100.100.202
```

Example 11-6   *Details of a Particular BGP EVPN Route type 2
Advertisement at a Remote Leaf*

```
L12# show bgp l2vpn evpn 0011.0100.0001
BGP routing table information for VRF default, address family L2VPN EVPN
Route Distinguisher: 10.100.100.11:32867
BGP routing table entry for [2]:[0]:[0]:[48]:[0011.0100.0001]:[0]:[0.0.0.0]/216,
  version 1538
```

```
Paths: (2 available, best #2)
Flags: (0x000202) on xmit-list, is not in l2rib/evpn, is not in HW, , is locked

  Advertised path-id 1
  Path type: internal, path is valid, is best path, no labeled nexthop
  AS-Path: NONE, path sourced internal to AS
    10.200.200.11 (metric 3) from 10.100.100.201 (10.100.100.201)
      Origin IGP, MED not set, localpref 100, weight 0
      Received label 30000
      Extcommunity:  RT:65501:30000 ENCAP:8
      Originator: 10.100.100.11 Cluster list: 10.100.100.201
```

Example 11-6 verifies that the MAC address learned on the local leaf has reached the remote leaf via the BGP EVPN control protocol exchange. As was the case with the initial leaf, verification that the MAC address is correctly downloaded and installed from the MAC-VRF or EVI (EVPN instance), should be performed. Example 11-7 shows output from **show l2route evpn mac** on a remote leaf.

Example 11-7 *MAC Entries Received Over BGP EVPN at a Remote Leaf*

```
L12# show l2route evpn mac all
Topology    Mac Address    Prod    Next Hop (s)
----------- -------------- ------ ---------------
100         0011.0100.0001 BGP    10.200.200.11
```

Example 11-7 verifies that MAC address 0011.0100.0001 has been learned by BGP and installed into L2RIB for further processing. The output verifies that the MAC address has a next hop assigned, and it reflects the IP address of the VTEP where the MAC was learned.

Example 11-8 shows output from **show mac address-table**.

Example 11-8 *MAC Table Output at a Remote Leaf*

```
L12# show mac address-table
Legend:
        * - primary entry, G - Gateway MAC, (R) - Routed MAC, O - overlay MAC
        age - seconds since last seen,+ - primary entry using vPC Peer-Link,
        (T) - True, (F) - False
   VLAN     MAC Address      Type      age     Secure NTFY Ports
---------+-----------------+--------+---------+------+----+------------------
*  100      0011.0100.0001   dynamic  0          F      F    nve1(10.200.200.11)
```

Example 11-7 verifies that the MAC address has been learned via the BGP EVPN control protocol and that it has been imported into the MAC-VRF. Finally, the MAC address table on the remote leaf must be inspected to confirm that 0011.0100.0001 is indeed installed in the MAC table as shown in Example 11-8. From that point on, data traffic can be expected from the remote leaf to this MAC address and that it can be forwarded via VXLAN encapsulation. With the integrated Layer 2 and Layer 3 services, Layer 2 and Layer 3 learning and information exchange must also be verified. Continuing with the same flow, it is also important to verify the ARP information has been learned on the local leaf as well. Example 11-9 shows output from **show ip arp vrf**.

Example 11-9   *ARP Table Output at a Leaf*

```
L11# show ip arp vrf Org1:Part1


Flags: * - Adjacencies learnt on non-active FHRP router

       + - Adjacencies synced via CFSoE

       # - Adjacencies Throttled for Glean

       D - Static Adjacencies attached to down interface


IP ARP Table for context Org1:Part1

Total number of entries: 1

Address          Age       MAC Address      Interface

192.168.100.200 00:13:58   0011.0100.0001   Vlan100
```

The output derived from the ARP table shows that the MAC address previously tracked (0011.0100.0001) is associated with the IP address 192.168.100.200. A corresponding entry is installed in the Adjacency Manager (AM). This ARP and AM entry creation notification is also passed along to the Host Mobility Manager (HMM) component, which is responsible for installing the host route in the unicast RIB. Example 11-10 shows output from **show forwarding vrf**.

Example 11-10   *Adjacency Output for an ARP Entry*

```
L11# show forwarding vrf Org1:Part1 adjacency


IPv4 adjacency information


next-hop          rewrite info     interface

--------------- --------------- -------------

192.168.100.200 0011.0100.0001 Vlan100
```

Once the entry is received by the AM, the MAC and IP address combination is verified and learned in HMM as a local route. Then HMM forwards the information to the L2RIB. Example 11-11 shows the output from **show fabric forwarding ip local-host-db vrf** that displays the HMM learnt local routes.

Example 11-11 *Locally Learned Host Route (/32) Information*

```
L11# show fabric forwarding ip local-host-db vrf Org1:Part1

HMM host IPv4 routing table information for VRF Org1:Part1
Status: *-valid, x-deleted, D-Duplicate, DF-Duplicate and frozen,
        c-cleaned in 00:02:58


    Host                 MAC Address       SVI        Flags      Physical Interface
*   192.168.100.200/32   0011.0100.0001    Vlan100    0x420201   Ethernet2/1
```

Example 11-12 shows output from **show l2route evpn mac-ip all.**

Example 11-12 *IP/MAC Entries Advertised Over BGP EVPN at a Leaf*

```
L11# show l2route evpn mac-ip all
Topology ID Mac Address     Prod Host IP                                Next Hop (s)
----------- -------------- ---- ------------------------------------- -----------
100           0011.0100.0001 HMM  192.168.100.200                        N/A
```

The previous examples verify several steps (including local learning) and ensure that the information is passed from ARP to the AM to the HMM, as well as to the L2RIB.

Example 11-13 shows output from **show bgp l2vpn evpn,** which verifies that the MAC and IP address are locally learned in BGP and advertised to the remote leaf.

Example 11-13 *Details of a Particular BGP EVPN Route type 2 Advertisement with Both IP and MAC at a Leaf*

```
L11# show bgp l2vpn evpn 192.168.100.200
BGP routing table information for VRF default, address family L2VPN EVPN
Route Distinguisher: 10.100.100.11:32867    (L3VNI 50000)
BGP routing table entry for [2]:[0]:[0]:[48]:[0011.0100.0001]:[32]:[192.168.100.200]
 /272, version 1550
Paths: (1 available, best #1)
Flags: (0x00010a) on xmit-list, is not in l2rib/evpn

  Advertised path-id 1
  Path type: local, path is valid, is best path, no labeled nexthop
  AS-Path: NONE, path locally originated
    10.200.200.11 (metric 0) from 0.0.0.0 (10.100.100.11)
      Origin IGP, MED not set, localpref 100, weight 32768
      Received label 30000 50000
      Extcommunity:  RT:65501:30000 RT:65501:50000

  Path-id 1 advertised to peers:
    10.100.100.201     10.100.100.202
```

Example 11-14 shows output from **show bgp l2vpn evpn** on a remote leaf.

Example 11-14 *Details of a Particular BGP EVPN Route type 2 Advertisement with Both IP and MAC at a Remote Leaf*

```
L12# show bgp l2vpn evpn 192.168.100.200
BGP routing table information for VRF default, address family L2VPN EVPN
Route Distinguisher: 10.100.100.11:32867
BGP routing table entry for [2]:[0]:[0]:[48]:[0011.0100.0001]:[32]:[192.168.100.200]
  /272, version 1554
Paths: (2 available, best #2)
Flags: (0x000202) on xmit-list, is not in l2rib/evpn, is not in HW, , is locked


  Advertised path-id 1
  Path type: internal, path is valid, is best path, no labeled nexthop
  AS-Path: NONE, path sourced internal to AS
    10.200.200.11 (metric 3) from 10.100.100.201 (10.100.100.201)
      Origin IGP, MED not set, localpref 100, weight 0
      Received label 30000 50000
      Extcommunity:  RT:65501:30000 RT:65501:50000 ENCAP:8 Router MAC:f8c2.8887.88f5
      Originator: 10.100.100.11 Cluster list: 10.100.100.201
```

The BGP output helps verify that the MAC and IP addresses are correctly imported and installed from the MAC-VRF and IP-VRF, respectively. With the corresponding BGP EVPN Route type message, two labels are advertised and received. The label 30000 is attached to the Layer 2 VNI, and the Layer 3 VNI is represented with the label 50000.

Example 11-15 shows output from **show l2route evpn mac-ip** on a remote leaf.

Example 11-15 *IP/MAC Entries Received Over BGP EVPN at a Remote Leaf*

```
L12# show l2route evpn mac-ip all
Topology ID Mac Address    Prod Host IP                                 Next Hop (s)
----------- -------------- ---- --------------------------------------- -------
100            0011.0100.0001 BGP  192.168.100.200                         10.200.200.11
```

Example 11-16 shows output from **show ip route vrf** on a remote leaf.

Example 11-16 *Output of IP Routing Table for Received IPv4 /32 Route Installed in RIB*

```
L12# show ip route vrf Org1:Part1 192.168.100.200
IP Route Table for VRF "Org1:Part1"
'*' denotes best ucast next-hop
'**' denotes best mcast next-hop
'[x/y]' denotes [preference/metric]
'%<string>' in via output denotes VRF <string>

192.168.100.200/32, ubest/mbest: 1/0
    *via 10.200.200.11%default, [200/0], 6w1d, bgp-65501, internal, tag 65501 (evpn)
  segid: 50000 tunnelid: 0xac8c80b encap: VXLAN
```

At the remote leaf, the MAC and IP addresses are learned via the BGP EVPN control protocol, and they are imported into the respective MAC- and IP-VRFs. In particular, the import is controlled by the appropriate Route Targets import semantics, as is usually the case with BGP route prefixes.

Finally, the IP address is installed in the IP routing table in the respective VRF. At this point, it should be possible to send both routed and bridged traffic to the endpoint (represented with MAC address 0011.0100.0001 and IP address 192.168.100.200) from anywhere in the VXLAN BGP EVPN fabric.

Example 11-17 shows the output from **show nve internal bgp rnh database**, which verifies that the VXLAN data plane encapsulation is established from the remote leaf, and specifically captures the router MAC addresses for routing, as well as the associated tunnel ID.

Example 11-17 *VTEP Peer Information with a Recursive Next Hop on a Remote Leaf*

```
L12# show nve internal bgp rnh database
Showing BGP RNH Database, size : 3 vni 0

VNI     Peer-IP           Peer-MAC        Tunnel-ID   Encap    (A/S)
50000   10.200.200.11     f8c2.8887.88f5  0xac8c80b   vxlan    (1/0)
```

By verifying the recursive next hop (RNH) database on the remote leaf, on the tunnel ID, on the associated peers' router-MAC, and on the Layer 3 VNI, validation of the various pieces of information that control forwarding in a VXLAN BGP EVPN network is now complete.

Example 11-18 shows output from **show nve peers detail** on a remote leaf.

Example 11-18   *Detailed VTEP Peer Information on a Remote Leaf*

```
L12# show nve peers detail
Details of nve Peers:
-----------------------------------------
Peer-Ip: 10.200.200.11
    NVE Interface       : nve1
    Peer State          : Up
    Peer Uptime         : 8w1d
    Router-Mac          : f8c2.8887.88f5
    Peer First VNI      : 50000
    Time since Create   : 8w1d
    Configured VNIs     : 30000,50000
    Provision State     : add-complete
    Route-Update        : Yes
    Peer Flags          : RmacL2Rib, TunnelPD, DisableLearn
    Learnt CP VNIs      : 30000,50000
    Peer-ifindex-resp   : Yes
```

Additional verification of the data plane peering ensures that the correct tunnel is not only instantiated but also in a working state, with the correct configuration. The output also verifies the uptime in addition to the flags to ensure that the traffic is correctly forwarded in the VXLAN BGP EVPN network to the endpoint in question. However, potential issues may still be present with the hardware programming that is platform specific. To determine how this can be validated, please refer to the relevant Nexus switch–specific guides.

This section shows how to verify that the VXLAN BGP EVPN setup and configuration through relevant outputs and explanations. Likewise, it shows how to verify that MAC and IP learning in the data center fabric is occurring correctly. The preliminary trouble-shooting steps in this section demonstrate a sequence of events to better understand the flow of information and what configuration settings can be derived from various outputs. As a result, several insights are provided beyond the basic examination of the BGP output previously discussed in Chapter 2, "VXLAN BGP EVPN Basics."

VXLAN OAM (NGOAM)

The growing deployment of overlay networks in the data center has placed a great deal of focus on the operations, management, and life cycle of multiple stacks. Historically, troubleshooting and management involved some Layer 2 and Layer 3 basics, along with the specifics of certain routing protocols used in the network. Overlays bring an additional layer of virtual wires along with the associated protocols. These additional layers add a level of indirection and abstraction from the underlying network as well as additional complexity.

Abstraction provides a simple and efficient way of providing services without considering intermediate devices. However, when it comes to service degradation or performance drops, a physical infrastructure that contains multiple paths is challenging. For example, when an operator is trying to determine the specific path an application is taking from one endpoint to another in the data center fabric, there is no simple tool for providing this visibility. In other words, it is not easy to determine the path without investing a fair amount of time and energy.

In a VXLAN network, entropy is achieved by changing the UDP source port number so that traffic between the same pair of VTEPs is spread across all available paths. The intermediate nodes use an appropriate hashing algorithm, based on the outer packet header fields of the VXLAN-encapsulated packet. The hashing algorithm used on the ingress VTEP may be different from that used at the intermediate nodes. This results in challenges for specific troubleshooting efforts related to path selection from the ingress VTEP to the egress VTEP.

VXLAN Operations, Administration, and Management (OAM)[31] is part of Cisco's Next-Generation OAM (NGOAM) framework for a Connectivity Fault Management (CFM) approach. NGOAM provides a simple and comprehensive solution to address these problems. VXLAN OAM and Cisco's NGOAM are both evolutions of Ethernet OAM, known as IEEE 802.1ag.[32] In addition to generating synthetic traffic to probe all available paths between ingress and egress VTEPs, OAM also provides an easy approach for determining the outer UDP source port number used by VXLAN for a specific application traffic flow.

Example 11-19 shows output from **ping nve**.

Example 11-19   *Sample Output from the* **ping nve** *Command*

```
L37# ping nve ip unknown vrf Org1:Part1 payload ip 192.168.166.51 192.168.165.51
  port 5644 25 proto 6 payload-end vni 50000 verbose

Codes: '!' - success, 'Q' - request not sent, '.' - timeout,
'D' - Destination Unreachable, 'X' - unknown return code,
'm' - malformed request(parameter problem),
'c' - Corrupted Data/Test

Sender handle: 410
! sport 52677 size 56,Reply from 192.168.166.51,time = 1 ms
! sport 52677 size 56,Reply from 192.168.166.51,time = 1 ms
! sport 52677 size 56,Reply from 192.168.166.51,time = 1 ms
! sport 52677 size 56,Reply from 192.168.166.51,time = 1 ms
! sport 52677 size 56,Reply from 192.168.166.51,time = 1 ms


Success rate is 100 percent (5/5), round-trip min/avg/max = 1/1/1 ms
Total time elapsed 42 ms
```

The command **ping nve** sends ICMP probes, simulating traffic in the VXLAN overlay. In Example 11-19, the destination endpoint has the IP address 192.168.166.51 within VRF Org:Part1. It should be noted that the source and destination IPs are in different subnets, resulting in a routing decision where the Layer 3 VNI that is assigned to the VRF (50000) is used in the VXLAN header.

ping nve has the ability to calculate the UDP source port used for the VXLAN encapsulation, which achieves entropy for ECMP in the underlay network. The UDP source port is generated based on the inner payload; in this example, the value is 52677. This example uses an inner payload with TCP (protocol 6), destination port 25 signifying an SMTP application (25/TCP), and source port 5644 for the e-mail connections. The result shows the acknowledgment and the reachability of the endpoint, using the outer UDP source port (52677) for VXLAN encapsulation. Instead of understanding all the algorithms or searching for the used paths, a single probe can provide the feedback and acknowledgment of the reachability of the destination endpoint or application.

In the event that one path is experiencing performance degradation, the probe can determine and detect this erroneous path by returning potential packet loss similarly to traditional ICMP **ping** or **traceroute** tools. The presence of an application or payload profile yields the exact path the application is using and plots the effective physical path taken.

Example 11-20 shows output from **traceroute nve**.

Example 11-20 *Sample Output from the* **traceroute nve** *Command*

```
L37# traceroute nve ip unknown vrf Org1:Part1 payload ip 192.168.166.51
   192.168.165.51 port 5644 25 proto 6 payload-end vni 50000 verbose

Codes: '!' - success, 'Q' - request not sent, '.' - timeout,
'D' - Destination Unreachable, 'X' - unknown return code,
'm' - malformed request(parameter problem),
'c' - Corrupted Data/Test

Traceroute Request to peer ip 10.1.1.140 source ip 10.1.1.37
Sender handle: 412
  1 !Reply from 10.1.1.38,time = 1 ms
  2 !Reply from 10.1.1.140,time = 1 ms
  3 !Reply from 192.168.166.51,time = 1 ms
```

The command **traceroute nve** issues a VXLAN traceroute and sends ICMP probe-simulating traffic in the overlay with incrementing TTL. Of note, TTL is copied from the inner header to the outer header to ensure that the intermediate routers will handle the VXLAN-encapsulated packets like regular IP traceroute packets.

In Example 11-20, the destination endpoint has IP address 192.168.166.51 within VRF Org:Part1. The source and destination IPs are in different subnets, which results in a routing operation using the Layer 3 VNI assigned to the VRF (50000). The output from the **traceroute nve** command provides the exact path that certain data traffic uses in the underlay routed network. Specifically, the IP of each intermediate node along the path is listed, as with the regular IP **traceroute** command.

With ECMP, traffic selects one of several equal-cost paths. **traceroute nve** simplifies the path-finding and troubleshooting exercise. The path generated is based on the protocol payload, thereby emulating a packet sent by the application or endpoint in question. As before, the example uses TCP (protocol 6) with destination port 25, emulating an SMTP application with the source port set to 5644 for the e-mail connections.

The output provides an understanding of the exact path being used in the underlay network, which enables the ability to pinpoint the exact spine that the data traffic is taking to the e-mail server. In addition, the destination VTEP has been set to "unknown," so the output of **traceroute nve** also provides the IP address of the VTEP (10.1.1.140) attached to the destination endpoint.

One additional tool within VXLAN OAM that is extremely helpful is the "tissa"-based **pathtrace** described in the draft-tissa-nvo3-oam-fm IETF draft.[33] This OAM tool provides the ability to list the exact underlay path that specific applications are taking, and it also derives the respective destination VTEP information and lists the ingress and egress interfaces at each of the intermediate hops (including the egress VTEP). In addition, it provides metadata information such as the interface load, interface state, and interface error counters of all the listed interfaces.

Example 11-21 shows output from **pathtrace nve** with interface statistics.

Example 11-21   *Sample Output from the* **pathtrace nve** *Command*

```
L37# pathtrace nve ip unknown vrf Org1:Part1 payload ip 192.168.166.51
  192.168.165.51 port 5644 25 proto 6 payload-end vni 50000 verbose req-stats

Path trace Request to peer ip 10.1.1.140 source ip 10.1.1.37
Sender handle: 416


Hop   Code   ReplyIP   IngressI/f  EgressI/f   State
======================================================
  1 !Reply from 10.1.1.38, Eth1/23  Eth2/2  UP / UP
  Input Stats:
PktRate:999  ByteRate:558873
Load:3        Bytes:2101901590781
unicast:3758851978  mcast:1487057
bcast:13     discards:0
errors:0     unknown:0
bandwidth:171798691880000000
```

```
  Output Stats:
PktRate:999  ByteRate:558873
load:3        bytes:2101901590781
unicast:3758851978  mcast:1487057
bcast:13      discards:0
errors:0
bandwidth:171798691880000000
  2 !Reply from 10.1.1.140, Eth2/3  Unknown  UP / DOWN
  Input Stats:
PktRate:0    ByteRate:860
Load:0        Bytes:5057292548
unicast:194899  mcast:1175038
bcast:13      discards:0
errors:0      unknown:0
bandwidth:171798691880000000
```

The command **pathtrace nve** issues a VXLAN path trace and uses special OAM probe-simulating traffic in the overlay. The same sample payload as that used for **ping** and **traceroute** is used here, with the destination endpoint corresponding to an SMTP application located at the endpoint with IP address 192.168.166.51 within VRF Org:Part1.

The output clearly lists the intermediate hops, the ingress and egress interfaces, and the associated load, statistics, and bandwidth. This results in an understanding of the exact path being used in the underlay network. It also provides the ability to pinpoint the exact spine that the data traffic is taking to the e-mail server, as well as the exact path/link being taken.

VXLAN OAM is implemented as NGOAM in the NX-OS platforms. This functionality is provided through both the CLI and the API, via NX-API. NGOAM not only executes the various probes across a programmatic interface but also provides the ability to retrieve statistical information from the VTEP. Both synchronous and asynchronous options are available.

With the preferred asynchronous option, a session handle is returned as an acknowledgment that the OAM probe execution request has been received. When the OAM probe execution is complete, the result is stored in the OAM database at the sourcing VTEP so that it can be retrieved at a later date since it is indexed via the session handle. In this way, the session handle enables retrieval of the current and historical statistics from the VTEP local OAM database via a programmatic API or CLI.

Additional enhancements in VXLAN OAM include the introduction of periodic probes and notifications to proactively manage the overlay network, along with the physical underlay. In order to make the collected path information and statistics meaningful, VXLAN OAM has been integrated with VXLAN management systems such as DCNM.

Summary

This chapter introduces the basic elements of fabric management, including POAP-based day-0 provisioning (using DCNM, NFM, Ignite, and so on), incremental configuration using day-0.5 configuration, overlay configuration using day-1 provisioning (using DCNM, VTS, and NFM), and day-2 provisioning, including providing continuous monitoring, visibility, and troubleshooting capabilities in a VXLAN BGP EVPN fabric. This chapter also provides a brief primer on VXLAN OAM, which is an extremely efficient tool for debugging overlay-based fabrics.

References

1. Cisco. *Using PowerOn Auto Provisioning. Nexus 3000 Series NX-OS Fundamentals Configuration Guide, Release 5.0(3)U3(1)*. www.cisco.com/c/en/us/td/docs/switches/datacenter/nexus3000/sw/fundamentals/503_U3_1/b_Nexus_3000_Fundamentals_Guide_Release_503_U3_1/using_power_on_auto_provisioning.pdf.

2. Jain, V., and B. Edgeworth. *Troubleshooting BGP*. Cisco Press, 2016. www.ciscopress.com/store/troubleshooting-bgp-9780134436548.

3. Cisco. *Using PowerOn Auto Provisioning. Nexus 3000 Series NX-OS Fundamentals Configuration Guide, Release 5.0(3)U3(1)*. www.cisco.com/c/en/us/td/docs/switches/datacenter/nexus3000/sw/fundamentals/503_U3_1/b_Nexus_3000_Fundamentals_Guide_Release_503_U3_1/using_power_on_auto_provisioning.pdf.

4. W3C. *HTTP—Hypertext transfer protocol*. 2003. www.w3.org/Protocols/.

5. TCL Developer Exchange. *Welcome to the TCL Developer Exchange*. www.tcl.tk.

6. Python. *Python homepage*. 2001. www.python.org.

7. OpenSSH. *OpenSSH7.3*. 2016. www.openssh.com.

8. Cisco. *Data Center Network Manager*. www.cisco.com/go/dcnm.

9. Cisco. *Network Fabric Manager*. www.cisco.com/c/en/us/products/cloud-systems-management/nexus-fabric-manager/index.html.

10. Github. *Date center ignite*. 2016. github.com/datacenter/ignite.

11. Cisco. *Cisco Dynamic Fabric Automation Configuration Guide*. www.cisco.com/c/en/us/td/docs/switches/datacenter/dfa/configuration/b-dfa-configuration/b-dfa-configuration_chapter_01001.html.

12. Cisco. *Virtual topology system*. www.cisco.com/go/vts.

13. Cisco. *NX-API. Cisco Nexus 9000 Series NX-OS Programmability Guide, Release 6.x*. 2016. www.cisco.com/c/en/us/td/docs/switches/datacenter/nexus9000/sw/6-x/programmability/guide/b_Cisco_Nexus_9000_Series_NX-OS_Programmability_Guide/b_Cisco_Nexus_9000_Series_NX-OS_Programmability_Configuration_Guide_chapter_0101.pdf.

14. *Yang Data Model for EVPN.* tools.ietf.org/html/draft-ietf-bess-evpn-yang.

15. Cisco. NX-API CLI. *Cisco Nexus 9000 Series NX-OS Programmability Guide, Release.* 2016. www.cisco.com/c/en/us/td/docs/switches/datacenter/nexus9000/sw/7-x/programmability/guide/b_Cisco_Nexus_9000_Series_NX-OS_Programmability_Guide_7x/NX_API.html.

16. Cisco. NX-API REST. *Cisco Nexus 9000 Series NX-OS Programmability Guide, Release.* 2016. www.cisco.com/c/en/us/td/docs/switches/datacenter/nexus9000/sw/7-x/programmability/guide/b_Cisco_Nexus_9000_Series_NX-OS_Programmability_Guide_7x/b_Cisco_Nexus_9000_Series_NX-OS_Programmability_Guide_7x_chapter_010001.html.

17. Cisco. *Virtual topology system data sheet.* www.cisco.com/c/en/us/products/collateral/cloud-systems-management/virtual-topology-system/datasheet-c78-734877.html.

18. Cisco. *Tail-f.* 2015. www.tail-f.com.

19. Cisco. *Virtual topology system data sheet*, Table 2. 2016. www.cisco.com/c/en/us/products/collateral/cloud-systems-management/virtual-topology-system/datasheet-c78-734877.html.

20. Cisco. *Nexus Fabric Manager.* www.cisco.com/c/en/us/products/cloud-systems-management/nexus-fabric-manager/index.html.

21. Cisco. *Nexus Fabric Manager data sheet*, Table 2. 2016. www.cisco.com/c/en/us/products/collateral/cloud-systems-management/nexus-fabric-manager/datasheet-c78-736499.html.

22. Cisco. *Data Center Network Manager 10 data sheet.* 2016. www.cisco.com/c/en/us/products/collateral/cloud-systems-management/prime-data-center-network-manager/datasheet-c78-736613.html.

23. Github. *Data center Ansible NXOS.* 2016. github.com/datacenter/Ansible-NXOS/tree/master/Ansible-NXOS/VxLAN-BGP-EVPN.

24. Puppetforge. *Puppetlabs/Ciscopuppet.* 2016. forge.puppet.com/puppetlabs/ciscopuppet#type-cisco_evpn_vni.

25. Cisco. *Python scripting.* 2016. www.cisco.com/c/en/us/products/collateral/cloud-systems-management/aci-fabric-controller/white-paper-c11-729385.html#_Toc459078278.

26. OpenStack. *OpenStack homepage.* 2016. www.openstack.org.

27. Cisco. *Cisco UCS Director.* www.cisco.com/c/en/us/products/servers-unified-computing/ucs-director/index.html.

28. Github. *Nexus fabric OpenStack integration.* 2016. github.com/CiscoSystems/fabric_enabler.

29. Cisco. *Cisco Nexus 9000 Series NX-OS Virtual Machine Tracker Configuration Guide, Release 7.x*. 2016. www.cisco.com/c/en/us/td/docs/switches/datacenter/ nexus9000/sw/7-x/vm_tracker/configuration/guide/b_Cisco_Nexus_9000_Series_ NX-OS_Virtual_Machine_Tracker_Configuration_Guide_7x/b_Cisco_Nexus_9000_ Series_NX-OS_Virtual_Machine_Tracker_Configuration_Guide_ 7x_chapter_010.html.

30. Cisco. *Virtual machine tracker auto-configuration*. 2016. www.cisco.com/c/ en/us/td/docs/switches/datacenter/pf/configuration/guide/b-pf-configuration/ Introducing-Cisco-Programmable-Fabric-Management-Operations-and-Provisioning. html?bookSearch=true#concept_ED66F638F46A4CA0BCA431E141345D15.

31. Cisco. *VXLAN OAM*. 2016. www.cisco.com/c/en/us/td/docs/switches/ datacenter/pf/configuration/guide/b-pf-configuration/ Introducing-Cisco-Programmable-Fabric-Management-Operations- and-Provisioning.html?bookSearch=true#concept_ 2359393ACD0E4159B0E3DFCE99C00BD0.

32. IEEE. *802.1ag—Connectivity fault management*. www.ieee802.org/1/ pages/802.1ag.html.

33. NV03 Working Group. *NVO3 fault management draft-tissa-nvo3-oam-fm-03.txt*. 2016. tools.ietf.org/html/draft-tissa-nvo3-oam-fm-03.

VXLAN BGP EVPN Implementation Options

This book encompasses details on building data center fabrics with open standards, specifically VXLAN, BGP, and EVPN. Although the primary focus is specific to the Cisco NX-OS implementation, the book also explains the fundamentals associated with the base technologies of VXLAN, BGP, and EVPN. Nevertheless, with open standards, the associated documented definitions in IETF contain some prescribed implementation options and additional functionality that will be briefly discussed here.

This appendix goes over some specific EVPN implementation options that are mentioned as part of RFC 7432 BGP MPLS-Based Ethernet VPN[1], the EVPN Overlay draft-ietf-bess-evpn-overlay[2] draft, and the EVPN Prefix Advertisement draft-ietf-bess-evpn-prefix-advertisement[3] draft. The option for EVPN inter-subnet forwarding specified in draft-ietf-bess-evpn-inter-subnet-forwarding[4] that relates to symmetric and asymmetric Integrated Route and Bridge (IRB) options is excluded as it has been covered in detail in Chapter 3, "VXLAN/EVPN Forwarding Characteristics," under the IRB discussion.

EVPN Layer 2 Services

EVPN defines different VLAN Layer 2 Services, as mentioned in RFC7432 Section 6. There are two options mentioned in Section 5.1.2 in draft-ietf-bess-evpn-overlay, which apply to the VXLAN-related implementation. The first option, implemented by Cisco, is called *VLAN-based* bundle service interface. The second option is called *VLAN-aware* bundle service interface.

In the VLAN-based option, a *single* bridge domain is mapped to a *single* EVPN Virtual Instance (EVI). The EVI provides the Route Distinguisher (RD) and controls the import and export of the associated prefixes via Route Targets (RT) into the MAC-VRF and in turn into the bridge domain (see Figure A-1). When using the VLAN-based approach, the EVI corresponds to a single MAC-VRF in the control plane and a single VNI in the data plane, resulting in a 1:1 mapping of EVI, MAC-VRF, and bridge domain (VNI). The disadvantage of the VLAN-based implementation is the configuration requirement of one EVI per bridge domain. This becomes an advantage for import/export granularity on a per bridge domain basis. Example 5-3 in Chapter 5, "Multitenancy," provides a configuration example for the Cisco VLAN-based implementation.

```
[2]:[0]:[0]:[48]:[0000.3000.1101]:[32]:[192.168.1.101]
```

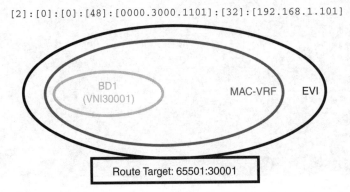

Figure A-1   *VLAN-Based Bundle Services*

In the case of the VLAN-aware bundle service interface, multiple bridge domains can be mapped to a single EVI. The VLAN-aware implementation allows a single RD and RT set to be shared across multiple bridge domains that belong to the same EVI. This results in a 1:N mapping for the EVI to MAC-VRF to bridge domain (see Figure A-2); resulting in the VNI in the data plane being sufficient to identify the corresponding bridge domain. The VLAN-aware implementation reduces the configuration requirements for EVIs. The disadvantage of the VLAN-aware implementation is that it does not allow the granularity of prefix import/export on a per bridge domain basis.

```
[2]:[0]:[30001]:[48]:[0000.3000.1101]:[32]:[192.168.1.101]
[2]:[0]:[30002]:[48]:[0000.3000.2101]:[32]:[192.168.2.101]
[2]:[0]:[30003]:[48]:[0000.3000.3101]:[32]:[192.168.3.101]
```

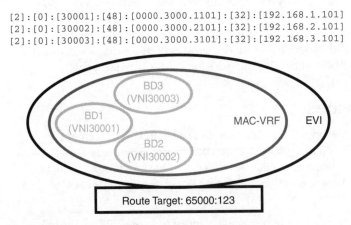

Figure A-2   *VLAN-Aware Bundle Services*

The big difference between the VLAN-based and the VLAN-aware implementation is the use of the Ethernet Tag ID field in the control plane. The VLAN-based option requires this field to be zero (0). The VLAN-aware option specifies the Ethernet Tag ID must carry the identification of the respective bridge domain (VNI). The difference in Ethernet Tag ID usage is described in RFC7432 section 6.1: VLAN-Based Service Interface and

6.3: VLAN-Aware Service Interface. It is important to understand that both options are valid and conform to RFC 7432 but are not per se interoperable.

EVPN IP-VRF to IP-VRF Model

In some cases, IP prefix routes may be advertised for subnets and IPs behind an IRB. This use case is referred to as the "IP-VRF to IP-VRF" model. As part of the EVPN prefix-advertisement draft, draft-ietf-bess-evpn-prefix-advertisement, there are three implementation options for the IP-VRF to IP-VRF model. The draft provides two required components and one optional component. For draft conformity, it is necessary to follow one of the two required component models. The main focus here is on the two required models; the optional model will be touched upon briefly towards the end. Section 5.4 in draft-ietf-bess-evpn-prefix-advertisement describes the three models, which will be briefly introduced in this section.

The first model is called the *interface-less* model where the Route type 5 route contains the necessary information for an IP Prefix advertisement. The Cisco NX-OS implementation uses the interface-less model. Within the IP Prefix advertisement, all the IP routing information is included-such as the IP subnet, IP subnet length, and the next hop. In addition, the IP-VRF context is preserved in form of the Layer 3 VNI present in the Network Layer Reachability Information (NLRI). The interface-less model also includes the Router MAC of the next hop as part of the BGP extended community. With VXLAN being a MAC in IP/UDP encapsulation, the data plane encapsulation requires population of the inner source and DMAC addresses. Although the local router MAC is known and used as the inner-source MAC, the DMAC address needs to be populated based on the lookup of the destination prefix. The Router MAC extended community will provide this necessary information, as shown in Figure A-3. Note that with the interface-less model, the Gateway IP (GW IP) field is always populated to 0. Example 5-9 in Chapter 5 provides a configuration example for Cisco's interface-less implementation.

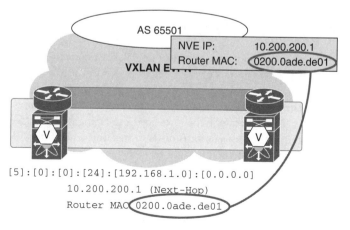

Figure A-3 *IP-VRF Interface-Less Model*

The second model is called *interface-full*, which has two sub-modes:

- Core-facing IRB

- Unnumbered Core-facing IRB

In both cases of the interface-full model, in addition to the Route type 5 prefix advertisement, a Route type 2 advertisement is also generated. With the interface-full core-facing IRB option, the Router MAC extended community is not part of the Route type 5 advertisement. Instead, the Gateway IP (GW IP) field is populated to be that of the core-facing IRB associated with the VTEP. In addition, the VNI field in the Route type 5 advertisement is set to 0. To complete the information required for the VXLAN encapsulation, a Route type 2 advertisement is generated, as shown in Figure A-4. The Route type 2 advertisement provides the IP, as well as MAC information for the next-hop core-facing IRB interface that in turn is used for the population of the VXLAN header. In addition, the VNI field corresponding to the tenant or IP-VRF is also carried in the Route type 2 advertisement.

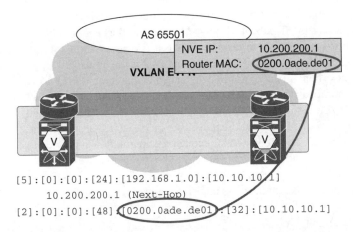

Figure A-4   *IP-VRF Interface-Full Model with Core-Facing IRB*

In the optional interface-full model of unnumbered core-facing IRB (see Figure A-5), the Router MAC extended community is sent as part of the Route type 5 advertisement in a similar way as the interface-less model. However, the VNI field in the advertisement remains 0, as does the GW IP address field. The associated Route type 2 advertisement is keyed by the Router MAC address associated with the next-hop core-facing IRB interface and also carries the VNI associated with the tenant or IP-VRF. In this way, when traffic is destined to the Route type 5 advertised prefix, there is a recursive lookup performed to verify the next-hop router MAC information, and it is employed to populate the corresponding VXLAN header.

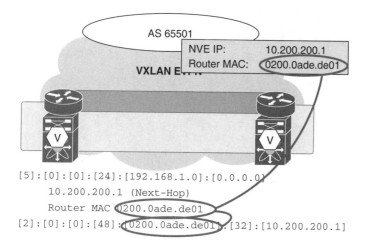

Figure A-5 *IP-VRF Interface-Full Model with Unnumbered Core-Facing IRB*

The difference between the interface-less and the interface-full model is mainly the presence or absence of an additional Route type 2 advertisement. The interface-less option expects the Router MAC in the Route type 5 advertisement and will not leverage the Route type 2 information advertised by an interface-full core-facing IRB model. Similarly, an interface-full option would expect the additional Route type 2 advertisement. In both cases, the VXLAN data plane encapsulation would have the information necessary for populating the inner DMAC address.

In summary, the different IP-VRF to IP-VRF models are described in the EVPN prefix advertisement draft, draft-ietf-bess-evpn-prefix-advertisement in section 5.4. It is important to understand what is required for each model so that they conform to the IETF draft; the different models are not per-se interoperable.

References

1. *BGP MPLS-Based Ethernet VPN*. IETF Website, 2015. Retrieved from https://tools.ietf.org/html/rfc7432.

2. *A Network Virtualization Overlay Solution using EVPN*. IETF Website, 2016. Retrieved from https://tools.ietf.org/html/draft-ietf-bess-evpn-overlay.

3. *IP Prefix Advertisement in EVPN*. IETF Website, 2016. Retrieved from https://tools.ietf.org/html/draft-ietf-bess-evpn-prefix-advertisement.

4. *Integrated Routing and Bridging in EVPN*. IETF Website, 2015. Retrieved from https://tools.ietf.org/html/draft-ietf-bess-evpn-inter-subnet-forwarding.

Index

J-K-L

P

S

T

U

W-X-Y-Z